Advance praise for
ABSOLUTE ETHICAL LIFE

"Bringing together Aristotle, Hegel, and Marx, Michael Lazarus's new book forcefully defends an expansive account of ethical life as a central concept for social and political theory. An important contribution to our understanding of Marx as an ethical thinker and essential reading for students and scholars of nineteenth-century philosophy."

—KAREN NG, author of *Hegel's Concept of Life*

"*Absolute Ethical Life* is both highly advanced and accessible, expansive and yet in-depth, philosophically patient and yet politically urgent. At a time when Marx is being revived, Lazarus is an exemplary guide."

—MARTIN HÄGGLUND, author of *This Life: Secular Faith and Spiritual Freedom*

"There is a long-standing discussion about the ethical aspects in Marx's critique of political economy. Michael Lazarus's book is the first contribution to link this debate directly to the value-form analysis. He shifts the debate to a new level. Only now it becomes really clear to what extent Marx was a theorist of the social. An enormously important book."

—MICHAEL HEINRICH, author of *Karl Marx and the Birth of Modern Society*

"This book establishes that Marx's critique of political economy is not simply a theory of economics. No less than Aristotle and Hegel, Marx was concerned with the good of the political community, claiming that a social world subject to the reign of capital cannot adequately further the good. Lazarus's presentation and defense of Marx's arguments are clear and convincing. Readers of this work will gain a deeper appreciation of Marx's immense contribution to normative social philosophy."

—TONY SMITH, author of *The Logic of Marx's "Capital"*

ABSOLUTE ETHICAL LIFE

CURRENCIES

New Thinking for Financial Times
STEFAN EICH AND MARTIJN KONINGS, EDITORS

Absolute Ethical Life

Aristotle, Hegel and Marx

MICHAEL LAZARUS

STANFORD UNIVERSITY PRESS
Stanford, California

Stanford University Press
Stanford, California

© 2025 by Michael Lazarus. All rights reserved.

No part of this book may be reproduced or transmitted in any form or by any means, electronic or mechanical, including photocopying and recording, or in any information storage or retrieval system, without the prior written permission of Stanford University Press.

ISBN 978-1-5036-4170-9 (cloth)
ISBN 978-1-5036-4285-0 (paperback)
ISBN 978-1-5036-4286-7 (electronic)

Library of Congress Control Number: 2024061998

Library of Congress Cataloging-in-Publication Data available upon request.

Cover design: George Kirkpatrick
Cover art: Detail of *Study for Coat Makers*, 2019, © Caroline Walker. Courtesy the artist; Stephen Friedman Gallery, London; GRIMM, New York / Amsterdam / London and Ingleby, Edinburgh. All rights reserved, DACS/Artimage 2024

The authorized representative in the EU for product safety and compliance is: Mare Nostrum Group B.V. | Mauritskade 21D | 1091 GC Amsterdam | The Netherlands | Email address: gpsr@mare-nostrum.co.uk | KVK chamber of commerce number: 96249943

To G. & E. Rousou

That's in the future. Our
present care is with the present.
The future will be shaped
by those who control it.
—Sophocles, *Antigone*

Contents

	Acknowledgments	xi
	Abbreviations	xiii
INTRODUCTION	Ethical Life and the Life of Capital	1

Part I

ONE	Politics as Action *Hannah Arendt*	37
TWO	Ethics as Virtue *Alasdair MacIntyre*	76

Part II

THREE	Shapes of Ethical Life *Ancient and Modern*	119
FOUR	From Shipwreck to Commodity Exchange *Robinson Crusoe's Adventure Through Social and Political Thought*	158

Part III

FIVE	Species-Being and Flourishing *The Young Marx*	193
SIX	Form and Fetishism *"Capital" and Misrecognition*	218
CONCLUSION	The Song of the Weavers	275
	Notes	293
	Index	357

Acknowledgments

This book has a long history. Its pages are much richer from discussions with friends and comrades, including Daniel Lopez, Gene Flenady, Emma Fajgenbaum, James Kent, Darren Roso, Conall Cash, Mathew Abbott, Steven Levine, Jesse Lambourn, Emma McNicol, Ali Alizadeh, Sarah Garnham, Sandra Bloodworth, Alex Cain and Robert Moseley. All of whom improved the work in one way or another. I would also like to thank Caleb Bernacchio, David Kretz, Ahmad Fattah, Peter Wicks, Kelvin Knight and others in the International Society for MacIntyrean Enquiry. Stuart MacIntyre kindly read an initial draft. I owe a great deal to Paul Muldoon's sound mentorship. Along with Michael Janover, Paul taught me how to think with and against tradition. In such a volatile job market, I would like to acknowledge the advice of Jane Kenway, Jean-Philippe Deranty, Michael Ure, Robert Lazarus, Amanda Gilbertson and Cat Moir.

It was a privilege to discuss the book with sharp respondents at a manuscript workshop at Leiden University. Thanks especially to David Lebow, Paul Raekstad, Matthew Longo and Lucas Entel, as well as to Jensen Suther for an excellent joint session. I benefited immensely from feedback received in numerous ways, ranging from detailed comments to conference questions. I would like to thank Miguel Vatter, Andrew Chitty, Terry Pinkard, Jay Bernstein and Michael Heinrich. Scott Robinson offered probing observations on several chapters while nursing his newborn, François, on his lap. I am very appreciative for the insightful notes made on the first draft by Tony Smith which helped me think about the project dramatically.

An enriching correspondence with Patrick Murray illuminated several issues with verve. Many thanks to Martin Hägglund, a generous interlocutor, who engaged crucial questions through wide-ranging conversations and philosophical friendship. On Martin's invitation I had the pleasure of finishing proofs for the book shortly after arriving at Yale University as a visiting postdoctoral research fellow.

I am very grateful to the series editors, Martijn Konings and Stefan Eich. Martijn has been a source of enduring encouragement and confidence. Stefan's precision pushed me on important points. Working with Caroline McKusick and Stanford University Press was a delight from beginning to end. Caroline's editorial direction and faith in the book provided the support I needed to get it to the finishing line. I would also like to thank the two anonymous reviewers for Stanford University Press. A grant awarded by the Australian Academy of Humanities assisted with production. Caroline Walker very kindly allowed me to use her wonderful painting for the cover.

Kate Meakin has been a big part in the making of this book. With E. P., Kate lived with me while I tried to bring it to life. Just as much as they made the work feel lighter, they helped weather the storms. My parents, Steven and Connie, my siblings, Charlotte and Darcy, and many dear friends maintained my spirit. This act of weaving is dedicated to the memory of my grandparents, George and Ellen Rousou.

Abbreviations

Aristotle

EE *The Eudemian Ethics*. Oxford: Oxford University Press, 2011.
NE *Nicomachean Ethics*. Indianapolis: Hackett, 1999.
Pol *Politics*. Indianapolis: Hackett, 2017.

All other references are from *The Complete Works of Aristotle*, 2 vols. Ed. Jonathan Barnes. Princeton, NJ: Princeton University Press, 1984.

G.W.F. Hegel

EL *Encyclopedia of the Philosophical Sciences in Basic Outline. Part 1: Science of Logic*. Cambridge: Cambridge University Press, 2010 / *Enzyklopädie der philosophischen Wissenschaften I* in *W* 8.
GW *Gesammelte Werke*. Hamburg: Felix Meiner Verlag, 1968–
NL "On the Scientific Ways of Treating Natural Law, on Its Place in Practical Philosophy, and Its Relation to the Positive Sciences of Right" in *PW* / "Über die wissenschaftlichen Behandlungsarten des Naturrechts, seine Stelle in der praktischen Philosophie und sein Verhältnis zu den positiven Rechtswissenschaften" in *W* 2.
LHP 1–3 *Lectures on the History of Philosophy*. London: Routledge, 1882, 1884, 1886 / *Vorlesungen über die Geschichte der Philosophie* in *W* 18–20.
PhG *Phenomenology of Spirit*. Cambridge: Cambridge University Press, 2018 / *Phänomenologie des Geistes* in *W* 3.

PR   *Elements of the Philosophy of Right.* Ed. Allen W. Wood. Cambridge: Cambridge University Press, 1991 / *Grundlinien der Philosophie des Rechts* in *W* 7.

PW   *Political Writings.* Ed. Lawrence Dickey and H. B Nisbet. Cambridge: Cambridge University Press, 1999.

SEL   *System of Ethical Life* (1802/3) and *First Philosophy of Spirit* (Part III of the *System of Speculative Philosophy* 1803/4). Albany: State University of New York Press, 1979 / "System der Sittlichkeit. Reinschriftentwurf" in *GW* 5.

SL   *Science of Logic.* Cambridge: Cambridge University Press, 2010 / *Wissenschaft der Logik* I in *W* 5 and *Wissenschaft der Logik* II in *W* 6.

W   *Werke* in 20 Bänden. Ed. Eva Moldenhauer and Karl Markus. Frankfurt am Main: Suhrkamp Verlag, 1969–1971.

When applicable the references will note the paragraph and page in the English edition, followed by the German. For instance, *PhG,* ¶177, 108/145. For references to texts not listed above, the relevant volume of *Werke* or *Gesammelte Werke* follows the English citation. For instance, G.W.F. Hegel, *Philosophy of Mind* (Oxford: Oxford University Press, 2007), §482, 214 / *W* 10, 301.

Karl Marx

Cap.1   *Capital,* vol. 1. London: Pelican, 1976 / *Das Kapital,* Erster Band. Berlin: Dietz Verlag, 1955.

Cap.1a *Capital,* vol. 1, 1st ed., "The Commodity" (1–48) and "The Form of Value" (49–70) in *Value.* Ed. Albert Dragstedt. New York: New Park Publications, 1976 / *MEGA2* II.5.

Cap.2   *Capital,* vol. 2. London: Penguin, 1978 / *Das Kapital,* Zweiter Band. Berlin: Dietz Verlag, 1953.

Cap.3   *Capital,* vol. 3. London: Penguin, 1981 / *Das Kapital,* Dritter Band. Berlin: Dietz Verlag, 1953.

CJM   "Excerpts from James Mill's *Elements of Political Economy*" in *EW* / "Auszüge aus James Mills Buch 'Klemens d'economie politique.' Trad. par J. T. Parisot, Paris 1823" in *MEW* 40.

CM   Karl Marx and Frederick Engels. "Manifesto of the Communist Party" in *MECW* 6 / "Manifest der Kommunistischen Partei" in *MEW* 4.

EPM   "Economic and Philosophical Manuscripts" in *EW* / "Ökonomisch-philosophische Manuskripte" in *MEGA2* I.2.

EW	*Early Writings*. London: Penguin Books, 1975.
Gr	*Grundrisse*. London: Penguin, 1973 / *Ökonomische Manuskripte 1857/58* in *MEGA2* II.1.1 (1–309) and II.1.2 (315–747).
M	*Marx's Economic Manuscript of 1864–5*. Ed. Fred Moseley. Chicago: Haymarket, 2017.
MECW	Karl Marx and Friedrich Engels. *Collected Works*, vols. 1–50. London: Lawrence & Wishart, 1975–2004. Cited by volume and page.
MEGA2	Karl Marx and Friedrich Engels. *Marx-Engels-Gesamtausgabe*. Berlin: Dietz Verlag/De Gruyter, 1975. Cited by section, volume and page.
MEW	Karl Marx and Friedrich Engels. *Marx–Engels Werke*. Berlin: Dietz Verlag, 1956–1990. Cited by volume and page.
NW	"'Notes' on Adolph Wagner" in *Marx's Later Writings*. Ed. Terrell Carver. Cambridge: Cambridge University Press, 1996 / "'Randglossen' zu Adolph Wagners 'Lehrbuch der politischen Ökonomie'" in *MEW* 19.
OJQ	"On the Jewish Question" in *EW* / "Zur Judenfrage" in *MEGA2* I.2.
RIPP	"Results of the Immediate Process of Production" in *Cap*.1 / "Resultate des unmittelbaren Produktionsprozesses" in *MEGA2* II.4.1.
U	"The Original Text of the Second and the Beginning of the Third Chapter of *A Contribution to a Critique of Political Economy*" in *MECW* 29 / *Zur Kritik der politischen Ökonomie*. Urtext in *MEGA2* II.2.

English page is cited before the German edition. For instance, *Cap*.1, 270/174.

Hannah Arendt

HC	*The Human Condition*. Chicago: Chicago University Press, 1998.
MCT	*The Modern Challenge to Tradition: Fragmente eines Buchs, Kritische Gesamtausgabe*, Band 6. Göttingen: Wallstein Verlag, 2018.

Alasdair MacIntyre

AMEM	*Alasdair MacIntyre's Engagement with Marxism*. Ed. Paul Blackledge and Neil Davidson. Chicago: Haymarket, 2009.
AV	*After Virtue: A Study in Moral Theory*. London: Duckworth, 2007.

INTRODUCTION

Ethical Life and the Life of Capital

"**So**, *this volume is finished*," Karl Marx rushes off in a letter to his dear friend and collaborator, Friedrich Engels, at two o'clock one morning in August 1867. Nestled in London's leafy northern suburbs, only a short walk from where another refugee, Sigmund Freud, would later settle, Marx's study enjoyed a view of Maitland Park. From this room, overflowing with books, papers and large printer sheets of proofs, Marx worked ever more frantically, desperate to complete the work. Writing to Engels in Manchester, the reason for such urgency was that he had just corrected the last sheet of a long-awaited manuscript. "Without your self-sacrifice for me," Marx remarks, "I could not possibly have manged the immense labour demanded by the 3 volumes," adding in English, "I embrace you full of thanks!" In the months preceding the letter, Marx had been working on an appendix, which he attached in fine print, titled "The Form of Value [*Die Wertform*]."[1] The forthcoming work, *Capital: A Critique of Political Economy*, was to be Marx's masterpiece. Despite his exulted frame of mind, the work was never finished. In his lifetime, only the first volume was published. *Capital*, volume 1, appeared in two German editions and a French translation, which Marx himself painstakingly corrected.

Earlier in June, again across letters, the two men discussed the merit of this appendix. Engels suggested to Marx that his discussion of the "form of value" should be simplified, quipping that it bears the "marks of your carbuncles." Marx's skin was red with boils, a condition which plagued him for over a decade and made it increas-

1

ingly hard for his body to keep up with his work schedule. According to Engels, the explanation of value should be made more accessible

> as your philistine really is not accustomed to this kind of abstract thinking and will certainly not torment himself for the sake of the form of value [*Wertform*]. At most, you could provide rather more extensive historical evidence for the conclusions you have here reached dialectically, you could, so to speak, apply the test of history.

While Engels acknowledges the dialectical structure of Marx's conceptual categories, where each category is developed immanently leading to the next, he advised that greater historical illustration will simplify the discussion for the reader and make it easier to understand. Engels also recommended that Marx follow a paragraph structure modelled on G.W.F. Hegel's *Encyclopedia of the Philosophical Sciences*, with section headings making clear each "dialectical transition" and, like a "school text-book," offering an explanation to "a very large class of readers" mostly unfamiliar with Marx's dialectical approach, since "one has to make it as easy for them as one possibly can."[2]

In his reply, Marx played on the idea that dialectical thought arrives at a new truth immanently, by both affirming and denying at the same moment. He joked "[w]ith regard to the development of the *form of value*, I have both followed and *not* followed your advice, thus striking a dialectical attitude in this matter, too." Marx adjusts the structure of his discussion and adds section headings to help the "'*non-dialectical*' [*nichtdialektischen*] reader." However, Marx maintains that the form of value "is crucial for the whole book" since "economists have hitherto overlooked" the way that value is expressed in commodities and money. Marx also retorts, "I hope the bourgeoisie will remember my carbuncles until their dying day."[3] Aware of such concerns, he wrote to *The Chronicle*, a Catholic newspaper in London that showed interest in "things German," including Hegel, to promote the publication of *Capital* to an audience more receptive to dialectical thought. Marx described the work as the "first attempt at applying the dialectical method to political economy."[4]

For the second edition in 1872, Marx altered the structure of the opening chapter, incorporating parts of the 1867 appendix and adding section headings. The treatment of value remains a much-contested aspect of his work—posing the question of Marx's philosophical influences and his particular method. Marx's dedication to dialectical thought and the abstractions of value has left many readers putting down *Capital* without progressing past the initial pages. "Beginnings are always difficult in all sciences," Marx warns the reader.[5] Indeed, the difficulty of *Capital*'s beginning prompted Louis Althusser to recommend the early sections should be rewritten "so that it becomes a 'beginning' which is no longer at all 'difficult,' but rather simple and easy."[6]

However, with all its Hegelian subtleties and seemingly obscure digressions, from Aristotle's *Nicomachean Ethics* to Daniel Defoe's *Robinson Crusoe*, Marx's first chapter and derivation of the value-form provides an opening to comprehend capitalism. Rather than rewriting the beginning of *Capital*, its fundamental conceptual categories should be unfolded to follow the path of critical investigation made possible by this sequence. The value-form is Marx's most significant contribution to critical social theory. It is the theoretical innovation which sets him apart from traditional political thought and political economy and accords his analysis of commodity production and exchange with the historical specificity needed to grasp, and critique, capital. In this book, I reject the traditional view of Marx's theory of value as simply a revision of the "labour theory of value" developed by Adam Smith and David Ricardo. Many economists, heterodox or otherwise, easily dismiss Marx's theory of value, assuming it rests upon the same fundamental premises of the classical view.[7] What emerges from Marx's *Capital* is an account of capitalism as a form of life which is constituted by social relations of domination that restrict in fundamental ways the ability of human beings to recognise each other as free and rational beings in a social world of our own creation. My task in this book is to draw out the normative stakes of Marx's critique of political economy as an understanding of capitalism as a form of life. For Marx, modern society consists of abstract and alienated social forms. His critique of the constitution of such social forms raises moral problems which stretch back through the history of philosophy, politics and economics. From Marx, as I argue, it becomes possible to see ethics, not just in terms of individual ideas of right and wrong behaviour, but as the goal-directed practices that structure social life and its ends. Marx's analysis of sociality must be reconstructed from his immanent critique of classical political economy. However his critical social theory must be distinguished from the object of this reckoning.

In a distinctive way, the dialectic between ethics and politics is part of Marx's adoption, adaptation and absorption of a tradition with an expansive conception of ethical life—a tradition he shares with Aristotle and Hegel. Marx finds an ontology of social being in Aristotle. Since human beings are political by nature, for Aristotle, the basis for ethical virtue is provided by the practical activity of rational agents as they contribute to the flourishing, what he calls *eudaimonia*, of the polis. As for Hegel, reality itself is ethical. The expression of decisively modern and collective self-understanding is the composition of rational institutions, constituted by subjects who can objectively determine social life beyond the egotism of civil society to the mutual recognition and self-consciousness of ethical life entwined in the fabric of the political community. Marx takes from Hegel the conceptualisation of historical forms of being as socially determinate and relational. Like Hegel, Marx seeks the realisation of social freedom in mutual recognition. Cut from the same cloth, Marx shares with Hegel and Aristotle the need for a politics that grasps human action as rational and goal driven. For all three thinkers, the end of social life is the living good of human flourishing. The exact practices and institutions which might realise the good might vary between them; however, each thinker looks to the dynamics of political life as a compass for normative meaning. I argue that Marx's value-form theory provides the crucial means for grasping the ethical dimension of his immanent critique. Marx's analysis of the specific dynamics of social life identifies the contradictions within the forms he sets out to investigate based on their internal logic and relationship to the social whole. Marx goes on to show the normative limitations apparent in these forms, which point to new social practices, activities and forms of life. Marx's theory of the value-form is the result of a close engagement with Aristotle and Hegel. The beginning of Marx's *Capital* bears the mark of Aristotle's *Ethics* and Hegel's *Logic*. As I will show, Marx's dialogic procedure redeems and reinvents the flourishing, *eudaimonia*, of Aristotle's political community and the living good in what Hegel calls *Sittlichkeit*, ethical life. I argue this normative antecedence shines through Marx's value-form theory and empowers his idea of emancipation.

My interpretation highlights the form-determinations operative in Marx's critique of bourgeois economic categories. The most basic category for Marx's theorisation of modern society is "the commodity." The commodity-form is the abstraction from which Marx derives the dual characteristics of wage-labour—the bifurcation between social and private labour in the production of commodities made specifically for exchange. Such objects are values in terms of their practical use and necessary exchange. Commodities appear before us reflecting both qualities and quantities. But commodities only realise their potentiality as value when they are socially actualised by sale on the market. Thus, "value" is the complex metamorphosis of social forms, which Marx unfolds across the volumes of *Capital*, beginning with the use and exchange of commodities and proceeding to the "trinity form" of capital-profit, land-rent and labour-wages. Marx shows the process in which individual and social goods are subsumed by the logic of exchange and equated with our ability to buy and sell on the market. However, as a result of the *need* to continue the accumulation and valorisation of surplus value, the end of human flourishing inevitably loses out to the ends of capital's reproduction. Things cannot be said to be created and exchanged based on how socially useful they are for human beings with complex and multifaceted needs living in communities. Instead, the market trades commodities based on their exchange principle, "value," to derive surplus and make profit. Individuals are pitted against each other, and the social logic of wage-labour means that a defining feature of our relationships to other human beings is as buyers and sellers of commodities. This form of life is premised on an abstract sociality, since the form of value-producing labour specific to capitalism contains both private and social activity. Value is a social relation, but it is an expression of human labour, depending upon the particular social organisation of privately performed labouring tasks. Labour tasks are equalised by the market, which socially mediates the function of this activity. Abstract labour is the social activity that produces commodities to be sold as values. In turn, value is actualised through its metamorphosis into different social forms and its realisation as capital. Capital becomes "self-valorising value"—a force acting on the world as if independent of human action. What Marx unfolds through his dialectic of the value-form is the manner in which value is a social category comprising abstract forms of life. Value, as Marx maintains, is "purely social."[8]

Marx, more than any other thinker, exposes the social mechanisms that underpin the whole process of capitalist production and exchange. For much of contemporary thought, "value" carries either a strictly economic definition (the monetary price of a commodity) or a seemingly moral usage (what *I* value). For Marx, the logic of commodity exchange means people come to associate what is of value with the exchangeable price of things. When put in a more determinate form, value is seen to be simply the *cost* of a commodity as expressed by money. But Marx suggests "value" in capitalist society is something distinct from price. Value, in his view, is a social relation mediated by commodities and their exchange. The commodity Marx identifies as playing the crucial role in this social relation is human labour-power. To see what Marx takes to be normatively unacceptable about capitalism requires confronting the character of value as both a relation and a real abstraction that carries in its common usage the antinomy of the commodity and its fetishism. Marx seeks to understand the full human consequences of value beyond either economic usage or individual decision-making.

Marx claims the essence of value is living labour which finds its necessary appearance in money. Capital is a relation of domination depending upon the extraction of living labour to derive value, which becomes a process that structures social life as a whole. In his writing, Marx returns to the evocative metaphor of capital as a vampire. The life of capital depends upon what it takes from human life:

> Capital posits the permanence of value (to a certain degree) by incarnating itself in fleeting commodities and taking on their form, but at the same time changing them just as constantly; alternates between its eternal form in money and its passing form in commodities; permanence is posited as the only thing it can be, a passing passage—process—life. But capital obtains this ability only by constantly sucking in living labour as its soul, vampire-like.[9]

Requiring the unity of production and circulation for its metamorphosis, value shifts forms in an attempt to valorise and expand through a socially determinate process of accumulation. Beyond providing what he considers facts about capitalist production and exchange, Marx argues that the social relations underpinning value are structured by domination because they rest on the generalised exchangeability of commodities created by value-producing labour. The reduction of human activity into what Marx calls "abstract labour" is the nexus between his mature value-form theory and the concept of alienation present in his early writings. What is important about Marx's concept of labour and his account of the value-form is what it suggests about the paradoxical nature of exchange in capitalist society. On one hand, exchange is generalised in such a way that relations can only be comprehended socially. On the other, exchange can only operate by atomising, individualising and dominating the seller of labour-power. From conceiving this fact objectively in all its determinations, what underwrites Marx's analysis of capitalism and its social forms of life is an embedded ethical claim. Marx's value-form theory concludes with the necessary negation of value. This instruction, at once theoretical and practical, invites normative reflection. By thinking with Marx, we can better see what is wrong about capitalism as a barrier to human flourishing and what it is about our lives as social, rational and historical beings that makes a life well-lived possible. Construed in this way, it becomes viable to interpret the normative structure of his critique of political economy in terms of a sustained ethical vision of the good life.

The domination of capital pervades modern life, and its logic seeps ever more into human relationships and interactions, inexorably subsuming and modifying the meaning of our feeling, treatment of others, as well as the measurement of our individual purposes, self-regard and value. Capitalism structures our ability to live happy lives as individuals and societies. Money-making is always in the foreground or background of our social relationships, no matter its worth. Marx's claim to have elucidated the essence of the processes that mystify and obscure social relations—which are, in fact, structures of domination—relies upon his conceptualisation of value-producing labour. Under capitalism, according to Marx, human labour is made abstract and alienated, which limits and constrains the ability of human beings to control our life activity. The omnipresent fetishism of the commodity shapes our forms of activity and social being.

It is crucial to understand that Marx is not simply a critic of "economics" but is concerned with a critique of capitalism as form of life. As he put it in 1858, "[t]he work I am presently concerned with is a Critique of Economic Categories or, IF YOU LIKE, a critical exposé of the system of the bourgeois economy. It is at once an exposé and, by the same token, a critique of the system."[10] Marx's work on a *critique* of political economy dated back even further. In 1851, he wrote to Engels that he was "so far advanced" in his work that he "will have finished with the whole economic shit in 5 weeks' time." Remarking that "this science [*Wissenschaft*] has made no progress since A. Smith and D. Ricardo," Marx wanted to be done with his research on political economy and be able to "throw myself into another branch of science at the [British] Museum."[11] Unfortunately, five weeks became sixteen years and Marx continued to refine and rework his critique of political economy. His dedication to this unfinished task, which engulfed his research, can make it appear as if Marx was fundamentally a social scientist exemplifying the transition (or break) from German Idealism, steeped in normative philosophy, to sociology, objective and value-free. As I will argue, such characterisation loses sight of the normative dimension of Marx's idea of value and, at the same time, reduces its critical thrust.

In its earliest form, Marx had been working on a critique of political economy since 1844. But even before it became the fully fleshed research program of *Capital*, his turn to this inquiry was envisioned from the very beginning in normative terms. In a remarkable section of the *Economic and Philosophical Manuscripts of*

1844, Marx diverged from his exploration of the intricacies of political economy to draw a picture of the early Parisian working-class movement:

> When communist *workmen* [*Handwerker*] gather together, their immediate aim is instruction, propaganda, etc. But at the same time they acquire a new need—the need for society—and what appears as a means has become an end. This practical development can be most strikingly observed in the gatherings of French socialist workers. Smoking, eating and drinking, etc., are no longer means of creating links between people. Company, association, conversation, which in its turn has society as its goal, is enough for them. The brotherhood of man [*Brüderlichkeit d[er] Menschen*] is not a hollow phrase, it is a reality, and the nobility of man [*Adel der Menschheit*] shines forth upon us from their work-worn figures.[12]

This quotation provides a useful point of departure for the argument I want to advance in this book. Marx does more than reflect on the cultural activity of a newly emerging working-class movement. More significantly, he also demonstrates his developing philosophical claim, an articulation emanating from his understanding of capitalism as a social form of life. This critique emerges in conjunction with a newfound analysis of the content of labour activity as alienated under capital production and reproduction.

Marx comes to the view that capitalist social relations limit the potential and capabilities of human beings as subjects, the type of flourishing and good realisable if we act together. In this passage, association does not simply arise from working together, but from the creative act of collective decision-making. Labour becomes an act of self-conscious intersubjective social connection, rather than alienation. Marx offers a way to think about the sociality of labour in both the process of productive activity itself and in the social relations which constitute its social form. The young Marx articulates a conception of freedom in teleological terms, as a potential to be realised in and by the actions of human beings aiming at a life which looks beyond the alienation of wage-labour. *Capital* carries forward this immanent critique by putting into view the very contradictions within the dynamics of capitalism that make possible emancipation. Marx's thought is fundamentally motivated by the central question of ethics: how we should live? His analysis of capital is nothing but the working out of why capitalism cannot provide the good life.

Marx's portrayal of the Parisian workers brings into focus crucial aspects of the ethical dimension of his thought that will be explored in this book. Marx's ideas went through many changes, modifications and innovations as he continually sought to develop the concepts most adequate to grappling and grasping social life as a whole. But he never gave up the normative claim that underwrites his thought. As I argue, this through line shows that we should not understand his later work from the prism of the young Marx, but view his mature formulations of the form of value as a means to tarry with alienation critique. Marx conceives of our activities as conscious, rational, historical and goal-directed. He considers human needs as capabilities that can be met in accordance with collective association and rational production. Marx suggests that means and ends are not counterposed; human beings cannot simply be taken as a means for others, but means cannot be reduced to their ends. The phrase "what appears as a means has become an end" expresses the sublation of this binary into the telos of ethical life, a society of free association. The collective means becomes an end in itself. For Marx, this association is conceived concretely in the practices which bring about the negation of capitalism as a form of life, defined by value-producing labour, commodity exchange and capital accumulation. Marx's analysis offers a way of conceiving ethical life as the concrete universality in which our social relations, our labour and institutions can become realised as relations of social freedom. Marx shows that capitalism as a form of life systematically precludes relations of recognition between human beings. Our social world is founded by relations of abstract action, from labour to our fundamental moral and political language. Social being and consciousness are made abstract by the social form of life under capitalism.

The work-worn figures Marx describes find dignity in a politics that seeks collective expression in rational association. This action expresses a form of self-consciousness that aims for universality, the collective rational agency that emerges from, and strives to transcend, the contradictions of life under capitalism as divided by class. The "brotherhood of man" (*Brüderlichkeit der Menschen*)[13] reconceives society, challenging the sociality of fragmentation and atomisation of "economic man." On such logic, just as the individual lives a private life at home, their activities at work are equally private. The sole autonomous producer is not the basis of society, but only reflects the abstraction of social forms under capitalism. In rejecting this alienated existence, Marx sees in the nexus of workers the reality of a shared political existence which he calls "a community of human beings." This *reality* is both the actualisation and realisation of socially transformative action, where association makes possible a social form of human activity in which human subjects are in collective control of the productive and political institutions of social life. To find meaning in such institutions requires social relations of recognition. Put this way, Marx's idea of freedom is an understanding of *ethical life*. Borne out of Hegel's appraisal of Immanuel Kant's moral philosophy as empty formalism based on "infinite autonomy,"[14] the guiding thread of Marx's thought traces the contradictions within social relations between human beings that define our activity and forms of life. This inquiry depends upon a conceptualisation of sociality that traces the social mediations between human beings as the basis for normative analysis and critique.

While few would dispute that Marx belongs to the canon of political and economic thought, usually this is seen in terms of the stagist politics attributed to "historical materialism" or the economics of an embodied "labour theory of value." To push past these interpretative impasses, I argue that Marx is foremost a theorist of "the social." Marx fuses political, economic and ethical thought to produce a dialectical account of modern life in the unfolding of social forms specific to capitalism. Marx does not have a single concept of "the social." In fact, ideas of sociality (*Gesellschaftlichkeit*) appear throughout Marx's work in various concepts. Marx speaks of "social relations," "social modes of production," "social division of labour," "socially necessary labour-time," "total social capital," "social labour," "social need," "social reproduction," and of course, "socialism." Fundamentally, Marx maintains that there is no form of human activity that is not social, since we are social beings. Communism can only be a possibility as a result of social forms of human activity, which Marx takes to be constituted by an immanent sociality, that is, life activity that is abstract, alienated and unrealised, but it could be otherwise. That it could be otherwise is a view that Marx develops immanently from his analysis of capitalism and the form of value.

What Marx means by his idea of a postcapitalist form of society requires unpacking the concept of "the social" in his thought. Marx considers "society" and "social" as categories which pertain, resembling Hegel's claim in the *Science of Logic*, to the "exact determination [*Bestimmung*] and discovery of *objective relations*."[15] By treating human beings as ontologically social, Marx assesses human action as embedded in a total social system of production and reproduction. Fundamentally, capitalism is not just an economic system, but a form of life. Marx's account of value shows the way in which social productive activity becomes an abstraction that obscures the actual relations of sociality apparent in the fabric of our lives. The sociality of capitalism is hidden from those who produce it. Capitalism as a form of life is constituted by labour that must be in essence social, even if the individuals who perform this activity are isolated and alienated. This is why Marx also uses "society" to mean a sublation of those relations into a social formation where relations between human beings are readily apparent and rational.

This social view criticises, and goes beyond, Enlightenment conceptualisations of society as a contract between singular individuals. From the perspective of the individual, society is a collection of atomised persons, entering via contract into a governed state with sovereignty. This ontology generates a view of freedom as the protection of individuals against the threat of "the social," which is collapsed into the question of the state and government. The atomist view advances both a critique of government as such (negative liberty) and an affirmation of its necessary power to secure authority and order (ranging from Leviathan to the nightwatchman state). In this view, the separation of individuals is the necessary condition of private interest, which motivates human action. Society arises from the need to regulate and legitimise the interests of private interaction by exchange. Gain is supposed to be the compelling feature of human interaction and rationality. Hegel described this understanding and its reflection in bourgeois "civil society" (*bürgerliche Gesellschaft*) as "the spiritual animal kingdom," a world of "deceit" in which "this individuality which is real in itself is again *singular* and *determinate*. The absolute reality which it knows itself to be is, as it will become aware, therefore the *abstract universal* which is without fulfillment and without content and is only the empty thought of this category."[16] With the idea of "civil society," many Enlightenment thinkers contributed to the creation of a model individual fundamentally bourgeois in nature. In Marx's view, the methodological individualism of Thomas Hobbes and John Locke defined a social theory which was then translated by Adam Smith and David Ricardo, despite protestations, into political economy. Marx picks up the paradox of civil society that troubles Hegel's *Philosophy of Right*. If Hegel sees it that civil society serves a necessary but contradictory system of needs, Marx demonstrates that these limits—poverty, exploitation and alienation—are inherent within capitalist social forms. By doing so, the immanent insight of Hegel's own interpretation of the social contract tradition and political economy are vindicated. Marx shows the insights of both political and economic traditions are undercut by the naturalisation of historically specific social forms. Marx insists the thread that runs throughout is the depiction of human nature as an ongoing tension between benevolence and self-interest in the individual.[17] In this way, the social contract thinkers created an ontological starting point of the atomised individual and a *model* for thinking about society that still acts as a barrier to normative conceptions of the good life.

The notion of civil society expresses a fundamental split between the world of politics and that of commerce. Society itself is conceived as divided between two contradictory notions: the world of the private individual who is the producer, owner, buyer and seller of commodities, and the realm of government, which is the nexus of social structures and interactions that make it possible for individual sellers of commodities to meet each other at the market. This bifurcation presupposes an extant *social* system that has been created by human agents. By drawing attention to this contradiction, Marx highlights the limitations of ahistorical and particular standpoints. He has this in mind in the tenth of the *Theses on Feuerbach*, "[t]he standpoint of the old materialism is civil society [*bürgerliche Gesellschaft*]; the standpoint of the new is human society, or social humanity [*die menschliche Gesellschaft, oder die vergesellschaftete Menschheit*]."[18] Marx's inquiry is a distinct way of conceptualising society. The *Theses on Feuerbach* strike an immanent vision of the possibilities of critique, grasping the present with the demands of a future conceived as a new form of freedom. In the process of the new society emerging from the remnants of the old within the antagonisms of contemporary life, Marx finds revealed an image of transformative possibilities: "The emancipation of the oppressed class thus implies necessarily the creation of a new society [*neuen Gesellschaft*]."[19]

The most fundamental aspects of Marx's immanent critique of the atomistic position are cast in his value-form theory. Crucially, Marx does not adopt the ahistorical and physiological "labour theory of value" found in the traditional view spanning Locke to Ricardo, but instead sets forth an immanent critique of this conceptualisation.[20] Marx's value-form theory is better understood as a "value theory of labour," a historical and critical concept of human activity, abstract labour and social form.[21] As I will argue, the value-form provides the key to open up the normative resources in Marx's thought.

In this book, I trace the importance of Marx's political and economic thought by excavating the specific usages of the category of "the social." This task is primarily developed by locating the ancestry of his thought in Aristotle's social ontology and Hegel's speculative *Realphilosophie*. I group the three philosophers—Aristotle, Hegel and Marx—together as constituting a shared tradition of thinking about society that locates ethics within social relationships which are, in turn, mediated by political concerns and action. All three assess social life in terms of the normative relations of human activity and rational institutions in which human beings might be free. For Aristotle, society is prior to the individual. Ethics must be understood in terms of political life and organisation. Human beings are conceived of ontologically as distinctively rational and political animals, where politics is the exercise of our ethical natures. For Hegel, the human subject seeks social recognition. Conflict and domination are life-and-death struggles for subjectivity that must be sublated through mutual relations of recognition. Individuals are seen not in isolated singularity but in relation with others, both in terms of their conflicts and dependence. Marx detects domination in the social relations of production and reproduction.[22] When the form and content of these relations are defined by capital, they take on characteristics seemingly independent of human control and agency. Thereby, the products of human creative activity become fetishistic, appearing as objects beyond our control. If Aristotle sees freedom in the teleological function of the polis and Hegel perceives it in the rational state, Marx discovers the telos of human beings in a society of freely associated producers.

For Marx, following Hegel, the Enlightenment was unable to provide a coherent account of social reality. Political economy sought to ground an understanding of society in the individual producer—the free commodity owner and seller. Marx's reckoning with political economy establishes a mode of thinking about society and sociality that regards the form of social interaction in question as an expression of relations inherent to capital itself. For Marx, human relations are mediated by things. But these things, although embodied in various objects and means of production, derive their meaning from estranged social relations. Thus, capital itself is a relation and *"simply takes the form of a thing."*[23] This specific social form is paradigmatic of the way human relations are mediated in capitalist society.[24] Marx's thought aims to advance human possibilities, which would require the negation of capital for there to be any hope for such potentiality to be realised. In conceiving of emancipated human activity as "freely associating production," Marx's thought follows Aristotle's definition of the good life as human flourishing. Simultaneously, he also affirms an association of collective institutions, a view in basic accordance with what Hegel finds in ethical life, *Sittlichkeit*. Thinking with Aristotle and Hegel illuminates the ethical dimension of Marx's thinking that has been insufficiently recognised.[25] In reinstating these links, the ethical dimension of his thought comes to the forefront, and it becomes clear that Marx belongs to a tradition of critical inquiry that conceives of ethics as a historically and socially embedded rational practice. Central to such a conception of rationality means articulating the manner in which social life is constituted by practices and institutions. Aristotle's notion of the practices of the virtues is manifest in Hegel's conception of rational agency and in Marx's articulation of political action. Practices aim at the good; they require cultivating the virtues of human action for the end of flourishing, and as such require that human beings make decisions and act on reasons that help bring about that end as the good of collective enterprise.[26] Marx's writings express a view of rational agency as the collective subjectivity in the practice of working-class action. My claim that Marx enables us to think about ethical life brings to bear his normative assessment of modern social forms and the corresponding human rationality and activity that is alienated in such forms of life.

Marx's analysis of capitalism demonstrates the normative barriers to an ethical life. From this position, it becomes possible to generate a conception of mutual recognition where agents give and find meaning in the normative fabric of social life and action informed not narrowly by individual self-gain and interest, but by a rational conception of what a good life for everybody requires. By examining the historical and social form of capital, Marx illustrates that its sociality is in an essential way abstract. Individuality and collectivity are seen in antinomic opposition, rather than in an essential unity.

The intellectual landscape traversed in this book shows that rational inquiry is always set within social, historical and intellectual traditions. In a similar manner to what Alasdair MacIntyre calls "tradition-constituted enquiry," I argue that Marx's social thought and its relevancy today can only be understood "when placed in the context of traditions."[27] The conception of rational enquiry, is "embodied" in tradition. As MacIntyre points out, "the standards of rational justification themselves emerge from and are part of a history in which they are vindicated by the way on which they transcend the limitations and provide remedies for the defects of their predecessors within the history of that same tradition."[28] This insight is suggestive of the reading of Aristotle, Hegel and Marx in this work. It helps push past the tired tropes of Marx scholarship, especially the Althusserian legacy which argues that Marx decisively "breaks" with Hegel and in doing so drops his alienation critique and its normative character. Another influential perspective, critical of Marx, but which helps elucidate the problem of tradition is offered by Hannah Arendt. For Arendt, Marx "adopts" the Hegelian tradition but at the same time, maintains "a concurrent rejection of its authority."[29] While I challenge Arendt's understanding of tradition and her view of its rupture in Hegel and Marx, the advantage of her insight is that the relation between Hegel and Marx is an open question.

By arguing that Hegel and Marx are best comprehended as parts of a shared rational tradition, I mitigate the danger of allowing one tradition to foreclose the other: both the self-referential closure of absolute idealism and the presumed infallibility of the materialist conception of history are avoided. Instead, I focus on their shared attempts to realise the forms of rationality required for human beings to become at home in our social world. This helps us to read tradition not as fixed and settled, but as I argue, a dynamic relation of possibility. Framed in this way, in a world as inhospitable as we find in our contemporary life, critical social theory can lend currency to the Adornoian insight that the bad life cannot be lived rightly, not to recant the possibilities of emancipation, but to show the normative import of holding fast to an idea of the good life.[30]

Clearly, Marx differs from Hegel and from Aristotle in his vision of what exactly this good life constitutes. But the project of this book, and the concept "absolute ethical life," which gives the book its title, is to show that occupying the point of departure between Hegel and Marx requires first unifying Aristotle, Hegel and Marx. *Sittlichkeit* is what Hegel calls "ethical life," the form of life that preserves, but goes beyond, the morality of the individual and realises social freedom in the ethical relations of self-conscious and rational institutions. "Absolute ethical life" is the concept that brings together Hegel's critique of atomised and relative notions of morality (Kant's practical reason) and the historical value of community into a normative theory of recognition. The three key terms in this concept each have significant meaning in Hegel's thought. By "life," Hegel is referring to the specifically rational agency of the human being, who as a living being, strives for self-consciousness. An "ethical life" is the shape of life in which human beings can institute their self-consciousness in relations of recognition between social subjects, which enables our freedom to be shared and sustained.

The "absolute" is Hegel's master concept. While there is a long line of critics (including infamously, Karl Popper) who see this concept as explicitly authoritarian, the absolute is nothing but the philosophical name Hegel provides to articulate freedom. Despite the high altitude of Hegel's writing, his concept of the absolute attempts to render visible the unity of thinking and reality in social life. In many of Hegel's most important texts, the concept of the absolute appears at the end. However, the process of thinking through the relationship between thought and reality also means that a unity is always present, despite its appearances. According to Hegel, the absolute shows itself as the process inherent and necessary to grasp reality in thought and at the same time, as the unified ends, the concrete totality of concept and reality. The journey of forms of historical consciousness as traversed in the *Phenomenology of Spirit* culminate in "absolute knowing," the self-knowledge of spirit. In the *Science of Logic*, the "absolute idea" is the concept that comprehends itself. To know in terms of the absolute is to conceive the possibilities of freedom. For thought to gain self-consciousness, Hegel insists that the speculative position of the absolute must be obtained:

> Free and genuine thought is *concrete* in itself, and as such it is an *idea,* and in its full universality *the* idea, or *the* absolute. The science of the latter is essentially a *system,* since the true insofar as it is *concrete* exists only through unfolding itself in itself, collecting and holding itself together in a unity, i.e. as a *totality.* Only by discerning and determining its distinctions can it be the necessity of them and the freedom of the whole.[31]

To think the absolute entails unifying theoretical and practical reason and by doing so educing "the unity of the idea of life and the idea of knowing." Hegel directly evokes Aristotle's idea of *noêsis noêseôs*, thought thinking itself, to entwine the unity of reason with life. To reason in such a sense is the form of absolute living good.[32] From this view, I draw out the normative aspects of Marx's attempt to systematically unfold the determinations of value specific to capitalism as a form of life. I argue the debt to Hegel stretches beyond logic, since the entire point of mapping such forms is to think the possibility of freedom. For Marx, concrete freedom exists in the living good of the whole, which enables human flourishing.

My idea of "absolute ethical life" seeks to develop the concept by building on Gillian Rose's highly generative interpretation of Hegel. Rose examines the split between theoretical and practical reason in post-Kantian philosophy as a contemporary crisis which demands Hegel's notion of the absolute as the identity of thought and being. Rose's arresting interpretation brings Hegel close to Marx to offer the radical potential of an idea of ethics as a mutually reciprocal form of life. She maintains:

> For Hegel, the whole aim of absolute ethical life was to eschew the domination of the *concept* of pure practical reason. Absolute ethical life is a critique of bourgeois property relations. It may be elusive, but it is never dominant or pre-judged. Minerva cannot impose herself. Her owl can only spread its wings at dusk and herald the return of Athena, freedom without domination.[33]

Expanding on this idea of ethical life, I argue that any Hegelian notion of freedom requires Marx to make good on a conception of the historical conditions of bourgeois life as both property and productive relations. Marx's conception of capitalism spells out that modern rationality is itself beholden to fetishism in the metamorphosis of value as commodity, money and capital, and as such, our form of life is one of misrecognition. This social critique is required for the call of Athena's speculative moment to be realised as a transformative journey worth taking. *Absolute Ethical Life* is the account of why sociality must go beyond capitalism as a form of life.

To comprehend the possibilities of emancipation, critical social theory must grasp the present. The challenge social theory faces today is to provide a conception of modern life that allows the present to be known as both conflictual and transmutable. The conflicts of modern politics, emanating from the public life of citizens and institutions, are by no means unrelated to the conflicts of private life, emanating from the decisions of moral agents, sellers and buyers. However, emancipatory thought too often dissociates these spheres into isolated realms, a procedure that Theodor W. Adorno names the "severance of morality from politics," which results in an "extreme contrast between public affairs and private existence."[34] Ideally, critical social theory should provide a bridge between these two realms; instead it has tended to reproduce this tension between political emancipation and individual morality. Precisely what intellectual resources might enable this tension to be transcended thus remains an open question. Curiously, however, the tendency has been to look everywhere but at Karl Marx.

This work is a reconsideration of Marx's social theory and its relation to other traditions of critical inquiry. But why "reconsider" when Marx's place in the pantheon of modern thought is hardly under threat? Marxism was so prevalent as a form of intellectual critique during the twentieth century that in 1981 MacIntyre could call it "the most influential adversary theory of modern culture."[35] Yet, it was during this period, beginning in the late 1970s, that Marxism started to lose its coherence and authority in theory and practice. This deterioration corresponded with the popularity of various currents, such as "post-structuralism," which moved markedly away from the traditions of critical inquiry established in close reference to Marx's social theory. In effect, these trends sidelined Marx in a way that has been slow to recover.[36] Marx might be seen as foundational and historically significant, but his value as a thinker of the present remains disputed at best and repudiated at worst. Even those intellectual traditions derived from Marx (notably Frankfurt School critical theory and some strands of post-structuralism) are hesitant to posit the immediate relevance of his social theory.[37] Such disregard notwithstanding, during the last two decades an undercurrent has emerged which rejects this common sense, insisting instead on Marx's contemporaneity.

Following the Global Financial Crisis—the biggest crisis of capital since the Great Depression—serious interest in Marx has flourished, no doubt due to the pressing need to understand the structure and nature of contemporary capitalism. Remarkably, "the critique of capitalism has come back into vogue," as Nancy Fraser and Rahel Jaeggi observe in their book *Capitalism*.[38] Despite a proliferation of interest in capitalism, a focus on normativity has often come at the cost of the immanent critique of political economy. As Martijn Konings notes, "a growing emphasis on communitarian or civic-liberal principles of interaction is accompanied by a steadily declining ability to offer penetrating readings of the capitalist economic structures whose oppressive operation and colonizing dynamics are taken to require the need for critical interventions in the first place."[39] My argument in this book is that a normative critique of social forms of life *needs* Marx's critique of the value-form. *Capital* is precisely the text to offer such a vision.[40]

Of further concern, is the little conceptual clarity on the relationship between the concept and the reality of capitalism in much of contemporary political theory. In his book on the history of the word "capitalism," Michael Sonenscher declares that although the term "is still quite hard to define, it remains quite easy to see."[41] He argues that "capitalism" needs to be reinterpreted to consider the background of many earlier concepts into this nineteenth-century word, especially the specific context to the notions of commercial society, the division of labour and civil society expressed by Hegel, Smith, Ricardo and Marx. However, Sonenscher never ventures a definition of capital and simply assumes that capital is the "thing" that people own to produce profit.[42] In this view, "capitalism" and "capital" are conceptually distinct. Yet, he does not see that capital is the necessary condition of capitalism as a social system once it becomes generalisable as a social form. Capital does predate *capitalism*, but as Søren Mau explains, what "distinguishes capitalism from other modes of production is not the mere existence of capital but its social significance; only in this particular mode of production is the accumulation of abstract wealth the basis of social reproduction."[43] Sonenscher claims that the concept "capitalism" needs historical excavation, but in doing so, he leaves untouched the definition of "capital" in mainstream economics and overlooks its historically definite existence.

Marx's own analysis of capital points to foundational conceptual issues in Sonenscher's view. Capitalism cannot be grasped without theorising the historical and social form of wealth. The "social wealth" that Smith termed "the wealth of nations," Marx makes clear, is "a specifically capitalist form of the process of social production" defined by "the self-valorization of capital."[44] For Marx, capital is a social relation between human beings, which appears as a relationship between things. His critical social theory attempts to show the "connection" between

> the simplest categories of the capitalist [*kapitalistischen*] mode of production, in connection with commodities and money, the mystifying character that transforms the social relations for which the material elements of wealth serve as bearers in the course of production into properties of these things themselves (commodities), still more explicitly transforming the relation of production itself into a thing (money). All forms of society are subject to this distortion, in so far as they involve commodity production and monetary circulation. In the capitalist mode of production, however, where capital is the dominant category and forms the specific relation of production, this bewitched and distorted world develops much further.[45]

Capitalism is the social form in which capital is dominant, and its movement defines social relationships well beyond economic ownership as a total form of life.[46] It must be explained through examination of the conceptual makeup of capital as a social form of value. Thus, social forms "are not defined in independence from the object being valued; they emerged from and constitute that object."[47]

This task is pressing since life following the pandemic is more unequal and unstable, with the spiralling cost of housing and stagnant wages. While this book does not explore the contours of the contemporary financial world, it is intended to provide insight into the conceptual genesis of capital and illuminate the connection between political, ethical and economic life. With this theoretical construction, it becomes easier to see that the current crisis is much more than an economic one—it is a crisis of the "conjuncture."[48] The reverberations of surging living costs have exacerbated an existing crisis of political legitimacy for mainstream political institutions. In a situation of global unease, the public sphere has seen a collapse of the political centre. Social movements against inequality, racism and environmental destruction have disrupted typical ideological narratives. The formal freedom of individuals under the law is constantly contrasted with the experience of systemic oppression. The once accepted neoliberal economic and political paradigm is now widely viewed as a failure and is subject to mounting challenge—although as yet, it has by no means been overcome. In the midst of austerity and depression and in the face of an intensifying global growth of the far-right, critical social theory is necessary. In today's world, ordinary people are increasingly seeking theoretical explanations with which to make sense of the contemporary conjuncture. The mounting irrationality of our world demands rational theorisation.

It is here, as a theorist of society, and capitalist society in particular, that Marx is particularly indispensable. Marx helps us comprehend the alienation experienced in everyday life and the persistence of inequality in a world dominated by capital. In this book, I take it that Marx's critique of liberal political and economic theory offers insight into the nature of neoliberal capitalism today.[49] This mode of abstraction avoids the danger of representing "neoliberalism as a return to a more basic form of capitalism modelled on the experience of nineteenth-century liberalism."[50] Instead, by clarifying Marx's critique of political economy, I aim to show fundamental points of connection between capitalism and liberalism and the resonance between economics and political theory in terms of the fundamental categories of capitalism as a social form of life.

My interpretation of Marx offers a basis to reconsider disciplinary boundaries which assume a great deal of distance between economics and politics. I maintain that the development of economic theory is nothing other than the history of political thought. Marx's critique of political economy is the name he gives to his systematic critical reconstruction of the economic categories that comprise the modern world.[51] I argue that Marx *politicises* economics by conceptualising a critical social theory that grasps economic phenomena as social relations that are anything but natural and outside the control of human beings. "Economics" is itself a modern category, and while it is possible to use modern categories to understand the past, there is no "economics" as such before capitalism.[52] The "illusion of the economic," as Patrick Murray calls it, is the view that there is "production in general" which "involves no particular social forms and no particular way of life."[53] By denaturalising "the economic," it becomes possible to draw the connection between modern capitalism and our political and ethical lives.

For this reason, an account of contemporary capitalism must come to terms with Marx's critique of political economy since he demonstrates that any antinomy between politics and economics is untenable. Marx's challenge to contemporary economic thought is that its foundational ideas and categories fail to conceive their conceptual underpinning. Essentially, in his view, economic relations are social. The distinctiveness of Marx's claim that capital is a social relation makes possible an assessment of wealth creation as the accumulation of capital derived on the infinite valorisation of value. Marx's critical social theory establishes a critique of economic thinking on its most fundamental level and in doing so, allows us to rethink the presence of economic logic in our day-to-day lives and our political and social institutions. From Marx, we become better able to assess the domination of our political lives by economic forces once his concept of capital is understood as a political theory of economic logic.

This book maps out a conceptualisation of Marx's idea of capital as a social form of value. By investigating the ethical formation of Marx's concept of capital, I hope to achieve two things. First, I seek to clarify the way in which economic theory has always expressed a moral position, despite foundations in the modern dualistic split between fact and value. Second, by examining the germination of Marx's critique of political economy, I want to show the enduring importance of his thinking about sociality. From this critical project, I argue that Marx's concept of capital provides normative resources to understand crucial ethical questions. Marx's theory of value helps assess the structuring conditions of action in the modern world which make ethics possible.[54] However, Marx's voluminous work—as neither his critics nor his defenders would dispute—contains extended reflection on class, ideology and economic theory. The role of ethics within his theoretical architecture is, however, less easily gleaned. Vulgarised politically and philosophically in traditional Marxist understandings, Marx's thought has often been read as a positivistic science concerned with economic distribution rather than an immanent critique of modern social forms.[55]

When Marxism is reduced to a programmatic demand for the common ownership of the means of production (as opposed to being understood as the moreover *critique* of the very form of capitalist production and exchange), the normative and ethical aspect of Marx's social theory is lost. Such a view assumes that communism retains the same structure of value production while changing the way the results of production are distributed. This vulgarisation renders the key conceptual function of Marx's thought as workers' control of the existing form of production.[56] By comparison, a normative view holds that Marx's critique of value illuminates the necessity of overcoming the form of capitalism itself through rational action. Further, through his explication of sociality, Marx identifies the way in which the entire fabric of social life under capital is dominated by the form of value. For Marx, the social conditions for fully actualised, concrete freedom are immanent in the overcoming of capital. Action can only be conceived as rational insofar as it pursues that end and can only be *realised* as rational insofar as it achieves it. Rather than something that hinges upon individual choice, therefore, Marx's construal of the good life is the realisation of a particular kind of social world—a social world in which rationality prevails and human beings can recognise each other in reciprocal relations of freedom. I call this theory "absolute ethical life." Under the value-form, actualised rationality is impossible, although it is promised. To be truly free, subjects must overcome the forms of domination which mask and mystify the social world (including "bourgeois morality" itself) and ask a wider set of questions about the total composition of social life.

I argue that an idea of ethical life motivates Marx's thought, and this idea allows his theorisation of modern social relations to be adequately critical. Marx's account of alienation and abstract labour does not just amount to an analysis of how capitalism is reproduced; it accords for an immanent critique of modern social relations. Within this examination resides his critical account of the human capacity, rationality and self-consciousness which are present under capitalism, but are not fully realised and constituted as actual. Until the very end, Marx's vision of emancipation is underpinned by a concept of human flourishing. While this concept is discerned via critical social inquiry within capitalism, wherein human virtues do exist, albeit in stunted or one-sided forms, the concept may only be actualised by a free humanity, flourishing in the fertile ground and clear light of a society built around interdependent social relations of freedom. However, locating this conception of ethics requires a reconstruction and elaboration of both the form and content of Marx's thought.

With his immanent critique, Marx calls attention to a paradox that goes to the heart of the modern meaning of freedom. Few normative ideals have been so closely associated with the emergence of modernity as freedom, and under this banner, the spread of capitalism globally was accompanied by many assurances to newly learnt freedoms, despite the colonial processes that brought it about. Freedom from the bonds of direct coercion and personal domination was promised in the equal rights of all human beings as individuals. It is essential to Marx's account that capitalism not only brings about unheralded productive powers but acts to establish social relations on the norms of natural equality, rather than in natural hierarchy.[57] There is no mistaking Marx's appreciation of capitalism for exactly what it promises: freedom. But just as capitalism brings about freedoms that are real and instigates revolutionary advances, Marx's analysis magnifies the contradictions between the norm and reality of freedom that run in both directions. "Immanent critique not only measures reality against the norm," as Rahel Jaeggi contends, "but also *the norm against reality.*"[58] While calls for freedom inspire and capture something real about the emergence, actuality and possibilities that arise with capitalism, for Marx, such a notion of freedom was always deployed at the same time to justify the limitation and curtailing of freedom. Freedom under capitalism is always limited, since the very relations of equality brought about by capitalism are undercut by the processes that made this dynamic and its reproduction impossible.[59] An evocative section of *Capital* parallels the "very Eden" of the Genesis story of the creation and fall of man with the veneration of freedom as "the innate rights of man":

> the exclusive realm of Freedom, Equality, Property and Bentham. Freedom! Because both buyer and seller of a commodity, let us say of labour-power, are determined only by their own free will. They contract as free persons, who are equal before the law. Their contract is the final result in which their joint will finds a common legal expression. Equality! Because each enters into relation with the other, as with a simple owner of commodities, and they exchange equivalent for equivalent. Property! Because each disposes only of what is his own. Bentham! Because each looks only to his own advantage. The only force bringing them together, and putting them into relation with each other, is the selfishness, the gain and the private interest of each. Each pays heed to himself only, and no one worries about the others. And precisely for that reason, either in accordance with the pre-established harmony of things, or under the auspices of an omniscient providence, they all work together to their mutual advantage, for the common weal, and in the common interest.[60]

Marx's appraisal of formal equality raises two crucial points. First, the inalienable human rights so essential to modern normative ideals of freedom are undermined by the emptiness and formalism of its actual expression. By pointing to the distance between the norm and reality (and vice versa), Marx is not denying the normativity apparent under capitalism, but illustrating the variance from the conception of freedom and dynamic of capitalism that on one hand lends legitimacy to its reproduction and on the other, cannot possibility live up to its principles.[61] Such rights are contradictory since not only do the norms prove to fall short of their aspiration, but the promise of autonomy in commodity exchange results in the social compulsion for self-gain. The "universal" freedom of the individual becomes the freedom of private interest.

Second, Marx attributes this tragic symptom of modern freedom to be manifest in moral thought. Invoking Jeremy Bentham's utilitarianism, Marx points out that if freedom is reduced to formal equality under capitalism, then modern morality is reduced to individualism. Marx calls attention to the impossibility of a moral philosophy that centres its standpoint narrowly on the individual, since it loses sight of the broader social relations that human beings are embedded within. So imagined, morality is just as limited as the freedom to buy and sell one's labour-power. But in this forceful appraisal of the norms of freedom under capitalism by the lights of its central claims, Marx is not disavowing normativity all together. The "soberly pedantic and heavy-footed oracle" of Bentham might act as a stand in for bourgeois morality, but he does not represent normativity as such.[62] Instead of a morality of mutual self-gain, inscribed in Marx's insight is that each sphere—freedom, equality, property and morality—must be made social. His immanent critique is not to deny, but to show their meaning could only be sustained through the mutual recognition of human beings who see their normative practices not in self-gain, but in social freedom. Marx's contribution as a thinker of freedom should not be understated.

The normative dimension of Marx's critique of modern social forms challenges, and provides insights to overcome, contemporary conceptions of ethics as merely proper individual behaviour.[63] This critical comprehension enriches recent debates in political, moral and economic theory. To do this, I bring Marx's early texts into dialogue with the contemporary literature on *Capital*. One vital strain in recent discussions is the effort to contest traditional "substantivist" understanding of Marx's "labour theory of value" that takes value to be primarily an account of the quantity of physiological labour necessary for a commodity to be created.[64] The problem with such views is that not only is the value of a commodity simply equated with labour, but the necessary connection between the social forms of the commodity, money and capital is elided. Further, the recent revival of work on *Capital* has coincided with the emergence of growing interest in Hegel in Anglo-American philosophy from the pioneering work of scholars including Robert B. Pippin, Terry Pinkard and Robert Brandom.[65] Despite their general disinterest in Marx, this renaissance of post-Kantian thought sets the ground for reinterpreting the Hegel-Marx relation afresh.[66] I engage with their normative reading of Hegel, which advances a highly generative picture of rational agency as a space of reasons, to develop the implications for coming to terms with the normative aspects of Marx's social theory.[67] These discussions have helped push Marx's thought back into the theoretical problems of post-Kantian philosophy and away from the monopolies of economists.

Drawing on normative philosophy helps assess the status of "the economic" and Marx's critique of economic thought as such. Impressive recent work on the relationship of Marx to his philosophical ancestors recasts the role of Hegelian logic in his critique of political economy.[68] However, the normative dimension of Marx's mature work is often missing from accounts that stress its logic. Questions about the ethical implications of his critique of political economy have often been relegated to the background. I pursue these questions through the prism of Marx's social ontology and the ethical dimensions of his value-form theory. The approach makes it possible to think beyond the classical fact/value distinction by instead conceiving of Marx's immanent critique as also developing a concept of ethical life. This concept builds off and incorporates other traditions of ethics. Concurrently, a renewed interest in Marx's attitude towards ethics has resulted in a series of scholarly collections in the last several years.[69] However, no full-length work has reassessed the relation between Marx's social and ethical thought and recent work on his value-form theory.[70] This work aims to initiate a sustained discussion within that space.[71]

This book contributes to the renewal of Marx's social thought in terms of his critique of modern social life and the modes of existence characteristic of capitalist social relations. I suggest that modern life cannot be reduced to the latest economic stage of the capitalist mode of production. Instead it ought to be understood as the distinctive paradigm of social relations dominated by the value-form. In Robert B. Pippin's account, modernity is understood in terms of autonomy, "the nature of both the independence and the dependence or finitude of modern communities and individuals."[72] For Hegel, this requires a historical and collective view of subjectivity, born by the concept of absolute spirit. Marx's critique of modernity is similarly conscious of the antinomy between independence/dependence and communities/individuals. However, he denies that autonomy (understood as it has been from Kant onwards) can be assessed independently of the determinations of capitalist social forms.[73] Marx's critique of political economy comprehends the systematic nature and structure of capitalism from a dialectical logic that identifies the antinomies of bourgeois categories and social forms.

Marx's ongoing dialogue with the tradition of ethical life in Aristotle and Hegel establishes an important philosophical component of his critique of political economy. His value-form theory builds upon Aristotle and Hegel while making his contribution distinctive. Marx turns to Aristotle and Hegel in order to show that the hidden "secret" of the commodity form is capable of grounding a coherent account of an abstract form of sociality which is historically specific to capital. By comprehending the capitalist mode of production in its conceptual determinations, Marx comes to understand the present in thought; the modern world cannot be known without deciphering capital.

In a highly perceptive comment, made only in passing in *Hegel Contra Sociology*, Rose observes that the theory of commodity fetishism is "the most speculative moment in Marx's exposition of capital" since it "comes nearest to demonstrating in the historically-specific case of commodity producing society how substance is ((mis)-represented as) subject, how necessary illusion arises out of productive activity."[74] While Rose does not demonstrate the insight and leaves it unpursued, I take this proposition to have considerable benefits for working out the conceptual categories that run across *Capital*. Rose alerts us to the ethical and normative purpose inherent in this theoretical critique. Marx's dialectical procedure parallels Hegel's speculative philosophy and should be seen not just in terms of logical derivations and transitions, but also with the normative dimension that such a procedure necessary involves. For Hegel, *Geist*, as absolute spirit, is the self-moving "reflection on the essential self-identity of the human community" and the subject of social life.[75] Marx extends this insight to theorise the self-movement of value, which in its self-valorisation, its constant reproduction, creates a logic which defines social life and subjects all forms of being and social practice under its force. On this basis, he finds that the alienation and domination of social being is intrinsic to capital. Marx's deployment of Hegel prompts vital questions of subjectivity and consciousness, since for Hegel, *Geist* is the self-consciousness of historical and social life. Capital, on the other hand, is an alienated social form. But Marx's interest in *Capital* is to unfold the social ontology of value. Capital is value-in-process, the limitless, infinite movement of things which take their socially recognisable form in commodities and money. In its continued accumulation, its limitlessness, capital is a force that self-creates by extracting the living and creative activity from human labour. The contradiction here is between the prevailing social relation which is both dynamic and self-valorising and its abstract and alienated condition of existence.

The practical life of capital, by necessity, produces and reproduces social domination.[76] This domination can only be undone by agents who become aware of this logic and act practically and rationality to overcome it. In the negation of these relations, Marx conceptualises a new social form as rational and concrete sociality as relations of interdependence. Emergent subjects with a commitment to breaking with this logic must recognise that their collective task requires the negation of capital and the establishment of institutions which are rational and enable people to see their freedom actually realised in themselves and others. The ethical organisation of free institutions must be seen in political terms since the ethical composition of social life is organised politically. Marx sees the overcoming of abstract social forms and the creation of institutions of self-rule as the form of concrete sociality that might realise the concept of freedom. This realisation is the human control of the social world, to grasp the human potential beyond the life of individual buyers and sellers of commodities. For Marx, a society of associated producers allows rationality to be institutionalised and mutually recognised.

This book is divided into three parts, each containing two chapters. Part I introduces key contemporary debates concerning political and ethical action in Marx's thought. I examine the critical appraisals of Marx made by Hannah Arendt and Alasdair MacIntyre. Both thinkers offer compelling accounts of the crisis of modern human activity in terms of a loss of meaning in political action and ethical virtue. Arendt and MacIntyre advance decisive insights into the composition of modern political and ethical life. Arendt's theory of political action is a crucial means for comprehending the limits of economic thinking and the value of political deliberation. MacIntyre offers a sweeping critique of modern moral philosophy. According to MacIntyre, modern moral language is severed from socially intelligible practice. To challenge the individualism of today's world, he suggests the fostering of ethical practices conducive to the human good. Both Arendt and MacIntyre set forward theories of political and human action with the depth of perception that dramatically advances our understanding of modernity and its differences with forms of politics and ethics that preceded capitalism. Each rejects the prioritisation of economics and the reduction of human action to its dictates. As such they share considerably with Marx, yet both put substantial attention in refuting his thinking about human action. For this reason, I intently scrutinise their misreadings of Marx, since as I see it, to best fortify his conception of political action and social ontology depends upon animating the most crucial insights in Arendt and MacIntyre. By designing their theories in explicit opposition to Marx, in one respect Arendt and MacIntyre confirm his import for contemporary political and ethical action. Through examining the misapprehensions that shape both interpretations of Marx, I propose that Arendt and MacIntyre ask the right questions about Marx. Despite the substantial textual problems in their answers, their provocations bring to the surface the vitality of political and ethical action. By giving an account of human action in these terms, the essential motivations of Marx's critical theory of society are clarified and enriched.

Chapter 1 maps out the radical possibilities and limits of political action in Arendt's thinking. In her remarkable intervention into the Western tradition of political thought, Arendt sees human freedom in the capacity of political action to spark new beginnings. People acting together in the public realm offers a political life well beyond the limits and constraints of bureaucratic parliamentary models. As she argues, modern politics is reduced to economic life. Interestingly, she locates this argument not just in early economic theorists, but in Marx. In a direct sense, although often misunderstood, Arendt's conception of political action is conceived as a response to Marx. In this chapter, I draw on the strength of her concept of action but show that her construal of Marx is faulty. In particular, I address Arendt's interpretation of Marx as it evolved through the 1950s. What she first calls Marx's "turning operation" of Hegel and the Western tradition of political thought becomes the infrastructure for her critique of labour and "the social" in *The Human Condition* (1958). Arendt dismisses "process thinking," which she associates with Marx's inheritance from Hegel, and rejects Marx's social ontology which she associates with his inheritance from Aristotle. According to Arendt, Marx's idea of politics collapses the possibility of action since it is grounded in the biological necessity of life rather than the distinctive public realm of political freedom. Arendt argues that Marx's concept of politics is inadequate for the modern world. In *HC*, Arendt specifies her challenge to Marx's concept of labour. In an all-out attack on his social ontology, Arendt argues labour is glorified, reducing politics to necessity and erroneously folding ethics into the fact of labour. However, I contend that Arendt's distinction between "labour," "work" and "action" fails to capture the richness of Marx's theorisation of labour.[77] Contra Arendt, I emphasise the extent to which Marx's political writings offer a concept of action, which is advantaged, by its relation to a normative account of the social form of labour.

In chapter 2, I undertake a throughgoing examination of MacIntyre's major contribution to ethical theory, *After Virtue* (1981). The book is a brilliantly conceived and executed diagnosis about what has gone wrong in modern moral philosophy, composed from wide-spanning philosophical, historical and political reflection on social forms of moral life. In Jaeggi's words, MacIntyre is "one of the most dazzling figures in Anglo-American analytic philosophy," but the interpretation of his work has tended not to stray far beyond *AV* and as a result he is seen almost "exclusively as a proponent of virtue ethics and as communitarian critic of modernity."[78] I argue that the brilliance of MacIntyre's project can be better understood and its ethical and political potential expanded by analysing his engagement with Marx. I contrast *AV* with his New Left writings in the late 1950s to highlight elements of clarity and anticipate lines of departure. Ultimately, MacIntyre makes the case that Marx is unable to initiate a conception of ethical action that avoids the dominant moral dualisms of modernity. As he sees it, Marx does not take enough from Aristotle and thus falls victim to modern individualism. MacIntyre advocates a type of practice-based virtue ethics which contests individualist approaches to morality. However, this account loses coherence when trying to articulate the upshot of his historical argument. In his rehabilitation of the virtue ethics of the Greek tradition, I find that MacIntyre neglects a convincing explanation of the relation between individuality, particularity and universality in modern politics. Both MacIntyre in *AV* and Arendt in *HC* look for possible solutions to the modern bureaucratic world by amplifying the variance between our political and ethical life and the meaning it had for the Greeks. This contrast acts not to insist on a return to the polis, but to trace just how much our modern sense of politics and ethics has shifted away from its basis in the shared interaction of political and ethical life. I suggest each approach fails, in part, since Arendt and MacIntyre in turn dismiss Marx. Through his intellectual genesis in Aristotle and Hegel, Marx critically appreciates Greek freedom but looks to analyse a distinctly modern form of social life with a depth of vision that goes further than Arendt and MacIntyre. In evaluating the limits of these readings, which rely on thin repudiations of Marx's thought, I endeavour to retain the centrality of political action and ethical practices. Indeed, I contend that Marx helps empower these concepts in ways that support Arendt's and MacIntyre's insights but gives direction to a stronger conception of social freedom. This discussion prepares the ground for an immanent reconstruction of his social theory and its inheritance.

In part II, I examine the intellectual tradition shared by Aristotle, Hegel and Marx to stress the dialogic partners needed to overcome the aporia in the scholarly discussion. I trace the conception of ethical life in Aristotle and Hegel and propose lines of continuation in Marx. In this way, I directly situate Marx within broader traditions in the history of political thought, allowing a better construal of his thinking of sociality contra various forms of methodological individualism. Tracing these issues in reference to the history of social theory, I argue Marx's thought must be read as an expansive dialogue with Aristotle and Hegel. This dialogue is outlined in chapter 3. Together Aristotle and Hegel locate ethical life in the socially recognisable forms of action related to the polity and chart the realisation of human rationality, as a teleologically informed process, in political terms. What conceptually constitutes the good life in Aristotle's Athens bears a striking resemblance to the social substance of Hegel's rational state. Both construe human flourishing in terms of practices that are socially validated and collectively shared. A practice is an activity that is defined by an internal dynamic of cultivation and purpose. Together they provide an ontology of political and social beings, understood teleologically in Aristotle and then historically in Hegel. The conversation between these two thinkers becomes a richer dialogue still when Marx enters the agora. I discuss the three thinkers as constituting a tradition of thinking about ethics and politics together as *ethical life*. This concept understands social life in terms of the shared rationality and mutual recognition which make political life ethical.

The tradition of ethical life runs against the prevalent methodological individualism of contract theory and classical political economy. Chapter 4 examines this ontology of individualism as presented in Daniel Defoe's 1719 novel *Robinson Crusoe*. Robinson Crusoe is a mythic character who lives not only in the popular imaginary but through the history of political and social thought. Defoe's protagonist lives marooned on his island, isolated and apart from society. At the same time, the novel tells a story about colonial domination and expansion. The narrative is a perfect naturalisation of the "bourgeois" world and its colonial conditions of possibility, dependent on an ontology of the self-sufficient individual. This chapter analyses this lineage in the social contract theory of Hobbes, Locke and Jean-Jacques Rousseau. Later, Hegel used the novel to illustrate his dialectic of mastery-servitude. Challenging the atomism of the state of nature, Hegel's theory of recognition gives an account of social freedom, where the individual is formed in and through social interdependence. This sociality is continued by Marx, who satirises Defoe's novel in his value-form critique of political economy. The value-form provides insight into Robinson's labour and Marx's difference with Locke and the classical labour theory of value. For Marx, the myth of "natural man," typical in liberal economic and political theory, hides the domination and imperial expansion of capitalist development. Robinson Crusoe reflects the internalisation of the abstract rationality of commodity production and exchange. However, Marx's immanent critique of the novel points to a radical idea of social life and freedom.

Part III offers an interpretation of Marx's social ontology and his value-form theory. Chapter 5 explores Marx's social ontology in his 1844 writings. Through his concept of "species-being," Marx advances an account of the alienated social form of labour under capitalist production. In his early examination of political economy, Marx calls into question the normative foundations that underpin the theories of Adam Smith and James Mill. Marx embraces Aristotelian social ontology to conceptualise the distinctly rational form of human life as "species-beings." But Marx modifies Aristotle's view, historising his idea of sociality with a conception of alienated labour. In Marx's view, capitalism as a form of life systematically prevents human beings from having self-control of our free activity, since production involves the alienation of human beings. In his incredible early manuscripts, Marx insists that capitalist production rests upon a form of domination that renders human life alienated and, in a fundamental way, impedes our flourishing. In Marx's account, the social form of labour under capitalism limits the ability of human beings to exercise the ends of our distinctively human capabilities. This form of alienation atomises and separates, privatising social acts, so that human beings relate to each other through the logic of capitalist production and reproduction. Our normative social roles and practical identities are shaped by our place within a system of capital, where individuals sell their labouring capacity only for this activity to become the source of another's profit. In turn, money becomes the form of value which binds us to each other—we relate to each other through the hostile exchange of the market. We "treat each other as the private owners" of external and alienated things in a "relationship of reciprocal isolation and foreignness."[79] This normatively impoverished form of life is characterised by the dominance of economic interest. The individual's being-for-self is alienated from their being-for-others. Marx conceives of alienated production and value accumulation as a relation that fundamentally denies the potentiality of human beings to rationality and collectively realise our capacities in concert with others as an end in itself. In this sense, Marx's idea of labour is teleological since abstract labour and the capitalist form of life shape sociality and our normativity to the logic of the market. Marx's early analysis of alienated labour shows that this activity results in a pernicious form of life and social domination. But in his critique of this historical form of activity, Marx sees the immanent possibilities in productive activity to endow a normative sociality that could foster, rather than hinder, creativity and potential. Marx's theory holds fast to flourishing of human beings.

Chapter 6 examines the normative stakes of Marx's value-form theory. Crucial to my interpretation is that Marx's idea of value is an immanent critique, rather than a simple modification of the classical labour theory of value. If Marx's 1844 writings anticipate a construal of value as a social form, defined by alienation, his mature theory comes to a new level of sophistication to understand both the historical form of life activity and its alienation under capitalism. Marx's concept of capital employs a speculative logic that grasps the composition of social relations via an immanent critique of economic categories. He charts these relations in the social forms, commodity, money, capital, which are derived as dialectical unities that shape the domination of human activity in capitalist society. Tracing the normative elements of Marx's idea of sociality articulates his contribution to comprehending ethical life. Drawing on the *Grundrisse* and *Capital*, as well as lesser-known texts, this chapter focuses on the way in which Marx's theorisation of the fetish character of the commodity is essential to an ongoing critique of capital. Marx develops his critique of political economy not just in response to the classical view, but by bringing Aristotle and Hegel into the centre of his analysis. Across *Capital*, especially in the early chapters, Marx contrasts Aristotle's idea of wealth creation to the modern self-valorisation of value. This chapter supplies justification for the work as a whole and legitimises the approach set out in part I and part II. The chapter brings to bear the full conceptual and normative shape of Marx's thinking about society and the form of value constitutive of modern capitalism. In his conception of society, Marx attempts to unveil the fetishism of modern domination by the speculative unfolding of social relations in terms of a logic of social forms.

To conclude I explore the aspects of my normative interpretation that could furnish further thought about emancipation. I frame my conclusion with that of Adorno, since he is the thinker after Marx who most explicitly addresses the ethical absence at the heart of late capitalism and raises the ensuing problems for emancipation we currently face. Further, I reflect on five threads that are woven through the normative fabric of Marx's thought. First, I discuss Marx's concept of needs. This recurring idea, articulated in various guises across his texts, is that capitalism not only fails to meet the needs of human beings, but its constitute structure actively prevents it from doing so. Second, I make clear that his concept of social individuality found in his mature work sustains a notion of human flourishing. Third, I make some brief remarks about the significance of time in Marx's thinking about the rational organisation of human activity. Fourth, I suggest Marx's idea of rational organisation involves a conceptualisation of what it would mean for human activity to be self-conscious. His idea is motivated by the goal-directed practices that give normative meaning to our action and enable the good to be shared between human beings. Fifth, I reach the end of Marx's argument, his idea of a free society, which he fittingly sees as a new beginning. Steeped in Aristotelian and Hegelian thought, Marx's idea of emancipation is not a rupture with this tradition, but its most adequate idea. It is an idea of absolute ethical life.

This work presents Marx as a thinker for today.[80] His critique of capitalism exposes the manner in which capital valorises itself by absorbing living labour. Capital is a dead weight that bears upon the living and "lives the more, the more labour it sucks."[81] The history of society has been the history of the denial of human beings the ability to rationally control our own labour by the structures of division and separation imposed by entire epochs of domination and servitude. Modern life is mediated by economic markets and political institutions that not only seem out of the control of human subjects but objectify that lack of control in forms of domination. Further, the domination of modern life distorts and fetishises the social forms that mediate experience. If social theory is to provide a conception of freedom from this domination, it must reveal the origin and function of these fetishistic relations. In doing so, social theory must investigate the barriers to the rational self-consciousness which would allow human agents to realise a rational and recognitive social world.

The politics of the modern world are shaped by the domination of racial and gendered oppression, imperialism and state repression, set against the disequilibrium of labour relations and market exchange. The politics of freedom relates not just to the nature of political structures, but to the forms of human action which motivate the questioning of these relations. For freedom to be thought in political terms, freedom must become the concern of ethics and simultaneously its principle and ground. Simply put, political life must meet ethical life. A rational social order is one in which rationality is realised in the social forms that enable freedom to be embodied in the ethical life of the polity; in the institutions self-created and self-controlled by human agents aware of their roles and responsibilities as recognised in their social individuality. This idea of political emancipation relies upon a conception of ethical life. A form of freedom that can realise itself absolutely—as self-conscious and universal—is *freedom without domination*. To struggle against domination on the basis of a shared social existence gives an ethical status to Marx's thought that is both located in the activity of collective labour, in the objective labour process itself, and at the same time, in the subjective potential for agency. For all the freedom denied to human beings under the abstract sociality and the domination of capital, potentiality remains an enduring *reality and hope*.

PART I

ONE

Politics as Action

Hannah Arendt

IN EARLY 1951, HANNAH ARENDT sent Karl Jaspers, her former dissertation supervisor and lifelong friend, a copy of her first major book, *The Origins of Totalitarianism*. It was a birthday gift and yet to hit bookshops. In their letters, they exchange their ideas, plans and spirits. On 4 March, Arendt ruminates on the far-reaching political issues raised by *Origins* which require going back to the philosophical tradition to better answer. "Western philosophy has never had a clear concept of what constitutes the political, and couldn't have one, because, by necessity, it spoke of man the individual and dealt with the fact of plurality tangentially," Arendt commits to paper, only to retract the thought immediately. "But I shouldn't have written all this. None of it is thought through at all. Excuse me." However, from this point in her life, Arendt became centrally concerned with this question, and it comes to entirely define her thought. Not by coincidence, in the same letter she raised another issue that will occupy her future thinking: the relationship between Marx and freedom. Reading his early work, she reflected that "the de-humanizing of man and the de-naturalizing of nature—are what Marx means when he talks about the abstraction of society, and a rebellion against these things seems to me to be still alive in the later Marx as well."[1] For the next several years she worked on Marx's thought to help work out "the political," even as she ultimately rejected Marx as a suitable thinker of freedom. *The Human Condition* (1958) reflects her grappling with both problems.

In what becomes *HC*, Arendt traces the lost meaning of human action in the modern world. She puts forward a sweeping account of the fundamental aspects of human life, "labour," "work" and "action," which she categories as the *vita activa*. This term is itself "loaded and overloaded with tradition," and the task of *HC* is to show the impact of these distinct activities on the condition of human beings living together.[2] Arendt's account of tradition assesses the loss of action with the collapse of political life and the growth of "the social realm" in modernity. As she sees it, modern thought has obscured the ancient distinction between private life and public action. Arendt evokes a vision of politics in which public speech and action allow for a distinctive space of "plurality" for human beings to define ourselves as equal and free beings living with others. The good life is one lived in the public realm. Accordingly, the modern "rise of the social" has come at the expense of our ability to express our plurality as human beings by acting together as a political community of citizens. Once the public realm vanished, passivity imbued modern politics and came to define the operation of representative forms of government. To most in our contemporary world, living well is a private concern without political character. For Arendt, the private realm of economics has become dominant and diminished the political meaning and possibility of the good life. Modern mass society has stretched over the public realm and destroyed its vitality. By confusing activities that were once properly distinct, "labour" and "work" corrode the public realm and "exclude the possibility of action" since "society expects from each of its members a certain kind of behavior, imposing innumerable and various rules, all of which tend to 'normalize' its members, to make them behave, to exclude spontaneous action or outstanding achievement."[3]

In Arendt's account, "the social" packs together economic life, morality and political action into a single category, and in doing so our public life, which provides the space for moral and political action, is closed. Rebranded as "the social," economics, which was once the private matter of the *oikos*, household, has become the primary mode of modern life. Arendt insists this predicament is entrenched in the modern tradition of political thought that has dominated the West. Arendt looks to revive an Aristotelian conception of human beings as political animals, in which logos, reasoned speech, is the very condition of human action. For Arendt, speech and deed in the public realm allow our character as political beings to be defined; it is the place for individuality, where human beings can prove themselves in concert with others. In Aristotelian terms, this action is conceived as *eudaimonia*, the flourishing life well-lived. Arendt finds inspiration in the ancient polis, presenting a vision of political freedom in the words and deeds of individuals interacting in the public realm. She exalts the Greek definition of politics as persuasion. The political life of the polis consisted in decision "through words and persuasion and not through force and violence."⁴ The polis helps shape her concept of action, but her thinking cannot be seen as a nostalgic demand for its return. Rather her idea of the polis is deployed as part of her provocation that without action modern politics is not free. The word and deed of the polis demonstrate that political action is crucial to our freedom as human beings and as such can inspire political participation and shared decision-making today. But recalling the ancient priority of words and deeds cannot supplant modern politics. Indeed, in her exaltation of the council movements in the Russian and German revolutions and the 1956 Hungarian Uprising, the polis helps motivate her understanding of their promise. From the polis, Arendt sets forth a theory of participation and democratic founding to promote a vision of the good life that might challenge the lack of meaning human action has in modern mass society.

Arendt's critique of modern politics is arresting. She identifies serious problems in modern representative politics and in looking to restore the dignity of action, points to a vital issue: the action of human beings is reduced to economics and the motivation of self-interest, gain and competition. Today, participatory political action is derided by mainstream institutions, especially political parties and legal systems. Public politics is often reduced to the logic of self-interest and economic organisation, whereby the "winners" and "losers" of state policy assumes human subjects are simply economic units who make decisions based on their "hip pocket nerve."⁵ In the modern world, political opinion is simply equated with economic preferences. The "bourgeois man" has eclipsed the citizen. Arendt's council model of democracy articulates participation as the decisive salvo to bureaucratic representative systems, logics and structures. With acerbity, Arendt's gives the lie to any institution that proports to value democratic practices, but rather is controlled by an elite with a contempt for democracy. By addressing the loss of political action in modernity, she brings to light the engulfment of economics in a "consumers' society" which has fundamentally obscured freedom by reducing human action to economic function. Arendt's political theory has major implications for economic and moral thought. Without political action, modern society normalises economic behaviour in moral terms.

Significantly, Arendt's idea of action has helped motivate political movements and public confrontations to bureaucratic embodiments of politics. From her popularity in the New Left to struggles against climate change and the Black Lives Matter movement today, Arendt is looked to as a theorist of political protest.[6] A prominent trend in contemporary social theory has drawn on her idea of the spontaneity of political action to help theorise democracy, stretching from what Jacques Ranciére called the "hatred of democracy" to Miguel Abensour's idea of "insurgent democracy" and Adriana Cavarero's "surging democracy."[7] For such theorists, defending democracy against domination entails giving space to politics as human action in the public realm. Arendt's idea of spontaneous action is not reducible to "fleeting or momentary surges of horizontal power," but involves a commitment to what comes next, to the longevity of political involvement, in organising and creating the space of politics.[8] Interestingly, Arendt generates this conception from her frontal critique of the Western tradition and its foreclosure of political action.[9]

Arendt's analysis in *HC* is generative. Her assessment of the encroachment of economics on political life in modernity is a rich source of imagination and insight for public action. Since Marx's eleventh thesis on Feuerbach, few thinkers have been so centrally occupied with the problem of political action and its vitality for human life and meaning. Yet, intriguingly much of her argument in *HC* is motivated by a critique of Marx. Her close engagement with Marx throughout the 1950s did not lead to loud endorsement or quiet acquiescence, but instead to sharp disagreement. In the midst of McCarthyism, Arendt set out to evaluate Marx's mantle as a thinker of freedom, in terms she considered apart from the traditional right and left interpretations. Not only did *HC* originate as an attempt to address this question, but the dismissive stance ultimately taken towards Marx in the book can easily obscure her motivation to respond to his idea of social freedom. Even as she ultimately disagreed with him, I suggest there is a significant upshot to restoring Marx's constructive role on Arendt's central arguments in *HC*. With Arendt, Marx's idea of action can be better enunciated; and with Marx, Arendt's idea of democracy can be given a definite social content. Understood together, we can better identify the barriers to, and the necessity for, political action against capitalist domination.

To put this problem into relief, her interpretation of Marx will be considered in detail. For Arendt, the problem of "the social" is bound up with Marx's concept of labour. In discerning the loss of political action, Arendt proposes what action in modernity would have to look like for it to be meaningful. On both scores, she lays blame on Marx, since in her view, he promotes economic life as the basis of all action and in doing so confirms the ascendency of "the social" and the forfeiture of political action. Accordingly, Marx marks a definite turn away from politics. As she would have it, Marx's thought is burdened by his Hegelian and Aristotelian inheritance. Marx borrows Hegel's idea of absolute spirit and repackages it as class struggle, but as a result is unable to rid the theory from the determinism of dialectical "process thinking." Marx's attempt to overthrow Hegel's metaphysics seeks to ground history not in spirit (*Geist*), but in labour. In doing so, Arendt argues that Marx takes recourse in an Aristotelian social ontology to rejuvenate labour by giving it the status of life activity. Marx transforms Aristotle's political animal to a social animal and thus, glorifies labour as a political and ethical activity, rather than the bare existence of life—simple reproduction. If Marx attempts to offer a critique of modern economic life, Arendt contends that in fact he reinforces its central premise by elevating labour. Arendt's account of action explicitly calls into question Marx's dialectical thought and social ontology.

In this chapter I will focus on Arendt's evolving reading of Marx in the seven-year period between *Origins* and *HC*, focusing in particular on her 1954 lecture series, "Karl Marx and the Tradition of Political Thought." Her work in this period, intended for a book project titled "The Totalitarian Elements of Marxism," eventually resulted in *HC*.[10] By shedding light on this period, I argue that *HC* is the culmination of Arendt's struggle with Marx. Her work on this project is largely found in the fragmentary essay drafts and lectures from 1952 to 1954 published in her *Kritische Gesamtausgabe* (2018).[11] While sections of this material have been previously available, only now with a scholarly edition of her drafts can the development of her engagement with Marx be properly assessed, including her reading of the source material.[12] Coming to terms with this period of Arendt's thought puts pressure on existing interpretations of *HC*. First, in examining the evolution of her interpretation of Marx and in the way core arguments are first presented and reworked, *HC* is shown to contain a much more serious engagement with Marx than previously assumed. Evidently Arendt thought deeply about Marx's idea of human freedom even as she seriously objected to his theorisation of labour. Second, given Arendt's attention to Marx, her commentators require a more substantial reading of his texts themselves if they are to analyse Arendt adequately.[13] Despite her enduring popularity as a theorist of democracy, Arendt's relationship to Marx has presented serious difficulties for commentators. Many sympathetic Arendt scholars neglect any serious assessment of the detail and validity of her criticism of Marx. Some simply assume Arendt to be correct;[14] others "deliberately leave aside questions about the accuracy or otherwise of her interpretation of Marx."[15] However, the dominant interpretation is best exemplified by Seyla Benhabib's claim that the distinction between "work" and "labour" correctly identifies Marx's latent romanticism, and as such "Hannah Arendt became one of the most useful and creative critics of Marxism."[16] I suggest holding to Arendt's conclusions lose sight of the potential of Marx's idea of action. At the same time, many on the left have taken Arendt's attitude towards Marx to betray a "preference for metaphysical construct or poetic feeling over reality"[17] and her characterisation of "the social" to bring her "into proximity to a then-standard Cold War liberal critique."[18]

I assess Arendt's interpretation of Marx to avoid the pitfalls of both approaches. Arendt raises the question of Marx's relationship to freedom by returning to his dialogue with Aristotle. Just as praxis in Marx cannot be conceived without Aristotle, Arendt contributes to the same conversation about the status of action. Paradoxically, while Arendt wants to get away from Marx—and is almost entirely critical of his work—her concept of action shares much with Marx's own confrontation with the tradition of political thought in the name of praxis. In an important sense, Arendt's thinking about action would be impossible without Marx. While I ultimately conclude that her reading of Marx is substantially flawed, I offer an immanent critique of Arendt to show her idea of action detects a crucial absence in the political experience of modern life. As I argue, her portrayal of Marx's place within the Western tradition and his concept of labour raises questions about the full political potential of her idea of action. Despite her assessment of the dominance of economics over politics in modern life, Arendt consistently neglects to connect this problem to capitalist social relations and the social form that both economics and politics becomes subsumed under: value. This analysis shows that failures in Arendt's critique of Marx, once properly considered, could deepen her own account of action in the council system. Marx's account of social forms could supply Arendt with the historical dimension that would enhance her assessment of the potentiality of action in the council movement. By putting her interpretation of Hegel and Marx in a critical light, I aim to show that her motivations share crucial parallels. Tracing these lines of connections helps secure both the viability of her idea of action and highlights its importance for Hegel and Marx. When dialectical thought is understood precisely as allowing for the very conceptuality of human action, the contemporary applicability of Arendt's theory of action would not be weakened, but concretely strengthened. The possibilities of Arendt's idea of action lends currency to think with Marx, rather than against him. Her theory of action can be freed from its polemical shell and further enrich its potential for politics today. Political action is not opposed to "the social" but interwoven with it. Emerging from this picture is the necessity of political action to the life well-lived.

In this chapter, first I trace Arendt's critique of Marx as it evolved through the 1950s and into *HC*. Arendt pinpoints Marx's idea of "the social" as the decisive point of rupture with the Western tradition of political thought and maintains he takes up Hegel's faulty philosophy of dialectics. Also apparent in the initial research, which would evolve into a much deeper criticism in *HC*, is her thesis that Marx problematically adopts Aristotle's social ontology. Then, I address Arendt's characterisation of dialectical thought by tracing the saliency of rational agency in Hegel's *Phenomenology of Spirit*. Contrasting Arendt's notion of word and deed with Hegel's, I maintain that his idea of action (*Handlung*) and deed (*Tat*) is much more complex, and persuasive, than Arendt permits. My account draws on the understanding of agency advanced by Robert Brandom, who takes discursiveness to be the social and historical structure for normativity and recognition.

If Arendt identifies Marx's concept of labour as a major roadblock to conceiving freedom, on the contrary, I attest that his critique of alienated labour entails a strong normative dimension as a theory of human action and political freedom. Next, I examine Arendt's thesis that Marx's Aristotelian inheritance has the dramatic political implication of sacrificing action for labour.[19] Evidently, for Arendt, crucial questions for thinking about human action and freedom derive from the relation between Marx and Aristotle.[20] Marx's Aristotelianism furnishes decisive insights pertaining to the connection between labour and action. By investigating the social form that labour takes in modern life, Marx is able to grasp the interrelation between economic, political and moral activity within a totality of human activity. Each thread is woven together in his idea of praxis.

I develop an immanent critique of the content of Arendt's concept of action by arguing that her interpretation of Marx eschews this very concept in his theory and practice. Both Marx and Arendt prize action as the expression of collective and participatory decision-making, which is founded through the expression of word and deed. Arendt *and* Marx insist that politics must be located in the shared interaction between human beings acting in the world. I contend she misconstrues Marx's idea of freedom and that it in fact meets the demands of her concept of action and brings its most salient features to life. Connecting language and action, Marx's idea of labour is much more complex than Arendt admits. Further, Marx's political writings dissolve Arendt's firm distinction between the *vita activa* and the *vita contemplativa*. Significantly, she ignores that Marx's writings are a product of political action. While there is much to value in Arendt's eudaemonic concept of action as word and deed, in seeking to separate action from labour her council model of democracy lacks concreteness. Arendt considered it a strength of her concept of action that labour is dislocated from praxis.

However, this separation has consequences for her model of action in the council system which explicitly detaches the idea of direct democracy from the actuality of the social form and content of its political expression. Arendt's idea of action combines a vision of the ancient polis with a distinctive reading of modern revolutionary movements. Last, I demonstrate that her disregard for the social content of the council movement is exacerbated in her idealised construal of the ancient polis. Detached from its social form, she celebrates ancient political life precisely because of the distinction between the private and public sphere. Arendt's idea of the polis risks abstractly negating the content of action, obscuring both ancient and modern political life. But this is not because Arendt calls for a nostalgic return to the polis, but as Patchen Markell observes, because of her "simplified description of it."[21] Similarly, I argue this simplification applies also to her conception of the council system.

Marx's critique of the social form of alienated labour establishes a valuable perspective to assess Arendt's own argument. The difference between them demonstrates what is at stake for thinking about human freedom in theorising labour. However, failures in Arendt's critique of Marx, once properly considered, could deepen her own account of action in the council system. If rendered in such a way, her picture of the ancient polis would feel less like a simplification and help reanimate the history of political action. When Marx's dialectics of social forms is understood as an attempt to grasp the conceptuality of human action and its historical concreteness, the democratic aspects of Arendt's theory of action become more germane and robust.

Tradition and "the Social"

HC prompts us to think about what it would mean to revive the *vita activa* and its greatest activity, which appears eclipsed to us moderns, human action. Through "word and deed we insert ourselves into the human world" and make ourselves known as political and ethical agents.[22] Action is the unique human activity of freedom, higher than the necessity of labour and the fabrication of work. Action allows for natality, for something *new*, for a second birth. In our words and deeds, we actualise "the human condition of plurality, that is, of living as a distinct and unique being among equals."[23] Arendt's political theory hinges on the significance of the distinction between the public and private realms. The meaning of politics itself has changed from the life of the polis to the mass society of today. Arendt's idea of the *vita activa*, a Latinisation of Aristotle's *bios politikos*, acts to restore a lost notion of political life back into a tradition of political thinking that has faded from view and is no longer readily apparent in our lives. Arendt holds to Aristotle's idea of a political animal (*zōon politikon*), "man who acts and speaks" in the public realm.[24] For Aristotle, human beings are distinctly political since through our logos we give reasons for our actions within communities functioning to best enact the good characteristic of human life.[25] "Action alone is the exclusive prerogative of man," she writes, "neither a beast nor a god is capable of it, and only action is entirely dependent upon the constant presence of others."[26] Arendt's provocation is that politics correctly understood, as the life of action—words and deeds in the light of the public sphere—has vanished. Drawing on Aristotle's idea of *eudaimonia*, Arendt argues that since "'the work of man' *qua* man" is living well (*eu zēn*), politics as such seeks no physical product or ends; it exists as a virtuous activity, "sheer actuality."[27] The translation of "political" to "social" animal, Arendt maintains, "betrays the extent to which the original Greek understanding of politics had been lost."[28]

Arendt looks within the Western tradition of political thought to locate the exclusion of political action from this very tradition. Her interpretation is at once expansive and critical. *HC* centres on a tradition that is born with the trial of Socrates and ends with Marx.[29] In this period, *contemplation* dominated the tradition, recognisably in Plato's forms and Hegel's absolute spirit.[30] For Arendt, the lamentable loss of the notion of political action can be traced back to the belief that labour, the bare necessity of life, has become the highest expression of the human condition. According to Arendt, Marx's glorification of labour is what confirms this loss.

This thesis has its genesis in the period after the first publication of *Origins* in 1951.[31] While the "dignity of our tradition" is foundational to her account of the social and historical context for twentieth-century totalitarianism, there is an ambivalence towards Marx in the original text.[32] *Origins* tells the story of the development of totalitarianism in class terms, drawing heavily on Marxist accounts of the accumulation of capital, especially on Rosa Luxemburg, in the masterful chapter on imperialism, "The Political Emancipation of the Bourgeoisie."[33] Arendt's understanding of the modern world here is that it is *bourgeois*, formed by classes and the modern relations between bourgeois civil society and the nation-state.[34] But surprisingly, given her attention in the text to Stalinism as a form of totalitarianism, direct discussion of Marx is minimal and always fleeting.³⁵ When he does appear, Arendt is mostly critical of what she takes as his inability to appreciate the historical significance of modern antisemitism.

In Marx's discussion of Judaism in his 1843 essay "On the Jewish Question," Arendt believes that he prioritises class struggle over the question of antisemitism and in effect sides with "the anti-Jewish radicals." Noting that this essay is "sufficiently well known not to warrant quotation," Arendt's discussion suffers from common misconceptions of Marx's object of critique.³⁶ There is only a fleeting hint of what is to become a main part of her position. She accuses Marx of an "utter neglect of political questions" by narrowing his view of society to only include those who sell their labour-power.³⁷ While there are more points of connection than she would like to admit between her view of the relationship between the state and civil society and the young Marx, Arendt omits an explanation of his overall significance for her conceptual scheme. Significantly, in the first edition of *Origins* there is little sense of Marx's place within the tradition of political thought that Arendt's inquiry addresses. Principally she takes issue with Marx's "great attempt to rewrite world history in terms of class struggle" informed by "hopeful predictions" for a classless society.³⁸ Arendt traces the root of Marx's theory of history—defined by a view of the "proletariat as the protagonist of mankind"—to Hegel's dialectics. Since both Hegel and Marx believe "in the process of history in which ideas could be concretized only in a complicated dialectical movement" this means that individual moral responsibility is absorbed "automatically" into the idealised values of a broader mass movement.³⁹

In subsequent editions of *Origins*, Arendt left these passages unchanged. However, the entire emphasis of these earlier remarks is transformed when she replaces the initial conclusion with the essay "Ideology and Terror: A Novel Form of Government" in the 1958 edition. Written in German in 1952, this concluding theoretical chapter dramatically shifts the depiction of Marx found in the book and reflectively effects how the reader should understand her previous remarks.⁴⁰ Arendt is markedly more hostile towards dialectical thought and now identifies Marx's concept of labour with a kind of biological naturalism. She posits that Marx and Darwin share "basic philosophies" where "ultimately the movement of history and the movement of nature are one and the same." Natural movement is "unilinear, moving in an infinitely progressing direction." According to Arendt, Marx's concept of labour as the human metabolism (*Stoffwechsel*) with nature means labour "is not a historical but a natural-biological 'force.'"⁴¹ In this change, she saw fit to add an overarching theoretical evaluation of Marx's legacy largely absent from the first edition. Significantly, in "Ideology and Terror," Arendt gestures at the critique of Marx she comes to advance in *HC* and subsequently retains.

It was only after publishing *Origins* in 1951 that Arendt felt Marx's thought required greater investigation and immediately started to work on a book project.⁴² She expanded her existing criticisms to include his concept of labour and discarded her own use of the category of class entirely. As she saw it, Marx is an heir to the Enlightenment, despite his thought becoming the ruling ideology of totalitarian terror under Stalin. The working title of the project, "The Totalitarian Elements of Marxism," hints at her initial thesis, but in what becomes *HC,* Arendt shifts her focus from an investigation of Marxism as a political movement to the investigation of Marx's political thinking and its place in the Western tradition.

In late 1952, Arendt starts to work on Marx extensively.⁴³ The evidence from the lecture notes from this period show that several of her central arguments to be found in *HC* begin to emerge clearly. In lecture notes from winter 1952, she outlines three important arguments. First, she states there is a distinction between Marx "the scholar—economist, sociologist (perhaps founder of this science) and historian—and philosopher." Second, she characterises the popular "impact" of Marx's view of human beings as "primarily" labouring animals ("Labor is the creator of all values"), where labour is necessity and in contradiction to "animal rationale" and "freedom." This formulation carries her distinction between human beings as "*homo faber*" and "*animal laborans.*"⁴⁴ Arendt purports that for Marx labour is a category that enforces a "new standard of productivity" in necessity. Third, she claims Marx shares the very contempt of politics which has plagued the Western tradition since the Greeks, since history takes pride of place at the expense of politics. In doing so, Marx was

> the first to see history in terms of past politics, made by men as laboring animals. Then it must be possible to make history in the process of Labor, of Productivity, to make history as we make things. Marx discovered Labor and identified it with work, discovered Politics and identified it with History. Marx the Traditionalist as against the usual idea.⁴⁵

Arendt addresses the relationship between Hegel and Marx directly in a Berlin radio broadcast and transcript from May 1953. Here she uses the language of Marx's "turning" of Hegel on his head and connects this inversion with Marx's glorification of labour.⁴⁶ To confront the problem of tradition, Arendt needed to confront Marx since "within the framework of the tradition which Marx always worked, there could be hardly any other outcome than a new twist in determinist philosophy."[47] Arendt's increasingly critical interpretation of Hegel and Marx situates her broader rethinking of the Western tradition.

According to Arendt, Marx not only assumes Darwin's naturalism, but he also inherits Hegel's dialectic. She describes dialectics as a "formal methodology," "the familiar three-step process" of a thesis, antithesis and synthesis. Arendt considers the movement between these triads as "automatic." She takes Hegel's idea of the absolute, "the world spirit or godhead" which divulges itself to human consciousness, to be taken up by Marx and "formalised" as "development," the automatic process of historical change as the natural evolution of the laws of history.[48] Furthermore, at this time Arendt portrays dialectical thought to be little more than delusion and absurdity, resulting in Marxism's distance from reality.[49] Arendt makes the assertion that dialectics is ultimately a "turning operation" where evil is transformed into good, insisting that "the sophistic-dialectical" view of history considers every event as a moment of development in the inevitable victory of progress.[50]

Dialectics and Self-Consciousness

Arendt's characterisation of dialectical thought is highly problematic. In reducing Hegel's speculative proposition to "thesis, antithesis and synthesis" and attributing this formula to Marx's theory of history, ironically Arendt reproduces aspects of Soviet Marxism. Her interpretation of dialectics as a game or formal method wheeled out to justify the work of God or historical progress fails to be very convincing as a criticism of Hegel or Marx.[51] Hegel's speculative thought operates not as a method of *thesis* plus *antithesis* equals *synthesis*, but the determinate negation and immanent unfolding of social forms by an analysis of their conceptual content.[52] For Hegel, spirit is not a prescriptive force bending the world to its cosmic will, but instead the embodiment of reason as it is realised in the world. Its movement traverses progress and failure as spirit emerges through historical shapes of consciousness. The development of consciousness is historically contingent.[53] But it is crucial to note that dialectics does not serve to justify the way historical change has until now occurred.[54]

Arendt's description of the dialectic as "thesis, antithesis and synthesis" and her assumption that Hegel's theory of history is highly deterministic were both relatively conventional views amongst traditional mid-century interpretations.

Arendt's caricature of Hegel is surprising considering her training in the German phenomenological tradition in the 1920s suggests a richer engagement with Hegel. In Paris, she attended Alexandre Kojève's famous 1930s lectures that advanced his influential, if idiosyncratic, reading of Hegel's *Phenomenology*.⁵⁵ It is hardly the background of typical mid-century hostility to Hegel and Marx, exemplified in Karl Popper's virulent *The Open Society and Its Enemies* (1945). However, Arendt's engagement with Hegel is quite limited and focuses mainly on Marx, who she is much more interested in. Despite this context, such a construal of Hegel's thought as deterministic is spurious and highly misleading as a foundation to explaining his relation with Marx.

In Hegel's account, dialectics is much less an instrument for affirmation than the need to follow the self-critical path of consciousness phenomenologically. Dialectics requires embarking on a path of doubt and despair, confronting ordinary consciousness and navigating the contradictions immanently apparent in the appearance, constellation and breakdown of inadequate forms of knowing. Hegel does not assume his approach is right from the start but seeks to justify the demands of such an analysis. He makes the procedure in which knowledge seeks truth—his own approach included—an open question. For Hegel, the dialectical movement of thought and being speculatively derives the relationship between both in the form of consciousness. Self-consciousness, the unity of thought and being, proves itself in the process of cultivation which consciousness traverses (*durchläuft*) on its path to establish an account of agency.⁵⁶

In contrast to traditional interpretations, recent Hegel scholarship has emphasised the normative aspect of his idea of history to dispel assumptions about determinism. What has emerged is a richer reflection on Hegel's dialectics as an exposition of the possibilities inherent in historical forms of self-knowing to provide acceptable reasons for action. "Dialectics," as Terry Pinkard glosses it, "looks at *accounts* that forms of life give of what they take to be authoritative for themselves, and how those accounts are transformed in terms of considerations internal to the accounts themselves."⁵⁷ Hegel's phenomenological explanation advances an immanent unfolding of the possibility of action. The character of our agency as rational beings is embedded within a form of life that is susceptible to breakdown and failure. By reflecting on our action, we become able to see how our decisions have meaning for us as historical beings engaged in social practices. For Hegel, the formation of human agency is predicated precisely on the process of becoming aware of the failures in previous forms of understanding, since these forms of life did not instantiate in their social and institutional form the possibility for self-conscious reflection. Pinkard explains that Hegel's reflective, conceptually comprehended history (*begriffene Geschichte*) explains "its own possibility" as "part of the larger field of possibilities that make us who we are, and our reflections on them are themselves only part of that self-enclosed circle of human practices and the ways in which we have developed the practices of reflecting on them."[58] When Hegel is understood in this manner, a very different picture emerges than Arendt's idea of dialectics as a sophist tool.

Just as the historical aspect of Hegel's thought is what gives his notion of agency such normative force, Marx's own dialectical approach holds that conceptual categories are always manifestations of historically specific social forms. Indeed, for Marx, dialectics is also an immanent unfolding of social forms.[59] His critique of the economic logic of the categories specific to value is the determinate negation of the conceptual content of capitalism as a form of life. Marx's concept of history is not the familiar one-dimensional characterisation of a march of inevitable stages of history culminating in communism, but is instead a multilinear study of historical social forms, which he calls "modes of production."[60] Despite her disavowal of dialectical thinking and a certain enmity to the Hegelian Marxism of her contemporaries,[61] Arendt's attention to Marx brings into focus the importance of action in the modern world.

Further still, Arendt's polemical remarks about dialectics have an interesting argumentative context. First, she takes her assessment of Hegel and Marx to dispute then popular understandings, and her reading of Marx's early texts are notably before their exposure and popularity with the Anglophone New Left. The second contextual aspect is her construal of Hegel and Marx in terms of the trajectory of the Western tradition of political theory. For Arendt, while Marx ends the tradition, his fidelity to Hegel means that in important ways he remains within it. The distortions in this appraisal diminish the overall persuasiveness of her concept of tradition. In the remainder of this chapter, I will argue while Arendt dismissed Marx and Hegel as ultimately unable to conceive of freedom as action, in their thought we can find resources for precisely such an account of action. Comparing Arendt's idea of action with the concept in Hegel and Marx helps illuminate this problem.

Arendt is right to tie Marx closely to Hegel and to see him as inheriting the mantle. However, her charge that Hegel produced a deterministic view of history that politically comes to an end with the existing modern state is dubious. Hegel does not present a closed system which reconciles rationality with the Prussian state, but instead suggests that the modern world furnishes a unique ability to assess the rationality of our lives from our own self-conscious agency. As a result, Arendt misconstrues Hegel's idea of recollection as a justification of the most traditional view of Western thought, the supremacy of the philosopher, which Marx is supposed to break.[62] Put differently, Arendt misses a crucial element of Hegel's argument in the *Phenomenology*. Hegel tells the story of the subjectivity of action within the contradictory forms of consciousness that constitute the modern world. The contradictions themselves facilitate action and herald the breakdown of that expression of consciousness. The journey of self-consciousness experienced phenomenologically pertains to the very possibility and ends of action. Spirit, *Geist*, is not a quasi-religious force but articulates the historical forms of consciousness in which knowledge comes to express itself. The *Phenomenology* is an account of the "social space" of reason, which structures beliefs, norms and ethical life.[63]

In Hegel's view, human action strives for recognition. There is no human action that is not bound by recognition. The rationality distinctive to human beings depends upon relations of reciprocity with others to award ethical meaning and status as free beings. This idea of recognition is not reducible to expressions of singular consciousnesses, but to the type of consciousness characteristic of human being qua human being. Implicitly or explicitly, ethical meaning depends upon the individual finding satisfaction in their own actions as a mutually interdependent relationship with others. Notably, in the *Phenomenology*, Hegel writes, "*[s]elf-consciousness [Selbstbewußtsein] attains its satisfaction [Befriedigung] only in another self-consciousness.*"[64] Towards the end of the "Spirit" chapter, Hegel examines how this satisfaction necessitates that the individual allows themselves to be *bound* by their acts and deeds to others. In action we bring something about together—to share social space as equals. Similarly, for Arendt, the significance of speech and action is realised when human beings share space in their "togetherness": "In acting and speaking, men show who they are, reveal actively their unique personal identities and thus make their appearance in the human world, while their physical identities appear without any activity of their own in the unique shape of the body and sound of the voice."[65] Action is only worthy of its name when it is unpredictable. Deeds require saying something about who we are, and action must contain the willingness to "risk the disclosure."[66] Arendt's concept of action revels in the distinctiveness of words and deeds. At the same time, she believes Hegel's determinist philosophy of history sacrifices action upon the alter of *Geist*. Arendt's conceptualisation of this tradition hinges upon this highly problematic characterisation of Hegel. However, her own concept of action depends upon a discursive notion of act and speech which would benefit from Hegel's insights.

Robert Brandom's normative reconstruction of the *Phenomenology* in his *A Spirit of Trust* helps secure this claim. As Brandom points out, in Hegel, ""spirit" means the community."[67] For Hegel, history is not one of "stages" but historical "shapes" of life: "*moments* of spirit as a whole (consciousness, self-consciousness, reason, and spirit) have, [and] because they are moments, no existence distinct from each other."[68] Spirit is purposeful precisely because it is the activity of the historical subject. Hegel's conception of language has significant parallels with the importance of speech in Arendt. Language (*Sprache*) is, in Hegel's words, "the existence of spirit [*Dasein des Geistes*]. Language is self-consciousness existing *for others*."[69] Brandom emphasises the discursive aspect of Hegelian recognition: "One of the distinctive features of modernity is the way in which language mediates the relations among individuals, their acts and attitudes, and their norms, institutions, and communities. Language becomes the medium of recognition."[70] Speech acts help make commitments *explicit*; in public logos enables subjects to own our commitment and hold ourselves responsible to others.

Hegel's conception of agency renders the reciprocal relations necessary for ethical life, *Sittlichkeit*, as the unity of action *in* and *for* the individual ("as self-conscious selves") and community ("as recognitive communities that comprise and are instituted by them").[71] Brandom takes up Hegel's idea of recollection as the distinctive normative aspect of the *Phenomenology* which enables human subjects to reflect on what our commitments are in respect to the consciousness of "how things *really* are, how they are *in themselves*."[72] Hegel seeks to make explicit the way in which norms are located both objectively and subjectively in our social and historical lives.

In Brandom's interpretation of Hegel's concept of action, he suggests that first we must know that the act is ours: we must take responsibility and authority for the action.

> What makes what is done (the deed) *mine* is, an *action*, rather than just something that happens—its relation to a purpose . . . The distinction among features of the deed that is induced by the purpose is what determines the deed as the agent's doing, in the normative sense of being something the agent is *responsible* for. *What the agent thereby becomes responsible for* (doing) is the whole deed (what is done). And that fully developed deed reveals an intention that extends beyond what is merely "meant" or purposed.[73]

For Brandom, intention makes clear that our actions are motivated by practical reasons; that we have reasons for what we do, that we act in light of ends, specific outcomes, goals, purposes, commitments, and so on.[74] Intention endows a normative character for practical reasoning; it sets the horizons of our responsibility for our actions. Of course, we can act for the wrong reasons and make mistakes, but there is always something at stake for us normatively in acting.[75] Brandom maintains this idea of reasoning is recognitive since "the agent specifically recognizes or acknowledges himself as responsible, and those under which the community specifically recognizes the agent as responsible—are essential to the unity and identity of the action."[76] This structure of normativity means that action is public through relations which are fundamentally social. The recognitive community has *authority*, and individual agents have *responsibility* for our deeds and actions. A Hegelian view of agency does not hold that the private life of individuals is disregarded, as Arendt maintains in her objection to "the social," but suggests that as individuals we always occupy "social roles" mediated by historical and normative life. The distinctiveness of individuals is made possible by relations with others, which found our normative commitments and give us reasons to act. "Roles are public," Jaeggi notes, "even when performed in private."[77]

In a striking argument, Brandom characterises three differences in the historical structure of normative life. He contrasts the changing nature of normative attitudes (what individuals take to be correct, authoritative or responsible) with normative statuses (the normative standing of appropriate, authoritative and responsible action).[78] First, in the traditional phase—akin to the beautiful *Sittlichkeit*, ethical life of the Greek world—objective normative statuses structure normative attitudes. Social life is dependent. Brandom follow's Hegel's account of the breakdown of this form of life in the *Phenomenology* with the discussion of Sophocles's *Antigone*. The second phase, modernity, is one of subjectivity and independence; normative attitudes structure normative statuses. This form of life is alienated. The third phase is most novel, since Brandom introduces a "postmodern" *Sittlichkeit*, which brings together both subjectivity and collective freedom.[79] This form of life is structured by relations of normativity and braids together the authority of norms and attitudes that make possible recognition as self-consciousness practical agency. For Brandom, recollective recognition is the type of distinctly modern form of rationality that allows agency to be normative as both authority and responsibility and what makes it possible to move beyond alienated modernity. Recognition is universal consciousness, the trust that my actions are normatively binding and that

I act in a social world I am at home in. Free from modern alienation, Brandom's idea of *Sittlichkeit* is one that does not see reconciliation with the existing state of affairs as normatively acceptable.

With this notion of act and deed, Brandom advances a rich Hegelian account of the necessity of norms in any historical conception of subjectivity. However, Brandom's idea of alienation is limited to his model of discursiveness and lacks an account of the varieties of human action which might inform our normative attitudes and statuses. In this sense, Marx's account of alienation can expand Brandom's Hegelian picture by grasping labour as practical consciousness, the ontological life activity that shapes any structure of normative attitudes and normative statuses. The modern configuration of normative relations reflects forms of mastery and domination that are reproduced abstractly in commodity production and exchange.[80] While Brandom asks the question "[w]hat is modern alienation?," his definition does not go beyond a pathology of "undercut" norms which lack "bindingness."[81] However, Brandom's argument that alienation is a deeply normative concern for social life opens the door to Marx. Marx's normative critique of modern life depends upon an understanding of the distinction between labour as human productive activity and alienated labour as social domination. Brandom's conception of alienation needs to be expanded by Marx's insight that specific social forms of human activity in the modern world are normatively unacceptable because the very structure of that activity restricts recognitive relations.

The specific social forms of human activity pertain directly to Marx's idea of history. His much-maligned terminology of "modes of production," *Produktionsweise*, contra Arendt, does not advance a determinist idea of progress, but is constituted by an analysis of the logic of specific and historically determinate relations of social forms. Determination figures in Marx not in the sense of a mechanical causal determinism, but is instead a category of concretisation in his dialectical thinking. Marx's claim that the "ultimate aim" of *Capital* is "to reveal the economic law of motion of modern society" is to trace the historical and social processes specific to capitalism by a mode of abstraction that derives the movement of "economic laws" determinately by tracking their social content.[82] Contrasting this view from the absence of abstraction in Marx's vulgar interpreters, who take *concrete determination* to be *lawlike determinism*, Jairus Banaji argues:

> The dialectic in *Capital* was thus nothing else than the rigorous, systematic investigation of the laws of motion of capitalist production, in the course of which a series

of simple abstractions ("wage-labour," money, etc.) were historically concretised as bourgeois relations of production, or abstractions determinate to capitalism as a mode of production; that is, reconstituted as "concrete categories," as historically determinate social forms.[83]

By using determinacy as a dialectical category, as the logical structure of a form, Marx is offering an analysis of the conceptuality of social forms and the dynamic of forms of existence (*Dasein*) historically specific to capitalism.[84] Marx's critique of capitalism looks to the immanent and determinate processes which could negate the form itself. Arendt's contrasting view of determination as a mechanical motivating force of historical change has no truck with the logic of Marx's dialectic.

Moreover, in Marx's theory, a mode of production analyses the distinct social form of productive relations and processes, not causal necessity. This approach is apparent from the early articulation of "modes of production" in the 1845/6 "The German Ideology" manuscripts.[85] The concept of a "mode of production" equips Marx (and Engels) with a way to articulate the historically specific social relations which make human agency intelligible. Human productive activity is understood as a social mediation. Crucially, economic life is not a mechanical power but *made*. A mode of production designates the specific form of economic life as it is historically constituted in the physical and conscious life activity of human beings. Marx notes that "men [*Menschen*] have history [*Geschichte*] because they must *produce* their life, and because they must do it in a *certain* way: this is determined [*bestimmt*] by their physical organisation; as well as their consciousness [*Bewußtsein*]."[86]

Fundamentally, Marx's idea of consciousness is that it is a component of social life which arises from the interaction human beings have with each other and is made explicit through language. He writes "language [*Sprache*] *is* practical [*praktische*], real consciousness [*wirkliche Bewußtsein*] that exists [*wirkliche*] for other men as well, and only therefore does it also exist for me; language, like consciousness, only arises from the need, the necessity, of intercourse with other men."[87] Language makes possible the practical activity of human beings. There is no social life without this form of consciousness. A mode of production *does* require necessity, but Marx is clear that language and consciousness are always imbedded in human action. The young MacIntyre detected that for Marx, human history begins "with the family of concepts which belong to what he called 'practical consciousness': the concepts of intention, deliberation and desire, those concepts which are essential to understanding men as agents and not a mere passive reflexes of non-human forces."[88] MacIntyre captures the insight that language is a crucial element of the rational and conscious human activity within Marx's idea of labour and that such a view entails normativity. However, Arendt's objection to Marx stretches beyond his idea of history to concentrate on the implications of his thinking about labour for political action. This focus motivates the research program Arendt sets out after first publishing *Origins*.

The Straight Line from Aristotle to Marx

In a fragmentary draft, the first material she prepared for her 1953 Christian Gauss Seminar in Criticism at Princeton University, Arendt begins with an enigmatic appeal: "It has never been easy to think and write about KM."[89] On one hand, little critical interpretation of Marx's philosophy was produced in the USSR, where Marxism was the state theory in the form of "dialectical materialism" and "historical materialism." On the other hand, McCarthyite America made discussion of Marx's theories dangerous. To both Stalinists and conservatives, Marx was partisan in a way that bypassed his actual thought. However, Arendt goes back to Marx's writings to assess his contribution to the Western tradition. She remarks, "Marx's roots go far deeper than he knew it himself. I think it could be shown that the line from Aristotle to Marx shows much less and much less decisive breaks than the line from Marx to Stalin."[90] In this sense, Arendt's attempt to interpret Marx's impact on political thought and modernity itself importantly predates New Left "Marxology." The earliest of these interpretations tended to revel in Marx's early writings (often at the expense of *Capital*).[91] Arendt's reading is more circumspect. She draws widely on Marx and Engels's writings to argue something distinct.

Arendt's novel claim identifies what she takes to be the basic paradox in Marx's thought.[92] Marx locates true freedom in a world where labour has been abolished and specialisation is gone, but at the same time as identifying labour as freedom, he aspires to strike it entirely from life. What Arendt tries to show is how Marx breaks with tradition insofar as he attempts to give labour a conceptual status at odds with the Western tradition; however, he remains with the tradition insofar as he thinks nobody can be free of necessity.[93] By glorifying labour and equating necessity with freedom, Marx creates a rupture in the tradition. Against this depiction of freedom, Arendt calls attention to "those activities concerning the common-public realm which comes into being whenever men live together, of all dignity of their own."[94] Action brings about something new as the light of the public realm illuminates the capacity for political judgement by equal individual citizens. Arendt wants to free what has been lost from Marx and from the tradition, the content of human freedom in the capacity of speech. This line of argument becomes the architectonic of *HC*.

Arendt's opening argument in *HC* establishes the political significance of the distinction between the public and private realms and focuses her account in the dramatic change from the political life of the polis to "the mass society of today."[95] Arendt's discussion is comparable in a certain respect to Marx's "On the Jewish Question."[96] For Arendt, as with Marx, the tension between the two realms structures the possibility for politics and articulates modern, historically specific, contradictions. Arendt points out that the location of freedom shifts from the political realm of the Greeks to the social realm in Marx.[97] In the text, Marx demarcates the difference and relation between bourgeois, political emancipation and social, human emancipation. However, as Arendt insists, the notion of freedom as not "political" but "social" blurs the line drawn between private and public and brings about a crisis for the individual. In a conflict-ridden existence, the individual is not at home in the mass society of the modern world, nor able to live outside it. Political action has lost its meaning and private life has become the space for disagreement and difference.[98] For Arendt,

> In the modern world, the social and political realms are much less distinct. That politics is nothing but a function of society, that action, speech and thought are primary superstructures upon social interests, is not a discovery of Karl Marx but on the contrary is among the axiomatic assumptions Marx accepted uncritically from the political economics of the modern age.[99]

This position entails a direct critique of Marx's social ontology, relying on a strong distinction between "labour," "work," and "action." Arendt's argument here is phenomenological, drawing on the changing linguistic usages, reflected in political theory and culture, in which it is "a simple fact that every European language ancient and modern, contains two etymologically unrelated words, for what we have come to think of as the same activity."[100] For Arendt, the synonymous use of "labour" and "work"—fully expressed in Marx's political economy heritage—is in actuality "the glorification of labor."[101] In the activity of labour, the *animal laborans* is "enslaved by necessity." Labour is toil and suffering, the bondage of natural life. Work, however, is creative and formative. With work, man is the maker (*homo faber*) of the "unnaturalness of human existence," of the "'artificial' world of things." The third category, action, is Arendt's governing concept. Action allows for political life without the mediation of "things or matter."[102]

For Arendt, "[w]hile dire necessity made labor indispensable to sustain life, excellence would have the last thing to expect for it."[103] This expectation is precisely the problem with Marx's social ontology, which elevates production to an idealised social standpoint, but really its "sole purpose" is the "entertaining of the life process—and this is the unfortunately quite un-utopian ideal that guides Marx's theories." A footnote to this sentence, adds the suggestion that for Marx social humanity (*der vergesellschafteter Mensch* and *die gesellschaftliche Menschheit*) and "species-being" (*Gattungswesen*) paint an ideal society as "a state of affairs where all human activities derive as naturally from human 'nature' as the secretion of wax by bees for making the honeycomb; to live and to labor for life will have become one and the same."[104]

Arendt's critique of Marx is not just that he elevates labour to such a high conceptual position as "socialised man," but that his concept of labour also maintains the political economists' reduction of politics to the egoism of interests.[105] She writes:

> Behind Marx's theory of interests stands the conviction that the only legitimate gratification of an interest lies in labor. Supporting this conviction and fundamental to all his writing is a new definition of man, which sees man's essential humanity not in his rationality (*animal rationale*), or in his production of objects (*homo faber*), or in his having been made in the likeness of God (*creatura Dei*), but rather in labor, which tradition had unanimously rejected as incompatible with a full and free human existence. Marx was the first to define man as an *animal laborans*, as a laboring creature. He subsumes under this definition everything tradition passed down as the distinguishing marks of humanity: labor as the principle of rationality and its laws, which in the development of productive forces determine history, make history comprehensible to reason. Labor is the principle of productivity; it produces the truly human world on earth.[106]

As Arendt sees it, this is how Marx occupies a paradoxical relationship to the Western tradition of political thought. The break with the tradition is in his definition of human beings in terms of labour, which reduces life (including action) to production. At the same time as Marx makes this challenge, Arendt stresses his place *within* the tradition. Marx is a "traditionalist" since he tries but, in her account, fails to resolve Aristotle's preoccupation with the relationship between freedom and necessity.

The full extent of the critique of Marx's social ontology comes into view when Arendt draws a straight line—"given by Aristotle on one side and Marx on the other"—between the definition of the human being as a "political animal" and the definition of the "animal laborans."[107] Central to both Aristotle and Marx is the conception of social ontology based on the *bios* and the distinctiveness of human beings as rational animals. As a result, Arendt believes that Marx's economic thought is marked by this "reliance on Aristotelian philosophy."[108] Further, in her view, Marx takes the productivity of the political economists and through Aristotle further naturalises labour. Biological life is elevated over human reason.[109] The deficiency in his concept of labour is its veneration of society and labour over politics and action. Insofar as political action exists for Marx, it is now "past" as history.[110] Human beings might make our own history, but the emphasis on *making* reveals Marx's proclivity for elevating productivity over action. Further, by identifying his attempt to overcome the distinction between the "realm of freedom" and the "realm of necessity," "by abolishing labor," Arendt argues that Marx's social ontology results in folding the latter into the former.[111]

In her interpretation Arendt is right to emphasise the Aristotelian aspect of Marx's social ontology and to recognise that this ontology decisively shapes his concept of labour. However, Arendt's depiction nonetheless does serious violence to his thought. As I will maintain throughout this book, the conflation of necessity and freedom that Arendt takes Marx to endorse, is in fact a problem he identifies precisely because human activity is reduced to the necessity of alienated production. For Marx, the negation of this social form is contingent on the establishment of a public realm in which motivation is not defined by the dominance of private interest, but the free activity of recognitive social roles and practical identities. Freedom in Marx's sense requires a condition of life in which human activity is untied from the necessity of capital accumulation. Capital is dead labour. As such, it is parasitic. The entire point of Marx's delineation of the concept is to set out the reasons why it must be overcome as a social force.

Rather than glorifying necessity, Marx theorises the production and reproduction of value in terms of human activity and in doing so, captures what is distinctive about a form of social life defined by unfree forms of activity under capitalism. What Arendt overlooks is that integral to the concept of alienation is the integration and transformation of necessity into the historical conditions for freedom beyond capitalist social forms. Just as Marx thinks freedom must go beyond bourgeois right, necessity is also shown to be conditioned by the historically specific dualism between freedom and necessity.[112] The movement from the realm of necessity to the realm of freedom requires a form of action which is dependent on the rationality of human beings to articulate and decide on a shared sense of the right reason (what Aristotle calls *orthos logos*) for the flourishing of the political community. In the sublation of necessity to freedom, Marx construes the realm of freedom as a *higher*, rather than *separate*, sphere from the realm of necessity. Necessity is an essential condition for human activity to be concretely free. What follows is that practices that function for social need or as leisure are both free. No concept of leisure time could be intelligible without a prioritisation of our activity in terms of necessity, and Marx's discussion insinuates that purposive labour is the social mediation of necessity and leisure, not the obliteration of either.

Arendt fails to realise that Marx's concept of labour depends upon the critique of alienated labour. Marx's critique of political economy is precisely that it conceives of labour transhistorically as economic nature, rather than the specific social form of alienated labour under capitalism. Once clarified, Marx's concept of alienation—absent in Arendt's criticisms—makes it possible to grasp labour as an activity not just of necessity but of substantive freedom. This insight supplies a prism to see that Marx shares with Arendt an understanding of the *necessity* of political action. Rather than conflating freedom with necessity, Marx should be understood in line with Arendt's commitment to the freedom which arises with human action. The notion of freedom is not an added extra, but central to Marx's social theory.

At one level, Arendt's distinction between labour, work, and action deliberately runs against the "process" character of Marx's dialectical thinking.[113] Her problem with Marx positing human activity in the physical metabolism with nature and reduction of freedom to the process of biological necessity is that it flattens vital differences in the singularity of the human condition. Arendt agrees with Marx that surplus value provides for social reproduction. Her move to disembody political theory from the necessity of labour in Marx's social ontology aims to identify the human qualities that separate the life activities of labour, work, and action and uphold freedom as political action.[114] In the light of the public realm, there is the space for freedom. Significantly, Arendt's exposition calls for key aspects of Marx's concept of labour to be clarified. Her interpretation points to the impossibility of a concept of action derived from an activity of unfreedom.

However, Arendt fundamentally misconstrues the relationship between labour and freedom in Marx's thought. Pointing to Marx's idea of free labour, she asks, "[i]f labor is the most human and most productive of man's activities, what will happen when, after the revolution, 'labor is abolished' in the 'realm of freedom,' when man has succeeded in emancipating himself from it? What productive and what essentially human activity will be left?"[115] To seek answers, Arendt turns to the famous 1845/6 "German Ideology" manuscripts. But her analysis relies on a remarkably literal interpretation of the text. Arendt writes, "Marx's self-contradiction is most striking in the few paragraphs that outline the ideal future society and that are frequently dismissed as utopian. They cannot be dismissed because they constitute the centre of Marx's work and express most clearly its original impulses."[116] Arendt takes Marx not to be a utopian, but as offering a revised picture of the Athenian polis, "an almost complete leisure society where the time and energy for making a living, was, as it were, squeezed in between the much more important activities of *agorein*."[117] Marx "banishes" not only labour performed by slaves, but also "the *banausoi*, craftsman and artists"—communist society is without painters, only those who paint.[118] For Arendt, once Marx abolishes labour, the worker becomes a kind of Greek aristocrat.

In her view, Marx's biological and naturalistic idea of labour glorifies what for the Greeks was *pre-political*. Since slaves laboured, the necessities of life occurred before politics began. The problem, as Arendt sees it, is once again Marx tries to both uphold labour as freedom and abolish it altogether. But in this "contradiction," Marx is unable to grasp the idea of freedom known to the Greeks, certainly to Aristotle, as logos.[119] Instead, due to his dialectical conception of history, necessity brings about freedom. The violence of historical change, praxis, is mute to speech.[120] Even Arendt's most rigorous commentators assume the soundness of this interpretation. Dana Villa notes this point "seems undeniable and even obvious," but neglects to interrogate the validity of her claim.[121] However, Arendt misses the irony of the manuscript passages and instead takes it to be representative of the full extent of Marx's notion of freedom. She looks past the playful intent of Marx's argument and at the same time, more importantly, misses the creativity of feeling and emotion so crucial to his idea of labour. The famous examples of painting without painters and after-dinner critique serve Marx's insight that alienated human activity cannot provide normatively acceptable meaning to our practical identities.[122]

Considerable caution is necessary when considering Arendt's interpretation since she dramatically mischaracterises Marx. The weight of Arendt's criticism rests in what she sees as the "basic contradiction" between Marx's desire to "abolish labor" in the realm of freedom and his idea of labour as human essence. However, there is good reason to doubt this is a contradiction. Marx's own distinction in the early writings between labour as alienated activity and productive activity as an ontological life activity cannot be overlooked. In his later writings, the categories are clarified as abstract labour and labour. Her criticism of Marx's concept of labour only holds if these distinctions are disregarded. Most significantly, the key interpretive distinction between alienated labour and free labour points to the flaw in Arendt's critique of Marx. To "*abolish* labour" is not to rob human beings of our essential powers, but to end the objectification of subjective activity in its determinate social form. Marx grasps productive activity as a thoroughly mediated relation, not a category that can be abstractly negated.

Her critique of his "basic inconsistency,"[123] idealising a life without labour and labour as freedom, needs to be questioned by examining Marx's own categories. He certainly wants to abolish *alienated labour* which he understands not as a natural condition of humanity but instead as a historically specific form of domination.[124] Marx's critique is of the social form of labour as it is constituted under capitalism.[125] Alienated labour is ruled by necessity in a double sense: for the worker who must work to live and for the capitalist who relies on the worker's labour-power to derive value. Marx distinguishes between alienated labour and human labour as creative life activity. In this sense, what Marx thinks of as communism is conditional on unalienated labour as creative activity lived out in the public realm.[126] Marx's idea of unalienated labour politicises labour as an activity of meaningful cohabitation since it now becomes open to rational discussion and decision. Communism is predicated on the possibility of labouring activity having normative meaning for human beings who act for reasons decided in concert with each other. If put this way, then Arendt does not point out a "self-contradiction" but confuses two distinct but inseparable aspects of Marx's concept: alienated and unalienated labour. For it to be Marx's "self-contradiction," would mean ignoring his analysis of social form including the relation between concrete and abstract labour.[127] Privately performed concrete acts of labour are set within specific value-forms, which means that this same activity is objectified as abstract labour when it takes on the function of value production and is socially validated. Marx's distinction between concrete labouring acts and the socially specific form of abstract labour means that this conception is not physiological, but detects that the logic of commodity exchange makes labour unfree in a very particular way. Labour under capitalism takes the social form of abstract labour. Arendt's reading thus elides the central aspect of Marx's critique of political economy, his critique of the social form of value.[128]

Further, Marx's analysis of wage-labour not only generates an account of the work process under commodity production but also maintains that alienated and abstract labour produce value, the historically specific social form wealth takes under capitalism. In Marx's view, labour-time is the immanent measure of value, which must be expressed as money.[129] Marx's concept of labour maintains that human activity is only intelligible in its determinate social form. The social form of labour is the production of values which are both private and social. Commodities are produced and exchanged for private gain and profit, but only as a result of the social meaning that this process takes between people. Capitalism depends upon the continual metamorphosis of productive activity between social forms. Labour is the activity that mediates the private and social interactions of human beings, which are unified under the social form that labour generally takes in capitalism as value-producing activity. Arendt elides this central aspect of Marx's notion and, in Patrick Murray's words, conceives of labour "devoid of social form."[130] For this reason, Arendt does not grasp the distinction between political economy and Marx's *critique of political economy*, which is a criticism of the dismal science in toto.

Without assessing the complexity of Marx's understanding of social form, Arendt omits the historical dimension crucial to his position and mistakenly attributes the errors of political economy to Marx's view, in effect ignoring the substance of his critique of this tradition. Also, at risk is the problem Arendt identifies in "the political importance of the emancipation of Labor and Marx's corresponding dignification of Labor as the most central of all human activities."[131] But this criticism omits the critical content of Marx's difference with political economy, first evident in his 1844 writings.[132] By leaving the alienated social form of labour unexamined, Arendt is unable to register the basis of Marx's critique of the form of labour and ultimately accepts the transhistorical concept of labour posited by political economy.[133]

Once Marx is interpreted as a critic of the social form of alienated labour, it becomes evident that the very things Arendt misreads in Marx are real problems in her thinking. If labour as such is seen as inherently unfree and a form of slavery, the dualism between freedom and necessity is reinforced rather than determinately mediated and sublated. In this respect, the central difference between Marx and Arendt can be located in their contrasting interpretations of a passage from the *Politics*:

> For if each instrument could perform its own function on command or by anticipating instructions, and if—like the statues of Daedalus or the tripods of

Hephaestus (which the poet describes as having "entered the assembly of the gods of their own accord")—shuttles wove cloth by themselves, and plectra played the lyre, an architectonic craftsman would not need assistants and masters would not need slaves.[134]

Since for Aristotle, slaves are natural instruments of their masters, he invokes the idea of machinery (as nonhuman instruments) to imagine the freedom human beings might have if they could be free from production. Quoted in full in *Capital*, volume 1, Marx contrasts Aristotle's imagined future with modern realities. Marx is making a point about the "dialectical inversion" of human activity and the instruments of modern production.[135] Rather than using technology to reduce labour-time, its advancement becomes a means to further the valorisation of capital, with its necessary increases in productivity.[136] However, Arendt takes the passage to point to the limitations of modern tools to free human beings from labour, affirming Aristotle's division between production (*poiesis*) and action (*praxis*).[137] She notes, "[m]an cannot be free if he does not know that he is subject to necessity, because his freedom is always won in his never wholly successful attempts to liberate himself from necessity."[138] While Arendt takes the passage to confirm the slavery of labour, Marx gives insight into the historical relation of unfreedom in the organisation of human activity. What Arendt sees as the cause, labour as such, Marx diagnoses as the symptom of alienated labour.

Importantly, Marx stresses the modern dualism between freedom and necessity. Rather than considering freedom to be in inherent tension with necessity, necessity is the condition of possibility for freedom. Marx puts this clearly: "[t]he true realm of freedom, the development of human powers as an end in itself, begins beyond it, though it can only flourish with this realm of necessity as its basis."[139] This "realm of freedom" sublates necessity when human flourishing is considered as essential to human life activity and an end in itself. Crucially, the realm of freedom is not independent from necessity but a dialectically surpassed realm that preserves necessity while altering its fundamentally unfree characteristics. The realm of freedom can then condition necessary activity and provide a structure of reasoning to ask and respond to the normative questions involved in the reproduction of social life.

The salient point that arises from Arendt's criticism is to sharpen the manner in which Marx's position seeks to confront the bifurcation of necessity and freedom.[140] Freedom cannot be located in the distribution of the products of alienated labour, but consists instead in the overcoming of the form of wage-labour itself, with its division between mental and manual labour.¹⁴¹ Productive activity allows for human beings to become free *through activity* rather than in its subservience.¹⁴² For Marx, as for Aristotle, properly understood, action is the "subject matter" of politics.¹⁴³ Rather than reducing labour to nature, Marx envisions a type of political association which demands sociality as expressed in the public realm.¹⁴⁴ His insistence, however, is that unalienated labour is a condition of possibility for actualised public freedom. This claim buttresses Arendt's argument that Marx's future society would be without politics.¹⁴⁵ For Marx, labour itself must be grasped politically.

In Arendt's view, Marx understands history to be a story of economic forces continuingly equating necessity with freedom.¹⁴⁶ For Arendt, the activity of politics is citizens participating freely, which can only be performed in a space totally distinct from the necessity of labour, which is always a compulsion. However, Marx's idea of freedom as a historical process conceives of necessity in two senses. First, necessity is expressed in the fundamental aspects of practical consciousness required for social life, and language is in this sense is necessary for self-conscious action. Second, Marx understands necessity in relation to the historically specific demands of social forms. He locates in the capitalist form of life a distinct separation between the "realm of necessity" and the "realm of freedom." But contra Arendt, Marx's idea of communism is not to glorify necessity but to maintain that freedom must determine necessity. Marx's concept of a society of associated producers understands the political and social constitution of life as one in which collective decision-making allows necessity to be discussed rationally amongst equals.¹⁴⁷ Arendt's division between public and private realms preserves the dualism between freedom and necessity. This dualism is overcome once Marx's idea of freedom is understood as allowing for human activity to be collectively decided.

The aim of Marx's politics is for the distinction between necessity and freedom to be traversed and negotiated by a type of collective activity that breaks from the domination of capital. Life activity is transformed from alienation to freedom. Fundamentally, Marx does not aim to abolish necessity and uphold every mundane task as one of liberation but instead to conceptualise the historically specific conditions for freedom. Accordingly, if labour is unalienated, human activity could be negotiated in such a way that necessity is understood not as an unfree activity, but as essential to socially free forms of interaction. This social freedom determines the necessities of production.¹⁴⁸ Martin Hägglund elucidates this idea by suggesting free activity "enables us to live our lives in the realm of necessity *in light of* the way we lead our lives in the realm of freedom."¹⁴⁹ In this way, necessity becomes a normative dimension of social life and can be evaluated as a question of social priorities and decisions.

Further, unalienated labour is the precondition for Marx's concept of democracy in a postcapitalist society. The questions of political life can be understood, contested, and collectively owned as *political questions* since it will be possible to democratically make decisions concerning both the demands and ends of production and the organisation of the polity, rather than the demands and ends of capital accumulation carried out under a division between economics and politics.[150] The issue of political decision-making in public life requires the substantive reevaluation of what constitutes political activity. For Marx, engaging in this activity freely requires that social production is also a political activity, and in turn, political life *orders* "economics," thereby expanding political decision-making to areas of life seen as merely necessary.

Labour and Action

The central question which arises from this analysis, however, is how to draw out the political consequences. What is at stake in this critique is whether Marx's concept of labour is adequate for the human activity of politics. As I want to stress in this section, in certain respects, there are close similarities between Marx and Arendt in terms of political action, and these points of contact help illuminate the democratic commitment of both thinkers. By reading Marx as also a theorist of action and freedom, rather than following Arendt's own dismissive rendering, we can place the two into a more productive conversation and reveal shared concerns. Marx's discussion of the Parisian communist workers, which I quoted earlier, for instance, demonstrates this motivation. Marx's claim that when they "gather together" for "immediate" political organisation, "they acquire a new need—the need for society—and what appears as a means has become an end ... Smoking, eating and drinking, etc., are no longer means of creating links between people. Company, association, conversation, which in its turn has society as its goal, is enough for them."[151]

The "society" that Marx deems to have emerged when the workers come together for political discussion is very close, phenomenologically, to what Arendt calls action. His suggestion that in these moments the means (getting together in order to strategise about improving their lot) becomes the end (getting together as a pleasure and joy in its own right) coincides importantly with Arendt. In *On Revolution*, she discusses the American revolutionaries in remarkably similar terms:

To them, power came into being when and where people would get together and bind themselves through promises, covenants, and mutual pledges; only such power which rested on reciprocity and mutuality, was real power and legitimate, whereas the so-called power of kings or princes or aristocrats, because it did not spring from mutuality but, at best, rested only on consent, was spurious and usurped ... This confidence moreover, arose not from a common ideology but from mutual promises and as such became the basis for "associations"—the gathering-together of people for a specified political purpose.[152]

While gathering together to decide on the shape of the constitution, the revolutionaries discover that the gathering itself founds the space for politics to become an actually collective and mutually reciprocal experience. Association provides for the development of public flourishing through political means.

Marx's political writings exemplify his concept of action. For instance, consider his analysis of the French Constitution of 1848 written for the Chartist newspaper *Notes to the People*. Marx assesses the constitution's republican demands for liberty in terms of the exceptions and limitations it makes to political freedom (press, association and public meetings) and the incapacity for this constitution to empower the "courage, sense, and union" of "the People." The concern of this article relates closely to the theme of founding in Arendt.[153] Ironically, despite Arendt's account of the split between political action and philosophical contemplation, she avoids taking Marx's political interventions seriously. Although Arendt was right to examine Marx's work beyond the partisan positions of her time, she ignores that his thought was advanced from his own public realm. While she claimed to be interested less in Marx's figure as a scholar or philosopher, but "as a rebel and a revolutionary," the relationship between his thought and his action is absent and uninterrogated in her analysis.[154] The result of this reading is that Marx's work is abstracted from his *vita activa* and his thought treated as *vita contemplativa* within the Western tradition (and hence a process of selection and inclusion by the philosopher). Marx's political life and concrete intervention are discounted, and the world of action that informs his authorship is hidden. However, Marx's authorship is precisely the rupture of any division between philosopher and political actor.

Further, throughout his political and journalist interventions, political action carried out in the public sphere (in Arendt's sense) informs his argument.[155] In *The Civil War in France* (1871), Marx's reflections on the Paris Commune, he spoke (in terms parallel with Arendt) about the need for a "Communal constitution" which would allow for political unity and for the "legitimate functions" of government to be a function of "the responsible agents of society," as a political form which disrupts the capitalist state by the worker-run Commune.[156] In this text, Marx articulates a concept of action very close to Arendt's own idea. *The Civil War in France* begins when the Parisian workers "proclaimed the republic."[157] This pamphlet is full of speeches,[158] denunciations,[159] public placards[160] and slogans.[161] Marx is not telling a story in which violence directs the narrative, but he is giving an account of proletarian power enmeshed in speech and action. Workers' self-emancipation is heralded in public, with declarations, words and deeds. Marx's thought is concerned foremost with human action.[162] Crucially, "every class struggle is a political struggle."[163] Such a conception of power can be emphasised with Arendt's words, since it only exists as the "potentiality in being together" and as such "power, like action, is boundless... Its only limitation is the existence of other people, but this limitation is not accidental, because human power corresponds to the condition of plurality to begin with."[164] Put this way, Arendt's conception of action helps grip the centrality of these aspects of Marx's political practice, not only as a complement, but as an essential feature of his theoretical innovation. It is now easier to resist traditional portrayals of Marx's political thought as an exercise in base-superstructure, little more than a reflection of the contradictions between forces and relations of production. Instead, it becomes clear that Marx's political theory is fundamentally concerned with human action. For human beings to make history, action must be constituted in the public realm.

Marx's most important political writings were often first *spoken* to other political agents with the intention to persuade and shape collective decision-making on the basis of his analysis.[165] This is the case with the *Communist Manifesto* and *The Civil War in France*. Both spoken, one to the Communist League, the other to the First International. Marx is not writing from the standpoint of contemplation but of the *vita activa*. His intention is to rally other political agents and convince them of the power of acting together. What Arendt appreciates in the "revolutionary spirt" of founding, especially in the men of action of the American Revolution and the communal council system, could equally be said to apply to Marx himself. But Arendt flouts Marx's own political action and the efforts to persuade that frame his speeches and pamphlets, instead describing him as a "mere witness" to the Commune.[166] This characterisation distorts the aims and function of the First International and Marx's strategic battle within it to further the aims of the Commune through his interventions.[167] *The Civil War in France* was derived from the General Council's collective discussion of the implications of the Commune. In Arendt's own terms, this work can be seen as itself an "act of founding," an address from the General Council of the First International (as the resulting pamphlet's subtitle notes) to its members across Europe and the USA. Adopted after a unanimous vote, *The Civil War in France* was printed and published by the First International.[168] Considering the agitational nature of the text and his involvement in the First International, Arendt's interpretation reads Marx in abstraction from his political activity and, thereby, the very politics of the work. Marx's political participation destabilises Arendt's criticisms, which exclude his own speech from the very public sphere which gave his ideas meaning. The significance of *The Civil War in France* is its assessment of the Commune as a new beginning, a form of action which allows for a development in the conception of political power along the lines laid out by Marx's connection between consciousness and labour. Workers' councils are predicated upon the constitution of democratic bodies founded in the politics of action. Labouring activity mediates and shapes their collective practice, and self-consciousness in the form of class agency founds the normative institutions of self-rule. Marx's insight is captured by Arendt's reflection of what could arise from the "potentiality in being together."

Of the Commune, Marx writes "the old world writhed in convulsion of rage at the sight of the Red Flag, the symbol of the Republic of Labour, floating over the Hôtel de Ville."[169] Revolutionary action establishes institutions of self-conscious rule that can be seen as normatively justified. Human action takes different determinate forms both in terms of the reasons for acting and in the institutions of organising founded by subjects. For Marx, the Commune as an institution of political rule can only be conceived as the goal-directed ends of working-class action. The Commune demonstrated that workers struggle beyond immediate economic interests and seek to create political institutions that provide normative justification of their legitimacy. The "Republic of Labour" is a democratic form of rule which articulates a new beginning and hence a "model" through the organisation of "the Communal constitution."[170]

The "spirit of revolution" is what Arendt extolls as "the act of founding a new body politic," with this experience bringing "the exhilarating awareness of the human capacity of beginning, the high spirits which have always attended the birth of something new on earth."[171] However, the genuine expression "of something new" in Marx's writing on the Commune is deliberately ignored. Marx makes the point that this is precisely the problem with contemporary commentators on the Commune, who cannot see it as unprecedented and instead take it to be medieval or traditional.[172] Marx's claim in *The Civil War in France* is that it is a "completely new" social form "which breaks the modern State power" by organising a revolutionary government.¹⁷³ However, Arendt argues that Marx considers revolution to be "the result of an irresistible force rather than the outcome of specific deeds and events." Thus, as she interprets Marx, the Commune was not seen as "possible germs for a new form of government" but "mere instruments to be dispensed with once the revolution came to an end."¹⁷⁴ Arendt notes the passage where he identifies the "true secret" of the Commune as "the political form at last discovered under which to work out the economical emancipation of Labour,"¹⁷⁵ but alleges that Marx never held the view very seriously or for very long.¹⁷⁶

This claim is dubious. Not only did Marx persist in his celebration of the Commune but he sustained its political defence. For Marx, the Commune founded an embryonic political form for future revolutionary action. As Peter Hudis notes, Marx's view of the Commune is of a "non-statist and *freely-associated* form of self-governance...an exemplar of the political form best-suited for exiting capitalism."¹⁷⁷ In 1880, Marx wrote the Preamble for the electoral program of the French Workers Party and its minimum demands with Jules Guesde. In the Preamble, Marx maintains that "the collective form" of production brought about by the "revolutionary action of the producing class," would ensure their freedom and the emancipation of "human beings (*Menschen*) without distinction of sex or race."¹⁷⁸ The minimum demands include political and economic programmes formed in direct reference to decrees of the Paris Commune from April 1871. In his correspondence, Marx writes: "The economic section of this very short document consists (apart from some introductory words which define the communist aim in a few lines) solely of demands that have, in fact, arisen spontaneously out of the workers' movement itself."¹⁷⁹ Not only is it clear that Marx takes the spontaneous nature of workers' action as crucial to political contestation, but the relation between his presentation of the "communist aim" and the minimal demands confirms that he understood the Commune as embodying the political form of rule which brings together the collective making of a constitution with the collective self-control of production. By holding the political and social content of action in relation, Marx posits the possibility of bringing "the economic" under the remit of political decision-making. Arendt's insistence on the persuasion necessary for plurality brings out that "demands" are essentially a "specifically human way of answering, talking back and measuring up to whatever happened or was done."¹⁸⁰ Seen this way, Marx's argument to bring "the economic" under "the political" does not run together two distinct things, but holds that action can be limitless in the manner that Arendt suggests.

However, Arendt's distorting reading of Marx not only eschews the normative upshot and political significance of his conception of action, it also consequently overlooks that his discussion of the Commune bears similarities with the account she is herself elaborating. While she treats labour and action as a tension in Marx's thought with devastating consequences for politics, it would be more accurate to say that he seeks to politicise human activity by transforming the organisation of labour from forms of domination to spaces defined by the practice of logos.

Arendt's idea of the *vita activa* involves an insightful critique of representative democracy and electoral government. She describes elected politicians as "either glorified messenger boys or hired experts who, like lawyers, are specialists in representing the interests of their clients."[181] The council system constitutes the space of freedom. Instead of opposing these insights to Marx, we can now see how they reinforce something crucial in his account, even if she misses the way in which the resources in his idea of freedom *confirm* her idea of action. In the Commune, Marx describes the operation of a new form of democracy with a series of assemblies and recallable delegates "bound by the *mandat impératif* [formal instructions]" of their constituents. For Marx, the Commune gave birth to a different form of power. He writes, "[w]hile the merely repressive organs of the old governmental power were to be amputated, its legitimate functions were to be wrested from an authority usurping pre-eminence over society itself, and restored to the responsible agents of society."[182] In this claim, Marx's idea of a new form of rule instituted by rational political agency is concrete. Crucially, he does not see the violent and repressive arms of the capitalist state as able to be wielded for working-class purposes since they lack normative justification. The activity of the Commune presents a novel development since it exposes the failure of bourgeois revolution to actually establish democratic rule. Marx remarks, "[t]he Commune made that catch-word of bourgeois revolution, cheap government, a reality."[183] Contra Arendt, Marx's political writings do not promote an idea of freedom conceived simply in terms of biological reproduction, but instead are imbued by the persistence of human action. His articulation of the dynamic of political activity bears reminiscence to the best of what Arendt imagines by founding. Marx learns from the action of the Commune, suggesting in the 1872 preface to *The Communist Manifesto*, co-written with Engels, that the text would be "improved" with a discussion of this new form of political power and "the practical experience" gained by the working class.[184] Marx's fundamental claim in *The Civil War in France* is that the emancipation of the working class can only be achieved by working-class action.

Arendt finds the promise of politics in the revolutionary council, exemplified in the council movement in Hungary in 1956, not unlike how Marx finds the promise of politics in the constitution-making of worker's control in France in 1871. For all her celebration of the action of the workers' councils, which gain their power in the immediacy of speech, Arendt's workers express little self-awareness.[185] Once they enter the political realm, Arendt has no room for the emancipation of the realm they leave behind. Political participation is given an autonomy which leaves Arendt blind to the social preconditions for politics that animate Marx's idea of action. Ironically, in her analysis of the institutions of the council movement she imposes firm boundaries between the political functions of the revolutionary councils and the economic functions of the workers' councils, occluding their political accordance. Even if the revolutionary and workers' councils "emerged together, [they] are better kept apart," as Arendt writes in her 1958 essay on the Hungarian revolution.[186] Despite the twin birth such revolutionary founding might appear to share within the council movement, labour and action are held in inextricable tension. But given the demand of her idea of natality is expressly to consider the radical potential of beginnings, Arendt's own remarks betray the limits of posing labour and action as fundamentally opposed. The consequence is that action becomes restricted in the critical moments where it would be enlightening and help understand what the revolutionary councils and the workers' councils meant for modern politics. Further ambiguities arise when it comes to describing the labour movement in terms of action.[187] Despite Arendt's protestations, the lines between labour, work, and action blur and bleed together.

In terms of a politics of action, Arendt is closer to Marx than it might appear at first sight when we follow her main lines of criticism. Arendt is compelled by the aspiration for political action to be carried into the light of shared political association. When Marx is put in that same light, he can be better seen as revealing the dynamic character of human activity and its expression in contradictory social forms. He does not reduce politics to labour but goes on to show why "economic life" can be politicised and made rational by human action. Action binds the narrow sense of "the economic" within the broader sense of "the political." For Marx, the ends of human activity make intelligible politics as a dynamic relation between participation and self-made institutions. What Abensour observes in reference to Marx's early writings applies to his thought in general: "The advent of 'true democracy'" signifies only the disappearance of the political State qua organizing form and separate realm, and not at all the extinction or the disappearance of the political."[188]

Despite her critique of Marx, assessing Arendt's interpretation allows the radical democratic aspects of his concept of labour to be understood in terms of action and the importance of the public realm in terms of political participation.

Conclusion: From Revolutionary Council to Ancient Assembly

In *The Eighteenth Brumaire of Louis Bonaparte*, Marx wrote that "heroes as well as the parties and the masses of the old French Revolution, performed the task of their time in Roman costumes and with Roman phrases, the task of unchaining and setting up modern *bourgeois* society."[189] Arendt reverses this image. The heroism of antiquity is reborn in the powdered wigs of the founders of the American Revolution and the hobnail boots of the delegates to the German *Räte*. Notwithstanding the birth of something new that Arendt extols in such movements, there is a definite sense that their natality appeals to the "lost treasure" of ancient political life.[190] Their heroism is in the story that could be told, in the "free men" of Homer's poems, where courage finds its expression in the "willingness to act and speak at all, to insert one's self into the world and begin a story of one's own."[191] For Arendt, the modern revolutionaries might be able to restore the dignity of politics, but in their explicit aims, the content of their politics is much less of a concern. Foremost, action "reveals" our distinct identities and by doing so, resists content.[192] As Cavarero observes, "Arendt is first and foremost interested in the concrete relationality of embodied political actors, not in the contents of their discourse, nor as one says today, in their political agenda."[193] For Marx, however, the consciousness involved in praxis is the very realisation of the "concrete relationality of embodied political actions." In this respect, Arendt's reversal misses the significance of consciousness in Marx's idea of action. Ancient costume and terminology give the modern revolutionaries a sense of inspiration and world historical purpose, but they create new meaning through their action—"in creating something that has never yet existed"—and action makes freedom conscious and concrete.[194] Just as action for Arendt creates our identities, for Marx, it enables the collective consciousness that directs action towards specific goods and rational ends.

Arendt's idea of council democracy reanimates the spirit of the Athenian polis directing action to the words and deeds of the public realm.[195] The Greeks, as Hanna Fenichel Pitkin notes, "authorize and explicate her vision of free citizenship, connecting her concept of action with politics."[196] Putting aside the controversies about the extent in which Arendt is a "modernist" or "anti-modernist,"[197] the issues in her interpretation of Marx exacerbate and weaken her use of the polis as a metaphor for political action. Despite her remarks about Marx's idea of communism as some kind of leisure society, Arendt herself sees the possibility of modern freedom in the scission of the political and social, pivoting her notion of modern freedom in reengaging a political equality that expresses the conditions for being political that the Greeks once appreciated. In this sense, the Greeks bestow a light to shine in the modern world and open the path for our own words and deeds. She writes:

> Let us therefore go back once more to antiquity, i.e., to its political and pre-philosophical traditions, certainly not for the sake of erudition and not even because of the continuity of our tradition, but merely because a freedom experienced in the process of acting and nothing else—though, of course, mankind never lost this experience altogether—has never again been articulated with the same classical clarity.[198]

This is why when Arendt invokes the polis, she is not calling for some kind of return to the "city-state in its physical location." Instead, Arendt views the polis as an ideal, "the organization of the people as it arises out of acting and speaking together, and its true space lies between people living together for this purpose, no matter where they happen to be."[199] The polis acts as a metaphor for the possibilities of politics. But in representing the polis as an ideal that arises in public, a tension emerges concerning the content of the workers' councils. The ancient polis was remarkable to Arendt precisely because production was a private concern. The polis provided a space for everyone "capable of deed and word," even if "most of them—like the slave, the foreigner, and the barbarian in antiquity, like the laborer or crafts man prior to the modern age, the jobholder or businessman in our world" did not occupy the public realm.[200] The public realm is a necessary condition of politics for Arendt and since she transplants the ancient structure of action onto the council movement, she is unable to explain the relationship between politics and economics in those movements. In looking to ancient political life to cure modern ills, Arendt's political solution is an abstract negation of the present content of social forms for the image of a political life long past.

In Marx's account, the concrete and determinate overcoming of the social form of labour under capitalism means that both dominant forms of politics (as representation) and economics (as alienated labour) must be negated in the birth of the councils. Without an account of the social form of labour, Arendt's concept of action lacks the historical dimension which would allow her to appreciate just how central Marx's politics were to the praxis of the council movements.[201] Arendt's concept of action is abstract when removed from the concrete content of working-class action so central to the council movement. As a result, Arendt's idea of action affirms the traditional separation between politics and economics. Her critique of Marx as elevating economics above politics misses the mark. Rather, Marx's challenge to tradition is that he seeks to transform the way "economic life" could be a component part of a larger and more expansive political form of life.

Arendt's argument that freely spent time will always end in consumption— "the more time left to him, the greedier and more craving his appetites"—betrays not Marx's "illusion in mechanistic philosophy," but a fundamental contradiction in Arendt's thought.[202] Her praise of the council model flouts that it is precisely the "time left to him" which compels the politics of the councils. Therefore, the activity of politics incorporates economics to create a realm in which democratic human action and deliberation has authority, rather than the "mute compulsion [*stumme Zwang*] of economic relations."[203] Arendt's separation of labour from the activity of politics restricts her concept of action dramatically. Her emphasis on beginning is stimulating for a political world which today seems to be exhausted of options. However, rather than sidelining Marx, "the social" should be seen as the category to grasp both private and public as mediated relations within historical forms of human action. For Marx, the criticism of capitalism involves a critique of the historical and social form of labour and the arising relations of commodity production and exchange absent in Arendt.

Arendt tars "the social" with economism. But rather than confirm economic life, Marx's thinking about the social develops a rich normative account of the interrelation between economic, political and ethical action and the necessity for human action to realise a comprehensive idea of freedom. Marx's account of the Commune is so important since as a new form of power, the bond that allows for its birth is the vision of equality between human beings acting in the public realm. In this sense, Marx and Arendt articulate the very same impulse. However, the positive moments of Arendt's concept need to be synthesised into a more expansive normative idea of action, which I argue can be found by tracing Marx's Aristotelian and Hegelian inheritance as a tradition which looks to make possible political action, rather than hinder it. Part II and III of this book attempt to make good on this claim. Having interrogated Arendt's political critique of Marx, and before excavating the wider intellectual ancestry, I next turn to Alasdair MacIntyre's ethical critique of Marx.

TWO

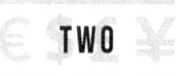

Ethics as Virtue

Alasdair MacIntyre

IN 1994 GIOVANNA BORRADORI PUBLISHED *The American Philosopher: Conversations with Quine, Davidson, Putnam, Nozick, Danto, Rorty, Cavell, MacIntyre, and Kuhn*, interviews with many of the most influential and renowned analytic philosophers of the postwar period. That the volume included Alasdair MacIntyre was perhaps a surprise since he was born in Scotland and published prolifically in England in the 1950s and 1960s, well before moving across the Atlantic at the onset of the 1970s. Hardly a likely candidate for *The American Philosopher*. However, it was in America, in 1981, when MacIntyre published *After Virtue*. Borradori directs her questions to push at the connections between different and rival traditions of philosophy. She is particularly interested in MacIntyre's relationship to politics and to Marx. After MacIntyre affirms a point from Georg Lukács, Borradori prompts him, "[t]hen even in this you assume a Marxist voice." MacIntyre replies:

> An Aristotelian critique of contemporary society has to recognize that the costs of economic development are generally paid by those least able to afford them; the benefits are appropriated in a way that has no regard to one's merits. At the same time, large-scale politics has become barren. Attempts to reform the political systems of modernity from within are always transformed into collaborations with them. Attempts to overthrow them always degenerate into terrorism or quasi terrorism. What is not thus barren is the politics involved in constructing and sustaining small-scale local communities, at the level of the family, the neighborhood, the

workplace, the parish, the school, or clinic, communities within which the needs of the hungry and the homeless can be met. I am not a communitarian. I do not believe in ideals or forms of community as a nostrum for contemporary social ills. I give my political loyalty to no program.[1]

With great precision MacIntyre lays out a biting appraisal of modern politics and an image of the community that eschews the label of communitarian. This response captures much of what is worth emphasising about his thinking as it becomes known in *AV*. At once there is a forceful critique of modernity and at the same time, lines of tension are apparent. How do modern politics and ethics converge for a thinker who gives their political loyalty only to Aristotle?

In *AV*, MacIntyre puts forward a grand vision and critique of the antinomies of modernity. MacIntyre points to ways in which the historical and cultural processes that riddle modern society with contradictions and bifurcations in turn fragment modern thought. His interpretation of modernity is provocative and strikes at fundamental aspects of modern morality philosophy. Tracing the genesis of this fragmentation to the European Enlightenment, MacIntyre argues that the dominant conceptions of moral understanding—utilitarian and Kantian—are unable to offer a coherent account of the moral good. *AV* delivers a probing assessment of the moral poverty of "the dominant social, economic, and political order."[2] MacIntyre looks to identify and confront the incoherence of moral meaning in the modern world, where life is often alienated and disenchanted. In diagnosing this situation, MacIntyre finds that the deficiency of ethical meaning can be remedied by cultivating ethical traditions and shared practices of the human good. MacIntyre revives the standpoint of Aristotle's teleology, centring his view on the conception of human nature as goal-directed potentiality that is fulfilled in the good life of *eudaimonia*. Against modern individualism, MacIntyre deploys Aristotle's social ontology. He specifically argues for an ethics based upon Aristotle's understanding of the virtues, which allows a full account of the rationality of human practices and traditions. On its initial publication, *AV* attracted considerable interest and has rightly become a landmark text of Anglo-American moral philosophy.

What is often overlooked in his reception, however, is the impact of the origins and initial growth of MacIntyre's philosophy in a pioneering and creative Hegelian Marxism. His luminous essays published as part of the British New Left shine light on his most fundamental claims in *AV*.[3] These origins manifest in his enduring attraction to Marx. Throughout his career, MacIntyre has continued to argue that modern moral philosophy and social science require engaging with Marxism as a critical tradition which offers a perspective into the character of modern thought as a whole. Marxism as a standpoint "made it possible for me to recognize the nature of the dominant contemporary morality." The influence of Marx runs from MacIntyre's involvement in the Communist Party of Great Britain at Queen Mary College of London in the 1940s, where: "I had become and to this day remain convinced of the truth and political relevance of Marx's critique of capitalism" to Trotskyism in the 1950s and 1960s.[4] MacIntyre's recent autobiographical reflections affirm his lifelong debt to Marx and Marxism in his critique of modern morality and twentieth-century moral philosophy. Marx's presence in his mature thought continues to be felt—serving not only to guide his analyses of modernity—but to shape his sense of a "revolutionary Aristotelianism."[5]

In the middle of the twentieth century, Marx was not seen as a serious topic for Anglo-American scholarship, and when he was, interest was often narrowed to "economic" topics.[6] MacIntyre's first publication, *Marxism: An Interpretation* (1953), was an inventive work, undertaking a very early philosophical reading of Marx (drawing on the *EPM*, yet to be published in English).[7] MacIntyre is one of its first Anglo-American interpreters. In the book, he focused on the Hegelian foundations of Marx's early writings. His understanding of Hegel is also noteworthy, considering it precedes the revival of Hegelianism that followed J. N. Findlay's *Hegel: A Re-Examination* (1958).[8]

As MacIntyre's thinking evolved throughout the 1950s and 1960s, he looked to establish a normative interpretation of Marx by reintroducing Hegel's idea of rational agency into the centre of the concept of "class struggle." With Marx, MacIntyre sought a comprehensive diagnosis of the ills of modernity and an ambitious account of the ethical resources needed for its critique and overcoming. His writing during this period were aimed at transforming the conception of Marxism from its dogmatic and deterministic versions to a sophisticated philosophical standpoint that could help inform moral and political action. This perspective was a result of MacIntyre's involvement and prominence in the British New Left.[9] This movement was born from the "twin crimes" of the conjunctional crisis in 1956: the challenge to Stalinism (brought about by the Soviet Union's crushing of the Hungarian council movement) and the disillusion with liberalism (sparked by the Suez Crisis).[10] MacIntyre intervened to interpret Marx against both Stalinist orthodoxy and liberal morality, often taken as the only available positions. His way to avoid this dualism involved centring the Hegel-Marx relationship to redeem normativity in Marx's theory of action. MacIntyre thought that Hegel needed Marx to be *realistic* and Marx needed Hegel to be *dynamic*.

Throughout his writings during the British New Left, MacIntyre turned to Hegel to radicalise understandings of freedom and emancipation. In his view, the "dilemma" of modern intellectual life "arises from a failure" to see the applicability of Hegel and Marx for a conception of freedom and "this failure is endemic not just in the minds of our sociologists but in the life of our society."[11] Despite his considerable status as an analytic philosopher, his writings in the 1960s defied what he took as the typical empiricism and dualism of academic moral philosophy by engaging directly with Marx.[12] He was explicitly influenced by the sociological and philosophical currents within Marxism as an intellectual tradition.[13] But by the close of the 1960s, MacIntyre had distanced himself from his political associations on the Marxist left and no longer considered himself writing from a tradition derived from Marx. However, in crucial ways the influence of Marx still informs MacIntyre's mature "revolutionary Aristotelian" conception of an emancipatory project centred in the ethical practice and belonging of local communities.

One cost of the success of *AV* was that MacIntyre's background and familiarity with Marxism were quickly forgotten, and his philosophy was stamped with the label of "communitarian."[14] Frequently *AV* is depicted as a response to John Rawls's *A Theory of Justice* (1971). Regardless of the unprecedented impact of Rawls's text, *AV* tells a much broader and more encompassing story about modern philosophy and the social world than such a depiction makes out.[15] Rawls called MacIntyre "one of the three stooges" to his liberal theory of justice (along with a neat list of communitarian critics including Michael Walzer, Michael Sandel, and often Charles Taylor).[16] Rawls's quip merely reflected an already accepted classification. In her perceptive history of this period, Katrina Forrester calls into question many of preconceived assumptions of Rawls's reinvention of postwar analytic philosophy by pointing out the political and social basis for its emergence and success. Unfortunately, however, the throughline of MacIntyre's debt to Marxism is overlooked, and Forrester repeats the long-standing accusation of his conservatism. This complaint shrouds MacIntyre's legacy and distorts both his interest in Marx and the political aspects of his ethical theory. If in the New Left, as Forrester narrates, MacIntyre had "combined critiques of analytic ethics with Marxism,"[17] by the 1980s his criticism had shifted dramatically: "MacIntyre, who had journeyed from Marxism to Christianity and a trenchant rejection of the modern, condemned the 'emotivist self,' devoid of social identity, and praised a premodern and anti-Enlightenment vision of the self constituted by kinship and motivated by virtue."[18] But MacIntyre is no conservative or reactionary, and this gloss misses what is profound about the depth of vision in his critique of modern moral philosophy. Rejecting the title and grouping of "communitarian," MacIntyre sees his project as a much more radical enterprise. His journey from Marxism is less a reactionary departure and more a story of his thinking through of modernity in terms already indicated in his earlier Marxist work.

A similar attitude is prevalent for many radical theorists. According to Chantal Mouffe, MacIntyre holds an "extremely ambiguous attitude towards the advent of democracy and tend[s] to defend premodern conceptions of politics, drawing no distinctions between the ethical and the political."[19] Such interpretations reduce MacIntyre's ethical theory to a kind of moral relativism and misconceive his politics. Recent attempts to understand MacIntyre's relationship to Marx have dramatically helped to remedy this attitude.[20] These reinterpretations have opened the way for reading MacIntyre as a significant commentator of Marx in his own right.[21] Adding to MacIntyre's standing as a "fierce critic of modernity,"[22] I unify MacIntyre's commentary on Marx and his overall philosophical project to provide a departure point to reassess Marx's own thought in relation to modern politics and ethics. When *AV* is read as a *response* to Marx and Marxism as a tradition, the lines of proximity and demarcation are better put into relief. The upshot of such a procedure is that the most generative aspects of MacIntyre's diagnosis of modernity and his conception of social life in terms of the narratives and practices of rational agents can be affirmed within an emancipatory politics that goes beyond what his vision allows.

Despite his enduring interest in Marx and Marxism, in *AV*, somewhat paradoxically, MacIntyre rejects Marx's critique of capitalism as ethically impoverished. He concludes *AV* with a severe, yet inchoate appraisal of Marx, encouraging readers to locate his text (and politics) beyond and without the conceptual categories of Marx's thought. To MacIntyre, Marxism itself is exhausted. As a tradition, its pretensions to supply a convincing critique of liberalism have failed.[23] Without an adequate moral philosophy which can guide moral practices, MacIntyre believes Marxism collapses politically. Deemed by MacIntyre to be suffering from a type of utilitarianism, as a tradition Marxism is declared unable to overcome the ethical crisis of modernity. This fault line is a direct result of an ethical lacuna in Marx.[24] I suggest this conclusion is misguided. In implicitly accepting and explicitly disavowing Marx in this way, MacIntyre introduces a certain tension into his work, inviting closer scrutiny to his own analyses of modernity and his critique of Marx as inadequate to its challenges. The task of this investigation is to show that there is a valuable convergence between MacIntyre's account of the virtues and the normative elements of Marx's depiction of rational action, especially as I elaborate later in this book. Both Marx and MacIntyre envision political collectivity organised around the good of goal-directed practices and the practical reasoning of human flourishing.

However, MacIntyre's conclusion in *AV* loses sight of the ethical potential of Marx's thought, which would help support his own political alternative to the modern market and state. This foreclosure results from a misreading that fails to come to grips with the residues of Marx and Hegel in his own thought. I argue that the most fruitful articulation of the normative dimension of Marx's thought depends upon a reconstruction of his social ontology and value-form theory in light of Aristotelian and Hegelian philosophy. Marx conceives of the human essence and the flourishing of human life in relation to the distinctively social and rational activity of labour. On this basis, Marx makes a historically specific critique of the naturalisation of capitalism in the methodological individualism of liberal political and economic thought. It is because MacIntyre jettisons Marx on precisely these points that a series of contradictions begins to surface within his analysis. When Marx is read with the rich determinations of both Aristotle's teleology and Hegel's conception of rational agency, it becomes apparent that the solution offered by MacIntyre is much less convincing than his overall diagnosis. But just as Marx learnt from Aristotle, MacIntyre's Aristotelianism has much to recommend it for those trying to come to terms with the poverty of ethical life under capitalism. In my interpretation, Marx's social ontology takes up an Aristotelian conception of human flourishing. As such, there is plenty to gain from MacIntyre's efforts to elaborate such a standpoint.

To his disadvantage, in *AV* MacIntyre does not seriously consider Marx's value-form critique of capital and the fetishism of social forms. Since he disregards Marx's idea of value, MacIntyre is unable to appreciate that the critique of fetishism is precisely the critique of individualism in modernity.[25] Without an analysis of capital as the universalising social relation of the modern world, MacIntyre cannot adequately analyse the specific logic of modern thought and being. Despite earlier elaborations of Marx's idea of "practical consciousness" as a theory of human action, MacIntyre forsakes the originality of Marx's understanding of productive activity as the mediation of modern social relations and overlooks its significance for a concept of collective agency and flourishing.

In this chapter, I begin by suggesting that in *AV*, MacIntyre provides a compelling historical critique of modern moral thought. MacIntyre points out how contradictions in thought reflect real contradictions in social being, and consequently, his work pivots around a critique of dualistic modes of thought: fact/value, is/ought, theory/practice, etc. As MacIntyre would have it, these antinomies limit not just how we see, but also how we act upon the world. Having become firmly embedded not just in our thought but in our social practices, according to MacIntyre, such antimonies are inclined to be resistant to anything less than a radical praxis. His historicist notion of the narrative structure of social life is inscribed with Marx's theory of history. But in *AV*, MacIntyre is less interested in the class dimensions of Marx's idea of social contradiction. The central dualism that structures modern life, for MacIntyre, is the antinomy between the individual and the community. The result is that modernity is premised on an "emotivist" culture that paints personal preference as moral justification and makes it difficult to see collective good beyond an idea of mutual advantage. The task of instituting a coherent tradition of ethical inquiry is thus a standpoint that does not simply mediate this dualism in theory but overcomes it in practice.

Believing such an ethics cannot be found in Marx, MacIntyre instead looks back to Aristotle. I assess MacIntyre's rejection of Marx, which neglects the normative potential of his value-form critique of capitalism as a form of life. Despite relying on aspects of Marx's historical insight, MacIntyre advocates a politics derived in local ethical communities. In my view, while local communities may develop practices that promote ethical reasoning, a normative theory of modernity must go beyond the *particularity* of small communities to a *universal* conception of absolute ethical life. This conception relates the particular community, made up of individual subjects acting in social roles, to a universal moral and political practice of ethical life. Next, I advance my immanent critique of MacIntyre's mature position by returning to the perspective of his early writings. *AV* is a both an elaboration of his early writings and a move away from Marx's fundamental normative insights, some of which MacIntyre articulated in the 1950s. His New Left essays serve as prolegomena for thinking about Marx and ethics. MacIntyre understood Marx as fundamentally a thinker of freedom who brings to life a normative vision of ethical action. He brought this acuity to bear upon the history of moral philosophy, pointing to the anatomies of bourgeois thought and capitalism as a form life. MacIntyre's early critique of capitalist modernity presents a sense of what is lost in his mature thought. MacIntyre's New Left writings establish a highly generative Hegelian Marxist perspective on the ethical import of Marx's idea of practical consciousness, even if he later denies this possibility. By failing to appreciate the synthesis of Aristotle and Hegel in Marx's value-form theory, MacIntyre cannot come to terms with the ethical resources within his critique of political economy. Indeed, as I go on to show, the power of Marx's social thought lies precisely in the preservation and animation of Aristotelian and Hegelian themes in his critique of capitalism as a social form of life.

Modern Moral Philosophy

In MacIntyre's account of modernity, the fundamental breakdown in the intelligibility of morality occurs in the European Enlightenment. The "Enlightenment project"—best represented in Hume and Kant—eschewed Aristotle's teleological conception of human nature and the corresponding view of moral rationality in the socially recognised practice of the virtues. MacIntyre contends that modern bureaucratic and individualist culture is predicated on the loss of a collective morality which was once socially constituted in a shared notion of the virtues. The severance of the link between the shared practices of the virtues and the philosophical justification of moral action resulted in a dualistic and partial comprehension of social reality. Isolated from the social processes and language that would permit rational and shared understanding of ethical meaning and action, modern morality reflects the antinomic nature of society. MacIntyre declares that moral philosophy is in a "grave disorder," where "[w]e possess indeed simulacra of morality ... But we have— very largely, if not entirely—lost our comprehension, both theoretical and practical, of morality."[26] Thus, modern thought after the Enlightenment is predicated on a crisis of moral intelligibility. Seen from his perspective, attempts to counter the Enlightenment—either by Marx or Nietzsche—are limited by Enlightenment presuppositions that went unquestioned. These viewpoints are compromised by the very alienation and amoralism they detected in modern society but could not surpass.

In *AV*, MacIntyre opens his critical appraisal of modern moral philosophy with the problem of disagreement. Modern philosophy, he suggests, uses the nomenclature of morality—"right," "virtue" and so on —but lacks any coherent account of ethical life because it has become divorced from the normative framework in which it once had meaning.[27] Attempts at constructing moral theories can now only be made using the fragments of traditions long destroyed, ripped from their social content and reified into empty abstractions.[28] As a result, moral language no longer serves as a compelling and motivating force that can clarify what moral action is and why it bears upon us as ethical beings. Contemporary morality can appeal to the terms, concepts and motivations of moral language, but this can only result in the incommensurability of competing views to settle moral disputes. In one of the early examples presented in *AV*, MacIntyre glosses a standard argument for and against state welfare. Despite the prominence of this debate in the public sphere, from the news headline and campaign rhetoric to the lectern or barstool, MacIntyre considers it to be "shrill." Both positions "for" and "against" rest upon notions of justice and freedom, but reflect dramatically different ideas of equality and liberty. Each position can be expressed in a way that is "logically valid." However, the rival positions are marked by their "morally incommensurability." That is, there is no way to assess the claims of one side against the other since as we know them "each premise employs some quite different normative or evaluative concept." Since the language used has little shared content, we are unable to meaningfully assess each claim next to each other. As such, appeals to equality or liberty ultimately become assertions. We can provide detailed reasoning for our view, but the use of moral language cannot help in solving the conflict.[29]

What makes this disagreement worse, according to MacIntyre, is that the moral language used is most often expressed as arguments that are "impersonal." When giving reasons to others for action, it is not sufficient to direct someone to act (excepting various types of authority) by simply asking someone to do it. Reasons must be given for why that action should be done, and so the benefits and positive consequences for a group, or alternatively, the responsibility or principle involved in doing that action are called upon. MacIntyre considers this kind of reason-giving as appealing to objective standards that merely "masquerade" as moral since the plea relies upon dissolving an important link between the agents and the motives of personal context, preferences or desire. What frames both the inability to assess rival claims and the appeal to impersonal standards of argument is that the concepts and notions of morality employed are ripped from their histories as ideas and expressions of moral meaning. Moral concepts are adopted without making sense of the variance of their content. As MacIntyre depicts it, this shift in meaning in our basic moral language has gone largely unnoticed. For instance, "virtue" is treated as if it meant the same thing for Aristotle, the *metic*, writing in Athens in the fourth century BCE, as for the eighteenth-century Kant, a Prussian who never left Königsberg.[30] Stripping ideas from their history and cultural contexts distorts the meaning of those ideas from the ground up.[31]

The source of this problem, according to MacIntyre, is the shift in culture that was brought about by the rise of individualism in modernity. His strategy is to show that if modern moral thought is detached from collectively understood and rational frameworks that provide moral knowledge with content, moral practice becomes unintelligible.[32] As MacIntyre would have it, the impasse of morality is not limited to the generally internal perspectives of particular branches or schools of philosophy. It fundamentally frustrates all efforts to settle philosophical problems in modernity and undermines reason-giving between agents. Deprived of a shared rational conceptual scheme, modern moral thought becomes "emotivist." In a culture of individualism, regardless of the moral language, moral meaning itself becomes little more than an expression, or in MacIntyre's words, a "mask" for individual preferences.[33] Thus, appeals to morality and the giving of reasons, regardless of the intention of the actor, are set within a moral culture that is underpinned by the dualism between individual and collective. Without a shared criterion of what constitutes moral value and the virtues, we can only appeal to "the good," but this is ultimately unintelligible.[34] We do not know or agree about what the good life looks like.

MacIntyre builds this thesis by providing an intellectual genealogy that ties social practice and structure to moral philosophy. Conceiving "advanced modernity" as "one distinctive type of social order" defined by a market economy and bureaucratic state, MacIntyre suggests that modern fragmented societal structures are reproduced in moral philosophy with the abstraction of "the individual."[35] In modernity, the individual is isolated from history and becomes the primary unit of moral reflection. This specific crisis of moral knowledge and action that brings about such a transformation arises from the culture of the European Enlightenment. The inherent problem of this intellectual vicissitude is not simply the falsity of the positions made by the particular theorists themselves, but the faulty foundation upon which all their constructions were predicated. The paradoxical effect was that the very historical processes that heralded the theoretical innovation of the Enlightenment remained partly obfuscated for its most important theorists. Notably, Kant, Diderot, Hume and Smith "inherited incoherent fragments of a once coherent scheme of thought and action and, since they did not recognize their own peculiar historical and cultural situation, they could not recognize the impossible and quixotic character of their self-appointed task."[36] The philosophers of the European Enlightenment lacked the self-awareness to apprehend the full extent of the "process of historical transformation" at hand—they failed to grasp their own time in thought—and thus could only inherit and build their positions on a fragmentary understanding.[37] Even the most profound thinkers, like Kant and Hume, were unable to recognise the social and historical conditions embedded in the disjointed and disparate schemes of moral philosophy they confronted. Lacking consciousness of the total process, but attentive to the demands of specifically modern problems, such as the relation of scientific knowledge to experience, reason and moral autonomy, Kant and Hume theorised *within* the limitations of the fragments, rather than confronting the barriers to thought and action presented in modernity in totality.

MacIntyre seeks to historicise this impasse with a history of philosophy, or what "Hegel called philosophical history" which establishes the structure of his argument in the first half of *AV*.[38] By tracing the changing meaning of morality beginning with the Enlightenment, MacIntyre constructs a *social* history of philosophy on the conviction that the meaning of morality is embodied in the composition of social life as a whole.[39] The historical narrative is crucial to MacIntyre's account in another way. This setting grants a distinct advantage over the "persistently unhistorical treatment of moral philosophy ... [the] abstraction of these writers from the cultural and social milieus in which they lived and thought and so the history of their thought acquires a false independence from the rest of culture."[40] Crucially, by "historicising" modernity, MacIntyre is able to identify both the inability of Enlightenment thought to self-understand the relation between social life and thought and the subsequent, persistent problem of philosophy that is unable to give an account of its own history. Blinded to its social determinants, the failure of Enlightenment philosophy to think its own history, means for MacIntyre that modern thought is largely unaware of the crisis at hand. Thus, on MacIntyre's analysis, moral philosophy must also be sociological.[41]

In *AV*, the rise and emanation of the European Enlightenment is seen as a distinctly modern process of transformation and fragmentation of social life. MacIntyre dates the transition between 1630 and 1830.[42] What he does not mention, but is important to note, is that these dates mark the ruptures of bourgeois revolutions and the consolidation of the capitalist state in Europe. Punctuated by the English Civil War in the mid-seventeenth century and the July Revolution of 1830 in France, the dates demarcate the beginning and primacy of bourgeois rule in Europe.[43] More specifically, MacIntyre focuses on the progression of Enlightenment thought that makes possible the shift that comes *after* the French Revolution of 1789. An intellectual culture in Europe had germinated well before this event. This Enlightenment culture encompassed increasingly secularisation, an educated middle-class bureaucracy and the proliferation of universities in European cities. As such, the French *philosophes* were alienated by the comparative backwardness of their context, when compared to social transformations in other European cities and nation-states. As MacIntyre puts it, "at least the first phase of the French revolution can be understood as an attempt to enter by political means this North European culture and so to abolish the gap between French ideas and French social and political life."[44]

This characterisation of the cultural formation of modern Europe echoes aspects of Marx's understanding of bourgeois revolution as a contractionary process pertaining to class tensions and fractures within a total social form. According to Marx, the French Revolution helped destroy European "feudalism" and marked a new epoch with a historically specific social form based on capital accumulation and the split between the individual and collective.[45] This interpretation locates a shift in thought from the pre-revolutionary period (intellectual movements against the *ancien régime* and absolutism) and that of post-revolutionary thought (attempting to understand the new paradigm).[46] MacIntyre shares with many Marxist accounts the basic view that the post-revolutionary thinkers of the eighteenth-century reflect on a world that is distinctively bourgeois, and the problems that arise from these social relations are specifically *modern*.[47] Conditioned by new realities, post-revolutionary thought becomes increasingly concerned with the nature of these unfamiliar conditions and at the same time, increasingly critical of the new social order. The political revolution spurred revolutions in thought. The ambition of German Idealism was to achieve in thought the implications of the French revolution of 1789–1815.[48] MacIntyre follows this narrative, noting that "Kant recognized the French Revolution as a political expression of thought akin to his own."[49]

This view closely resembles Lucien Goldmann's Marxist account of the history of philosophy in *Immanuel Kant* (1945) and *The Hidden God* (1955).[50] Following Georg Lukács's early writings, also a crucial influence on MacIntyre, Goldmann sees Kant's philosophy in light of the French Revolution and a "bourgeois worldview" that advances a moral individualism. By setting out a "sociological analysis of the basic elements of philosophical thought," Goldmann looks to establish the connection between conceptual knowledge and its creation by particular groups insofar as it impacts human life for the collective subject.[51] Kant's individualism is contrasted with a philosophy of history that underpins collective subjectivity and action, which Goldmann tasks with shaping the future of the human community.[52] For Goldmann, as for MacIntyre, the formation of philosophical thought requires historical and sociological analysis. Further, the tie between human action and human community that can be grasped from this analysis is central to addressing Kant's question, "what is the human being?"

This question and its consequences animate MacIntyre's mature work. Interestingly the impact of Goldmann's Marxist approach is explicit in work written well before *AV*. In a review of the English translation of *The Hidden God* from 1964, which shows familiarity with *Immanuel Kant*, MacIntyre declares the book is "a model of how to write moral philosophy."[53] MacIntyre appreciates two methodological aspects. First, Goldmann's advantage over crude "self-styled" Marxists who explain thought as simply a result of social forces is that he distinguishes the background of a thinker through the thinker themselves, "seeing in the coherence of great art or great philosophy something that is only implicit in the thought and action of ordinary men."[54] MacIntyre affirms the need to grasp both the thought itself and its manifestation in social life. Second, MacIntyre highlights the ahistorical approach of Anglo-American moral philosophers who overlook fundamental changes in the structure of concepts and as a result typically take disagreement about moral concepts (such as "good" and "ought") to reflect "rival and competing views of the same concepts, rather than elucidating very different concepts from very different historical periods."[55] This insight lays the groundwork for MacIntyre's argument in *AV*.

While MacIntyre shies away from Goldmann's conclusion that Kant's legacy should be readily incorporated within Marxist philosophy, he appreciates the depth of analysis.[56] In his review, MacIntyre praises Goldmann's identification of a major historical and moral juncture in Kant's dualism: "the related rifts between fact and value and between virtue and happiness." As MacIntyre interprets the argument, for Kant,

> the highest good is still virtue crowned with happiness; but virtue and happiness cannot be brought together within the world. It is only beyond the present world by a power outside it that they can be reconciled. Practical life is intolerable unless there is such a divine power, but theoretical inquiry cannot show either that there is or is not such a being. So, for Kant, moral rules are independent of how the world goes, to be obeyed whatever the consequences of obeying them; and yet there would be no point in obeying the rules unless the universe were of a certain kind.[57]

This line of inquiry, acknowledged in appreciation of Goldmann's approach, takes full form in *AV*.[58] There the historical account of Enlightenment thought, and Kant in particular, is shown to have resulted in a kind of moral incoherence that opens the way for an appraisal of modern individualism.

Kant is the foremost antagonist in *AV*.[59] In Kant's practical philosophy, MacIntyre finds the distinctive expression of the individualism foundational to modern moral thought.[60] Kant is presented as the vital turning point, for both the seriousness of the attempt to postulate a rational basis for morality and the consequence of the failure to provide sufficient justification.[61] According to MacIntyre, Kant based his moral philosophy on two points. First, for morality to be rational it must be uniform (in the same way as "the rules of arithmetic") and "*binding* on all rational beings." Since the moral law is universally applicable and inclusive of all rational beings, moral justification is the design of maxims that conform to the law. It is the duty of individual subjects to act in such a way that complies with the moral law. Hence a key element of morality is the task of determining a test for moral maxims. Kant rejects a traditional test of moral justification in the desire and realisation of happiness,[62] believing, as MacIntyre puts it, that "our *conception* of happiness is too vague and shifting to provide a reliable moral guide." Secondly, Kant rejects another traditional view which tests moral maxims in the belief of God. Since if one was to accept God's commands as what one "ought to do," it would be necessary prior to this knowledge to have an existing set of maxims to judge action by.[63] Instead, Kant's practical reason is determined by "principles which both can and ought to be held by *all* men, independent of circumstances and conditions, and which could consistently be obeyed by every rational agent on every occasion. The test for a proposed maxim is then easily framed: can we or can we not consistently will that everyone should always act on it?"[64] MacIntyre finds the basis of such justification question begging. Specifically, he attests that moral and non-moral positions can *both* be made universal by Kant's supreme moral principle. Since moral maxims are supposed to be binding on all rational beings, for Kant, morality is seen in terms of obedience to the categorical imperative by the individual will. According to MacIntyre, by locating morality in the moral law rather than happiness as the end of moral action, Kant problematically holds that moral justification must be the conformity of willing agents to moral maxims. In effect, desire cannot guide moral action since justification must be grounded in the supreme moral principle.[65]

MacIntyre's stress on Kant's departure from the traditional foundation of morality in happiness, desire or religious belief is important for his argument since it locates a pivotal transitional moment. The rupture point is Kant's attempt to ground morality in what is given by reason alone, and its justification in individual autonomous will proves vulnerable to failing on its own criteria. MacIntyre takes Kant's revolution in moral philosophy to be underwritten by the inheritance of certain conservative Lutheran presuppositions. He sardonically remarks, "Kant never doubted for a moment that the maxims which he had learnt from his own virtuous parents were those which had to be vindicated by a rational test."[66] MacIntyre's sharp exposition poses the Kantian formulation of moral autonomy within its historical and cultural context to show that it assumes a social content that the formal aspect of Kant's moral law claims to be free from. In this assessment, MacIntyre maintains Kant is not just a precedent historical forerunner, but the heir of such dualistic schemes as established by Diderot and Hume.[67] Diderot divides natural desires from the "artificially formed and corrupted desires" of society. Following suit, Hume looks to ground moral judgements in our passions, since our moral feelings, and not reason, prompt us to first act.[68] The opposition between the passions and reason for both Hume and Kant is just that each of their respective arguments have precluded the possibilities of founding moral judgement on either.[69] MacIntyre represents Kant and Hume not as the great antagonists of moral philosophy, where one can be validated against the other, but as philosophically conjoined, sharing the same historical presuppositions and thus the same historical failure.

AV presents the problem of moral fragmentation as the central, unavoidable, feature of Enlightenment dualism. MacIntyre's declaration of the failure of the Enlightenment project depends on a historical analysis. But moral philosophy as advocated by Kant and Hume fails on a second front—the nature of the social transformation undermines any hope of the consistency of their philosophy in the exact terms they understood it. In this sense, MacIntyre argues it is wrong to understand these thinkers as a series of "contributors to a timeless debate about morality." Rather they should be seen as the "inheritors of a very specific and particular scheme of moral beliefs, a scheme whose internal incoherence ensured the failure of the common philosophical project from the outset."[70] He remarks that this project was "bound to fail."[71]

MacIntyre draws out the implications of his critique of the Enlightenment for an analysis of advanced modernity. The dualistic conceptual scheme he identifies in Hume and Kant expands well beyond moral philosophy and shapes the dominant intellectual foundations of modern social science. Accordingly, moral "value" becomes severed from the "facts" of social science. MacIntyre deems this view as mechanical, since no fact is given a value: "'Fact' becomes value-free, 'is' becomes a stranger to 'ought' and explanation, as well as evaluation, changes its character as a result of this divorce between 'is' and 'ought.'"[72] As MacIntyre would have it, the division between "is" and "ought" is institutionalised by the structures of modern society and its corresponding systems of knowledge. As a result, moral philosophy becomes unable to coherently articulate moral action, and social science becomes positivistic, positing individual empirical facts as the basis of truth. The notion of "fact" is drawn from the same fraught history as moral philosophy: "'Fact' is in modern culture a folk-concept with an aristocratic ancestry."[73] MacIntyre is not claiming we cannot know truths about the world, but rather that empiricism elevates fact and leaves reason unknowable in conceptual terms, creating a division between facts and morality.[74] In Hegel's locution, it is the dialectical opposite of Kant's rationality, which in effect takes on the same one-sided shape.[75]

MacIntyre detects the progression and intensification of the fact/value distinction most clearly in bureaucratic rationality. He maintains that positivistic sociological thinking has become entrenched in the institutional and bureaucratic mentality and practice of modern society. For this reason, he describes the "contemporary vision of the world" as Weberian, essentially defined by the rationality of bureaucratic institutions and limited by a sociological mode of thinking about moral action.[76] Max Weber argues that means-end relationships are understood quantifiably, measured and supported by the "scientific" status of varying modes of social knowledge which are said to encompass "a set of universal law like generalisations."[77] The prediction and advice of managers and experts provide policy sets, detailed research and dominant ideological support for the operation of the present social order, precisely from the positivistic claims of this knowledge.[78] Weber can shed considerable light on the nature of bureaucratic organisation but ultimately replicates rather than overcomes the dualism within modern thought.

MacIntyre's argument, as I have presented it so far, is an account of the origins of the fact/value distinction in the Enlightenment and its longevity as the dominant form of rationality into the "culture of bureaucratic individualism."[79] The first half of *AV* is an assessment of this crisis, closely relating the incoherence of ethical thought to "the politics of modern society."[80] MacIntyre's own conception of politics is important, since he distances himself explicitly from the prevailing orthodoxies of modern political thought, especially liberalism.[81] This clears the intellectual space for his promotion of Aristotle and the practices of the virtues, which occupies the second half of *AV*. If modern ethics and politics can be deemed in every respect compromised, then looking for an alternative in Aristotle appears plausible.

Revolutionary Aristotelianism

MacIntyre calls for a return to Aristotle's conception of the virtues to help found a rational basis for ethics. Yet he seeks to treat Aristotle's ethics *historically*. This requires MacIntyre to conceive Aristotelian ethics, firstly, as an expression of the relationship between ethical and political life in Ancient Athens and secondly, as a historical tradition capable of improvement and modification.[82] MacIntyre looks to refashion Aristotle's ethical theory for modern conditions and model it with a politics that contradicts the established order, his self-described "revolutionary Aristotelianism."

In *AV*, MacIntyre renders visible fundamental issues that emerged with the formation of modern moral philosophy and social thought. However, his account is less clear when he attempts to define an Aristotelian ethical theory that can ensure a sufficient political basis for an emancipatory position. This weakness is evident in his treatment of Marx. MacIntyre's claim that the individualism of the Enlightenment is replicated in Marx's thought (and continued in Marxism as a political practice) is particularly problematic because it neglects the extent of the ethical dimension of Marx's social ontology and its specifically Aristotelian character. For Marx, the telos of human beings is realised in the flourishing made possible by the collective agency and rationality of labour as ontological activity. This view is evident in Marx's early concept of "species-being" (*Gattungswesen*) and is further enhanced in his critique of political economy. Marx provides an account of the fragmentation of modern social relations in the contradiction between private commodity exchange and social labour and the fetishism that arises from the production and reproduction of value. Although in *AV* MacIntyre adopts a political and intellectual history indebted to Marx, he distances himself from precisely this critique of capital and the immanent idea of ethical life that arises from Marx's notion of social activity. As a result, the book ends with a politically hesitant and largely unpersuasive call for the revival of the local community. It is worth examining how MacIntyre arrives at this position.

When MacIntyre's conception of modern politics is examined closely, Marx's presence is felt in implicit and explicit terms. Most clear is the imprint of Marx's theory of history. MacIntyre is a critical but close reader of *The Eighteenth Brumaire of Louis Bonaparte*, which is discussed in *AV* at important points. MacIntyre maintains "there is much to learn" from Marx's historical approach,[83] especially in "the classical, if not entirely satisfactory account of human life as enacted dramatic narrative."[84] From Marx's theory of history, MacIntyre articulates a conception of the narrative structure of social life. The drama of human life is written by those who also play their part in the action. Every narrative begins in the middle, as it were, with a history that precedes and shapes what story can be told. The possible actions available to human agents are always a question of uncertainty, but the social context and backdrop inescapably bear upon the stories of human life. MacIntyre perceptively draws from Marx to inform this normative conception of narrative as the expression of human action. However in the same breath, MacIntyre indicates that Marx subsumes this narrative structure to law like predication.[85] But on the lights of MacIntyre's own idea of narrative, his construal provokes a generative point that can be enhanced to show the normative aspects of Marx's idea of action.

My interpretation of Marx advances MacIntyre's insight that class struggle is an expression of political action that depends upon the practical identity of human beings who in narrative form articulate reasons for acting, reflecting on their consciousness and collective agency. The *Eighteenth Brumaire* helps render visible the dynamism of historical action as an interplay between traditions inherited from the past and the possibilities for social change in the face of reaction. Marx investigates, through a chronicling of Louis Napoleon Bonaparte's 1851 coup d'état, the relation between class interests, political forms, individual motivation and collective action. In this text, he offers an array of historical factors which condition, motivate and propel the opposing political factions into conflict. Tradition, for Marx, is itself the transmission of consciousness, articulating the historical and collective memory of classes and providing inspiration for action.

> And as in private life one differentiates between what a man thinks and says of himself and what he really [*wirklich*] is and does, so in historical struggles one must still more distinguish the language and the imaginary aspirations of parties from their real organism and their real interests, their conception of themselves from their reality.[86]

Marx does not reduce individual motivation to the most immediate and predictable class interest but reveals the way in which individuals are always part of a wider fabric of class relations. Political action weaves from these threads, and the conflicts between agents must be viewed through their entwinement. Tradition bears upon class struggle and political strategy, shaping the form of consciousness and expression of rational agency. Consciousness renders visible social relations and allows reflection as to what forms of organisation and action subjects might take.

Marx's historical mode of analysis is central to *AV*, where the European Enlightenment is interpreted as a qualitative transformation of thought synchronising with a universalising social transformation. In this way, MacIntyre's detailing of the shift in modern thought follows Marx in charting this intellectual movement as part of larger social processes. MacIntyre draws on the *Theses on Feuerbach* in his account of the dualism of Enlightenment materialism.[87] He refers to, but does not cite, the third thesis, which reads:

> The materialist doctrine concerning the changing of circumstances and upbringing forgets that circumstances are changed by men and that it is essential to educate the educator himself. This doctrine must, therefore, divide society [*Gesellschaft*] into two parts, one of which is superior to society.
>
> The coincidence of the changing of circumstances and of human activity or self-changing [*Selbstveränderung*] can be conceived and rationally understood only as *revolutionary practice* [*revolutionäre Praxis*].[88]

Marx compares the mechanical materialism that imposes a dichotomy between objective circumstances and subjective motivation to the transformative and rational action of praxis. "Circumstance" denotes the empirical world, which mechanical materialism places above conscious action. By contrast, Marx maintains that society is a dynamic totality, in which human beings transforms ourselves through enacting goal-directed practices. Productive activity mediates social practices and imparts rationality and universality to such activities. As Ernst Bloch suggests, "Marx is waging a war on two fronts: against mechanistic environmental theory, which tends ultimately to fatalism with regard to existence, and against the idealistic subject theory, which culminates in 'putschism,' or at least in excessive optimism with regard to activity."[89]

MacIntyre endorses the critique of Enlightenment dualism that Marx offers in these famous lines. However, he elides the central mediation that empowers Marx's position. The *Theses on Feuerbach* seizes upon the antinomy between nature and society in Enlightenment thought that, by holding each separate, reduces both to mechanistic explanation. Marx's response is to cast practice in terms of the mediations of consciousness that arise from human activity, since "[a]ll social life is essentially *practical*."[90] Seen as ontological activity, Marx attributes the mediating relation between subject and object to the human practice of labour. Through acting on the world and changing it, human beings prove the inseparability of nature and society.

By contrast, MacIntyre leaves the relation between forms of human activity and social practice undetermined. This means his concept of social life fails to account for the mediations between human beings and our productive activity (social relations) and between the objectification of production and circulation (fetishism) that configure the abstract sociality specific to capitalist modernity. Modern fragmentation does not mean total disassociation but instead relations of misrecognition between human beings. Nevertheless, MacIntyre pulls from Marx's third thesis a stark antinomy expressed in materialism. He points out that mechanical accounts of human action contain an inherent form of manipulation. Mechanical materialism relies upon the acceptance of laws which regulate the probability of particular behaviours and concurrently conceives of ways to control these behaviours. The materialist claims to know the laws that govern action. If the agent discerns the relevant laws, they can attempt to engineer an outcome. MacIntyre credits Marx with understanding that in this scheme "such an agent is forced to regard his own actions quite differently from the behaviour of those whom he is manipulating." Those manipulated are assigned presupposed laws in the terms already set by the mechanical account while the social scientist or manager must be an exception to the account they rely upon. Variations within this account appear to the manipulated agent as expressions of will but are in reality deceptive.[91] MacIntyre adopts Marx's *Theses* to give a prognosis of a mechanistic tendency in modern social science. It should not be overlooked that Marx's portrayal of the transition in modern philosophy to mechanical explanations of human behaviour is a crucial stage in MacIntyre's account.

AV is underpinned by a historicism that grasps practical reasoning in terms of the ability of human agents to comprehend the social embeddedness of our flourishing.[92] Moral philosophy must provide rational knowledge on which human beings can act. Without a shared comprehension of what moral action consists of, moral language will invariably reflect dualistic antinomies. Thus the modern epoch itself is unintelligible in the terms internal to its own frame of understanding. This paradigm is challenged by MacIntyre's presentation of his own Aristotelian position, where "the facts about human action include the facts about what is valuable to human beings (and *not* just the facts about what they think to be valuable)," justified teleologically, where "a hierarchy of goods" establish "the ends of human action."[93] Aristotle shows that human action aims for the good of a virtuous life. Our specific reasons for action vary infinitely, but every action, no matter how bad the reason, is defined by what we take to be the good of its end. Practical reasoning is constituted by learning processes of failure and success as we try to work out and move towards the living good. While we can reason badly, as it were, human beings are rational animals, and our activity is motived by the question of what it means for a life to be well-lived.

Marx stands in the shadows compared to the overarching theoretical import of Aristotle in *AV*. The second half of the book acts as a vindication of Aristotle's ethics.[94] When MacIntyre makes explicit the basis on which the Enlightenment project fails to offer a rational justification for morality, he points to the rejection of Aristotle's notion of a teleological human nature. In this teleological conception of ethics,

> there is a fundamental contrast between man-as-he-happens-to-be and man-as-he-could-be-if-he-realised-his-essential-nature. Ethics is the science which is to enable men to understand how they make the transition from the former state to the latter. Ethics therefore in this view presupposes some account of potentiality and act, some account of the essence of man as a rational animal and above all some account of the human *telos*. The precepts which enjoin the various virtues and prohibit the vices which are their counterparts instruct us how to move from potentiality to act, how to realise our true nature and to reach our true end. To defy them will be to be frustrated and incomplete, to fail to achieve that good of rational happiness which is peculiarly ours as a species to pursue. The desires and emotions which we possess are to be put in order and educated by the use of such precepts and by the cultivation of those habits of action which the study of ethics prescribes; reason instructs us both as to what our true end is and as to how to reach it.[95]

Ethics is understood, in this distillation of the crucial upshot of *AV*, in terms of the fulfillment of human potential by reasoning agents. Ethical life realises human potentiality over a morality of immediacy, teleologically mapping out the movement from one relation to the next. In this sense, ethics is the science of knowledge that grasps reality and realises rationality as it moves human agents to the end of human flourishing. In such a view, the truth of our species-specific natures is in the rational practice of the virtues. As comprehension and achievement, ethics is the unity of thought and action. The essence of the human form of life is rationality, and the specific goal-directed practices that habituate the virtuous life, help organise and direct our desire and sustain the success of our flourishing. Ethical practices direct action towards the end of rational happiness. Failure is just as essential to understanding as success, since it is the capability to achieve or to fail to achieve, which provides human beings with the knowledge of what we want or desire. We are beings that structure our practices on narratives of social meaning and ethical standing. Cultivating a rational life means upholding these goods, with awareness of the risks of success and failure inherent in any conception of happiness. This theory of ethics has much to recommend. From MacIntyre, the dynamic between actuality and potentiality moves rational activity and motivates the realisation of human good and flourishing.

MacIntyre shows it is the rational ordering of these human capacities through practices that endows us with a comprehension of the possible paths to the end of flourishing. His teleological notion makes rationality intelligible by the shared practices that would make possible the movement towards, and cultivation of, the human good. Ethical action expresses socially shared and constituted normative practices. In this way, ethics is conceived as a collective process of reasoning, embedded in the context of social bonds, relations and structures. MacIntyre charts this conception in a history of the virtues as the socially recognised form of morality. Accordingly, every moral view reflects a kind of social structure. For the Greeks, virtue is defined in relation to the excellence (*arête*) of human practices. First in Homer's epics, "morality and social structure are in fact one and the same."[96] Then, in Ancient Athens, virtue is located in relation to the moral community of the polis. In Sophocles's *Antigone* and *Philoctetes*, the tragedy is in the realisation of the impossibility of moral resolution. What reveals itself to be tragic is the knowledge that the conflict cannot be rectified. The conflict between two collectively understood social roles (the family and the state in *Antigone*) comes into opposition when the accepted notions of resolution no longer hold. Both social roles relate to the laws of the polis. It is precisely this impasse that deems it tragic.

In Athens, according to MacIntyre, the virtues are inherent in the conception of citizenship. To exercise the virtues is to be a good citizen.[97] Aristotle generalises this position to present "the rational voice of the best citizen of the best city-state." Ethics is itself political, since the "city-state is the unique political form in which alone the virtues of human life can be genuinely and fully exhibited."[98] For Aristotle, as for MacIntyre, the telos is the good life. Not interested in simply rehearsing Aristotle's position, MacIntyre instead attempts to outline a conception of the virtues that is both at one with Aristotle's teleological view and decisively modern.

Aristotle's virtue ethics is presented as the beginning of a long tradition, now mostly lost, of conceiving the practices that best habituate the fostering of internal goods and flourishing ends. Virtue cannot be reduced to the Kantian narrowing of morality to "distinct criteria by which to judge the goodness of a particular individual." Instead, the virtues of character and practical wisdom braid together to form "a complex measure" of the human good.[99] MacIntyre calls attention to the modern expert whose very professionalism depends upon their neutrality in connecting means to ends and the ubiquitous assumption that morality follows a similar path. As he reconstructs Aristotle, ethics depends upon the connection between practical wisdom (*phronesis*) and the virtues exercised through practices and habituation. We cannot hope to be good practical reasoners if our moral learning is simply dependent on rule-following, rather than cultivating and putting into practice the virtues as they ensue when we seek the good. Picking up a similar thread, Aryeh Kosman notes that "choice" in the Aristotelian view, is "not a concept having to do with individual moments in an agent's life, nor with individual single actions, but the practices of that life within the larger context of the character and intentions of a moral subject, ultimately within the context of what it has become fashionable to call one's life plan."[100] If modernity separates theoretical and practical knowing, reducing both to individual choice, MacIntyre suggests this division has both moral and political consequences.

The measure of the good in liberal societies is decidedly minimal, demarked by the boundaries of a very wide and anaemic conception of the good to what does not restrict individual freedom or harm others as each pursues their own interests. Accordingly, such a measure cannot judge individuals alone, but must be constituted in the relation between virtues:

> The application of that measure in a community whose shared aim is the realisation of the human good presupposes of course a wide range of agreement in that community on goods and virtues, and it this agreement which makes possible the kind of bond between citizens which, on Aristotle's view, constitutes a *polis*. That bond is the bond of friendship and friendship is itself a virtue. The type of friendship which Aristotle has in mind is that which embodies a shared recognition of and pursuit of a good.[101]

For MacIntyre, the incoherence of this measure of the good results in the atomism of liberal political philosophy, in which "political society" is little more than a "collection of citizens of nowhere who have banded together for their common protection," and relationships between people are structured by "mutual advantage."[102] The social contract view of citizenship fails to recognise that our relationships can not only be in terms of political sovereignty but must involve a stronger claim to shared goods. Modern politics requires a normative conception of ethical life for members of political communities to exercise standing as citizens who can sustain meaningful and rational relationships together. In MacIntyre's view, the polis establishes the rational criteria for the good within the norms that constitute social connection between its members.

The second half of *AV* develops this approach, pitting Aristotle's citizen, by nature a polis-dweller, against liberal "citizens of nowhere." This sharp contrast between the social ontology of an Aristotelian conception of citizenship (as a kind of political friendship that acts as the adhesive to "hold cities together") and a liberal notion of citizenship (founded on mutual self-interest and benevolence) enables MacIntyre to flesh out the ethical and political status of community.[103] In a community constituted by collective goods and shared norms, ethical virtues can be formed and recognised as worthwhile for its members acting together for such goods. The social practices of the community enable reasons for action to be established by the goods that will be realised in and though that action. When these goods can be exercised by the virtues in view of their collective meaning, the social freedom of human beings is realisable. Collective rationality offers the realisation of ethical life, rather than simply reflecting individual conflict masquerading as ethics. Thus, a rejection of the present *moral* order necessitates a rejection of the present *political* order, since "the tradition of the virtues is at variance with central features of the modern economic order and more especially its individualism, its acquisitiveness and its elevation of the values of the market to a central social place."[104] With Aristotle, MacIntyre looks to provide a tradition of ethics that accords to human practices the generation of goods internal to rational action. The unity of human life unifies these goods teleologically as *eudaimonia*.[105] The good of such a life is fulfilled in the making and sustaining of human flourishing. In these terms, MacIntyre's elaboration of Aristotle's practical reasoning is persuasive.

However, I am much less convinced on his second aim, which I will dissect at length. The second task of MacIntyre's project is to chart a modern conception of the virtues, and it is here that the argument breaks down. As MacIntyre himself acknowledges, Aristotle needs to be conceived historically.[106] At this point of *AV*, the political resources available for this historical rehabilitation become increasingly pertinent. But MacIntyre does not offer the depth of argument put in the first half of the book. His strategy involves a key distinction between practices and institutions. Practices, like chess, physics and medicine, are internal to the cultivation of the virtues. To learn, teach and exercise those skills means developing goods internal to that activity, and by doing these practices, our actions bring about the good as an end in itself. Institutions, like chess clubs, laboratories and hospitals, are external to the cultivation of the virtues. They are compelled by necessity to operate and survive amongst other institutions which compete over resources such as money, power and status. Institutions are bound by the logic of modern politics, and while all practices need institutional support to be maintained and reproduced, there is a tension between the end that both seek.[107]

While this criticism is well founded, such a division between practices and institutions does not capture the relationship between practical agency and its social form. Institutions are better seen as the social form of norm-bound and goal-directed practices. The goods internal to practices might be exercised in an institution in a way that eschews modern instrumentality if the social form and dynamic of such an institution is conducive to such goods. The question of rational action leads to the rationality of its institutional expression. The contrast between practices and institutions that MacIntyre draws is too restrictive. Clearly MacIntyre appreciates that the practical reasoning of communities will also take institutional form. But the boundaries he draws between the particularity of the community and the wider forms of political institutions depends upon the countenance of the local in contrast to the bureaucratic. As a result, he loses sensitivity to the acute political dynamic between them. MacIntyre frequently uses examples from the workers' movement. Consider the trade union official who comes into tension with the practical goods and flourishing of the workers' movement, precisely because of the institutional role they occupy involves bargaining with employers in such a way that relies upon a devastating utilitarianism.[108] Indeed, trade union officials often set aside the democratic decisions of the membership and readily preside over lowering the aims of the movement. This example is a salient one, and MacIntyre takes it that trade unions and trade union organisers are central to cultivating the virtues within local communities.[109] However, he does not bring into view the specific goods that might arise when trade union members contest their officials at an institutional level, not just to protect their local communities on specific issues, but with a wider political purview that can set into train other contestations across institutions and communities. The goods involved in such a dispute and the possibility for an institution that puts power in its members democratically are unconsidered. MacIntyre's concerns about modern bureaucratic institutions, as well justified as they are, prevents him from considering the further possibilities for cultivating rational practices precisely in the contestation and growth of political institutions.

If MacIntyre shies away from the politics of institutions, his premise is further undermined by the position of the individual—a historically specific type of agency that Aristotle could not account for. While MacIntyre is right to characterise modernity as fundamentally individualist, any modern conception of ethics must grasp the historically specific type of agency that arises with the individual subject. A view of ethical life must eschew both one-sided individualism and one-sided collectivism. For MacIntyre, the individual subject is the representative of modern politics and as such, is not easily integrated into ancient ethical frameworks. If the ancient conception of ethics was predicated on Greek public life, any contrast of this ethical unity with modernity cannot just implant this model or leave the question of modern subjectivity unanswered. MacIntyre's way of addressing this tension involves small modifications to Aristotle's picture of the practices, such as emphasising the role of conflict in discerning and navigating our individual and collective ends and purposes.[110] He recognises individuals who are exemplars of specific virtues and whose narratives illuminate an internal relation to the good, including figures as diverse as St. Benedict, St. Francis of Assisi, St. Teresa, Friedrich Engels, Eleanor Marx and Leon Trotsky.[111] However, he cannot fully make good on this insight, since the individual moral will is reduced to self-interested "individualism" and largely presented in terms of the problems that result from its emanation.

What is left out of the picture is the possibility in individual moral will for a new form of subjectivity and collective life, which is available only to us moderns. Seen narrowly as a problem of "individualism," MacIntyre loses sight of individual subjectivity as a constituting element of any collective freedom. While, like Arendt, MacIntyre does not offer the simplistic polis nostalgia that some critics claim, the contrast between the type of individualism that marks modernity and the collective rationality of the ancients also requires a political assessment of modern collective action in much richer detail than he sets out. MacIntyre considers the modern subject in too one-sided a way, jettisoning an explanation of subjectivity that could sublate the kind of premodern collectivity with the practical identity of individuals that is brought about, but not realised, in modernity. MacIntyre neglects furnishing Aristotle's conception of practical reasoning with a modern idea of the living good that can adequately articulate the relationship between practices and institutions. In effect, MacIntyre risks schematising Aristotle's ontology rather than successfully integrating an Aristotelian conception of ethics into a view of modern politics. This tension diminishes the power of his own historical account.

Marx's Robinsonade

To this end, problems transpire when attention is given to MacIntyre's interpretation of Marx. There is a divergence between his ontological position (which relies on a critique of Marx) and the radical diagnostic power of *AV* (especially the parallels with Marx's theory of history). There is some reason to doubt MacIntyre's own comment that "Marxism itself is only a marginal preoccupation," which obscures how Marx is simultaneously a figure of utility and of critique in *AV*.[112] MacIntyre regards Marxism as the most significant, yet failed critique of liberalism.[113] Marx's historical thought is presented as insightful, but when generalised into a theory, Marxism became just "one more set of symptoms disguised as a diagnosis."[114] While MacIntyre is correct to criticise the reductive and dualistic base/superstructure model featured in the most reductive interpretations, he is wrong to generalise this schematic model with Marx and Marxism as a whole.[115] Despite little engagement with Marx's idea of the "law of value," MacIntyre argues that Marxism adopts the same "law-like" predictive powers of social science and is fundamentally Weberian.[116] Therefore, this view becomes especially important for the practice of Marxism, since as Marxists "organise and move towards power" they take on the bureaucratic and managerial logic of modern thought rather than politically challenging the modern state. Accordingly, Marxism replicates liberalism by means of a Weberian embrace of the instrumentality of political power.[117] Marxists become authoritarian in power, using whatever means are necessary to defend their self-prescribed rationale.

Pushing his argument further, Marxism's failure to effect a coherent moral standpoint is attributed to an original sin. To MacIntyre, Marx's thought does not overcome the antinomies of modernity but is similarly marked. This tension is shown in "Marxism's own moral history," which betrays "relatively straightforward versions of Kantianism or utilitarianism."[118] MacIntyre extends his critique of Marxism to its founder, claiming its defective moral standpoint results from Marx's social ontology:

> Secreted within Marxism from the outset is a certain radical individualism. In the first chapter of *Capital* when Marx characterises what it will be like "when the practical relations of everyday life offer to man none but perfectly intelligible and reasonable relations" what he pictures is "a community of free individuals" who have all freely agreed to their common ownership of the means of production and to various norms of production and distribution. This free individual is described

by Marx as a socialised Robinson Crusoe; but on what basis he enters into his free association with others Marx does not tell us. At this key point in Marxism there is a lacuna which no later Marxist has adequately supplied. It is unsurprising that abstract moral principle and utility have in fact been the principles of association which Marxists have appealed to, and that in their practice Marxists have exemplified precisely the kind of moral attitude which they condemn in others as ideological.[119]

This assessment of Marx refers to a significant passage, one of the few in *Capital* which directly discusses communism, or what he calls in his later writings, "the free association of producers." Marx asks us to "imagine" that productive activity will have the same determinations as Robinson Crusoe's work on his island—the immediate interaction with nature for need—but production will be on a social rather than individual basis.[120] MacIntyre accuses Marx of simply accepting the ontology and individualism of Defoe's hero. Far from it, to locate a "socialist" Robinson requires a detailed investigation of Marx's social ontology, as I argue throughout this book.

MacIntyre paints Marx's evocation of *Robinson Crusoe* as emblematic of a social theory with an individualist core. What he fails to recognise is the depth of Marx's critique of political economy. It is essential to Marx's evaluation that bourgeois political thought not only posits an abstract individual that stands apart from history, but this ontology presents an ideological barrier to the formation of a social individuality through collective agency. When severed from history, human beings play no other role than bearers of economic categories. Marx's social ontology renews an Aristotelian conception of sociality in the practices and forms of human activity. Human flourishing is the sublimation of the individual with the collective as a kind of *social individuality*. Social forms contain the inner movement and unfolding of mediations of ontological and historically constituted life activity. Marx points to the processes that condition our present individuality as forms of domination that are structurally determined by the logic of capital itself.

MacIntyre's insistence on Marx's individualism does not hold up to a reconstruction of the role of social ontology in the theory of the value-form and as a result occludes compelling reasons why it simply inverts liberalism.[121] *AV* lacks serious exposition of the relation between political and social relations manifested by the operation of commodity exchange and the production and reproduction of value. Apart from an approving but unsubstantiated reference to commodity fetishism and a vague gesture towards production, work and the division of labour, a direct consideration of the logic of modernity in terms of capitalism is absent.[122] By forsaking Marx's theorisation of the social form of value, the connection between the logic of the market and state and modernity as such is lost. Without this investigation, MacIntyre is incapable of assessing the extent of the reach of the abstract sociality of capitalist modernity in shaping the lives of human beings. What MacIntyre constantly overlooks is that value is a social form and its movement is best captured in ontological terms. For Marx, value is shaped by the social relations of capital, and its self-expansion expresses the domination of processes of individualisation. Social labour takes the form of abstract and privately performed activity. By such logic, human beings appear to each other as buyer and sellers, impeding our self-conceptions of sociality and the conditions in which meaningful human relationships could flourish.

AV concludes with the desire to go beyond Marxism. MacIntyre's attempt to locate a politics to combat advanced modernity ends not with a confrontation but by taking refuge. Since as MacIntyre would have it, Marxism is spent as a political tradition, this "exhaustion" is "shared by every other political tradition without our culture." The significance of MacIntyre's singling out of Marxism signifies the seriousness he affords to its depth as "the most influential adversary theory of modern culture."[123] But against this, the only solution MacIntyre can offer is the holding project of fostering the virtues in small-scale communities. As he puts it in the closing paragraphs of *AV*:

> What matters at this stage is the construction of local forms of community within which civility and the intellectual and moral life can be sustained through the new dark ages which are already upon us. And if the tradition of the virtues was able to survive the horrors of the last dark ages, we are not entirely without grounds for hope. This time however the barbarians are not waiting beyond the frontiers; they have already been governing us for quite some time. And it is our lack of consciousness of this that constitutes part of our predicament. We are waiting not for a Godot, but for another—doubtless very different—St. Benedict.[124]

Through the practices and moral questioning cultivated in the community, MacIntyre does envision a critique of the status quo to emerge—since practical reasoning requires a confrontation with governing powers. *AV* is ambiguous about how this might occur given the locality of the small-scale community, stressing that the "particularity can never be simply left behind or obliterated."[125] By making the particular community the focus of his account of ethical cultivation, its relation to the universal is indistinct and undefined. In MacIntyre's account there is a tensity between what he sees as the ability of communities to exist in antagonism with the social order and the possibility of advancing a whole-scale questioning of that social order. Problematically, he tends to put weight on the presence of factors like the overdetermined desires of capitalist consumer culture.[126] This assessment cannot help but reduce the community to the nature of its *particular* aims.

While MacIntyre offers a modern conception of politics to scaffold his analysis of modernity, his return to Aristotle at the expense of Marx negates the historical and political specificity on which his critique relies.[127] Rather, MacIntyre exemplifies (and in an amplified way) precisely the problem he finds in Marx; namely, the adoption of "a vantage point outside their own society and culture."[128] If MacIntyre was more circumspect in labelling Marx's ontology as individualist, there would be a stronger basis to locate the Aristotelian dimensions of Marx's critique of capitalism. Instead, he opts to build a critique of modernity predominately on premodern moral philosophy.[129] His sketch of classical Athens and medieval Europe may be insightful for shared moral codes before the modern dichotomy of individual and collective, but it falls short of providing the mediations required to bridge modern antagonisms and the antinomies of thought and social being *historically specific to capitalism as a form of life*.

Politics and the Universal

To overcome dualistic thinking is to reconcile reality and an objective standpoint for reason. For MacIntyre, dualism is socially produced and embedded in modernity. A critique of modern thought necessitates a critique of modern society. MacIntyre understands Athenian political life as a reflection of ethical life, now lost but in need of recovery, albeit transformed and reconfigured in the present. In this sense, MacIntyre's project is a political intervention, since he is not warning of a future risk, but of what has already come to pass: "the barbarians" are well and truly in power.[130] The loss of ethical life from the modern world has made the poverty of modern culture ubiquitous. Dualism governs modern culture and its dominant political institutions. MacIntyre supplies a social theory of ethical life that rejects the individual as the protagonist of positivistic social science and demands the return of a collective rationality. Dualistic modes of thinking—radical or otherwise—are equally unable to bypass the status quo. For this reason, MacIntyre calls for a serious ethical reevaluation of the resources of political thought.

Difficulties arise from the attempt to challenge the prevailing logic of modernity on his reconstruction of Aristotle. The tension is not so much the contrast of the perspectives of modernity with that of premodernity. It is clear that MacIntyre's Aristotelianism is one informed by the political realities of the modern age. For instance, he disassociates himself from Aristotle's view of slavery, women and foreigners. The issue is more that the basis for the refoundation of the good life is in the lost Aristotelian community. Aristotle's idea of politics is premised on the particular and cannot offer an adequate concept of the universal, absolute ethical life. My claim involves rejecting the particular community as in itself an adequate foundation for politics. "Politics begins not when you organise to defend an individual or particular or local interest," as Rose puts it, "but when you organise to further the 'general' interest within which your particular interest may be represented."[131]

MacIntyre's politics do not sufficiently mediate the particular and universal. How can moral reasoning progress to a point where collective agents might pose a challenge to the political status quo without a wider universalisation of that political direction? How can the particular struggle transform into a politics of the city as the universal, the polis? Considering MacIntyre's critique of Marxism's inability to confront the state, it appears that he becomes a victim of his own critique and that his refutation of Marxism reduces his own vision of an emancipatory politics. When MacIntyre rejects Marx's critique of capitalism and its portrayal of the kind of rational action that could lead to an ethical life, he limits the potential of his own conception of what human beings *could be*. Without a universal idea of emancipatory politics, MacIntyre's idea of human flourishing is undermined.

AV contains his most well-known argument for the politics of local communities. In his view, "plain persons" are best able to live as moral reasoners in everyday life by sustaining practices that cultivate the virtues. In his later elaborations of this position, he is explicit that developing one's ethical reasoning develops one's political outlook. By living and making a life together as ethical reasoners in local communities (schools, unions, small businesses, clinics, families), which often come under threat from up high, MacIntyre claims that we are *forced* to confront the question of the state. In *AV*, he remarks that the modern state is *neither* a "necessary" or "legitimate" form of government.[132] In *Ethics in the Conflicts of Modernity*, he repeats this language and in a short, but illuminating, discussion points to the unity of the ethics-of-the-market and ethics-of-the-state in terms of the bureaucratic nature of representative democracies and the "parodies" of morality which are expressed by its functionaries.¹³³ Like Marx whose analysis he often takes for granted, MacIntyre also notes the contradiction between formal political *equality* and increasing economic *inequality*.

However, MacIntyre also rejects Marxist approaches to the state, which he takes to be in conflict with an adequate tradition of the virtues. Once power is wielded, as he would have it, Marxists reveal themselves as utilitarian, and hence Marxism proves itself to be morally deficient. I agree that MacIntyre is right insofar as many traditional versions of Marxism take the modern state to be an institution which is both necessary and legitimate, and these understandings *should* be rejected.¹³⁴ However, his account of the utilitarian kernel inside the Marxist shell misses the insights to be gleaned from Marx's own Aristotelian heritage. Tellingly, MacIntyre's focus on the state as the measure of Marxism's failure reflects his own inability to theorise a politics adequate for modernity. On this point, MacIntyre's model of local community offered in *AV* resists universal political claims. His criticism of the modern state prevents him from conceptualising political power beyond the local community. From Aristotle, MacIntyre ties particular virtues with archiving the ends needed for practical reasoning but cannot envision the universalism modern politics requires. This would involve going further than the particular concerns of the community and for these concerns to become universalisable in challenging the capitalist state by establishing rational institutions of collective agency. But such an appeal would also mean challenging the capitalist market and its role in reproducing the logic of modern individualism on which bureaucratic rationality depends. I agree with MacIntyre that the modern state, as he understands it, is neither a "necessary" or "legitimate" form of government but disagree that a politics of universality inescapably becomes utilitarian in power. More recently, in response to criticism of his idea of emancipation, he suggested the leap from "good politics to bad metaphysics" was too easy for Marxists.¹³⁵ This remark does not absolve MacIntyre of the need to formulate a robust account of the capitalist state if his politics are to live up to their "revolutionary" ambitions.

As strong as MacIntyre's assessment of modern moral destitution is, he eludes the necessary discussion of the state and in particular, the capitalist state (i.e. the role of capital within the state form). *Ethics in the Conflicts of Modernity* makes the link between capitalist markets and liberal democracy clear, and clear in a way that many of his more conservative followers ignore, but his focus here is on the politics of distribution, rather than a critique of the form of value itself: the social form in which the state and the market operate.¹³⁶ Distribution falls short of the account of the radically different form of life with which our needs—as social individuals—can be met. Freedom and democracy require institutional forms of social association that overcome the capitalist form of life. MacIntyre tells us how ethical practices can be cultivated, but eschews the social mediations which could transform politics from the particular and local to the universal political community. Interestingly, if we look back to the Hegelian Marxism of MacIntyre's earlier writings, we can find the universalism necessary for a sustained critique of liberal modernity which confronts the present political order. Properly understood, in the Hegelian Marxist view, universality does not see the modern state as a solution, since this social form is itself a particular and alienated social form. Freedom must be universal for there to be any freedom at all.

Freedom as Discovery

In the preface to *AV*, MacIntyre explicitly notes that the book is an attempt to answer questions he first raised in his Marxist writings.[137] The origins of his diagnosis of modernity as suffering from the moral deficiency of liberal individualism can be found in his early interpretation of Marx. But in *AV*, he sees Marxism as tradition itself suffering "from grave and harm-engendering moral impoverishment as much because of what it has inherited from liberal individualism as because of its departures from liberalism."[138] Significantly, the problems MacIntyre attributes to the moral defectiveness of Marx's thought are illuminated by the standards set out in his New Left writings. During this period, MacIntyre followed Marx to argue that ethical action is a form of practical consciousness. The rational activity that mediates consciousness and practical reasoning is labour, which is transformative since it allows for the discovery of human potential. In this normative view, ethical capabilities and the potential to flourish are systematically constrained by the alienation of human beings under capitalism as a form of life. The formation of practices conducive to the good requires confronting the way in which the alienation of labour restricts human activity and rational self-consciousness. In my view, many of these insights about the relationship between Marx and ethics deserve to be retained.

By detecting the limits of dogmatic Marxist philosophy in the 1950s, MacIntyre helped push against typical one-sided accounts of Marx's turning of Hegel on his head. To grasp the vitality of freedom in Marx, his debt to Hegel needs to be centre place. What MacIntyre demonstrated is that for Marx, freedom must be an ethical, as well as a political, concern. To deepen this idea, MacIntyre mobilised Hegel's idea of social freedom. The advantage of this approach to clarify key issues in Marxist theory is most evident in three major essays from this period, "Notes from the Moral Wilderness" (1958–59), "Freedom and Revolution" (1960) and "Breaking the Chains of Reason" (1960).

In "Notes" MacIntyre's specific concern was to offer an assessment and political intervention into public debates about the status of contemporary morality. In doing so, MacIntyre hoped to elucidate "what it is for men to make their own history, to act and not just suffer."[139] The analysis is centred in the rival moral positions of Stalinism and liberalism. MacIntyre argued that each share the same fundamental view of Marxism as a deterministic set of laws, which as "forces of production" mechanically develop as if independent of human action. In this sense, both Popper and Stalin agree.[140] MacIntyre eschewed "the contemporary anti-theoretical empiricism" of academic and political orthodoxies that depends upon a dualism between history and human agency. He attempted to work out a position independent of Stalinism and liberalism by elucidating a distinctive Marxist account of modern morality.

To grasp the idea of determination and historical change in Marx, MacIntyre argued for an engagement with Hegel's *Logic*. He explained that idea of "determination" in the infamous base/superstructure metaphor depends on Hegel's notion of conceptual determination and not the causal determination Marx is assumed to have advanced. This construal of Marx's idea of history rejects the utilitarian view that the forces of production drive history to progress and project justifiable means for the end of socialism. Instead, MacIntyre maintained that Marx's account of history is fundamentally an account of the possibilities of human action.[141] To grasp this significance, Marx's analysis of economic and historical forms needs to be situated in his understanding of human nature. This normative view is not an added extra to Marx's theory of history, but the motivation which underlies his entire idea of freedom. MacIntyre makes the argument, which he repeated frequently during this period, that Marx "inherits" Hegel's notion of freedom as "the human essence."[142] Human beings are in essence free, since we are conscious and rational beings who strive in our historical lives to realise freedom.

In a move that anticipates *AV*, MacIntyre responded to "traditional questions about human nature and morality" by providing a normative theory of human action based on historically constituted desires and needs.[143] Human actions require reasons, purpose and context which "point to a recognisable want or need served by my action . . . we make both individual deeds and social practices intelligible as human actions by showing how they connect with characteristically human desires, needs and the like." MacIntyre assessed both utilitarianism and Kantian morality as two sides of the modern moral dualism between "is" and "ought." If he associates the view of historical determinism with utilitarianism, MacIntyre took Kant's presentation of moral autonomy to offer the opposite problem. Kantian principles of moral "ought" are formed apart from the desiring "is." Turning to Diderot's writings on Polynesia, MacIntyre argued that since the Enlightenment, European morality "represses and distorts" the morality of desire Diderot observed in his Polynesian travels. As a result, the "myth of the natural man who spontaneously obeys desire is only comprehensible as the myth of a society where desire appears utterly cut off from morality."[144] Likewise *Rameau's Nephew* reflects the alienated conflict between norms and unconscious desire on an individual level.[145] Moral action has become a matter of individual choice and not a matter for the collective consciousness of the historical community. Explicitly enlisting Hegel's critique of the Enlightenment in a Marxist direction, MacIntyre attested that modernity has *objectified* morality.[146] In practice, the alienation of human beings from our social bonds severs individual decision-making from the meaning of our moral commitments.[147] Precapitalist notions of desire situated within ethical norms have been lost to view with the onset of modernity. Desire appears to us now only in a self-interested Hobbesian form as "warring desire."[148]

Against this picture, MacIntyre suggested "[t]he peculiar contribution of the Marxist critic here is the understanding that the 'I' can only be put back into 'I want' if the 'we' is put back into 'we want.'"[149] This position mobilises a Hegelian concept of recognition. According to Hegel, for consciousness to become self-consciousness, that is for an individual to realise themself as self-aware and free, they must articulate their freedom with other people whereby each recognises the other as free. Hegel's famously puts it as the "*I* that is *we* and the *we* that is *I*."[150] MacIntyre interpreted the Hegelian "we" in terms of the conceptual determination of class. Challenging the individualism of modern morality, MacIntyre argued that the "fundamental answer" to ethical consciousness and human action "is the whole Marxist theory of class struggle." In "Notes," class struggle is the specific human action in which self-consciousness overcomes the alienation of needs and desires. Class struggle in Marx is paralleled with Hegel's idea of reason. For both, human beings are rational and historical beings since "the history of man is seen as the history of men discovering and making a common shared humanity." But MacIntyre noted a fundamental difference:

For Hegel the subject of this history is Spirit. And individual human lives appear only as finite fragments of the Absolute. For Marx the emergence of human nature is something to be comprehended only in terms of the history of class struggle. Each age reveals a development of human potentiality which is specific to that form of social life and which is specifically limited by the class structure of that society.[151]

Class struggle allows for human beings to "re-appropriate" and "realise" our natures developed immanently from forms of social activity. MacIntyre's claim here seems to be vulnerable to Jaeggi's appraisal of the "trap" of essentialism in alienation critique.[152] However, his point is not that human nature is an authentic essence which can be returned to. Instead, with the historical knowledge of the norms of need and desire and the standpoint of working-class struggle against alienation, "[c]apitalism provides a form of life in which men rediscover desire" in the practice of finding what we "want in common with others ... a rediscovery of the deeper desire to share what is common in humanity, to be divided neither from them nor from oneself to be a man."[153] Put this way, class struggle is a rediscovery of the norms of need and desire through processes of collective action that prove their relation within the norms we come to share as ethical subjects who have constituted that normativity though acting together.

The pertinent point to emerge from MacIntyre's idea of class struggle as "rediscovery" is what it might mean for a concept of human nature. MacIntyre's enduring insight is that class struggle makes possible a discovery of human nature. It is through emancipatory and transformative acts that the potentiality immanent in our present form of life can be realised as rational. This discovery is the claim of self-consciousness realising itself as human freedom. Human beings can come to see ourselves as free. MacIntyre's use of the term "discovery," as opposed to the liberal "choice," makes good on the Hegelian claim of mutual recognition. MacIntyre tried to show that the contemporary debate between Kantianism and utilitarianism as rival moral positions are precisely "aspects of the consciousness of capitalism; both are forms of alienation rather than moral guides."[154] In *AV*, MacIntyre sets out a diagnosis of modern moral philosophy and its incoherence. His ambition in "Notes" is to locate a way out of this impasse in class struggle, as the normative form of human action which creates the historical possibility of discovering a mutual bond between human beings in a rational form of life.

MacIntyre went further in his normative understanding of class struggle in his 1960 essay "Freedom and Revolution." In this text, he drew on Hegel and Marx to argue that a political conception of emancipation must explicitly invoke an ethical idea of freedom. Building on Hegel's claim that the human essence is freedom, MacIntyre argued that unlike nonhuman animals, human beings fundamentally shape our "natural and social" conditions through our rational activity. However, this Hegelian idea of our

> specifically human initiative cannot be understood except in terms of the concepts that belong to what Marx called "practical consciousness," such concepts as those of desire, intention and choice. To say that men are free is to say that they are able to make their desires, intentions and choices effective.[155]

The efficacy of these concepts is an act of "discovery" of the "kind of life" which constitutes freedom. In the face of capitalist alienation, what is possible and desirable for human beings requires class struggle to gain conscious self-control of our actions and comprehend them as having normative force. From Hegel, MacIntyre highlighted the historical relationship between domination and human life, since "unless you are free you are not an authentic specimen of humanity, not really a man."[156] Capitalism as a form of life with unequal and conflictual social relations means that the desires, intentions and choices of the few are "effective at the expense of those of the majority."

Deploying Marx's immanent critique of capitalism, MacIntyre pointed to the "paradox of bourgeois society" as the cojoined "promise" for the expansion of freedom and the "denial" of that very freedom. Nature no longer rules over human life, as lawlike as the seasons, but "we come to feel inevitability and fatality is not in nature, but in society." Dependence is not tied in the natural hierarchy between peoples, but in the social hierarchy in which human beings are free to sell their labour "if there is a buyer, or starve." Characterising the specific ways freedom is systematically denied under capitalism, MacIntyre noted both the upfront "direct oppression" of unemployment, poverty and colonialism, as well as "the semi-automatic processes" that are tied to the fetishism of social forms. Commodities and money appear to have a power altogether outside the control of both the worker and capitalist alike.[157]

MacIntyre invested this Marxist perspective with his explanation of why social roles appear "outside of our control." Living amongst the paradoxes of freedom, it is not just a question of the objective structures that hang over us as forces acting upon us, but the hope that we can find meaning in our subjective action. The gulf between objective domination and subjective meaning appears natural, and as a result the alienated social roles we take on come to represent moral life almost exclusively.

Picking up the normative consequences of such a narrowing of the bounds of normativity, MacIntyre captured the porosity in the meaning we can possibly assign to our social roles. The choice seems to be between a conformism of established conventions in which social roles are (relatively or uncritically) adopted and a bohemian lifestyle that rejects these conventions outright. These two options often seem to be the only paths available. But MacIntyre claimed both positions are empty and simply inversions of the same lack of social meaning. The problem of alienated social roles cannot mean simply rejecting norms, nor can it mean simply affirming the alienation of daily life. Rather, freedom is not an act of the "conscious" individual alone but instead the commitment of political organisation which is "dedicated not to building freedom but to moving the working class to build it."[158] Regardless of the model of organisation MacIntyre advocated for, the broader normative importance is placed on the potential of political commitments to give meaning to our social lives, roles and identities. Despite the persistence of alienation, MacIntyre suggested that political commitments with others affords meaning to our desires, intentions and choices.

The concept of practical consciousness is delineated incisively in "Breaking the Chains of Reason" written for E. P. Thompson's collection *Out of Apathy* (1960). MacIntyre once again affirmed Hegel's "conviction that freedom is the core of human nature." He noted the "interrelationship" of the concepts of reason, freedom, human nature and history in both Hegel and Marx. MacIntyre quotes from Hegel's *Philosophy of Mind*,

> Since the free mind is the *actual* mind, misconceptions about it have the most tremendous practical consequences, and when individuals and peoples [*Völker*] have once got in their heads the abstract concept of freedom [*Freiheit*] that is for itself, there is nothing like it in its uncontrollable strength, just because it is the very essence of mind, and is in fact its very actuality.[159]

This passage is from the Remark to the final paragraph of "Subjective Spirit" before Hegel turns to the Objective Spirit of right, morality and ethical life in the *Encyclopaedia of the Philosophical Sciences*. The transition in this paragraph is useful since Hegel is connecting the freedom of will with objective freedom in the social world. He writes in the same passage,

> If knowledge of the Idea, i.e. of men's knowledge that their essence, purpose, and object is freedom, is speculative, then this Idea itself as such is the actuality of men

[*Wirklichkeit der Menschen*], not an Idea that they have about it, but an Idea that they are.[160]

Hegel argues that the idea of freedom is not separate from historical life, but that through human action, consciousness becomes increasingly self-aware and articulates an adequately social freedom. This concept of objective spirit articulates his ontological view of ethical life as the realisation of human good. As Frederick Neuhouser observes, Hegel's idea of "the goodness of the social order" can be "formulated in teleological language: the institutions of ethical life are rational because only within them are humans able to realize their *telos* (or essence) as self-conscious and self-determining beings."[161]

MacIntyre maintained that Hegel held fast to the spirit of the French Revolution and never jettisoned the idea that the essence of human beings is freedom and employs this view to render human action in normative terms. We act on reasons that have purpose and intention, since to grasp what an action is means knowing "what ends he is pursuing, what possibilities he is realising. Human history is a series of developing purposes, in which, through the exercise of reason in the overcoming of conflicts, freedom is attained." Human action is always informed by our present sense of purpose and our future direction. Imbedded in every action is a sense of the past and the future. Every action is set within a context. MacIntyre's view was that the very intelligibly of human action involves a dialectical conception in which possibility "grows through conflicts of principle and purpose" and "not as natural events are or as a machine."[162] Fundamentally, normative questions of human action require conceiving the inseparability of freedom and reason:

> Without freedom, reason operates only within limits, and so its constructions, however intricate, remain beyond those limits uncriticised, and, in so far as uncriticised, irrational. Without reason, freedom becomes merely a lack of constraint which leaves the individual the plaything of all the forces which impinge upon and influence him, but of which he remains unconscious.[163]

The status of reason *requires* an account of freedom. At this point, MacIntyre relied on Hegel to provide both the interconnection between reason and freedom and a historical account of the constitution of freedom. In this sense, MacIntyre appreciated that Hegelian freedom is "not something which at any given moment men either do or do not possess; it is always an achievement and always a task."[164] Different historical forms articulate specific relations of freedom and domination, which must be seen within the concrete unity of social life. As he saw it, Hegel's idea of negation identifies the need to overcome the alienation and objectification in our own creations as found in "God, the state, the Moral law ... The human task is to tear away the masks, to recognise our own faces behind them and so free ourselves from the domination of the mask."[165]

While the young MacIntyre followed crucial aspects of Hegel's idea of rationality, he ultimately came to affirm something akin to Marx's 1843 critique of the *Philosophy of Right*. MacIntyre believed Hegel distorts his notion of freedom by justifying the Prussian monarchy as the "authentic embodiment of freedom."[166] Holding onto this supposition in his recent work, such as *Ethics in the Conflicts of Modernity*, MacIntyre is more interested in the Marx who learnt from Aristotle than the Marx who learnt from Hegel.[167] This difference in emphasis demonstrates MacIntyre's own shift away from Hegelian Marxism to his "revolutionary Aristotelianism." In his later position, Marx might help an Aristotelian to see the modern world better, but fundamentally Marx's politics offer a sociological tool rather than a coherent basis for a normative critique. But as I argue throughout this book, a Marxist adoption of Hegel's idea of freedom offers a rich normative standpoint for a critique of capital and at the same time, builds upon the common ground of Aristotle's concept of practical reasoning and ethical cultivation. However, as I examine in the following chapter, Hegel's social and political thought provides a strong basis to enrich an Aristotelian idea of ethics in the form of universality.

Conclusion

MacIntyre's thought occupies a tense position in between Aristotle and Marx. Since he cannot integrate both thinkers, Marx is treated polemically despite playing a major role in the historical account of morality in *AV*. Since MacIntyre takes his critique of modern life to be in part a response to Marx, he can only go so far in his analysis of the influence of Aristotle on Marx. Unfortunately, this influence comes at the cost of Marx's Hegelian influence, which virtually disappears in *AV* and after. However, MacIntyre's reading of Marx throughout the 1950s initiated a normative understanding of human action and practical consciousness which could only be possible from interpreting Marx in light of Hegel. MacIntyre's advocacy of class struggle is understood as a form of purposeful self-activity which allows human beings to discover our self-consciousness as a process of shared ethical action.

In *AV*, MacIntyre maintains that Aristotle supplies the intellectual resources to remedy a body of social thought ridden with Kantian and utilitarian dualism and a set of social relations that are correspondingly fragmented. MacIntyre identifies the substantial methodological problems inherited in modern thought that must be confronted if there is any chance to challenge the status quo. MacIntyre's diagnosis can be affirmed and ratified by showing the lines of continuity in Marx's philosophical inheritance and critical absorption of Aristotle and Hegel. By reconstructing the concept of the value-form, I go on to show the normative value of Marx's thought. The next chapter details this beginning.

PART II

THREE

Shapes of Ethical Life
Ancient and Modern

THE CONCEPTIONS OF ETHICAL LIFE advanced by Arendt and MacIntyre are founded in the traditions of rational inquiry that originate in premodernity and look to the polis as an ideal. Both find in the ancient polis expressions of action and virtue that have been obscured by modernity, where traditions of politics and ethics lack coherent meaning. With such absence, tradition appears ordinarily as fragments and simulacra. Embedded in the fabric of social life, in the basic structures and institutions of the modern world, such traditions act against the kind of political and ethical beings that we are. Reconstructing meaning in reference to the polis hopes to revitalise the traditions of meaning that could inspire modern action and virtue.

In their respective ways, Arendt and MacIntyre take Marx to be a waystation and a roadblock between past and future traditions. While Arendt herself affirms Aristotle's distinction between production (*poiesis*) and action (*praxis*), in her account Marx borrowed too deeply from Aristotle and mistakenly elevates labour based on a defective social ontology. Further, for Arendt, Marx's unsuccessful Aristotelianism is a consequence of an only partial rupture with Hegel, which leaves him with a determinist notion of history. As we saw in the previous chapters, Arendt's idea of the lost meaning of political life, its "disappearing" with the historical ancient city-state, corresponds quite closely with the critique of modernity offered by MacIntyre. In his view, the term "virtue" lost its specifically *ethical* meaning with modernity and became a shorthand for the manifestation of individual preferences torn from their social fabric. Virtue came to correspond to the goods of discrete individuals, often taken to be in competition amongst other agents. Lost from view is the kind of shared ethical language that could articulate what a common good actually is, that is not reducible to individual agents, but requires that goods are cultivated with others for a shared purpose and end. In MacIntyre's account, Marx borrows too little from Aristotle and ends up affirming the individualism of modernity. The potential of human beings to become practical reasoners requires a conception of virtue not reducible to the kind of utilitarian instrumentality characteristic of many of Marx's supposed followers once political power is achieved. For Arendt, with the loss of our political lives, ethics means nothing. For MacIntyre, with the loss of our ethical lives, politics means nothing.

The life well-lived, *eudaimonia*, is central for both Arendt and MacIntyre. What Arendt calls "the Greek solution" is politics lived in the equality and plurality of the public sphere—where our legacy is left through the stories of our speech and action. In the "Action" chapter of *HC*, she suggestively invokes the unpredictability of well-being in its association with the *daimōn*, the way our identity is known to others. *Eudaimonia* is to "live well" and to have "lived well," and it is the "intangibility" of acting and speaking that is made "tangible only in the story of the actor's and speaker's life."[1] Our political action becomes an expression of our ethical life. *Eudaimonia* is the rational activity of the human good which motivates MacIntyre's virtue ethics. A life well-lived depends on cultivating, exercising and sustaining the virtues.[2] Both thinkers look for the forms of action expressed in the Greek polis that can be revived in the modern world to fill its political and ethical lacunas. Political action and virtuous practice are suppressed by modernity, but when they do appear, Arendt and MacIntyre take these moments as confirmation of a type of ethical life known to the Greeks and all but lost to us moderns. In doing so, both point to a missing aspect of human life, whether it be the action of politics or virtue, and trace this element through a historical narrative to diagnose the present crisis of meaning.

Despite their best efforts, however, Arendt and MacIntyre abstract the rediscovery of political and ethical action from the specific forms that define these practices in modernity. Arendt dislocates council democracy from the content of "social" struggles, and MacIntyre overestimates the capacities of local communities (in their relative isolation as localities) to cultivate practices that can act as a bulwark from capitalism. Without a conception of the way in which the social form of human activity under capitalism is shaped by the predominance of abstract, value-producing labour and its valorisation as capital, efforts to theorise political and ethical action cannot explain the fundamental conditions of rational agency as such. The immanent possibilities available to political and ethical agents can only be partially uncovered by Arendt and MacIntyre. Neither grasps the full extent of the normative implications of capitalism as a social form of life constituted by the self-valorisation of value.

Thereby, despite the sophistication in their thinking, Arendt and MacIntyre cannot help but be stranded in a conception of the polis as the "beautiful ethical life."[3] The polis features to both as providing a form of rationality needed to cure modern life. However, as Hegel argued against romantics of his day, the beautiful image of Greek life cannot offer a solution to the modern separation between individual and community. It might help us understand that an embedded ethical life is possible, but it will remain an ideal unless the universality of modern life is comprehended. Hegel maintains beautiful ethical life must be sublated by "passing through a series of shapes" which progressively reveal "they are real spirits, genuine actualities, and, instead of being shapes only of consciousness, they are shapes of a world."[4] As I argue in this chapter, Hegel's modernism preserves Aristotle's idea of *eudaimonia*, as "the living good," without longing for a return to the polis. I claim that Marx takes up this tradition. Marx's adoption, adaptation and absorption of Aristotle and Hegel emphasise the richest resources within his thought for a normative conception of modern life. Recovering these reworkings undercuts the criticisms Arendt and MacIntyre level at Marx.

As has already been intimated, I take the view that Aristotle, Hegel and Marx should not be seen as belonging to rival traditions,[5] but as thinkers that complement and conceptually reinforce one another by *sharing* a tradition of rational social theory. Against convention, I discuss these thinkers as part of a shared tradition, in a similar manner to what MacIntyre calls "tradition-constituted enquiry."[6] At the centre of this shared tradition is the conceptualisation of ethical life. Hegel's and Marx's social theories both respond to Aristotle's framing of ethics as "what constitutes a good life, and how it is to be attained."[7] The central purpose of this chapter is to trace the critical incorporation of Aristotelian insights into Hegel's speculative philosophy. The ethical tradition I seek to outline is one in which Aristotle's idea of the good is carried over and critically integrated by Hegel as the "living good," which magnifies the freedom of ethical life.[8] With this idea, Hegel retains Aristotle's idea of practical reasoning and develops it further to express the distinctive institutional forms of rationality that are only possible in modernity.

This intellectual and conceptual relationship sets the scene for Marx's social and political thought. In his social ontology and value-form theory, Marx's concept of sociality upholds and advances the rationality of these particular traditions, expressing a concept of ethical life which shares similar commitments to Aristotle and Hegel. To argue in this way is to suggest that Aristotle and Hegel are preserved moments in Marx's critical social thought. By tracing the way in which these intellectual threads are woven together, I render visible the drape of Marx's texts.

However, far from seeking to dissolve the insights of Aristotle and Hegel into Marx, my argument presents his critique of modern social life as their fullest realisation. As independent moments, Aristotle and Hegel are unable to fully articulate the immanence of social freedom. In Aristotle, human will remains unthought, since for him some unfreedom is natural. In Hegel, it is the domination of capital that remains unthought, since for him civil society (*bürgerliche Gesellschaft*) is a necessary condition of freedom and modern ethical life. Marx overcomes these limitations but preserves from both thinkers the resources needed to undertake a critique of modernity from the standpoint of absolute ethical life.

By introducing Aristotle's presence as a shared interlocutor, the relationship between Hegel and Marx is made more interesting, not by the common narrative typologies of character progression or materialist inversion—"Marx the Young Hegelian," "Marx the Revolutionary," "Marx the Economist" or "Hegel turned on his head"—but by an inquiry into the intertwining influences that are bound up conceptually in Marx's social thought. This conceptual rather than linear genealogy adds depth to an already well-discussed relationship. What is often missed in treatments of Hegel and Marx is the way both their attempts to confront modernity engage Aristotle in an ongoing dialogic. In the construction of their immanent modes of critique, Hegel and Marx reach back to Aristotle's teleological conception of ethics. While the concept of teleology is much maligned as a divine or deterministic notion of external causation, Aristotle, Hegel and Marx hold that teleology is internal to human purposeful and rational activity.

The nature and form of such purposeful activity as practical reasoning pertains to the development of political and ethical meaning, relationships and statuses. The Aristotelian connection between politics and ethics is enhanced by both thinkers. Yet neither Marx's nor Hegel's engagement with Aristotle is an ahistorical return. On the contrary, it is an integration of his conceptual thought in the attempt to comprehend the present and its contradictions. For Hegel and Marx, Aristotle's relevance lies in the thinking of political and ethical inquiry as socially constituted rational agency. This thread draws together a normative conception of ethics that refuses the idea of morality as confined to the private existence of the modern individual. Ethics is the fabric of the social good.

The thinking of ethical life shared by Aristotle, Hegel and Marx conceives of ethics as part of a larger architectonic. The good is not located simply in individual will or behaviour but in a richer conception of ethics that realises the good in socially ordered reasoning. Ethics relates to the question "how should we live?"[9] Aristotle, Hegel and Marx fundamentally think human beings are rational animals concerned with the possibilities of a social form of life that allows rationality to be realised as the human good. *Eudaimonia* is the living good of flourishing beings. The contours of this shared mode of practical reasoning have their conceptual genesis in the complex relation between Hegel and Aristotle. I argue that Aristotle's ethics are dialectically incorporated into Hegel's social thought, finding its final form in his concept of *Sittlichkeit*, ethical life.[10] Undertaking a genealogy of these dialectical concepts establishes a clearer basis for a discussion of Marx's confrontation with the ontology of individualism in liberal political philosophy and political economy. Marx's social ontology mobilises a concept of essence developed from Aristotle and Hegel. Essence denotes the nature and function of what a thing is. To ascertain the essence of a thing requires understanding its form, the totality of the relations that organise its purpose and activities.

Hegel's thought concerns the concrete totality, which he calls "the absolute." This totality is derived systematically, through the speculative unfolding of its determinations, forms which expand through the internal movement that is generated by the dynamic of identity and negation within shapes of thought and being. Absolute thought is Hegel's attempt to overcome Kant's antinomy between theoretical and practical reason and furnish an internal relation between these forms of reasoning. Hegel's absolute is not a metaphysical extra but what makes his theoretical and practical thought coherent.[11] Hegel's absolute unifies theoretical reason (the finite and infinite) and practical reason (morality and legality) in *ethical life*. The experience of consciousness moving through its own contradictions and concretisation expresses the possibility of self-consciousness to become realised and free in ethical life. The shape of ethical life, for Hegel, is the living identity of individuality, particularity and universality. According to Rose:

> The experience of philosophical consciousness in the *Logic* is to *rediscover* the unity of theoretical and moral reason and natural, finite consciousness through the con-

traditions of the history of philosophy. The *Logic* culminates in the notion of *absolute ethical life* [*Sittlichkeit*] which is reached in the two sections of the penultimate chapter, "The Idea of the True," and "The Idea of the Good."[12]

Hegel's takes Aristotle's *energeia* and mobilises it as *Wirklichkeit*. The Aristotelian dimension of this term is now expressed as "the unity of concept and reality, or true actuality [*Wirklichkeit*]," the absolute idea.[13]

Hegel's *Logic* and *Realphilosophie*, his political writings, are both motivated by the concept of ethical life. The *Logic* navigates the contradictions between theoretical and practical reason in the history of philosophy, and his *Realphilosophie* charts the internal logic of modern social forms. The *Logic* in its last (and authoritative) book is concerned with articulating the syllogistic structure of objectivity, that is, that individuals are determined by their own immanent universals, or substance-kinds. The *Logic* ends with an Aristotelian account of concrete universality as a condition of the coherent thinkability of *anything at all*. The *Realphilosophie* then attempts to present concrete universality as is proper for modern social life, which entails at its opening a critique of individuality as such, as incapable of grounding norms for collective life.[14] Hegel's political thought unfurls the social determinations necessary for ethical life to be actual *and* to be thought in the world.

The synthesis advanced in his *Realphilosophie*, stretching from Hegel's early writings on natural law to the mature *Philosophy of Right*, is the incorporation of a critique of the modern antinomies of social relations, especially those found in civil society, and the conception of the good life found in Aristotle. Further, Aristotle helps inform the metaphysical components of Hegel's speculative logic, particularly in the *Logic* where the categories of thought-forms progress by the inner development, negation and sublation of their being and becoming. In Hegel's systematic philosophy, it is the investigation of thought itself (understood as absolute knowledge) that informs the objective realm of human affairs in the categories of "ethical life." Partially, Hegel's debt to Aristotle is cashed out in his response to Kant's moral philosophy, where Hegel conceives of the content of ethical life as one that enables rational self-consciousness mediated socially between the collective good and the subjective will.[15] His critique of Kant turns on the idea that an account of the rational and autonomous individual cannot be understood in narrowly formal terms as the intention of following the dictates of the categorical imperative. For Hegel, as for Aristotle, ethics pertains to the realisation of *eudaimonia*, flourishing, in the shared life of a rationally organised society.[16] On his reckoning, individuality only becomes coherent in a concrete relation to the universal, where rationality is socially recognised. Considering the vast differences between ancient and modern politics, some commenters see a much stronger Aristotelian influence in the *Logic*.[17] My claim is that Hegel's task to show what an ethical life *actually is* takes inspiration from Aristotle's idea of the well-lived life. Hegel saw his own thought as an extension of Aristotle's concept of practical rationality in which the activity of human life has its end in *eudaimonia*.[18]

Hegel's thought centres on the idea of ethical life. By emphasising his early distinction between "relative" and "absolute" ethical life, I argue that Hegel's most generative insights about rational agency and freedom are best construed by seeing ethical life as the living good. This thought in Hegel establishes the main lines of dialogue with his precursor, Aristotle, and his inheritor, Marx. Lending currency to Aristotle's idea of the good life, Hegel cashes out the notion that the ethical life of human beings, as beings with logos, must be constituted in the political community since it is precisely that community which enables such rationality to come to fruition. This view is teleological since the rationality that is realised in such a life as the articulation of freedom is shown by the movement of self-consciousness. Hegel's account of progressively determinate shapes of self-consciousness developing and bearing upon world-spirit as reason is motivated by the idea that rationality must be embedded in a form of life that comprises ethical institutions. Consciousness is teleological, in the sense of the unfolding of an immanent dynamic between the natural and social. Nothing is automatic about this movement. Consciousness is not imposed upon the world, but essential to human beings as rational beings and inseparable from the manifestations of our social forms of life. Marx adopts, adapts and absorbs this tradition of ethical inquiry, deepening the insights set out by Aristotle and Hegel with a conception of social relations derived from his social ontology and value-form theory. The conception of essence and teleology that is so important for Aristotelian and Hegelian philosophy is vindicated in Marx's thought. He bolsters these conceptions of actuality and potentiality in his dialectical unfolding of modern social forms. Indeed, this philosophical pulse gives life to both Marx's political writings, which account for working-class activity as expressions of consciousness, and in his critique of political economy, which derives a conception of rational association from the immanent contradictions within capitalism. Historical actuality is always held in relation to what is possible for human beings to do as social and rational beings. In short, Marx's thinking of relation and form are structured on the interdependence of politics and ethics.

The inseparability of ethics and politics as forms of rational inquiry is made explicit by Aristotle and Hegel. Since Aristotle understands ethical life to be a component of political inquiry, ethics cannot be simply postulated as moral laws or principles but must be possessed and exercised as politics.[19] Likewise Hegel's ethical life comprises the rational institutions of society that enable the rational good to be lived. Ethics and politics are sublated in the self-conscious shape of *absolute ethical life*. In following this tradition, Marx incorporates the integral theoretical relation between both meanings in his mapping of social forms thereby offering an analysis of politics that preserves ethics within the ambit of his social theory. Hegel's concept of absolute ethical life gives definition to this moment in Marx's thought and clarifies a crucial element of his immanent and normative social theory. The ethical dimension of Marx's critique of political economy takes shape from the tradition shared with Aristotle and Hegel.

The concept of absolute ethical life in Hegel involves an explicit and important critique of Kant's moral philosophy. This criticism hinges on the strong distinction between Kant's idea of "morality" (*Moralität*) and "ethical life" (*Sittlichkeit*). Hegel's normative orientation leads him to construe ethics in terms of collective forms of recognition shared between rational agents.[20] This conception of ethics entails a rejection of both Kant's characterisation of moral action as a categorical "ought" and the empiricism of Hume's moral "is." In his critique of both antinomical positions, which rest upon a division between "is" and "ought," Hegel's ethical theory provides a normative conception that looks beyond individual action to socially constituted rational activity. Likewise, Marx's idea of collective agency expresses the deeply embedded ethical dimension of his thought. The shapes of ethical life found in Aristotle and Hegel give scope to a philosophical tradition within which Marx must be firmly located.

I construct a distinctive concept of ethical life from these thinkers. In my account, ethics concerns the forms of social life that enable rationality to be exercised in and through relations of mutual recognition. Ethics pertains to the conditions of life for rational beings in which normative action can be decided in such a way as to cultivate and sustain shared capabilities, commitments and potentials. Living well and human flourishing are fully actualised in the fabric of recognition. The identity of freedom with sociality in relations of recognition necessitates understanding the interrelationship between ethics and politics. The concept of absolute ethical life, developed from Aristotle, Hegel and Marx, establishes the necessary resources for a robust normative account that locates politics and ethics as component parts of a larger architectonic.

The upshot of this analysis is to suggest that reason is exercised in terms of a critical self-consciousness; the being-and-becoming of actualisation of one's own historical conditions of sociality. This process seeks the unity of the individual, particular and universal. The interdependence of each becomes validated and expressed as a totality in self-conscious social life. This freedom expresses the unity of self in others, the "*I* that is *we* and the *we* that is *I*."[21] This shape of social life as rational self-consciousness is then comprehensible in a world of our own making. The normative importance of this conception is that ethics can be seen as pertaining to the whole context of human life. Ethics is not relegated to a separate realm of private experience. Nor does such a view of ethics reduce normativity to the ought of our duties or the consequences of our actions. Instead, such a view sublates both. Ethics is woven out of the normative action that constitutes the very fabric of social life. Exercising and sustaining normative relations as acting in the space of reasons means that ethical action is embedded in political life.

I begin this chapter by setting out the early Aristotelian and Hegelian influences and themes within Marx's initial intellectual development.[22] This contextualises the detailed exposition of Hegel and Aristotle in the following sections of the chapter. I then introduce Hegel's confrontation of modernity in the philosophical project of realising what is real and what is rational in thought. Next, I investigate the basis of Hegel's recasting of Aristotle in his normative social philosophy and draw out the Aristotelian character of the holism which shapes his concept of absolute ethical life. I argue that the immanent and rational inquiry of ethical life must involve a critique of social relations. This inquiry finds its modern iteration in Hegel and sets the stage for Marx's critique of capitalism.

Modernity and Revolution

Marx's thought is born from two conjunctures. The first is the dual crisis of the French and Industrial Revolutions that propelled Europe into the new epoch of capitalist social relations and gave birth to a revolution in thought: the pressing task faced by philosophy was to comprehend and confront modernity.[23] The second is the particular character of the intellectual and social movements that emerged from these crises—the passage from the blossoming of the Enlightenment to a critique of its philosophical antinomies and private property relations. In this way, Marx's thought has clear origins, situated acutely between Hegel's philosophical modernism and the historical genesis and theoretical birth of the workers movement.[24] However, with this historical perspective in mind, mapping his intellectual development requires careful excavation. As Goldmann points out, "[t]he influence of one thinker upon another does not date from the first reading, nor even from the first borrowing of a few expressions, but only from the time when the ideas of the first become obstacles or essential contributions to the thought of the second."[25] Marx takes up and radicalises Hegel's modernism as a depiction of the world after the French Revolution, and this engagement presents a turning point. From Hegel, Marx is aware of not just the methodological elements of dialectical thought but also engages the problems of post-Kantian German Idealism. Most importantly, the relation between thought/being, essence/appearance and subject/object are all foundational issues for Marx. His analysis of alienation and fetishism can only be understood within these terms. Further still, Marx's idea of collective agency articulates a philosophy of praxis as human emancipation. This interpretation places Marx in dialogue with, and contributing to, a historical set of philosophical problems that are still alive in the conflicts of modernity. For this reason, Marx has a rightful place in contemporary debates about post-Kantian philosophy.[26]

Marx's intellectual development is located specifically in the legacy of German Idealism.[27] Recognition of the trammels of the post-Kantian paradigm are evident in his 1837 letter to his father. This letter marks the relinquishment of his early career ambitions in law and his abandonment of the idealism that had accompanied his early romantic poetry.[28] Here Marx is explicit about his conversion to Hegelianism:

> While I was ill I got to know Hegel from beginning to end, together with most of his disciples . . . I became ever more firmly bound to the modern world philosophy from which I had thought to escape, but all rich chords were silenced and I was seized with a veritable fury of irony, as could easily happen after so much had been negated . . . I could not rest until I had acquired modernity and the outlook of contemporary science.[29]

His embrace of the modernity of this science (*Wissenschaft*) registers his lifelong engagement with Hegel's philosophy but also, significantly, a movement away from the dualistic idealism in Kant and Fichte.[30] Marx writes,

A curtain had fallen, my holy of holies was rent asunder, and new gods had to be installed. From the idealism which, by the way, I had compared and nourished with the idealism of Kant and Fichte, I arrived at the point of seeking the idea in reality itself. If previously the gods had dwelt above the earth, now they became its centre. I had read fragments of Hegel's philosophy, the grotesque craggy melody of which did not appeal to me. Once more I wanted to dive into the sea, but with the definite intention of establishing that the nature of the mind is just as necessary, concrete and firmly based as the nature of the body. My aim was no longer to practice tricks of swordsmanship, but to bring genuine pearls into the light of day.[31]

Marx's association of the Hegelian position with the deduction of the idea *from* reality suggests a political reflection that critical thought must refuse dualistic conceptions. Rather than thought being conditioned in distinction from the world, the presence of the idea in reality itself binds philosophical reflection to social and political forms. This interpretation of Hegel pushes at an ambiguity between radical and conservative readings. In this view, the emphasis is firmly on the social and political intelligibility of thought. However, the most conservative Hegelians pushed in a different direction (most present in the *Philosophy of History*), taking the view that history had already realised rationality and as such freed thought to think itself.

The above passage points to an awareness of the political and philosophical implications of the contest between Kantian and Hegelian approaches. To locate the idea in reality entitles the concept to mediate the "ought" in the "is." This position rejects the rigid distinction Marx associates with Kantian and Fichtean antinomies.[32] While Marx is writing at a point of relative immaturity, the insight that emerges from this letter is the importance of the Hegelian concept mediating form-determinations. Marx is explicit: "The concept is indeed the mediating link between form and content."[33]

Marx's engagement with Hegel's thought, in connection with the currents of Hegelian philosophy in Berlin in the late 1830s, has often meant that his writings before the mid-1840s is simply labelled "Young Hegelian." Frequently, biographical treatments describe his 1841 doctoral dissertation more or less as a Young Hegelian exercise.[34] These types of categorisations serve more as a narrative function rather than an illumination of the themes Marx is considering within the broader post-Hegelian intellectual milieu.[35] Contrary to what is often assumed, in a sense, Marx was critically independent of the "Young Hegelians." Not only did the main currents within post-Hegelian philosophy fragment before his 1837 embrace of Hegel, but Marx also always maintained a distance from the mainstay Young Hegelian critique of Hegel.[36] These twists and turns are evident in Marx's dissertation, "The Difference Between the Democritean and Epicurean Philosophy of Nature." Although Marx has sympathy for "Young Hegelian" Bruno Bauer's critique of religion,[37] his comments on the relationship of philosophy to its "intellectual carriers" assess the Young Hegelians (which he terms the "liberal party") next to the Old Hegelians (termed as "positive philosophy"). Marx is certainly favourable to many figures in the Young Hegelian milieu, but he describes their responses to Hegel as a "duality": part of a "double trend, each side utterly opposed to each other." The Young Hegelians adopt social critique to make the world philosophical, turning *out* to the world; whereas the Old Hegelians "know that the inadequacy is immanent in philosophy" and turn philosophy inwards. Marx sees a need to relate the post-Hegelian trends as heirs to "the particular historical moments" of their development.[38]

For Marx, the corollaries between post-Aristotelian and post-Hegelian philosophy identify a turning point in the direction of philosophy. He sees the conjuncture in philosophy *after* Hegel in the same world historic terms as the period following Aristotle. Marx is cognisant, not just of the contested legacy, but of the impossibility of positing Hegel's philosophy as a closed mode of thought. While he appreciates that the great German idealist "has on the whole correctly defined the general aspects" of Greek thought, in Marx's view, Hegel had failed to offer a comprehensive account of the relation between its elements and history.[39] Marx appreciates the influence of Greek thought on Hegel himself, but finds the decline of the Greek systems of thought and Hegel's to be alike. According to Marx, Greek philosophy "reached its zenith in Aristotle" but "the death of the hero resembles the setting of the sun."[40] To write after Hegel demands the situating of thought in the reality of the historical present.[41] Marx's dissertation tasks the ancients with helping to shed light on the problems of modern philosophy.

Studying the philosophy of nature in Democritus and Epicurus permits Marx to examine the "riddle" posed by both philosophers who "teach exactly the same science, in exactly the same way," but inconsistently, "stand diametrically opposed."[42] For Democritus the atom contains objective and empirical nature, whereas for Epicurus, atoms are expressions of self-consciousness which are active and dissolve in "conscious opposition to the universal."[43] Marx's investigation pertains to the relationship between theories of atomism and the philosophical antimonies of thought/reality, phenomenon/truth, form/content, change/necessity, appearance/essence.[44] These antimonies are enduring problems of post-Kantian philosophy, and by looking at ancient naturalism, Marx is commenting on the "urge" (*Trieb*) for philosophy to realise itself in the world. He writes,

> the *practice* [*Praxis*] of philosophy is itself *theoretical*. It is the *critique* that measures the individual existence by the essence, the particular reality [*Wirklichkeit*] by the Idea. But this *immediate realisation* of philosophy is in its deepest essence afflicted with contradictions, and thus its essence takes form in the appearance and imprints its seal upon it.[45]

To make philosophy practical, critique must seek to clarify the individual and particular through the universal. Essence is shown to manifest in its appearances, allowing its contradictions to be exposed and put to critique. Marx's concern is that the distance between philosophy and politics, expressed in the Kantian dualism between practical and theoretical reason is apparent in the contradictions with the essence/appearance relation. The antinomy of essence and appearance has a direct correlation with the contradiction between theory and practice, which Marx voices in political terms as "critique." Moreover, the consolidation of the Prussian state deepened the existing crisis of German Idealism, now faced with the ruins of Hegel's system after his death. In this sense, there was a double crisis, the need for philosophical assessment of the politics of Prussia and the direction this philosophical assessment might go after the breakdown of Hegel's system. Marx's assessment of Greek atomism is an attempt to work out the relation of systematic thought to its collapse and the waning of its legacy. This concern is not abandoned with his turn to journalism in 1841 but expresses his view that political analysis was increasingly necessary.[46] By investigating Marx's early assessment of the breakdown of Hegelian philosophy, we can note resources that will become crucial elements of his critical social theory.

The towering influence of Aristotle is of particular significance. In the dissertation, he draws extensively on the Aristotelian corpus and produced an early annotated, but now lost, translation of *De Anima*.[47] During this period, he even entertained writing a book on Aristotle.[48] The idea of life in *De Anima* figures prominently in the dissertation. Marx describes the Aristotelian teleological structure of "birth, flowering and decline" as "commonplace," both an "iron circle in which everything human is enclosed" and a "very vague" notion, not sufficient in itself for understanding. Marx remarks: "Decay itself is prefigured in the living [*Lebendigen*]; its shape should therefore be just as much grasped in its specific characteristic as the shape of life [*Gestalt des Lebens*]."[49] In this post-Hegelian context, Marx is looking to push Aristotelian insights into in the modern world. Echoing the language of both Hegel and Aristotle, Marx's specification of the *shape of life* denotes that forms or essences are always related to their content. What many commentators fail to appreciate is the way in which Marx's adoption of Hegelian themes reflects and accentuates the Aristotelian dimension of Hegel's own thought. Marx's discussion of Aristotle cannot help but reflect his reception of German Idealism. Through his study of Aristotle and Hegel, the young Marx's investigation of naturalism locates the relation between philosophy and reality in the shapes of human life.[50] In this endeavour, there are strong points of continuation with his mature social theory. This point is not to derive programmatic Marxist slogans from Marx's earliest views, but to offer a sense of the impact of initial influences as *essential contributions* to his intellectual development.

Hegel's Modernism

Hegel's philosophy demands a comprehension of the present in thought.[51] This philosophical task requires a historically situated standpoint. To Hegel, the history of philosophy itself yields a philosophy of history.[52] His own departure point is distinctly modern: to think the consequences of the French Revolution. In the preface of the *Phenomenology of Spirit*, he notes

> it is not difficult to see that our own epoch is a time of birth and a transition to a new period. Spirit has broken with the previous world of its existence and its ways of thinking; it is now of a mind to let them recede into the past and to immerse itself in its own work at reshaping itself. To be sure, spirit is never to be conceived as being at rest but rather as ever advancing. However, just as with a child, who after a long silent period of nourishment draws his first breath and shatters the gradualness of only quantitative growth—it makes a qualitative leap and is born—so too, in bringing itself to cultural maturity, spirit ripens slowly and quietly into its new shape, dissolving bit by bit the structure of its previous world, whose tottering condition is only intimated by its individual symptoms. The kind of frivolity and boredom which chips away at the established order and the indeterminate presentiment of what is yet unknown are all harbingers of imminent change. This gradual process of dissolution, which has not altered the physiognomy of the whole, is interrupted by the break of day, which in a flash and at a single stroke brings to view the structure of the new world.[53]

The self-awareness of this moment of transition, in which the old world is wrecked on the shore of the new, makes this reflection a profound recognition of modernity.[54]

Hegel attempts to make coherent a philosophical comprehension of the present as our own time, to bring the "glorious dawn" (*Sonnenaufgang*) brought about by the "world-historical" event of the French Revolution to an understanding of what constitutes human freedom.[55] Spirit (*Geist*) is the collective historical subject, society, as it struggles to become aware of itself. Typically, Hegel's idea of absolute spirit is seen as a godlike deterministic force, outside of human control. However, this view is foreign to Hegel's thought.[56] As John McDowell points out, "[t]he philosophy of Geist is the philosophy of the human being."[57] For Hegel, the self-consciousness of spirit is its "self-sufficiency," its awareness of its "own nature" and its "activity of coming to itself, of producing itself, making itself actually what it is in itself potentially."[58] In itself, spirit is freedom. Absolute spirit is the shape of consciousness constituted by human beings who come to know reason as both bearing upon the objective world and as self-consciousness. Spirit is not a thing external to the world, but the normative rationality emerging immanently through the practices and institutions of social life that enable us to understand ourselves as self-conscious beings and to recognise others; who in and through this intersubjective relation, see ourselves as self-conscious beings. In a Hegelian view, spirit is the freedom that is inherent in human beings as rational animals *and* as something that is embedded in normative institutions that make possible agency "in the space of reasons."[59] Absolute spirit is self-consciousness and can only be grasped as the realisation of reason in a historical and social form of life which is structured on relations of mutual recognition. The "absolute" is not an idealism directed from up high, but the thinking of freedom as the self-realisation of rational human activity. As Pippin notes, Hegel's "entire philosophy could be summarized in one phrase, however initially opaque: that the Absolute is freedom."[60]

Hegel's concept of absolute spirit combines an Aristotelian view that human beings are ontologically rational animals with an argument about the inseparability of this rationality from history. In a clarifying passage, McDowell observes:

> Geist is Hegel's counterpart to what figures in Aristotle as the kind of soul that is characteristic of rational animals. It is human beings whom Aristotle defines as rational animals; that corresponds to Hegel's implicit identification of the philosophy of Geist with the philosophy of the human. On this account, then, Geist is the formally distinctive way of being a living being that characterizes human beings: in Aristotelian terms, the form of a living human being qua living human being … The idea of Geist is the idea of a distinctive way of living a life; often it is better to speak of Geistigkeit, as the defining characteristic of that distinctive form of life and thereby of the living beings that live it.[61]

For Hegel, our distinctive form of life needs to be grasped in its rational self-understanding. As consciousness, spirit takes passage through contradictory experiences. In this way, spirit comes to be through forms of consciousness constituted by self-conscious beings. Reason is realised in the world as relations of recognition. By understanding the genesis of modern society historically and the unity of the institutions of ethical life (the family, civil society and the state), Hegel situates the interaction of agents in a world defined by our subjective and objective social relationships.[62] The ethical world is the teleological movement of the universality of social life. Sublating abstract, subjective will, "ethical life" objectively allows self-determination in the forms of intersubjective recognition. Subjects understand their social world as one that encapsulates freedom in the normative social roles and institutions of their own making. Freedom is determined and discovered by human action, by the content of objective processes that take the form of subjective self-realisation, of consciousness realising itself, a dialectic of subject and object manifest in the totality of reason. Rational agents recognise the world and their place in it as free. But for this rationality to be real, the political community must be objectively free.

Therefore, Hegel's idea of rationality should not be seen as an apologia for an existing reality and political paradigm. Despite the argument in the *Philosophy of Right* that ethical life must be found in the spheres of the modern nuclear family, market exchange and the capitalist state, these instantiations do not need to be held up today as institutional rationality. Indeed, in my view, each sphere fails to be rationally acceptable in the modern world. But if a rational social order is one that realises the rationality latent in the actual world, in its concept as ethical life, this idea can point to different institutional and social forms from the ones Hegel himself suggests.[63] However, if Hegel's idea of freedom is understood immanently, it becomes possible to retain his concept of ethical life while going beyond the specific institutional forms he sets out.

Hegel's fundamental aim is to show that absolute ethical life is the realisation of social freedom that transforms and transcends the unity of the ancient Greek polis and the subjectivity of the modern world. Both shapes of life reveal aspects of freedom lacking in the other. The natural inequality of the polis and the social inequality of the modern world mean neither could make good on its normative promises for freedom. As Hegel sees it, subjective freedom is essential to any form of social freedom.[64] While he criticises Kant's idea of morality, Hegel goes on to show subjective will results in conscious activity with others and enables ethical life. For Kant, reason is distinctly modern in the sense that it necessitates individual autonomy and self-determination.[65] Kant's stress on freedom in these terms expresses a quintessentially modern understanding of subjectivity. Hegel appreciates the advance of this form of reasoning in terms of the identification of the individual subject. However, at the same time, he draws attention to the internal limitations of this view. Hegel sublates this understanding of the autonomous and self-determining individual subject into a conception of modernity that weaves together individual and collective flourishing in the ethical fabric of institutional rationality. The subject realises their distinctive autonomy and self-determination in a social world in which they recognise and are recognised by others who share their normative commitment to their mutual collective freedom.

Hegel's distinctive transformation of the modern idea of subjectivity is that rationality becomes self-conscious and is "at one with itself" only through its social determinations.[66] In Hegel, the unfolding of these relations in their rational institutional forms is the speculative task of the philosophy of right.[67] The concept of right (*Recht*) is developed from abstract will to its fully rational shape in ethical life. As "second nature," ethical life is "reason as it actualises itself in the element of self-consciousness."[68] The conscious nature of social intersubjectivity is mediated in Hegel's social theory by the determinations of modern life—the family, legal, economic and political institutions, and their socially constitutive normative practices. These determinations are conditioned by the industrialising economic paradigm of the modern era. Hegel seeks to understand the distinctly modern problems of market exchange, the division of labour, individual egotism and the ramifications of poverty and alienation on modern life. Individuals relate to each other through the particularity of the market, which enables each to seek their own ends ("all else means nothing to him") through "a system of needs" and thus mediates between individual family units and the substantial universal of the state.[69] The particularity of civil society is inherently contradictory, and its impoverished form of interaction results in the need for public authorities to ensure protection.[70] But the moments of individuality and particularity can only find rational expression in the universality of the state.[71] In his political thought, Hegel charts the conceptual progression of forms of subjectivity which culminates in ethical life but can be retrospectively understood in the "immanent principle," where the universal is made necessary by the concretisation of earlier particularities and in which the universal is always reflected.[72] The inconsistent or formal parts are redeemed only in terms of their universality.

Further, this process does not simply promote reconciliation within the modern world. Hegel's immanent principle is critical. Ethical life requires a concept of freedom which goes beyond the legality of constitutions. Freedom is inherent in the relations of right, socially instituted in rational association and community. This freedom must be universal—reciprocal and free from domination—for it to be actually rational. The radical character of Hegel's modernism is his theorisation of the present as fractured by alienation. However, the greatest puzzle of Hegel's social theory is how freedom can be realised in a rational political community with the inequality and dissatisfaction of civil society. At the emergence of modern capitalism, Hegel's growing pessimism about civil society should be read as a warning about the increasing irrationality of market exchange, not as a normative justification of its necessity in the modern world.

While rationality and freedom express the normative ideals and emancipatory promise of the revolutionary age, this new world arose disfigured, with upheavals inherent in its very fabric.[73] In an influential interpretation of Hegel's modernism in relation to the French Revolution, Joachim Ritter stresses the importance of the realisation of ethical life in the political realm.[74] He points to the central concern of Hegel's social thought as the "political realisation of freedom," which is left unresolved by the revolution and thus remains in our present.[75] With the revolutionary age, the possibilities of human freedom had been opened.[76] But, as Pinkard notes, the institutions of the modern world did not allow people to feel "at home," and therefore individuals "experienced freedom as a possibility rather than as something already established."[77] "In this time of critical enlightenment," Hegel observes, "the isolation of individuals from one another, and from the community as a whole" is the fundamental problem of modern life. Spirit is the "culture of a people" that acts in the world as "the thought of its life and condition, its laws, its system of rights and its ethical way of life."[78]

These problems are first evident in the Enlightenment struggle for reason against religious dogmatism. The idea that human beings have the inherent capacity as rational beings to act autonomously and exercise our will freely became embedded in the very logic of modern society. These new conceptions of freedom and reason took hold in the uneven global process of social transformation from precapitalist to capitalist forms of life. The fate of the modern individual became the very fate of modern society. With the demands of self-awareness, consciousness passes through the critique of religion and seeks truth in the capacity for self-knowledge that is now intelligible as reason. Kant stresses that to live in "an age of *enlighten-*

ment" is not to see the world as already enlightened, but the demand that human beings use our understanding to think and act freely, which are the conditions of possibility for self-awareness.[79] Kant's idea of enlightenment exposes a central contradiction in modern life. On one hand, his appeal to self-awareness articulates the significance of individual subjectivity. On the other, the type of freedom available to modern individuals is fundamentally shaped by a social form structured by the abstract domination of value that imposes an atomistic logic onto all subjectivity.

Hegel's thought is foremost concerned with the contradictions and possibilities of modern freedom. Self-awareness as "I" must become reason, the unity of "I" and "being" as spirit, conceiving of the shape of consciousness as changing form through interaction with the world. Ethical life is the historical realisation of self-consciousness in a social order of human making.[80] In this sense, the shapes of self-conscious knowledge won from the critique of religion and despotism are to become "genuine actualities, and, instead of being shapes only of consciousness [*Gestalten nur des Bewußtseins*], they are shapes of a world [*Gestalten einer Welt*]."[81] The passage of modernity through the European Enlightenment and French Revolution signified that subjectivity confronts the objective realm not externally (as in premodern social forms) but through internal relations of intersubjectivity, meaning that social agents only now have the possibility to make ourselves at home in our world through the institutions we create and control. The activity of this freedom is available to us moderns. This creation is the activity of normative self-determination. Hegel is cognisant that this rationality must be realised in a reality that has now been opened by modernity. The inseparability of revolution and modernity in Hegel's thought presents the distinctiveness of his conception of ethical life. He preserves but overcomes modern subjectivism (as in Kant's moral philosophy), in part, by mobilising the notion of collective freedom, the ethical life of the ancient polis, while resisting any romanticism towards its ideal. The radical feature of Hegel's modernism is that self-consciousness requires a relation between one's own historical condition and the sociality of reason.

Morality and Ethical Life

Ethical life, for Hegel, amounts to the realisation of the human good and the well-lived life. In this sense, "self-consciousness" and "recognition" are the terms he uses to express the process and form of rationality that is necessary for the good to be actualised as freedom in political institutions that are ethical. Rational agency is human action directed towards the good, which must be embodied as ethical life. The concept is first present in Hegel's *System of Ethical Life* and in the critique of empiricism and Kant in his *Natural Law* essay, both written in Jena in 1802/3.[82] The concept of ethical life crowns his mature "systematic exposition" of political and social theory, *The Elements of the Philosophy of Right: Or Natural Law and Political Science in Outline*, published in 1821.[83] The essential feature of this conception is his sublation of Aristotelian ethics into an understanding of modern subjectivity as mutual recognition. Hegel's concept of ethical life fuses individual will with the need for collectively constituted rational practices, norms and values. For subjects to find shared meaning with others requires a form of ethical life that orders norms rationally. If modern life is to be ethical, it must provide a sociality that enables every individual to be free.

In Robert Brandom's account, this phase of spirit is "post-modern," a recognitive community that upholds "a new, symmetrical normative structure of authority and responsibility: trust."[84] For Brandom, and other contemporary commentators, Hegel's analysis of alienation contributes a crucial account of the lack of moral freedom for both individuals and collectives.[85] However, despite his heralding of the need for a new age for spirit, Brandom fails to make explicit the relationship between agency, recognition and capitalism. The institutional forms that could structure such a recognitive community demand an analysis of the economic logic of political life under capitalism. Hegel's thought is squarely located in this problematic.

Many contemporary Hegelian assessments of the rationality of modern social forms occlude adequate assessments of economic rationality in terms of the basic categories of capitalism. While Marx's reading of Hegel leads him to develop exactly this kind of analysis, commentators like Brandom fail to take up Marx's most profound and speculative category: "value." Brandom assumes Marx's idea of "value" is a narrowly economic concept and struggles to discuss it in moral terms.[86] The lack of adequate attention to Marx in recent Anglo-American Hegel scholarship means that questions about the irrationality of civil society often lead to disconsolate conclusions. Regrettably, many of Hegel's finest commentators cannot go beyond his own pessimism. For Pinkard, the subject living under the alienation and looming abstractions of civil society and state institutions "must learn to live within these abstractions."[87] Pippin goes a step further concluding that capitalism today has "effectively destroyed the possibility" of the kind of "mutual recognitive status in modern ethical life" that Hegel sets out since it would require changes to such an economic system that is now effectively "without hope."[88]

I find Pinkard's "best we can have" picture and Pippin's hopelessness unnecessarily dejected. Both only go so far in determining the abstractions amongst which we live in the modern world. Engaging with Marx's analysis of capitalism makes it possible to identify the way in which the normativity of modern life and its institutions are shaped by the abstractions of the value-form. However, Marx's analysis also indicates that collective agency is always an immanent possibility since value is created by human beings. Practical consciousness is embedded in productive activity, which can take different social and institutional forms. Regardless, an assessment of subjectivity and the limits to our possible space of reasons necessitates a much stronger critique of the political economy of capital.

In this way, the contemporary stress on discursive practices that tends to underscore the "space of reason" interpretation put by many Hegelians today falls short of the full extent of the implications of Hegel's idea of social freedom. The role of economic life in a philosophy of right must reckon with the logic of capital as a social form for any picture of normative rationality to emerge. Hegel's own writings demonstrate that his ethical thought is always expressed in close reference to economic life. In the *Philosophy of Right*, Hegel unfolds the logical determinations of social being by abstracting the individual modern subject—the person—and tracing their relationship to the social world. The sequence moves quickly from abstract right and personhood to property. For a person to be free, according to Hegel, we need to externalise this freedom in property and through this relation we interact with the world.[89] Property requires possession that objectifies our need, drives or desire for things.[90] Hegel is very clear he means private property, which permits a need to be met through the object's use and its value to the individual.[91]

Modern life is decisively bourgeois, and the market relations of civil society establish a system of needs based on private property.[92] Hegel critically draws upon political economy to outline the sphere of civil society and its relation to ethical life. Hegel adopts Smith's account of the division of labour and frequently uses the famous pin-factory example.[93] Hegel carries over the emphasis on wage-labour and property in his own conception of modern subjectivity. The meeting of subjective needs requires both "external things [*Dinge*], which are likewise the property and product of the needs and wills of others" and "activity and work, as the mediation between the two aspects."[94] As he sees it, our own self-regard and status as a person is bound up in the social mediations of activity tethering my own will with others. But such activity assumes wage-labour.

To grasp the split between subjective will and political collectivity in modern society, Hegel investigates civil society in terms defined by the antagonistic character of modern property relations. The corresponding system of needs locates his ethical theory in a political assessment of modern social relations. In this respect, Hegel's account of Kantian morality is underwritten by a social perspective that is deeply aware of the contradictions of bourgeois property and the barriers it poses to the rational organisation of social life. Hegel's ambivalence about bourgeois life makes apparent the irrationality of constructing a moral philosophy apart from a substantive account of the sociality of freedom. In short, "morality" alone is too weak to support the institutional realisation of freedom he calls "ethical life."

The concept of ethical life which underpins Hegel's idea of freedom is developed through his critique of Kant's concept of morality.[95] Unlike many contemporary understandings of moral philosophy, Hegel's concept of ethical life (*Sittlichkeit*) hinges on its distinction from morality (*Moralität*). For Hegel, morality represents subjectivism, which he associates with both empiricism and Kantianism. Hegel insists that the dualism between "is" and "ought" in theoretical philosophy has devastating consequences for moral philosophy since it results in ontological individualism. His response here is configured chiefly in response to Kant's moral philosophy, which is structured around the judgement of the moral agent who ought to act in accordance with maxims and principles bound by the moral law. With his concept of ethical life, Hegel magnifies Aristotle's picture of the kind of shared reasoning that cultivates the political community. Ethical life encapsulates the living good of rational beings, a sublation of morality and politics into the shape of collective forms of social life. Both Aristotle and Hegel understand ethics as part of an architectonic form of political and social reasoning.

Kant's *Groundwork of the Metaphysics of Morals* presents the basic method of his moral theory. In this work, he begins by "carefully" separating an empirical "practical anthropology" and a rational moral philosophy.[96] Morality seeks its laws not in "the nature of the human being, or in the circumstances of the world in which he is placed, but a priori solely in the concepts of pure reason."[97] Kant's theory is based on moral will. This "subjective principle of acting" forms the basis of practical reason.[98] He asks the question: "What ought I do?" Kant's answer conceives moral action in accordance with duty, understood a priori. Duty is determined by the principles reason dictates and, in this sense, prevents self-interest. Duty must be done for its own sake and out of "respect" for the law.[99] The will aims at the good, which it achieves "not for other purposes *as a means*, but good *in itself*."[100] Duty forms the moral content of action, derived from reason and acting independently of desire.[101]

Kant explicitly rejects the justification of morality from experience.[102] Just as experience and feeling cannot ground morality, neither can "the particularities of human nature."[103] Instead, for Kant the moral will must come from laws we give ourselves.

Kant founds this idea of rationality by examining what he calls the "categorical imperative," the binding principle of moral *"ought [Sollen]."*[104] The categorical imperative is present in every person, irrespective of our consciousness of it, since we are rational beings.[105] The categorical imperative is pure form, demarcated by its indeterminateness, allowing reason to define morality without the imperative being shaped by contingency.[106] Unlike a hypothetical imperative that is a possibility when certain conditions are met, the categorical imperative is unconditional. He writes famously, "[t]here is therefore only a single categorical imperative, and it is this: *act only according to that maxim through which you can at the same time will that it become a universal law.*" This formula entitles moral justification.[107] Moral agents ought to make choices with the self-assurance that their action would constitute a universal law. In this sense morality must be "an *ought* without an *is*."[108] Kant codifies a method for thinking about morality as conforming to laws based on the "ought" of individual action. Each autonomous agent must adjudicate for themselves in their moral decisions, and the correct application of their reason will mean employing the same maxim. Action must meet this demand for it to be rational.

The categorical imperative brings subjects together in a "kingdom of ends," which proposes an abstract equality between individuals premised on their autonomy.[109] According to this conception of rationality, free will is autonomous and self-determining. Kant writes, "[s]ince morality serves as a law for us only as for *rational beings*, it must hold for all rational beings as well, and as it must be derived solely from the property of freedom, freedom must also be proved as a property of the will of all rational beings."[110] Desire and impulse are cast away as burdens to reason and the moral "ought" becomes the autonomous will of action, grounding morality in reason alone.[111] However, Kant's conception of reason falters in his final suggestion that the limit of moral inquiry is that we do not know "how freedom is possible."[112] For Kant, "reason would overstep all its bounds if it undertook to *explain how* pure reason can be practical."[113] The *Groundwork* ends with the insistence that the categorical imperative is both necessary but insufficient: all we can do is "comprehend its *incomprehensibility.*"[114]

It is precisely this limit that Hegel makes the object of his critique. The *Natural Law* essay establishes the main lines of his reckoning with Kant's moral philosophy that are subsequently developed in his mature work. In Hegel's account, the demands of Kant's moral law collapse and become subjectivist articulations of individual preference without adequate normative justification or determination. Central to this view is that Kant's concept of reason ultimately renders moral action and the condition for its possibility unknowable. Hegel observes that Kant must implicitly rely on experience but does not explain the mediation between pure reason and experience.[115] Kant's critique of empiricist justifications of morality in experience and desire is unable to overcome its one-sided determination and ends up falling into the opposite side of the problem. Rather than deriving morality from experience, for Kant, moral reasoning is "cleansed" of experience.[116] According to Hegel both claims share the "same" one-sided and atomistic starting point. His charge is that in the positing of the a priori as categorical and unconditional, Kant is forced to accept the empirical realm as a means of determining the relationship between the conditioned and condition. Hegel suggests this creates a loop, in which "formalism not only renounces all the advantages it has over what it calls empiricism; in addition, since the conditioned and the condition, as interconnected opposites, are posited as subsisting absolutely, formalism itself sinks totally into empirical necessity."[117] In this way, the formal dualism between experience and reason is left intact.

By pointing out the defects of empiricism and Kantian morality as both variants of atomism, Hegel opens the space in which he will chart his concept of ethical life. Hegel's alternative is to transcend the unmediated binary between particularity (experience) and universality (reason). Pinpointing the consequences of this antinomy in moral and political atomism, he maintains that

> we are left with the human being in the image of the bare state of nature, or the abstraction of the human being with his essential capacities, and we have only to glance at it to discover what is necessary. What is recognised as having a connection with the state must therefore also be separated out, because the image of the necessary cannot contain absolute unity, but only simple multiplicity [*Mannigfaltigkeit*], or atoms with the fewest possibility properties. Thus, whatever may come under the concept of a linking and ordering of these [atoms] as the weakest unity of which the principle of multiplicity [*Vielheit*] is capable, is excluded from this multiplicity as an adventurous and later accretion.[118]

With Hobbes in mind, Hegel rejects the model of human beings as abstracted entities "mutually opposed and in absolute conflict with each other." Rather, the ethical realm is the "architectonic" which locates the "the inner necessity" of human relations in the "the absolute unity of the one and many."[119] Hegel does not oppose the individual for the community, but in his view, it is the ethical realm that enables human beings to be at home in the world and creates the environment for individuals to actualise themselves in relation to others.[120]

Against Kant, Hegel turns to Aristotle. Hegel maintains that the moral law lacks the content that would give rational action meaning if individuals are to achieve their goals and purposes. As Jonathan Lear explains, Kant

> encourages the idea that in viewing the world objectively I reflectively detach myself from my present concerns, interests, and situation and conceive of myself simply as one agent among others. But if Hegel's Aristotelian criticism is correct, then if one actually succeeds in viewing the interests and concerns of all agents, including oneself, from a genuinely detached perspective, there will be no motivation left for acting in any particular way at all.[121]

Hegel's critique of Kant must be seen as an attempt to recover practical reasoning as a means of realising the good in the fabric of a social form of life. For Aristotle, it is society that cultivates practical reasoning. The virtues are constituted by rational agents as goods internal to the practices that foster flourishing.[122] If flourishing is "activity in accord with virtue" then "the just person needs other people as partners and recipients of his actions."[123] Ethical life must always correspond with the social form of life that is conducive to flourishing. In this way, subjective motivation for action can only make sense as a decision-making process with others.

In undertaking a critique of Kant's moral philosophy, Hegel is not in the least rejecting its fundamental claim of moral autonomy but making apparent that the categorical imperative does not provide justification for such a claim. As he sees it, the truth of Kant's idea of moral freedom can be retained, while overcoming the formalism that stops short of the critical insights such subjectivity could promise. Hegel points to problems that arise when we try to determine moral judgement and duty. Kant opens up a contradiction between his concern for the abstract nature of the moral will and the need to "look to this absolute practical reason for a moral legislation—which would have to have content—because the essence of this reason consists in having no content at all."[124] The result, in Hegel's view, is formalism. The determinacy is forced to supply content, which is then made into a moral law. Once it becomes a moral law, according to Kant, it must be universalised so as to guide action without contradiction. Hegel retorts, "[t]here is nothing which could not be made into a moral law in this way." If a moral law is premised on an arbitrary basis, then its supposed universality is also arbitrary. Hegel picks out Kant's famous "deposit" example to illustrate the point.[125] Kant puts the argument as follows:

> The most common understanding can distinguish without instruction what form in a maxim makes it fit for a giving of universal law and what does not. I have, for example, made it my maxim to increase my wealth by every safe means. Now I have a deposit in my hands, the owner of which has died and left no record of it. This is, naturally, a case for my maxim. Now I want only to know whether that maxim could also hold as a universal practical law. I therefore apply the maxim to the present case and ask whether it could indeed take the form of a law, and consequently whether I could through my maxim at the same time give such a law as this: that everyone may deny a deposit which no one can prove has been made. I at once become aware that such a principle, as a law, would annihilate itself since it would bring it about that there would be no deposits at all. A practical law that I cognise as such must qualify for a giving of universal law: this is an identical proposition and therefore self-evident. Now, if I say that my will is subject to a practical law, I cannot cite my inclination (e.g., in the present case my avarice) as the determining ground of my will appropriate to a universal practical law; for this is so far from being qualified for a giving of universal law that in the form of a universal law it must instead destroy itself.[126]

Someone who subsequently dies has placed a deposit into my hands but left no record of it. Kant is thus referring to a situation in which I can freely take the deposit (despite the wrongfulness of my action), because no one can conclusively prove the deposit does not belong to me. Kant's argument lays down the procedure involved in evaluating if a maxim might be consistently universal. If in taking the deposit I increase my wealth but deceive others, then a universalisable law on this action would make all deposits impossible.

Hegel makes the simple but powerful objection: "But what contradiction is there in no deposits being made?" If there are no deposits, then the prior determinations make little sense.[127] Further, if property itself is questioned, Kant's proposition is "tautological," and it would affirm property with the statement: "Property is property and nothing else besides." This does little more than affirm property:

> if there is property, there must be property. But if the opposite determinacy, i.e. the negation of property, is posited, the legislation of the same practical reason results in the tautology: non-property is non-property. If there is no property, anything

which claims to be property must be annulled [*aufgehoben*]. But the interest [at stake] is precisely to prove that there must be property; we are solely concerned with what lies outside the competence of this practical legislation of pure reason, namely with deciding which of the opposing determinacies must be posited. But pure reason requires that this should have been done in advance, and that one of the opposing determinacies should already have been posited; only then can it enact its now superfluous legislation.[128]

Hegel's charge is that on its own terms, the categorical imperative cannot permit *any* law to become a moral law.[129] Or, it can only do so on the basis of accepting as given (and thus as right) the existing conditions of society; for example, in the case referred to above, Kant does not question the underlying morality at work in the deposit-making society. The existence of capital (and of a society of self-valorising value) flies under his moral radar. In pointing to the presupposed content determinations that seep into the formalism of Kant's moral thought, Hegel mounts a remarkable challenge, with considerable implications for modern social theory.

First, he opposes the rigid imposition of form on social content. Law cannot be said to supply morality without reference to the totality of the social world.[130] Second, Hegel conceives of morality as a mediated moment in ethical and political relations. Here morality relates to the "relations between individuals" but closes itself off to the forms of social life that are necessary determinations for universality.[131] Morality itself is abstract, separate from the content that is filled by ethical life. But if morality is dialectically unfolded with the unity of ethical life, then the autonomy of moral will can be actualised as a component, but not reducible element, of social and normative practices.[132] For Hegel, freedom is realised in "the moment of the negatively absolute or infinity . . . which must be identified in *absolute ethical life*." The "shape" of absolute ethical life is constituted in "a *people*."[133] Ethical life is given definition by its actualisation in a political community, which Hegel sees as preserving the ethical ideal of the polis. Hegel's translation of polis as *Volk* carries this meaning.[134] Third, Hegel's reading of political economy is evidenced in this passage.[135] The concept of civil society is especially important for Hegel's social theory, namely that "property itself is directly opposed to universality." Civil society is the sphere of particularity and competition, whereas ethical life mediates the conflicts of the market and demands a universality that is concretely free.[136] Hegel's concept of ethical life attempts to make good on the possibilities of subjective action by going past the confines of its atomistic expression and posing this investigation in the form of social life itself. In this pursuit, Hegel sustains his critique of morality with newfound insights from political economy and furthers this case in the *Natural Law* essay.

For Hegel, the realm of civil society forms a "nexus of relations" in which economic functions, especially property and wage-labour, normatively shape human needs. Hegel considers the needs of human beings within a social system defined by inequality and "the process of acquisition" between "jealous" and competing "classes [*Stände*]." In his view, the necessary of absolute ethical life—a "genuine and complete justice and *Sittlichkeit*"—is in variance with the particularity of civil society. He maintains that "[t]his examination of the system of reality has shown that absolute ethical life must adopt a negative attitude towards this system ... the absolute ethical realm must take on a perfectly organised shape [*Gestalt*], for relation is the abstraction of the aspect of shape."[137] There is a definite Aristotelian character to this discussion. Like Aristotle, Hegel's organic language metaphysically situates parts within their unified whole. Ethical life must be understood in terms of the objective and subjective conditions which allow for the community to become concretely universal.[138] However, Hegel transforms this ontology with his modern idea of subjectivity.

Hegel holds that the "[s]hape of ethical life and its individuality" requires an account of "universal mutual dependence with regard to physical needs and the labour and accumulation [of resources]."[139] He draws upon classical political economy, assessing the modern division of labour. For Hegel, these relations are highly conflictual.[140] Unlike Smith's understanding of commercial society as the realisation of human nature, Hegel considers the modern division of labour to be abstract and in this way, begins to historicise this form of interaction.

In his early political writings, Hegel draws a distinction between *relative* and *absolute* ethical life. Rose sharpens the distinction between these concepts and applies them to Hegel's thought as a whole. She makes sense of this concept in terms of the division of labour found in *System of Ethical Life*.[141] The shapes of ethical life relate to the forms of identity in the social realm. First, experience is found in the individual, which is self-contained and limited. This is in turn negated by the immediate relation of individuals which come to see each other as particularities, means to their own ends. Hegel considers this to be "relative ethical life," since experience is oppositional. Relative ethical life is inorganic since it relates to the life dominated by the economic realm. Hegel's claim is that relative ethical life bases itself on particularity which reflects self-interested subjectivity. Absolute ethical life, however, is "organic" and relates to the immanent essence of individuals.[142] The importance of this distinction is that it allows Hegel to suggest the essence of an individual is not oppositional but socially constituted. Individuals are not simply opposed to the community, as categories that exclude each other, but Hegel investigates the immanent and ontological relation of dependency between the two categories.

Further, in the *Natural Law* essay Hegel analyses relative ethical life by the determinations of civil society, charting the unity of needs (subject), work and possession (object):

> Thus, two classes [*Stände*] are formed in accordance with the absolute necessity of the ethical. One of these is the class of the free, the individual of absolute ethical life; its organs are the single individuals. From the point of view of its indifference, it is the absolute living spirit, and from the point of view of its objectivity, it is the living movement and divine self-enjoyment of this whole in the totality of the individuals who constitute its organs and members. But its formal or negative side must also be absolute—namely work, which is directed not towards the nullification of individual determinacies, but towards death, and whose product is again not something individual, but the being and preservation of the whole of the ethical organisation.[143]

As Hegel understands it, the relation between individuals as mediated by economic relations is *abstractly* universal. The individual appears self-sufficient but really exists as part of a wider relation. Hegel is distinctly modern in this respect. Directly following the paragraph above, he compares the first class to what Aristotle knows as "πολιτευειν, which means living with and for one's people, leading a universal life wholly dedicated to the public interest, or philosophising." Hegel points to the passage in the *Politics* where Aristotle claims that "what the slave needs to scientifically know how to do is what the master needs to scientifically know how to prescribe. That is why for those who have the resources not to bother with such things a steward takes on this office, while they themselves engage in politics or do philosophy."[144] Hegel strongly rejects Aristotle's defence of slavery.[145] However, his attention to this passage does denote the seriousness Hegel afforded Aristotle's discussion of economic relations and the necessary link labour has to ethical life.

Hegel considers slaves, as an unfree class, next to a peasant class and to the modern earning class (*Klasse*). His aim is to understand how the classes fit within the relations of labour and property. Since the slave is someone else's property, the slave is not an abstract individual but a particularity of "domination and dependence." Hegel brings in this point to suggest the modern "system of property" conditions persons as "private individuals."[146] Hegel considers this private life as abstract freedom: "the individual is only free for himself as such, and enjoys citizen freedom alone—in the sense of that of a *bourgeois* and not that of a *citizen*."¹⁴⁷ The question of how the individual relates to the world needs to track the movement from the former to the latter.

In this way, Hegel seeks to reconcile the split between society and the individual that is endemic to modern life. Accordingly, for the Greeks life was *immediately ethical*, with practices and beliefs socially embedded as freedom. The Greeks "made their world their home."¹⁴⁸ Their culture reflected this freedom as the "spirit of ideally being-at-home-with-themselves in their physical, corporate, legal, moral and political existence."¹⁴⁹ Greek life was ethical, but limited and premodern since subjectivity was only comprehended as part of nature. If the polis allowed ethical life to be known in terms of a just community, the norms pertaining to the family and slavery were understood with regard to what is natural.¹⁵⁰ Subjectivity was limited since Greek life excluded some from the self-reflection of public life. Hegel makes this point in his critique of Aristotle's natural justification of slavery: "in Greece the few alone are free."¹⁵¹ Ethical life for the Greeks was "bound up" with, but not reducible to, slavery; it was "partly a matter of mere chance, a transient and limited flowering, and partly a hard servitude of the human and the humane."¹⁵² Hegel's treatment of Sophocles's *Antigone* in the *Phenomenology* dramatises the breakdown of Greek ethical life as subjectivity enters consciousness.¹⁵³

Despite this criticism, Hegel incorporates Aristotle's social ontology into his own ethical thought. Hegel explicitly differentiates morality as the "*individual's ethical life to the real absolute ethical life*" in which the "absolute ethical life is so essentially the ethical life of everyone that one cannot describe it as reflected, as such, in the individual."¹⁵⁴ Hegel quotes approvingly from Aristotle,

> The people [*Volk*] are more in accord with nature than the individual; for if the individual, in isolation, is not self-sufficient, he must—like all [other] parts—constitute a *single* unit with the whole. But anyone who cannot belong to a community [*wer nicht gemeinschaftlich sein kann*], or who requires nothing since he is self-sufficient, is not part of a people [*Volk*] and is therefore either an animal or a god.¹⁵⁵

Adapting the passage for his own purposes, Hegel's translation of the Greek *koinonein* into *gemeinschaftlich* emphasises the community as a form of political association in which social life is determined by the political life of the people.¹⁵⁶ Hegel fundamentally shares Aristotle's view that human beings are ontologically social beings, characterised by our political association. Without human sociality, there can be no ethical life.

For Aristotle, the cultivation of the good is the flourishing of both political and ethical dimensions of human life. This view is decisively expressed in the passage from the *Politics* which Hegel quotes. The remainder of the passage reads,

> Now, although the impulse toward this sort of community exists by nature in everyone, the person who first put one together was also the cause of very great goods. For just as when completed a human is the best of the animals, so when separated from law and judicial proceeding he is worst of all. For injustice is harshest when it possesses weapons, and a human grows up possessed of weapons for practical wisdom and virtue to use, which may be used for absolutely contrary purposes. That is why he is the most unrestrained and most savage of animals when he lacks virtue, as well as the worst as regards sex and food. But justice is something political. For justice is a political community's order, and justice is judgment of what is just.[157]

Aristotle's organic view of politics contains six components. First, the political community is a creation of our nature as human beings; second, such a community initiates the human good; third, the whole of the political community is prior to the individual parts;[158] fourth, human beings cannot discard our social natures and to try is to emulate beasts or gods; fifth, the political community founds social interaction and sets the standard for virtue; and sixth, without the political community there is no virtue and human life could not be rational. Aristotle theorises the sociability of human beings in the types of societal organisation that habituate ethical interaction in the very nature of this shared and organic existence. Not only is the good for human beings only possible with society, but when outside of it (and thus unrestrained by virtue), human beings are potentially "worse" than any non-human animal precisely when we possess the existential capacity, the weapon of reason, but cannot exercise it adequately or cultivate the good. Our behaviour is not unintelligible, it is simply unrestrained.

Society provides the normative structure to understand our desires and needs by practical reasoning. The cultivation of ethical behaviour and intelligibility comes through the practices and judgement of human agents. This ethical realm fosters human flourishing. Flourishing is understood as a concrete whole, a quality of a shared, habituated life rather than a passing state of feeling. Aristotle's philosophy is underpinned by a teleological conception of the good, specific to the reasoning of human beings. In Aristotle's organic terms, the definition of forms is in accordance with their proper function (*ergon*) and telos.

Hegel follows Aristotle in conceptualising the ethical life of political community as both organic and the realisation of human rationality.[159] His conception of the state as an organic whole is dependent on his immanent and teleological ontology.[160] Hegel adopts from Aristotle the view that for a human life to flourish, it must be realised in a form of human association that cultivates the good. However, unlike Aristotle, Hegel's ethical life incorporates modern notions of the will and rational agency of the individual subject.[161] But his idea of subjective freedom as individuals finding satisfaction in rational self-conscious action distinctively recasts Aristotle's insistence that the telos of a flourishing life is the "soul and determinant" of rational action.[162] In this way, Hegel's ethics weaves together Aristotle and modern understandings of individual will and self-consciousness. In short, "the absolutely ethical has its proper organic body in individuals; and its movement and life [*Lebendigkeit*] in the common being and activity of everyone is absolutely identical in its universal and particular forms."[163] The shape of ethical life, "like all living things, is simply an identity of universal and particular, and it is therefore an individuality and a shape."[164] This syllogism proposes absolute ethical life, which, once differentiated from morality, demonstrates that the individual is a mediated moment in a dynamic nexus of social relations. Hegel's claim is that for the individual's will to be realised it must be in the living shape of absolute ethical life. At a more systematic level, Hegel develops the inquiry of the *Natural Law* essay with the institutions of ethical life in the *Philosophy of Right*.

Ethical Life as the Living Good

The *Philosophy of Right* dares the modern person to find "delight" in reason, to recognise the role of reason in modern life.[165] Reason vindicates ethical life in the conflicts of modernity. Hegel's aim is to depict reason as objective spirit in the institutions of the social world.[166] He goes on to show in what way objective normative institutions constitute social life as "second nature."[167] In this sense, the *Philosophy of Right* deepens his criticism of subjectivism laid out in the *Natural Law* essay.[168] He argues not only that the world is inherently rational, but that this rationality can be actualised in the organisation of the social world. This attempt to systematise social theory into a philosophy of "objective spirit" culminates in "Ethical Life," the sphere of the family, civil society and the state. Hegel conceptualises the political structure of the modern world. The *Philosophy of Right* establishes a view of politics and ethics as essential parts of the same rational inquiry. His concept of ethical life is fundamentally an architectonic for the unity of political and social association in the open space of recognition and freedom.

The logical structure of the *Philosophy of Right* starts with the first sphere, "abstract right," which then transitions into "morality" before its transcendence into the sphere of "ethical life." Hegel again makes a sharp distinction between morality and ethics.[169] The latter concept integrates the abstract will of right and the subjective individualism of morality.[170] Beginning with the most abstract category of modern society, the "idea of right" (Recht), Hegel immanently unfolds from this starting point, which again returns in its final and most concrete iteration as actualised social freedom.[171] After the abstractness of abstract will, which is contained to the internal categories of personal property, contract and crime meet the "subjective individuality [*Einzelheit*]" of the sphere of morality. This sphere introduces the external aspects of moral responsibility, intention and duty, which mediate abstract right. According to Hegel, both moments are brought together in ethical life:

> the *unity* and *truth* of these two abstract moments—the thought Idea of the good realised in the internally *reflected will* and in the *external world*;—so that freedom, as the *substance*, exists no less as *actuality* and *necessity* than as *subjective will*;—the Idea in its universal existence [*Existenz*] in and for itself; [the sphere of] *ethical life* [*Sittlichkeit*].[172]

For Hegel, ethical life is the most concrete sphere of individuality and collectivity. Freedom and the human good are intertwined. Freedom cannot be understood as the absence of interference, nor absolute formal principles, but instead inaugurates its substantive meaning in the actualisation of the good of subjectivity through a political community and its objective institutions. This substantive good is considered teleologically in relation to a flourishing human life: "In so far as the determinations of happiness [*Glückseligkeit*] are present and given, they are not true determinations of freedom, which is not truly present for itself until it has adopted the good as an end in itself."[173] The task of human freedom is to not accept the status quo as happiness but to determine freedom in the fulfilment of the good life. In discussing happiness in such a way, Hegel makes good on Aristotle's idea *eudaimonia* as the telos of human life.[174] Hegel's concept of "the good" brings Aristotelian ethics to bear in his explicitly modern view of "*subjective freedom*, [which] is the pivotal and focal point in the difference between *antiquity* and the *modern age*."[175] The good life makes subjectivity possible by establishing that the particular goods of normative practices find their end in practical wisdom and the flourishing life of the human being. Aristotle argues that the virtues go beyond

> universals alone but must also be acquainted with the particulars: it is bound up with action, and action concerns the particulars ... As a result, one ought to have [knowledge of] both [universals and particulars], but more so of the latter. But here too there would be a certain architectonic [art or knowledge].[176]

Hegel follows Aristotle's reasoning in that ethical action requires a dialectic between the particular and universal. Despite this acceptance, Hegel moves explicitly away from Aristotle's distinction between production and activity.[177] For Hegel, action and production are part of spirit, which includes the determinations of labour and consciousness. Hegel reworks Aristotle's conception of political and ethical life *within* a modern conception of labour and political economy.[178] This reworking pushes against the limits of political economy and its foundations in methodological individualism and empiricism.

What is crucial for Hegel's idea of freedom is that ethical life is conceived in the political terms first set out by Aristotle. Hegel's telos of self-consciousness is collective and rational. To be at home in the world, as an individual and as a citizen, we require a political community of our own making. The good life is recognitive. "Ethical Life" is the culminating part 3 of the *Philosophy of Right*. According to its first paragraph:

> Ethical life is the *Idea of freedom* as the living good [*lebendige Gute*] which has its knowledge and volition in self-consciousness, and its actuality through self-conscious action. Similarly, it is in ethical being [*sittlichen Sein*] that self-consciousness has its motivating end and a foundation which has being in and for itself. Ethical life is accordingly the *concept of freedom which has become the existing* [*vorhandenen*] *world and the nature of self-consciousness*.[179]

By locating freedom in the living good, Hegel restores reason its legitimate place in the action of human beings. He points to an overcoming of the dichotomy between thought and being; thought can inform action and shape it towards a higher and developing truth. This "motivating end" echoes Aristotle, who writes in the *Nicomachean Ethics*, "thought by itself moves nothing; what moves us is goal-directed thought concerned with action."[180] Hegel comments, "Aristotle thus places virtue in knowledge, yet reason is not, as many believe, the principle of virtue purely in itself, for it is rather the rational impulse towards what is good; both desire and reason are thus necessary moments in virtue."[181] For "substance" to be borne out as "subject," Hegel is making explicit the way in which through rational agency we move towards the end of human flourishing.[182]

As Hegel sees it, Aristotle's notion of the cultivation of the virtues requires the activity of reasoning, practices that pertain to the end of a life well-lived. This reasoning necessitates that human beings act in accordance with the forms of activity which would cultivate a shared conception of the virtues. This activity is embodied in the life of the community. Moral decisions are oughts "in accordance with correct reasoning."[183] However, this ought is not derived from the supreme principle of practical reason as an abstract universal, but developed through the success and failure of the practices of the virtues embedded in social life. We act on reasons and decide what we ought to do as part of decision-making with others. The cultivation and process of acting in accordance with the good is the actualisation of potentials inherent in human rationality. The upshot of this conception of ethics is that it becomes possible to conceive of the living good in terms of the normative justifications of social rationality, eschewing both empty universalism and moral relativism by ordering the human good in normative practices and rational institutions.

After Aristotle and Hegel, it is not *any* community that allows rational practice, but the *free community*. The determinations of such a community require historical content, so we can be with Aristotle and Hegel *and* with Marx, by suggesting that community cannot be a state of domination. For Marx, it cannot be a state at all. However, the strain of ethical thought established in Aristotle and then Hegel and continued in Marx locates the potentiality of rational life in the socially determinate conditions of the political community. Rather than an ethical state, for Marx ethical life is conceived in the free association of social individuals.

Resulting from this shared tradition, ethical life is upheld as the concrete universal, a unification of the individual with society. This universal is mediated by the particular and individual in a process of increasing self-consciousness within the objective world. The whole can only be actually universal if the individual is free in every particularity. Hegel depicts this process as one of recognition. Starting with autonomy, the self seeks others, and in this unity, the individual is surpassed in their relations, now mediated, with others. Rather than individual difference at odds and in opposition with sociality, Hegel's concept of recognition ends with "release" (*Freigabe*), the opening and realisation of freedom. The individual is at home with the social world, which gives individuality its social shape.[184] Assimilating and surpassing the Kantian idea of reason as self-autonomy and self-legislation, Hegel manifests a richer sense of individuality in the universal forms of social life possible in intersubjective forms of recognition. Self-made institutions reconcile and harmonise the rift in modernity between the individual and the community. This act, the path of self-consciousness, is a historical task which develops immanently and teleologically:

> Here we can only point out that spirit begins from its own infinite possibility, but *only* from the possibility (which contains its absolute content implicitly). This is the purpose and the goal which it attains only as the end result, and which is only then its actuality.

Spirit comes to be from the contradictions, the urge striving for completion within its form. This immanent movement conceives of the development, the-coming-to-be, of a higher dialectical category within the existing form.

> In the same way, the possibility points (at least in thought) to that which is to become actual: more precisely the Aristotelian concept of potency [*dynamis*] is also *potentia* for it is force and power. Thus the imperfect, as its own opposite within itself, is the contradiction which certainly exists, but which is, by the same token, negated [*aufgehoben*] and resolved. This is the drive, the internal impulse of spiritual life, the drive to break through its own shell of naturalness, sensuality, and self-estrangement, in order to arrive at the light of consciousness, its own selfhood.[185]

The essential claim, for Hegel following Aristotle, that "*nous* rules the world" is that the struggle for self-consciousness to realise itself is the actualisation of a potentiality inherent in the shared ethical life of the modern world. There is a harmony of desires (individually and collectively mediated) with reason in the practices of the virtues, which allows desire to be rationally articulated. The relation between political and ethics is underpinned by a conception of the coming-to-be of the good life. Hegel brings Aristotle's teleological conception of the human good into the light of the modern world.

What is clear from Hegel's social thought is the impossibility of a rational life in a world in which "self-estrangement" predominates. With Hegel, the immanent critique of modern social relations from the standpoint of ethical life opens the possibility for a much deeper critique. This is the path Marx takes. Hegel is acutely aware that property relations configure modern life, and his critique of abstract right and morality gestures towards fundamental tensions resulting from private property relations and wage-labour. He highlights that the property relations of civil society tend to irrationality. Wealth is accumulated by a minority and poverty creates not only material destitution, but "moral degradation."[186]

In important ways, Hegel's attitude towards capitalism centres on his discussion of the "rabble." Hegel clearly sees that labour relations in civil society result in crisis and poverty: the creation of "a rabble" (*Pöbel*). However, the attempts to mitigate the effects of civil society in the *Philosophy of Right* are unconvincing. Although he mentions solutions, including welfare provision by the corporations and colonisation, they are obviously partial and temporary solutions.[187] His analysis is fleeting and pessimistic. Rebecca Comay is right to remark, "Hegel is not Marx. The rabble is not the proletariat."[188] However, the question Hegel raises with "the rabble" presents the necessary direction for any conception of ethical life along Hegelian lines.

Crucially, Hegel's desultory attempt to find a solution for the rabble, what he calls "the worm of civil society," is inadequate by the lights of his own idea of reason.[189] It is thus pertinent to mark this problem in the *Philosophy of Right* as provoking an evaluation of the normative demands of Hegelian critique. Frederick Neuhouser identifies this point as one "in which a contemporary critique of civil society might find a foothold in Hegel's account of what counts as a rational social order."[190] The pressing issue for contemporary Hegelians is whether this foothold leads to the institutions of a strengthened welfare state or to its negation and transcendence to a form of life beyond capitalism.[191] The stakes of advancing a rational critique of civil society are posed precisely by Hägglund: "The critical question is whether a capitalist society can avoid the production of a rabble and embody the commitment to the freedom of all in its institutional rationality. While Hegel's answer is yes, his own analysis of civil society confirms Marx's argument for why the answer is no."[192]

Without Marx, a Hegelian concept of rationality is bound to inadequately address this question. Modern civil society, as Marx demonstrates so vigorously in his value-form theory, cannot have a place within ethical life. The logic of civil society is one of misrecognition. In this sense, aspects of Hegel's painting of modern life need revising, for the specific reasons magnified in his own analysis. Hegel's pertinent insight that the organisation of the good life depends upon an elaborate "system of needs," in which human needs are met and "satisfied" in "the mutual condition" of recognition, cannot be met under the abstract social forms of value specific to capitalism. Hegel suggests, "[t]his universality, as the *quality of being recognised* is the moment which makes isolated and abstract needs, means and modes of satisfaction into *concrete*, i.e. *social* ones."[193] Freedom is realised in the living good of human flourishing, which demands human needs are organised systematically and rationally for that end. But as Marx points out, a society of commodity exchange is a system of capital. The social needs of human beings conflict with the compulsion of capital valorisation and accumulation. Hegel conceives of rational agency as the shapes of human freedom made possible by relations of recognition. Taking up Marx's account permits Hegel's profound observation to be redeemed and the forms of modern life assessed in terms of their concrete rationality. By assessing the normative aspect of Marx's analysis, it becomes evident that capitalism is a form of life based on *misrecognition*.

Conclusion

Hegel's often obscure writing has moments of brilliant clarity and poetic resonance. Two such moments reflect the need for reason in an account of ethical life. First, in the famous preface to the *Philosophy of Right*, Hegel claims the aim of philosophy is to "recognise reason as the rose in the cross of the present."[194] Modernity in its suffering is represented by the cross and reason as the rose that offers hope and solace in this suffering. The flourishing of reason can bring forward life from despair. In a less well-known passage, in his discussion of Heraclitus, Hegel describes universality as "the being of another for us." Reason is not the expression of individual knowledge, but a shared intersubjective relation. In this way, "[r]eason is this process with the objective: when we are not in connection with the whole, we only dream."[195] For Hegel, reason is mediated socially, its objectivity is realised through historical processes. Reason is not external to the world, but it develops its shape immanently from social life itself as the living good.

By reaching back to Aristotle's thinking about ethics as a relationship between the parts and the whole, Hegel theorises the immanent sociality of human action by investigating the relation between social forms of consciousness and their institutional form.[196] If philosophy must "reconcile thought or the concept with reality," then the reality of the present needs to be picked apart to equip rationally directed action.[197]

For Marx, reason has not only failed to be realised in the modern state, but this form is in itself a barrier to its actualisation. Marx is cognisant of the modernity of Hegel's thought, but becomes increasingly conscious that to make coherent an account of the modern world which retains from Aristotle and Hegel a vision of ethical life, a much deeper critique of social relations is necessary. In a letter to Arnold Ruge, he reflects:

> Reason has always existed, but not always in a rational form. Hence the critic can take his cue from every existing form of theoretical and practical consciousness and from this ideal and final goal implicit in the *actual* forms of existing reality he can deduce a true reality. Now as far as real life is concerned, it is precisely the *political* state which contains the postulates of reason in all its *modern* forms, even where it has not been the conscious repository of socialist requirements. But it does not stop there. It consistently assumes that reason has been realised and just as consistently it becomes embroiled at every point in a conflict between its ideal vocation and its actually existing premises.[198]

As the 1840s went on, Marx's attention was evermore directed towards developing a critique of political economy. As he surmised, the debates within German philosophy had now diminished and could not empower political critique. The promise of such an endeavour lay in the immanent investigation of the categories of political economy. Marx's theoretical engagement notes his increasing awareness of the theoretical stakes involved in such an inquiry. His realisation that the relation between individuality and sociality shapes the structure of economic thinking in a distorting way leads to his critique of the naturalisation of the individual in bourgeois political and economic thought, the shipwrecked Robinson Crusoe. This inquiry helps explain Marx's account of the inner workings of capitalist production and exchange, the metamorphosis of social forms, which subsume human activity through processes of accumulation including colonial expansion and the real subsumption of labour under capital. But under the guise of the atomised individual, an ideology arose which set sail in the theories of the social contract so foundational to the liberal tradition and the ontology of political economy. The tale of individual independence and isolation, Robinson Crusoe's adventure, continues in economic theory today.

FOUR

From Shipwreck to Commodity Exchange

Robinson Crusoe's Adventure Through Social and Political Thought

"DOES CRUSOE FINISH THE NOVEL a rich man or a very rich one?" *The Economist* asks in the article, "Why Economists Love 'Robinson Crusoe.'"[1] While a calculating logic seldom yields the most interesting literary insight, the analysis offered by *The Economist* counts the wealth of Robinson Crusoe for another reason. Like the earliest political economists, *The Economist* sees wealth as the truth of capitalist economics. Modern day prophets of the free market have always been fond of Robinson Crusoe stories.[2] Milton Friedman and Robert Nozick both refer to Daniel Defoe's character in hypothetical situations simulating the "ethics of distribution."[3] In their projections, the individual producer, alone on an island with only his property for company, is suddenly confronted by the knowledge of several other Robinsons. When beset with different islands, with different resources, owned by different Robinsons, the initial Robinson faces the dilemma of sharing. The question that concerns both Friedman and Nozick is the freedom of the individual.[4] They assume the first priority is to defend his interests against the coercion of others. For this paragon of atomist independence, the only objects within his moral world that bear any significance are those he possesses. Cooperation is a burden. Perhaps this is why, shortly after taking recourse to *Robinson Crusoe*, both Friedman and Nozick feel compelled to mention, if only to reject, Marx.⁵ In taking recourse to Robinson, his latter-day enthusiasts repeat a long-standing trope—one that Marx satirises in his critique of political economy.

The critique of political economy that Marx advances from the 1840s onwards is structured upon a core interpretive claim: in short, constrained by its own ideological limitations, political economy is unable to come to terms with the social form and dynamics of capitalism and produces a standpoint that naturalises social relations. The next two chapters detail the specific character of Marx's critique of political economy, from its first development in his 1844 writings to its mature expression in his later texts. This chapter traces the genealogy of the ontological individualism of political economy, which has its origins in the social contract tradition. If the free-market ideologues substitute a literary aesthetic for reality, by tracing the lineage of this aesthetic, the reality they occlude can be uncovered. I focus on a work of fiction, Defoe's *Robinson Crusoe*, as a way of illuminating, at its formation, the individualism of political economy. The novel serves as a moral justification for capitalism, which once examined, reveals the naturalisation of imperial expansion, profiteering and self-gain. The strong link Marx ties between *Robinson Crusoe* and political economy helps us to understand the character of his critique of the ontology of political economy and its theory of "natural man." More generally, Marx's ironic comments about *Robinson Crusoe* help elucidate the significance of his value-form theory. Even in island isolation, Robinson's account of his labour demonstrates that he not only depends upon modern tools, weapons and money, only available with capitalism, but also his actions are only intelligible with some notion of sociality at play, despite his efforts to eschew this company.

Marx's evocation of *Robinson Crusoe* stretches beyond the use of a well-known literary metaphor and pertains directly to the character of his immanent critique of modern society. In the 1840s—the major period of germination in Marx's writings—the authority of the English novel as an intellectual and aesthetic form dramatically increased.⁶ By calling on *Robinson Crusoe*, Marx is telling his readers, attentive to the high status of the novel as a cultural representation, that its fictions parallel the fictions of political economy. Literary or economic, thought represents a form of consciousness in social life. Immanent critique is the process in which the reality and the fiction of such representations can be assessed.

After an account of the primary narrative of the book, I chart the relation of *Robinson Crusoe* to social contract theory and the individualist standpoint common to Hobbes, Locke and Rousseau. Defoe gives in essential form the ideological expression of human nature readily adopted by political economy. I contrast this ontological individualism with Hegel's theory of recognition.[7] Hegel invokes the novel to illustrate the dialectic of mastery and servitude. While F. A. Hayek criticised his "hubris of collectivism," I show that Hegel establishes a rigorous concept of social interdependence, in which the individual is free in their relationship with others.[8] Next, I examine Marx's discussion of *Robinson Crusoe* in his critique of political economy. I demonstrate the importance of Marx's discussion of "original accumulation" in relation to *Robinson Crusoe*'s representation of colonial domination. Calling the mythmakers "Robinsonades," Marx produces his own highly distinctive interpretation of the novel. With a "socialist" Robinson, Marx theorises recognitive relations in the sociality of productive activity. I conclude with a discussion of Marx's immanent critique of the novel, which illuminates the truth of the story and helps articulate his concept of sociality and freedom.

Robinson Crusoe and Ideology

Robinson Crusoe is the story of an individual alone in a world that he fears as he attempts to survive by his intuition and resourcefulness. His successes are his own and his determination a model of innovation against adversity. Philosophers and economists find *Robinson Crusoe* to show a pristine example of how the individual would consider their isolation. Defoe's novel frequently appeared in nineteenth-century economic treatise and then became a standard feature of textbook treatments of the principles of supply and demand. Robinson Crusoe floats through the pages of modern economists as diverse as J. M. Keynes and Hal Varian.[9] Published in 1719, *Robinson Crusoe* is one of the earliest English language novels. It is a significant exemplar of the nascent novel form, initially the literary expression of bourgeois society.[10] The values of the emergent economic order set the scene for the book's popularity. In MacIntyre's words,

> *Robinson Crusoe* becomes the bible of a generation which includes both Rousseau and Adam Smith. The innovation of the novel, with its stress on individual experience and its value, is about to emerge as the dominant literary form. Social life becomes essentially an arena for the struggles and conflicts of individual wills.[11]

The birth of the novel marks an event for modern individualism. The novel recognised the individual as a distinct entity, uniquely expressing the emergence of the modern subject.[12] This subjectivity is characterised by the tension between moral internality and alienation. "The epic individual, the hero of the novel," as Georg Lukács notes, "is the product of estrangement from the outside world."[13] Its structure began to document, according to Terry Eagleton, the "individual psychology" of an "individual protagonist who moves through an unpredictably evolving, linear narrative."[14] This characteristic is evident in *Robinson Crusoe*, which "in the best Puritan tradition," is presented through the prism of a journal in which the protagonist painstakingly chronicles his life and adventures.[15] Famously, the novel centres on *his* island, where he is shipwrecked. Christopher Hill remarks that the theme of "traditional Protestantism is accompanied by prudential business morality."[16]

The adventure that motivates *Robinson Crusoe* is not just the determination of the individual subject, but also a portrayal of the cultural and ideological assumptions pertaining to the benefits of colonial expansion and imperialist domination. *Robinson Crusoe* epitomises the form of the novel as a way of telling the story of bourgeois ascendancy and the imperialist cultural values essential to this hegemony. It was one way, that "[s]lavery existed under the very eyes of eighteenth-century Englishmen," as Eric Williams suggests about material, rather than literary, culture.[17] The establishment of colonialism depended upon the construction of an ideology of slavery and domination from cultural products such as *Robinson Crusoe*.[18] "The novel," Edward Said observes,

> is inaugurated in England by *Robinson Crusoe*, a work whose protagonist is the founder of a new world, which he rules and reclaims for Christianity and England... Crusoe is explicitly enabled by an ideology of overseas expansion—directly connected in style and form to the narratives of sixteenth- and seventeen-century exploration voyages that laid the foundations of the great colonial empires.[19]

Defoe's novel is a founder of the "genre of adventure-imperialism" that comes to typify nineteenth-century realist novels.[20] Situating this lineage in the context of nineteenth-century intellectual cultural gives greater perspective to the readiness of *Robinson Crusoe* as a prominent representation that Marx could employ and upend.[21]

The novel follows Robinson's enterprising spirit. The chronicle begins in England before charting to unknown lands and after much ado, ultimately returning safely to the metropole. His narrative starts not with the shipwreck, but the calendar year of his birth, 1632.[22] From here, Robinson recalls his father's advice for "human happiness," a bourgeois "middle" station between the "labour and the suffering of the mechanic part of mankind" and the "pride, luxury, ambition and envy of the upper part of mankind."²³ Robinson's ambition escapes him, and against his father's wishes for him to pursue a career in law, he sets sail to chase fortune. Robinson's idea of enterprise is inextricable from colonialisation as an economic, political and cultural practice. He trades in new world plantations and slaves until his ship hits a storm. All aboard drown, save Robinson, who upon waking up on the shore, found "there should not be one soul sav'd but my self."²⁴ Robinson's first impulse is for survival, to get tools and instruments for his immediate existence. He is quick to declare the island barren and uninhabited and to focus his energies—his time and labour activity—to settlement of the island.²⁵ Finding himself in a place with "no society," Robinson plants crops,²⁶ raises cattle²⁷ and declares the island his own personal kingdom.²⁸ Robinson keeps a time-sheet account of each day's labour.²⁹ He captures a slave, who is given a name that denotes a day of the working week and the faith of His Lord.³⁰ Friday serves as an instrument of production for his master.

Robinson Crusoe is a transformative moment in the formation of the bourgeois imaginary, a mythological expression of an emergent social reality. The myth is the "natural man" who is divorced from society, alone in the world, but the basis of the world. The individual knows the world as *their world,* defined through and by their experiences, perspectives and actions. The world is the theatre in which the individual acts out their own singular narratives, confronting the world as an external entity, to be feared, manipulated, conquered and controlled. "Man" acts in this way because it is "natural" to do so, and this action is posited as instinctive and inescapable. "Natural man," once manufactured, is mythologised as ideology and then read back into history as an enduring truth. Defoe's novel is important, precisely because his picture captures a reality of human beings in the present. Hence, the truth of "natural man" is a *present truth,* and in this sense, the myth of "natural man" is a reality. The rise of individualism in the seventeenth century, as depicted in *Robinson Crusoe*, expresses real relations, real expressions of consciousness, embedded in an adventure fantasy. The picture presented by *Robinson Crusoe* is the simultaneous abstraction of myth and reality impelled by the logic of a fragmentary society. Its reality is the naturalisation of social relations defined by private property and the expansion of capitalism through conquest and empire.

The novel naturalises social relations by depicting labour processes in which the individual's productive activity—even when supposably abstracted from the social world—continues to be performed under the presupposition of empty homogenous time. Robinson's story is told through a linear and calendar time that imparts the temporal dimension of capital onto the desert island; the return to nature is given in an empty time and in empty space.³¹ Robinson's declaration of the island as his own assumes that non-European land is vacant and available for European occupation and control. His plunder, like the capitalist elsewhere, is justified through the sweat of his brow.

The myth of his isolation, however, masks the exchange relation which renders labour abstract. Defoe's story of how the lone individual rises from destitute survivor to thriving capitalist has been made idyllic in truncated children's editions and Hollywood films. Challenges to the cultural foundations of Defoe's tale of territorial possession and slavery, including in J. M. Coetzee's 1986 novel *Foe*, stress the colonial aspects of the novel.³² The imperialist drive to expand, to overcome every limit and barrier, is an essential component of capitalism's accumulative logic.

Robinsonades and the State of Nature

The vision of the modern world as formed by the rational considerations of atomised individuals finds its first political expression in the social contract tradition. Whatever variation in their ideas, the family resemblance in this tradition of theorising political right and natural law is their methodological atomism, in which the individual stands apart from, and prior to, society. The picture of the individual theorised by Hobbes, Locke and Rousseau becomes foundational. Offering wholesale opposition to Aristotelian conceptions of social ontology, Hobbes insists that individuals are fundamentally competitive, compelled by the fear and threat of death presented by others.³³ This idea of competition is passed into Locke's notion of labour and property. Rousseau's insistence that dependence limits freedom is defined by a similar individualism that underpins Hobbes and Locke.³⁴ Despite Rousseau's critique of civil society and private property, both Hegel and Marx are critical of his model of sociality. Rather, both see mutually dependent relationships as constitutive of social cooperation. *Robinson Crusoe* sits at the formation of the social contract tradition, not only sharing its presuppositions but advancing its central ontological premise. Robinson belongs as much on his island as in *Leviathan* and *Two Treatises on Government*, and as I will discuss, he already resides in *Émile*.

Defoe's narrative relies upon the notion of the individual that arises in early modern political thought. Like Hobbes, who constructs the state of nature as a negation of society (seen logically and not historically prior), Robinson's shipwreck is explicitly dramatised in the novel as a descent into the "State of Nature."³⁵ In Lawrence Krader's comparison:

The fable of the man-beast in isolation in the state of nature is a figment of the imagination of the same sort as Robinson. Both Hobbes, the author of the first fiction, and Defoe, the author of the second, anticipated the fable of the self-made man, the captain of industry who starts with nothing to become the hero in history.[36]

In Hobbes, the natural state of human beings is warlike. His natural human being is the individual, free and equal to others, but subservient to immediate base passions and driven by fear and competitive self-interest.[37] In turn, competition drives civil war and invasion: human beings invade for "Gain," "Safety" and "Reputation."[38] Hobbes writes,

> From this equality of ability ariseth equality of hope in the attaining of our Ends. And therefore if any two men desire the same thing, which nevertheless they cannot both enjoy, they become enemies; and in the way to their end (which is principally their own conservation, and sometimes their delectation only) endeavour to destroy or subdue one another. And from hence it comes to pass that where an Invader hath no more to fear than another man's single power, if one plant, sow, build, or possess a convenient Seat, others may probably be expected to come prepared with forces united to dispossess and deprive him, not only of the fruit of his labour, but also of his life or liberty. And the Invader again is in the like danger of another.[39]

Famously, Hobbes posits a state of inherent human conflict, where continuous fear dominates "the life of man, solitary, poor, nasty, brutish, and short."[40] Human beings meet each other not in cooperation but in competition, and this is the point of departure for thinking about human nature.[41] It is because "Gain," "Safety" and "Reputation" are in limited supply that human beings must compete, and that brings us into conflict. By finding these warlike motivations in the state of nature, Hobbes pens a fiction for the political present. As Giorgio Agamben notes, "the state of nature is a mythological projection into the past of civil war; conversely, civil war is a projection of the state of nature into the city."[42] If there are no norms in the state of nature, civil war becomes the norm in the modern world. In Hobbes's ontology, individuals are naturally independent and prior to society, defined by distrust and self-preservation.[43] Once formed by contract, social dependence is enforced by the sovereign.

Controversially, Hobbes's ontology denotes the "bourgeois" human being, a reflection of the early manifestations of market exchange and "possessive individualism."[44] According to Leo Strauss, Hobbes maintains that human beings "owe their good fortune exclusively to their own achievement and their own serious labour."[45]

The activity of labour makes it possible for individuals to gain reputation and assert values independent of nature. Hobbes links human labour to private property, noting "[t]he *Value,* or WORTH of a man, is of all other things, his price, that is to say, so much as would be given for the use of his power."[46] Marx highlights the role of labour in Hobbes's thought, pointing to this passage as a construal of value as the price of labour-power.[47] The war of all against all is not just physical but commercial. In this way, Smith understood the commercial motivation of the acquiring man: "Wealth, as Mr Hobbes says, is power."[48] For Hobbes, the individual's power comes internally from their labour.

Defoe's character shares the same inherent fear as Hobbes's natural man. He internalises war even when alone. After learning that he is not as isolated as he first thought, Robinson lives for a year and a half in constant fear of the neighbouring "savages."[49] Much of Robinson's character is prefigured in the atomism of Hobbes's ontology. However, Locke's additions to the concept of the state of nature, crucial to the foundation of liberal natural rights, are also carried into Defoe's construction. Locke inherits Hobbes's individualism but modifies in important ways the relationship between labour and private property.[50]

Whereas for Hobbes labour is a human activity that is sold for a price, Locke conceives of labour as the activity that bestows values on useful objects. For Locke, when human beings mix their labour with the natural world, it becomes their private property, since "[*a*]*s much Land* as a Man Tills, Plants, Improves, Cultivates, and can use the Product of, so much is his *Property*."[51] Once nature has been acted upon by human labour, value has been created, fusing the purposeful efforts of human beings with the natural environment. Useful labour produces exchange value, and by locating this idea of generation in the state of nature, Locke suggests this relation pertains across history. Locke naturalises both useful labour as the basis of value and private property. The state of nature is free since "he be the absolute lord of his own person and possessions, equal to the greatest and subject to no one." Not only the individual but the property owner also comes prior to the social order since the state acts to preserve the right to property. The function of society is fundamentally to uphold property. The individual only has an "interest" in society insofar as this aids the "mutual *Preservation* of their Lives, Liberties and Estates, which I call by the general Name, *Property*."[52] In this view, the state acts as a regulator and protector of property rights as bonds of trust.[53] The private property of individuals is prior to and constitutive of political rule.

This Lockean theme animates *Robinson Crusoe*, where the useful labour of the individual (or his slave) in the state of nature creates his property. At first, the protagonist's pride in the purposeful utility of his labour is not pride in the activity itself but in the creation of his own property. This logic encourages him to defend the island as "a right of possession" and to see that his hard work (felling trees, making boats, planting crops, herding, etc.) not just ensures his own survival but also his claim to property.[54] Since his labour has added value, in Locke's view, "improvement" has been made to the land.[55] By tying improvement of the land with value, in effect Locke's theory of property legitimised colonialism (especially in the New World) and capitalism in the metropole.[56] Just as with Locke's labouring individual, Robinson's property and colonial enterprise must be protected. As Ian Watt observes, Robinson "acts like a good Lockean—when others arrive on the island he forces them to accept his domination with written contracts acknowledging his absolute power (even when we have previously been told that he has run out of ink)."[57] In this way, Defoe explicitly adopts Locke's contract:

> My Island was now peopled, and I thought my self very rich in Subjects; and it was a merry Reflection which I frequently made, How like a King I look'd. First of all, the whole Country was my own meer Property; so that I had an undoubted Right of Dominion. *Secondly*, My People were perfectly subjected: I was absolute Lord and Law-giver; they all owed their Lives to me, and were ready to lay down their Lives, *if there had been Occasion of it*, for me.[58]

Once inhabited, Robinson's island could well be Locke's. Private property is directly connected with performed labour, and the individual is empirically shaped by this experience. Locke's explanation of private property as originating in the act of labour is an important moment in the development of the labour theory of value. According to Marx, "his philosophy served as the basis for all the ideas of the whole of subsequent English political economy."[59] Marx adds depth to this broader genealogy in the opening paragraphs of *Capital*. Marx starts with a double opening of the category of value: the most abstract category of modern wealth and the immediacy of the commodity. The commodity embodies value, the unity of use and exchange value. In defining this relation, Marx quotes Locke, "[t]he natural worth of anything consists in its fitness to supply the necessities, or serve the conveniences of human life," then comments:

> In English writers of the seventeenth century we still often find the word "worth" used for use-value and "value" for exchange-value. This is quite in accordance with the spirit of a language that likes to use a Teutonic word for the actual thing, and a Romance word for its reflection.[60]

What at first glance appears to be a simple remark about the etymology of economic terms, is better gleaned as highlighting the transitory nature of English political thought in this period. Marx sees the etymological difference as one way in which language reflects social categories. For the English writers, the identity of the words worth/use-value (Teutonic) and value/exchange-value (Romance) evidence the beginning of the abstraction of "value" over use-value.[61]

This conjuncture in English thought is where the modern understanding of labour value originates, to later assume more advanced iterations in classical political economy by Smith and Ricardo. In the observation that Locke understood the "natural worth" of a commodity in terms of use-values, Marx sets out a critique of this labour theory.[62] Commodities have use-values, irrespective of the amount of labour-time needed for their production. Marx's account of exchange value is not a naturalistic measure of amounts of concrete labour, but a theorisation of how value appears in exchange as "use-values for others, social use-values."[63] I differ from traditional interpretations that understand Marx as continuing a labour theory of the embodied kind articulated by Locke and the classical labour theory of value, rather than executing an immanent critique of the form of value specific to capital.[64] Marx analyses the distinctive way that value is produced and reproduced as a social relation.

Rousseau's critique of wealth inequality was revelatory, and Marx held it in high esteem.[65] Rousseau's understanding of "social relations" is specifically underpinned by a notion of labour as a social practice, where collective production is seen as both a product of industrial society and, within modernity, a necessity. As he writes in his educational treatise, *Émile*:

> The practice of the natural arts, for which a single man suffices, leads to the investigation of the arts of industry, which needs the conjunction of many hands. The former can be exercised by solitaries, by savages; but the others can be born only in society and make it necessary. So long as one knows only physical need, each man suffices unto himself. The introduction of the superfluous makes division and distribution of labour indispensable; although a man working alone earns only subsistence for one man, a hundred men working in harmony will earn enough to give subsistence to two hundred.[66]

This passage identifies the modern division of labour. Significantly, modern inequality has its basis in this division, interrupting the state of nature. To emphasise this point, Rousseau remarks "[w]hat important reflections on this point our Émile will draw from his *Robinson Crusoe*."⁶⁷ In Robinson's "natural man," Rousseau finds a fully formed ideological model of education, so much so that he recommends the book be interpreted practically. Defoe's novel instructs the (male) child to locate the problems of the modern division of labour in production. Rousseau posits that the individual producer is forced by industrial society to adopt collective labour processes and the separation of those processes by "division and distribution." Rousseau outlines a hierarchy of these divisions: the "first and most respectable" being "agriculture" and "ironworking in the second rank, woodworking in the third." He then asks what Émile might imagine, comparing this "subdivision" with *Robinson Crusoe*:

> What will he think on seeing that the arts [labour] are only perfected in being subdivided, in infinitely multiplying the instruments of all of them? He will say to himself, "All these people are stupidly ingenious. One would believe they are afraid that their arms and their fingers might be of some use, so many instruments do they invent to do without them. To practice a single art they are subjected to countless others. A city is needed for every worker."⁶⁸

The novel supplies educational value as an ideal picture of the state of nature. Rousseau contrasts the labour of industrial society, savage, dangerous and divided, with that of *Robinson Crusoe,* singular and authentic, where all labour processes are completed by the same instrument and individual. In presenting the novel as an ideological picture of natural man, Rousseau lays bare the disparity within the emergent social relations of industrial society.

However, Rousseau's social critique is undermined by his methodological individualism. Central to his claim is that dependence on others is a threat to the will of individuals, who he views from the standpoint of their isolation.⁶⁹ This position is evident in Rousseau's *Discourse on Inequality*, where "[t]he first man who, having enclosed a piece of ground, to whom it occurred to say *this is mine*, and found people sufficiently simple to believe him, was the true founder of civil society."⁷⁰ This quotation opens part 2 of the *Discourse*, which sets out his political account of inequality and socialisation to complement his narrative of the individual in the hypothetical state of nature in part 1. In part 2, Rousseau identifies the transition from "man's first sentiment" for his "preservation" to the love of the family and the formation of "nations," which he conceives as an early or pre-political "nascent Society," without laws or government but sharing a "kind of life" (a common region, language and customs).⁷¹ Inequality becomes an economic problem with the "great revolution" in metallurgy and agriculture, which not only expanded the population and forces of production with a modern division of labour, but also concentrated the means of production into private property creating a division between rich and poor. Thus, for Rousseau, inequality is not a product of nature but the effect of private property itself.[72] Rousseau's critique of private property supports his objection to the political domination of the powerful over the weak in the state.[73]

Rousseau's economic and political analysis is integrated within a broader social pathology which he calls *amour propre*, self-love.[74] His notion of *amour propre* expresses his concern for the individual's emotional life in modern society. *Amour propre* denotes the anxiety arising from the need for social standing, reputation and status; to feel acknowledged in the eyes of others.[75] Rousseau's position is that inequality is "born with society," and *amour propre* "inspires men with all the evils they do one another and is the genuine source of honour." *Amour propre* does not exist in the state of nature, where the individual "is the only being in the universe" which is able to give an account of "himself," "the only judge of his own merit."[76] Inequality, for Rousseau, is a historical problem that pertains to "the history of the social self."[77] Founded on private property, civil society is the source of the alienation, corruption and turmoil of industrial society. The presence of this socialisation, in contrast to the isolation of the state of nature, produces perpetual conflict and domination of the rich over the poor. Rousseau's analysis "Of the First Societies" in *The Social Contract* supports his earlier view of the integrity of the individual in the state of nature. Accordingly,

> it cannot be denied that Adam was Sovereign of the world as Robinson was of his island, as long as he was the sole inhabitant and what made this empire convenient was that the monarch, secure on his throne, had neither rebellions, nor wars, nor conspirators to fear.[78]

Rousseau is the first to see the fiction, however desirable for moral education, in Robinson's character.[79] Yet, his methodological insistence on independent individuals is a fundamental limit to his critique of the inequality of civil society and private property as the means of production.

Mastery and Servitude

Just as Marx's theoretical writings from the 1840s onwards are animated by his analysis of the naturalisation of capitalism in political economy, Hegel's *Realphilosophie* is conceived as a critique of the natural law tradition. In an early manuscript,

Hegel writes that "the spirit of the people [*Volk*]" is the movement of consciousness in which the individual comes "to itself in another" as a member of "an ethical essence"—the living good of "absolute ethical life [*absolute Sittlichkeit*]." In a note to this passage, he declares "no [social] contract, no tactic or stated or original contract; the single [person] gives up his freedom, [he surrenders] the whole of it rather, his singular freedom is only stubbornness, his death."[80] Hegel rejects the ontological foundation of the social contract and its implications for consciousness and the realisation of freedom. In his later lectures, in the same tone, he declares "[t]he term 'natural right' or 'natural law' ought to be abandoned." For Hegel, freedom cannot be found in "the soil of nature."[81] Instead of dividing nature and society, Hegel sets out to conceptualise freedom in the interdependent relations we have with others as self-conscious beings.

Hegel's concept of recognition presents an alternative to the individualism of the social contract tradition. However, Hegelian recognition should not be considered narrowly as merely a collectivist objection. Hegel considered "the principle of freedom," that is, knowledge directed at freedom, to have first been articulated in Rousseau's idea of individual will.[82] As he conceives it in the *Social Contract*, "[o]bedience to a law one has prescribed for oneself is freedom."[83] Hegel praises Rousseau's achievement in declaring individual autonomy to be self-legislating. However, he suggests that this notion must be expanded by grasping freedom as the *realisation* of social interdependence.[84] This idea of recognition is designed explicitly to incorporate Rousseau's idea of individual freedom, which Hegel takes to be lost as a consequence of the atomist character of the social contract model. Hegel characterises the contract as "the union of individuals [*der Einzelnen*] within the state."[85] In Hegel's alternative, recognition enables for both individual and social freedom to be articulated. Recognition is the condition of possibility for individuality itself to be fully developed.[86] Hegel goes beyond the paradigm of methodological atomism with the claim that social membership offers a positive sociality higher and irreducible to individuals, but still crucially preserving individuality.[87] Individual freedom is substantiated in and through relations of interdependence.[88] For Hegel, recognition is the form of sociality which realizes freedom in the concrete unity of individual and collective good.

According to the ontological individualism of the contractarians, the individual only enters or forms society once a compact has been made between an aggregate of individuals and the sovereign. This procedure abstracts individuals from the social settings that give individuality meaning. While this antinomy is methodologically essential for social contract theory, ontologically for Hegel, the individual is already social. An individual is only so by some relation to others. Hegel demonstrates that modern relations of individual personhood, properly conceived, necessitate a view of sociality in which the self and other are mutually dependent. Further, Hegel upholds the truth of the individual by showing through his dialectic of mastery and servitude that individual self-consciousness is measured against others as interdependence. The individual can only fulfill their freedom as social freedom, in which the subjective determinants of personhood are objectively substantiated and sustained by the sociality of its members.

Hegel's justification of this concept of sociality is provided in his dialectic of mastery and servitude. This dialectic plays an important part in the *Phenomenology of Spirit,* appearing as the transition from consciousness to self-consciousness. This knowledge is mediated by the self *through another*, reflecting the "*I* that is *we* and the *we* that is *I*."[89] Self-consciousness is the structure of agency in which the truth of the individual can only be sustained in another.

Hegel unfolds a concept of sociality, in which the distrust and fear of individuals proves inadequate as a means of grasping self-understanding. Hegel has Hobbes in mind in the first stage of this struggle, where a failure to gain respect between desiring individuals leads to war. The need for contract arises from the consciousness of this "undervaluing."[90] However, Hegel thinks this struggle must go beyond containment in a contract to a further contradiction. This moment is overcome when conflictual subjects come to see their own consciousness bound to the other. Their individuality is shown to be mutually dependent on their recognition as equals. The atomistic starting point of social contract theory proves to be impoverished since it lacks mediation with the other. Although the emergence of self-consciousness is put conceptually and not historically, Hegel understands this relation as manifest in the social world. He directly contrasts the "struggle for recognition" unfolded in this dialectic to "all *historical* views on the right of slavery and lordship, [which] depend on regarding the human being simply as a natural being."[91] Hegel *is* providing a historical account of freedom with his insistence that the relation to the self and the other is found in the historical shapes of consciousness.[92] However, this process is omitted by the atomism of social contract theory. Hegel elicits the dynamic in which the individual becomes *conscious* that their freedom is bound to another.

Recognition is actualised when self-consciousness exists "*in* and *for itself* while and as a result of its being in and for itself for an other; i.e., it is only as a recognised being."[93] When faced with another, consciousness finds itself in the other. First "it has lost itself, for it is to be found as an *other* essence. Second, it has thereby sublated that other, for it also does not see the other as the essence but rather sees *itself* in the *other*."[94] Recognition takes place mutually, as one recognises oneself, we at the same time recognise the other and the other in us. The relation between self and other, in which consciousness returns to itself and is superseded by a higher understanding of self, is played out in the dynamic between the master and the servant. This scenario is a "life and death struggle" since in the action "done *by the other,* each thus aims at the death of the other." Each side of the relation acts to subjugate the other and in risking their life, gain a truth of their own humanity—negating the early relation and rising to a higher truth.[95]

For Hegel, the risk of life allows for freedom since "it is solely by staking one's life that freedom is proven."[96] The master and servant begin in immediate opposition,

> because they are initially not the same and are opposed, and because their reflection into unity has not yet resulted, they are as two opposed shapes of consciousness. One is self-sufficient; for it, its essence is being-for-itself. The other is non-self-sufficient; for it, life, or being for an other, is the essence. The former is the *master* [*Herr*], the latter is the *servant* [*Knecht*].[97]

Each one-sided instantiation of the relation is dependent on the objectification of the servant to the desire and domination of the master. The master lives through the servant, mediating their own self through the thinghood of the servant, a negativity that subjects the other to their power. The master's "recognition comes about through another consciousness . . . for what the servant does is really the master's doing. The latter is only being-for-itself, the essence; he is the pure negative power for which the thing is nothing, and he is thus the pure essential doing in this relationship."[98] Mastery is the status of authority itself. By directing over "the space of reasons at work in a form of life," the master finds satisfaction in their desire and in doing so asserts that their will is supported by God, nature and reason itself.[99]

Looking for the most accessible way to elucidate this moment of the dialectic for the lectures he delivered to *Gymnasium* students, Hegel turned to *Robinson Crusoe*. In the section, "Relation between Master and Slave," he explains:

> This purely negative freedom, which consists in the abstraction from natural existence, does not, however, correspond to the concept of Freedom, for this latter is self-sameness in otherness, that is, in part the beholding of oneself in another self and in part freedom not *from* existence but *in* existence, a freedom which itself

has an existence. The one who serves lacks a self and has another self in place of his own; so that in the Master he has alienated and annulled himself as an individual Ego and now views another as his essential self. The Master, on the contrary, sees in the Servant the other Ego as annulled and his own individual will as preserved. (History of Robinson Crusoe and Friday [*Geschichte Robinsons und Freitags*].)[100]

Robinson's domination of his slave demonstrates the opposition between two self-consciousnesses. Defoe vividly describes Friday's servitude:

> His hair was long and black, not curl'd like wool; his forehead very high, and large, and a great vivacity and sparkling sharpness in his eyes. The colour of his skin was not quite black, but very tawny ... At last he lays his head flat upon the ground, close to my foot, and set my other foot upon his head, as he had done before; and after this, made all the signs to me of subjection, servitude and submission imaginable, to let me know how, he would serve me as long as he liv'd ... I made him know his name should be *Friday,* which was the day I sav'd his life; I call'd him so for the memory of the time; I likewise taught him to say *Master,* and then let him know that was to be my name.[101]

This submission occurs moments after Robinson steps in, guns blazing, to save Friday from a fate at the hands of cannibal "Savages" he notices arrive in canoes onto the island. Friday's submission is presented as if a contract, in which the protection Robinson can offer in the state of nature permits his authority. This representation serves to justify domination and mask the relations that constitute Friday's servitude.

Given the name of a day on an island without calendar-time, Friday is Robinson's slave. Friday functions as a "living labour machine [*lebendige Arbeitsmaschine*]" for Robinson, since his labouring activity is servile, not sold as "labour-power."[102] Instead, his activity is represented as if it were a gift, freely given to his master.[103] Friday is converted to the Protestant faith and work ethic, as Robinson wills it.[104] He is pleased that Friday "work'd very willingly, and very hard; but did it very cheerfully." As in Hegel's dialectic, Robinson increasingly sees himself in Friday. The slave becomes an expression of Robinson's egotistical self-love. He declares, "I believe he lov'd me more than it was possible for him ever to love any Thing before."[105] Robinson's understanding of Friday's love, who is supposed to find his own meaning in his subjection, holds to the logic of the master-servant relation. However, for Hegel, the negation of the thinghood of the servant in the struggle for recognition expresses the importance of social freedom for self-consciousness. What Hobbes took as natural existence, the moment of radical fear, Hegel shows to be a problem when human beings fail to recognise the sociality of human life.

The master-servant dialectic demonstrates the necessity of dependence. The life and death of conflicting consciousnesses is unfolded as a problem of acknowledging relations of interdependence. The labour of the servant is subjugated to the master's desire. His acknowledgement of the master's supremacy is in truth disregarded by the master since he knows his power over the servant.[106] Further, the master fails to recognise his real dependence on the servant since he refuses to recognise him as an equal being. Labour activity mediates this conflict and defines the relationship of servitude and domination. Hegel writes, "through work [*Arbeit*], this servile consciousness comes round to itself."[107] Labour is the "formative activity" which mediates and shapes the thing by its negativity, so that "the working consciousness comes to an intuition of self-sufficient being *as its own self*."[108] The significance of the dialectic comes in this disruptive moment. Through this subjected labour, the servant, made to create for their master, whose existence is predicated by their activity, becomes aware that their being-for-themselves exists not in the master but in their own life. This mediated relation defines the struggle for recognition. Through this conflict, the servant "comes to acquire through himself a *mind of his own*, and he does this precisely in the work in which there had seemed to be only some *outsider*'s *mind*."[109] This process of consciousness through the mediation of labour is transformative for the freedom of the servant. Once the servant comes into conscious recognition of their own self, at the same time, it means the death of the servile relation. Hegel grasps this as the moment of truth. In this relation, the other comes to be a self-determining end in themselves as they overcome the objectification and thinghood of servitude. This dialectic holds that dependency is built into the structure of human self-consciousness. Without recognising the other, the master debases themself. At the heart of the struggle for self-consciousnesses is the denial of dependence on another. Recognition shows that dependence is always at stake in human freedom and articulates the way in which labouring activity mediates and shapes domination and servitude.

Manifest in the historical world, the struggle for recognition substantiates the subjective action of human beings in the objective structure of the social order.[110] Recognition is the activity in which the individual's desires and wants are positively actualised as social freedom. For the social world to be free, its freedom is conditional upon the realisation of what Hegel calls the individual's "*inner* universality [*innere Allgemeinheit*]."[111] For the individual to be free, they must "belong" to a social order.[112] This idea of sociality entails that a political community needs to institutionalise relations of interdependence so that the recognised individual acts both for their good as a person with individuality and at the same time to "actively pursue" the good of the universal as their "*ultimate end.*"[113] Ethical actuality is located in the universality that only a mutually recognised rationality can constitute, in which the individual identifies their freedom with the freedom of the social world. This conception of freedom understands that the individual is a condition of the intelligibility of modernity, but the possibility of modern freedom requires that individuals recognise their essential dependence on the other. This idea of social interdependence is how Hegel's claim that "*Self-consciousness attains its satisfaction only in another self-consciousness*" should be understood.[114] Self-consciousness can only be satisfied when the opposition between self and other is transcended in a form of life. The demand of Hegel's dialectic of recognition is that freedom cannot be held or exercised by some at the expense of others, but self-consciousness requires universal freedom.[115] Although Hegel calls attention to historical manifestations and representations of the struggle for recognition (most clearly by drawing on *Robinson Crusoe*), the dialectic of mastery and servitude is not a literal representation.[116]

Recognition and Capital

The theme of recognition is carried into Marx's value-form theory. C.L.R. James maintains that Marx redeems Hegel's dialectic of mastery and servitude, and it is "one of the most powerful themes in *Das Kapital.*"[117] Although often seen in relation to the *Economic and Philosophical Manuscripts of 1844*,[118] I focus on the way Hegel's account of domination bears upon Marx's theorisation of capitalist social relations in the *Grundrisse* and *Capital*. His conception of the coming-to-be of capital develops the structure of recognition to incorporate the abstract dependence of value. Marx locates the dialectic of servitude in the relation between human activity and capital. As value-in-process, capital is dead labour, objectified living activity which has become the property of another. As the self-positing of dead labour, capital alienates subjective living labour. Here

> living labour appears as a mere means to realise objectified, dead labour, to penetrate it with an animating soul while losing its own soul to it—and having produced, as the end-product, alien wealth on one side and [, on the other,] the penury which is living labour capacity's sole possession.[119]

Marx illuminates the process in which the objectivity of living labour "in and by itself" becomes alienated "as the mode of existence of an alien person" and posits an "isolated and subjective labour capacity, wealth of and for the capitalist." In this way, productive activity becomes alien to itself, and the products of labour appear as a "combination of alien material, alien instrument and alien labour—as alien property." Production, in turn, becomes "poorer by the life forces expended, but otherwise begins the drudgery anew, existing as a mere subjective labour capacity separated from the conditions of its life."[120] The domination of capital *reconfigures* the dialectic of servitude between master and servant into the relation of formative activity between those who buy and those who sell their human activity as use for another. Concrete relations are rendered impersonal. Dependence is decisively abstract since capital spreads across the world and imposes the logic of commodity exchange upon every relationship, however indirectly.

Considering Marx's analysis in this way shows the politics of formal equality to be empty since this social relation mediates the abstract domination of commodity production and exchange. The self-relation of the individual is a form of *misrecognition*. The worker and the capitalist meet each other in the market as unequal, yet consciousness of this relation is obscured.[121] Capital and value are objectified forms mediated by alienated productive and circulative processes in which living activity is drained of its animating features and deadened. Domination is now abstract. Marx's analysis holds that basic conditions of human activity are determined by this relation. The necessity of recognition features explicitly, as the knowledge that value is realised "forcibly" as domination. Consciousness (*Bewusstsein*) of the process of capital production allows for *"the knell to its doom"* since like the struggle for recognition with the slave, the worker becomes self-conscious that their activity *"cannot be the property of another."*[122] This discussion helps reinforce the vital point for Marx, amplifying Hegel, to locate the overcoming of capital in the self-conscious activity that is given shape by the social form of labour. The immanent negativity of the worker threatens capital existentially. But the importance of this dialectic marks a larger thematic shift in political thought, one in which Marx follows Hegel. This is the shift from contract to recognition.

Marx's discussion of "primitive" or "original accumulation" (*ursprünglich Akkumulation*) unifies the Robinsonade theme of the individual producer with the creation of the wage-labourer through the development of capitalism, its colonial expansion and its specific relations of production and ownership. The individual producer is born not of natural accident but by a process of force and dispossession.

Original accumulation is the precondition for capital, the "historical movement" of capitalist development which separated precapitalist producers from their land and means of production, transforming them into wage-labourers and their land and means of production into capital.¹²³ Legal equality liberates the producer previously bound as a "mere appendage of the soil (in the form of bondsmen, serfs, slaves, etc.)" and at the same time involves "the expropriation of the mass of the people from the land."¹²⁴ This process involved the clearing and "forced expropriation" of vast amounts of common land in Europe, the enslavement of the Americas and Africa and colonialism in India, China and elsewhere.¹²⁵ Slavery and state coercion are different "moments" of primitive accumulation, where violence is essential to the emergence, domination and enforcement of the form of labour characteristic of capitalism.¹²⁶ In Marx's distinctive formulation, "the veiled slavery of the wage-labourers in Europe needed the unqualified slavery of the New World as its pedestal." Quoting Virgil, he notes ironically

> *Tantae molis eratt* to unleash the "eternal natural laws" of the capitalist mode of production, to complete the process of separation between the workers and the conditions of their labour, to transform, at one pole, the social means of production and subsistence into capital, and at the opposite pole, the mass of the population into wage-labourers, into the free "labouring poor," that artificial product [*Kunstprodukt*] of modern history [*Geschichte*]. If money, according to Augier, "comes into the world with natural [*natürlichen*] blood-stains on one cheek," capital comes dripping from head to toe, from every pore, with blood and dirt.¹²⁷

The existence of capitalism is as "natural" as the processes that force it into being. Specifically, the creation of private property and individualised labour through original accumulation was the "antithesis to social collective property." Private property is the corresponding form of ownership to the newly created wage-labourer who gains their "free individuality" through a fragmented production process, in which the free labourer sets "in motion himself" the conditions of labour. Marx points to how the concentration of private means of production is at the expense of cooperation, predicated on fragmented processes of production and the "social control and regulation of the forces of nature."¹²⁸

As a "new form" of production, capitalism is constituted by the abstract sociality of the individualised worker. Labour processes are socially dependent but performed as isolated and independent labour acts, contingent on the division of labour and the quantifiable measurement of labour activity in time as socially necessary abstract labour.[129] Labour-power is abstractly socialised as capital centralises and competes, accumulates and circulates as value. Marx theorises capitalist development as an uneven process of expansion, which depends upon colonialism. In the opposition between the "capitalist regime" and the colonial subject, there is a "struggle" between "two diametrically opposed economic systems." In a phrase reminiscent of the master-servant dialectic, Marx insists "the truth [*Wahrheit*] about capitalist relations in the mother country" is to be found "*in* the colonies."[130] The colonisers expand capital but are unwilling to recognise the racialised other this expansion is dependent upon. The truth of domination can only be understood by an investigation of the corresponding, historically specific social relations. Original accumulation forces the "freedom" of the wage-labourer by direct domination. Marx identifies the brutal role of slavery and violence in the creation of modern social relations and helps draw out the significance of the form of labour characterised in *Robinson Crusoe*.

In Robinson's settling of the island, replete with sourcing his own slave labour, the colonialist foundation of early capitalist expansion, an aspect of the larger process of "primitive" accumulation is given in pure form. Robinson, the individual, acts out each part of the process, turning an "uninhabited" island into a model of European settlement, where he owns the land and subjects the labour of others to his rule as forced dependants. By reducing externality to property, bourgeois social relations implicitly regard the precapitalist other in servitude, until such a time as they assert their own right.[131]

An important point about ownership arises from this discussion. Marx dispels the belief that the labour performed by the individual justifies private property.[132] Capitalist social relations depend upon the exploitation of labour-power as a commodity. This form of private property can only be constituted by the extraction of surplus value, the specific form of wealth under capitalism. Marx's notion of original accumulation traces this emergence historically. In doing so he is responding to a fundamental problem in political and economic thought since Locke: how is it that private property is justified? With Locke in mind, Marx delineates the contrasting claims:

> Originally the rights of property seemed to us to be grounded in a man's own labour. Some such assumption was at least necessary, since only commodity-owners with equal rights confronted each other, and the sole means of appropriating the commodities of others was the alienation of a man's own commodities, commodities which, however, could only be produced by labour. Now, however, property turns

out to be the right, on the part of the capitalist, to appropriate the unpaid labour of others or its product, and the impossibility, on the part of the worker, of appropriating his own product. The separation of property from labour thus becomes the necessary consequence of a law that apparently originated in their identity.[133]

What emerges clearly from this analysis is that the basic assumptions of capitalist property rights conceal not only its historical emergence, but the relations that comprise its essential dynamic. For Locke, value arises from the individual labouring acts that create private property. But as Marx points out, value can only be created by a general form of property that privatises the energy of human beings and separates the activity of labour from its products by extracting surplus value from those activities and offering the products for sale as commodities.

If *Robinson Crusoe* is interpreted as an ideological expression of the naturalisation of modern social relations, then the explicit origins and foundation of these relations as *historically specific forms of domination* is illuminated. What Marx makes explicit is that the "positing of the individual as a worker, in this nakedness, is itself a product of history [*ist selbst historisches Product*]."[134]

The problem both Hegel and Marx sought to overcome was the atomism presupposed by the social contract tradition. The answer, conceived in mutually inclusive ways, is an idea of sociality in which human activity and consciousness is intelligible as a product of history. For both thinkers, the actually free social order is composed of rational institutions which enable individuals to be recognised socially. Marx claims that such development must involve the freedom of the "entire social body," where human activity is rationality decided by "social individuals."[135]

Marx and the Robinsonades

Marx's interpretation of *Robinson Crusoe* has generally received little serious attention.[136] Many commentators have left their analysis to a simple remark on the employment of the literary metaphor and then proceed directly into an analysis of Marx's texts.[137] Even the most rigorous chronicler of his literary references, S. S. Prawer, fails to note the import of *the novel*: "What Marx really attacks . . . is not *Robinson Crusoe* itself but the illusions fostered in certain readers by lesser imitations, or by unperceptive and prejudiced reading, or by wishful thinking. He is attacking the *myth* of *Robinson Crusoe*, not the book itself."[138] But this view glosses over *Robinson Crusoe* as an expression of a symptomatic theoretical standpoint and in doing so, undercuts the weight of the metaphor. Considering Marx to be responsive *only* to the myth, and not the text itself, risks understating the representative role of the novel. *Robinson Crusoe* transmitted, by way of popular narrative, the conception of the state of nature and the solitary individual in modern thought. *Robinson Crusoe* is itself an expression of an emergent myth with an emergent logic. This insight is noted by Theodor W. Adorno and Max Horkheimer, who locate the significance of the narrative of the "solo manufacturer" in "bourgeois thinking." Robinson's "weakness"—the individual's separation from the collective—is his "social strength." Like Odysseus, Robinson is given up to the cruel fate of the sea. Once confined to his island, "helplessly isolated," he is forced "recklessly to pursue an atomistic interest" according to the "principle of capitalist economy."[139] Adorno and Horkheimer point to the infusion of the myth into bourgeois consciousness. This consciousness has deep roots, naturalising the interests of the individual. As Alfred Sohn-Rethel observes, commodity exchange necessitates "exclusive property" which promises that "[e]verybody could own the world as Robinson Crusoe does his island. We therefore state: that which constitutes the form of exchangeability of commodities is the singleness of their existence."[140]

Marx's repeated use of *Robinson Crusoe* in his drafting of *Capital* as a *critique of political economy* enmeshes his criticism of the standpoint of economic thinking with the individual postulates of bourgeois economics.[141] Marx exposes both the inner workings of political economy and the limitations and barriers of this standpoint. A central feature of his critique of economic thought identifies the ideological presuppositions embedded in an ahistorical notion of human nature.

Marx's *The Poverty of Philosophy* (1847) polemicises against Pierre-Joseph Proudhon's attempt to bring Ricardo into socialist theory wholesale, which results in an "ideological economics."[142] By starting with the "single individual" producer, Marx charges Proudhon with reproducing the ontological presuppositions of political economy. Canvassing *Robinson Crusoe* from the history of social and political thought, Marx writes: "M. Proudhon's supposition, have got no farther than the solitary and hardly social position of the Robinsons."[143] His point is that any theory which posits the pregiven individual outside the context of historical relations of dependence, even if socialist, falls victim to misconstruing capitalist social relations.

Robinson Crusoe is invoked again, a decade later in the 1857/8 *Grundrisse* notebooks, but with added importance. The introduction begins with the category of production; in a lengthy passage, Marx writes:

Individuals producing in society—hence socially determined individual production [*gesellschaftlich bestimmte Production der Individuen*]—is, of course, the point of departure. The individual and isolated hunter and fisherman, with whom Smith and Ricardo begin, belongs among the unimaginative conceits of the eighteenth-century Robinsonades, which in no way express merely a reaction against oversophistication and a return to a misunderstood natural life, as cultural historians imagine. As little as Rousseau's *contrat social*, which brings naturally independent, autonomous subjects into relation and connection by contract, rests on such naturalism. This is the semblance, the merely aesthetic semblance, of the Robinsonades, great and small. It is, rather, the anticipation of "civil society," in preparation since the sixteenth century and making giant strides towards maturity in the eighteenth. In this society of free competition, the individual appears detached from the natural bonds etc. which in earlier historical periods make him the accessory of a definite and limited human conglomerate. Smith and Ricardo still stand with both feet on the shoulders of the eighteenth-century prophets, in whose imaginations this eighteenth-century individual—the product on one side of the dissolution of the feudal forms of society, on the other side of the new forces of production developed since the sixteenth century—appears as an ideal, whose existence they project into the past. Not as a historic result but as history's point of departure. As the Natural Individual [*Naturgemässe Individuum*] appropriate to their notion of human nature [*menschlichen Natur*], not arising historically, but posited by nature. This illusion [*Täuschung*] has been common to each new epoch to this day.[144]

This passage contains a penetrating, if schematic, characterisation of the ontological individualism in political economy. Capitalist production is individualised, but not in the way that political economy presupposes. Production occurs within society, so "the individual and isolated hunter and fisherman" exemplified in *Robinson Crusoe* is the bourgeois individual projected by political economy back onto the past as nature. Rather than seeing production as a collective enterprise, free competition and capitalist social relations are read back onto history, packaging it anew for ideological purposes. The bonds of society are repealed and made digestible for political economy, the individual becomes detached from their social ties and reduced to "unimaginative" types. The individual now appears in "dot-like isolation [*Punktualität*]."[145]

The adoption of the Robinson story *unimaginatively* becomes the "Robinsonade" ideology advanced by the "prophets" of early bourgeois thought.[146] Marx directly references Rousseau, but, as I have outlined, the prophets in the tradition that precedes him also include Hobbes and Locke.[147] Marx, along with Hegel, finds that

Rousseau's model of social interaction is too limited to explain the historicity of human sociality. Rousseau conceives the social contract as the association between equal citizens which entitles freedom as self-autonomy and the common good.[148] However, Rousseau cannot overcome the dualism between individual and collective since he understands society as a union of individuals "forced to live together" rather than the actualisation of social individuality.[149]

Political economy takes its ideological presuppositions from the social contract tradition, and while it advances an understanding of social relations by investigating economic categories systematically, political economy takes too much from the conception of human nature found in bourgeois political thought.[150] Marx makes clear that the "Robinsonade" of bourgeois thought has a historical basis beyond the literary metaphor. To this effect, the "cultural historians," which Marx refers to in the above quotation, fail to note the full implications of *Robinson Crusoe* as a reflection of historically specific relations.

Further, Marx points to an internal contradiction in this conception of universal self-interest. If each individual is said to pursue their own private interest, this must hold universally: each person must serve "the private interests of all, the general interest, without willing or knowing it." This concept is necessarily abstract since it means that either there is a "totality of private interests" or that each individual acts to hinder the interest of others, and "instead of a general affirmation, this war of all against all produces a general negation." With this explicit reference to Hobbes, Marx points to the abstract negation made by the social contract tradition, especially in the attempt to define the concept of individuality simply in opposition to the unthought concept of sociality. The social contract theorists suggest mutually contradictory ontologies: one of shared private interest or self-interested hostility. Marx attempts to dissolve this antinomy:

> The point is rather that private interest is itself already a socially determined interest, which can be achieved only within the conditions laid down by society and with the means provided by society; hence it is bound to the reproduction of these conditions and means. It is the interest of private persons; but its content, as well as the form and means of its realisation, is given by social conditions independent of all.[151]

The response is not only to Hobbes, but also to Smith, since mutual self-interest is what drives the "invisible hand" of the market. Despite Smith's disagreement with

Hobbes, as Marx sees it, there is a parallel logic of economic self-interest.[152] Marx rejects the idealised and abstract notion of human nature carried in individualism and offers a concrete, historical and socially informed ontology.

The "Socialist" Robinson

Capital magnifies the ideological status that Marx's earlier reflections afford to *Robinson Crusoe*. However, through an immanent critique, Marx points to a "socialised Robinson." This approach adds to Marx's critical deployment of the novel, which acts to show the truth in Robinson's untruth. The novel features prominently in the pivotal opening chapter of volume 1 and the subsection, "The Fetishism of the Commodity and Its Secret."[153] The Fetishism section contains a condensed but lucid elaboration of the manner in which the relations between people are distorted into the "fantastic form of relations between things [*die phantasmagorische Form eines Verhältnisses von Dingen annimmt*]."[154] This takes place in the process of production for exchange, where articles of human use become profitable commodities, which in turn mediate human relationships. Marx suggests that money, in the "world of commodities" is the "finished form" of value, which "conceals the social character of private labour and the social relations between the individual workers, by making those relations appear as relations between material objects, instead of revealing them plainly."[155] Money establishes the socially objective measure for abstract labour and the token of social power.

The role of money in Defoe's novel is significant in this respect. The social importance of the money-form is expressed dramatically when Robinson scavenges through the shipwreck and comes across, "thirty six Pounds value in money, some *European* coin, some *Brazil*, some Pieces of Eight, some gold, some silver." His response demonstrates the novel's unity of myth and reality:

> I smil'd to my self at the sight of this money, O drug! said I aloud, what art thou good for? Thou art not worth to me, no not the taking off of the ground, one of those knives is worth all this heap, I have no manner of use for thee, e'en remain where thou art, and go to the bottom as a creature whose life is not worth saving. However, upon second thoughts, I took it away, and wrapping all this in a piece of canvass, I began to think of making another raft, but while I was preparing this, I found the sky over-cast, and the wind began to rise, and in a quarter of an hour it blew a fresh gale from the shore"[156]

Robinson's delight in finding money appears at first sight bizarre. Robinson sees "no manner of use" but cannot bear to let it sink to the bottom. He later reflects on the money as "nasty sorry useless stuff" and longs to trade it for some seeds or ink since the coins had "no manner of value to me, because of no use."[157] When ink serves him a real purpose on the island (to record his narrative), the money can be nothing other than a revelation of Robinson's capitalist presuppositions. On an island without a use for money, he chooses to hoard it; however, without commodity exchange, Robinson's money represents nothing. It has no *value*. In capitalist production, money is the necessary measure of abstract labour and the form in which products of labour are equated.[158] On the island, he can only measure his concrete labour against the sun. But despite his aspirations to labour under the laws of modern economics, his labour cannot produce value since his concrete efforts are not performed within the abstract social forms of commodity exchange. Robinson's useful objects are only goods for himself, they are not commodities that express their value through money. Regardless of its physical properties and the effort he goes to retrieve it, his money has no social weight without commodity exchange.

To the reader of the novel, the reality is that the money, island or not, still holds *social* significance. The retained money supplies Robinson with capital once he leaves the island, confirming the money's use. Adorno and Horkheimer suggest the furthering of the "new enterprise is evidence for the contention that the entrepreneur has always gone about his competitive business with more initial capital than his mere physical capacity." Even Robinson's miraculous labour efforts are of little import when compared to the socially recognised treasures retrieved from the shipwreck. Adorno and Horkheimer connect this ideology with political economy's concept of risk, in which "the possibilities for failure becomes the postulate of a moral excuse for profit." Robinson's "strange and surprising adventures" only make sense from the "standpoint of developed exchange and its individuals." Robinson's alienation, his isolation and disassociation, can only be comprehended from the perspective of the bourgeois social world. Robinson "produces" his own totality, which he realises "only in complete alienation from all other men" and meets the world seeing human beings "only in an alienated form – as enemies or points of support, but always as tools, and as things."[159] The individual is self-created, producing his world instrumentally and apart from society. Even alone on his island, Robinson cannot but think in terms conditioned by modern social relations and bourgeois presuppositions.

The "natural man" of the myth presents the distorted concept of society operative in bourgeois ideology. Relations are only reflected through the individual's own preservation, industry and utility. The moral justification offered by the novel serves as a bulwark for capitalist expansion. Marx's discussion of Robinson expresses the manner in which bourgeois ideology is individualist; promoting the isolated producer as a human ideal and masking the manner in which capitalist production *is* social, the generalised relation between people as mediated by things. This makes social production necessarily abstract and misrecognised. On his island, Robinson expresses both moments, promoting the former as a virtue of humanity and presupposing the latter.

However, in Marx's view, the categories delineated by bourgeois economics fail to grasp the historically specific relationship between "private labour and the collective labour of society" which conditions the social form of commodity-producing labour (including the duality of concrete and abstract labour).[160] With *Robinson Crusoe*, Marx wants to show how the classical labour theory of value fails to adequately conceptualise value. Marx sets up the problem:

> As political economists are fond of Robinson Crusoe stories, let us first look at Robinson on his island. Undemanding though he is by nature, he still has needs to satisfy, and must therefore perform useful labours of various kinds: he must make tools, knock together furniture, tame llamas, fish, hunt and so on. Of his prayers and the like, we take no account here, since our friend takes pleasure in them and sees them as recreation. Despite the diversity of his productive functions, he knows that they are only different forms of activity of one and the same Robinson, hence only different modes of human labour. Necessity itself compels him to divide his time with precision between his different functions. Whether one function occupies a greater space in his total activity than another depends on the magnitude of the difficulties to be overcome in attaining the useful effect aimed at. Our friend Robinson Crusoe learns this by experience, and having saved a watch, ledger, ink and pen from the shipwreck, he soon begins, like a good Englishman, to keep a set of books. His stock-book contains a catalogue of the useful objects he possesses, of the various operations necessary for their production, and finally of the labour-time that specific quantities of these products have on average cost him. All the relations between Robinson and these objects that form his self-created wealth are here so simple and transparent that even Mr Sedley Taylor could understand them. And yet those relations contain all the essential determinations of value [*Bestimmungen des Werths*].[161]

In identifying the determinations of value readily apparent in Robinson's account of labour-time, Marx suggests that political economy is fundamentally constrained by its individualist standpoint. Even if its practitioners adopt the myth, political economy is unable to grasp from this simple relation the form of value. Robinson's labour helps clarify a key aspect of Marx's value-form theory, the relation between concrete and abstract labour.

Robinson's labour is concrete in the simplest way. To survive, he must produce his own tools, fish and hunt for his own livelihood. Before he enslaves Friday, there is no division of labour since he produces each and every object. He creates useful products, but as Marx points out, Robinson brings with him the accounting methods of modern British industry. This act is reminiscent of Weber's discussion of the bookkeeping as the decisive "calculation" of capital, where the recording of money inputs, outputs, controls and balances leads to a "final balance sheet." Bookkeeping rationalises "the capitalist enterprise" on mathematical and quantifiable lines.[162]

Robinson rescues the instruments necessary to record the production and consumption of his labour *as if* producing commodities with exchange-values. But "[n]o producer considered in isolation produces a value or commodity."[163] Further, as Marx notes about bookkeeping, which requires both labour-time and the instruments of labour (ink, paper etc.), "[t]he movement of production, and particularly of valorization—in which commodities figure only as bearers of value, as the names of things whose ideal value-existence is set down in money of account—thus receives a symbolic reflection in the imagination."[164]

Even without commodity exchange, Robinson wants to stamp the products of his labour with the abstract categories of value. Although he can simply use what his work yields, he thinks he has created value in the capitalist sense. He does not just rely on his store of tools to survive; he implements an ideology of value-producing labour specific to capitalism. However, since he cannot actually trade the products of his labour, even if he measures and considers his labour abstractly in empty time, his labour is concrete and cannot create value in its historically specific meaning under capitalism. He can only produce value in Locke's ahistorical sense. Robinson does not make commodities, and so labour cannot take the socially specific form of abstract labour—the substance of value—which necessitates the sale of labour-power as a commodity. This sale is itself conditional on its place within the dominance of commodity exchange as the form of wealth "in which the capitalist mode of production prevails."[165]

Marx's critique of the labour theory of value holds that value is not created in production alone, but instead by the unity of production and exchange. For products of labour to become values, privately performed labour must become the historically specific social form which equalises labouring acts abstractly through the exchange of equivalents. Value is not the amount of time embodied in a commodity for its production, but the generalised social form of commodity-producing labour. Value is comprehensible as money, the measure of abstract labour socially validated through exchange. This social form expresses that private labour only becomes value after it is sold. If the creation of value necessitates private production and exchange, no matter how Robinson chronicles his time and hoards money, neither bind his activity to creating the capitalist form of wealth. Ironically, with both his time and money, the exchange principle that would give Robinson's labour value is only posited. Despite his island labour not taking the form of wage-labour and his coins not taking the form of capital, Robinson's assumptions are squarely "in line with the dominant mode of production," and in effect his labour which has "not been subsumed [*subsumirten*] by capitalism in reality are so in thought [*idealiter subsumirt*]."[166] The absence of commodity exchange on his island means not only is his production only for use, but the homogeneous empty time which rationalises his production is meaningless.

Marx highlights that without commodity exchange and the division of labour of modern industry, the products of Robinson's labour are directly apparent. How much time Robinson expends on each individual task is decided on the basis of the good of each accordingly. Marx's immanent critique of the novel makes it possible for him to appreciate this insight while pointing out the ideological rationalisation of Robinson's account-like attitude to his labour-time.[167] Marx finds fault in Robinson's view of the simple givenness of his activity which apprehends his world empirically, marked by the shopkeeper mentality of the early British ideologues. His world is the one he has made through his own individual efforts, representing his ingenuity, cunning and the practical assessment of his possibilities to advance and benefit from the uncharted territory in front of him. Marx makes the case that the determinations of value found in the Robinson story are unexamined and undeveloped by its storytellers. In extending the metaphor *beyond* its ideological function, he shows the immanent truth of the story.

The image of reality expressed by *Robinson Crusoe* is one where labour is "the living, form-giving fire [*lebendige, gestaltende Feuer*]; it is the transitoriness of things, their temporality, as their formation by living time [*lebendige Zeit*]. In the simple production process—leaving aside the realisation process—the transitoriness of the forms of things is used to posit their usefulness."[168] The myth is the isolation and ahistoricity of the production process, confined to the individual and removed from the realisation process—the exchange society which Robinson's accounting and time calculation presupposes. Yet Marx's comments entail a transformed and actualised sociality in which,

> it is neither the direct human labour he himself performs, nor the time during which he works, but rather the appropriation of his own general productive power, his understanding of nature and his mastery over it by virtue of his presence as a social body—it is, in a word, the development of the social individual [*gesellschaftlichen Individuums*] which appears as the great foundation-stone of production and of wealth.[169]

In light of this concept of sociality, it is possible to see how Marx *appreciates* the Robinson story. In one of the few passages in *Capital* that broach a postcapitalist society, Marx follows his preceding discussion of isolated capitalist production (and precapitalist production for consumption) with his conception of an emancipated society:

> Let us finally imagine, for a change, an association of free men [*Verein freier Menschen*], working with the means of production held in common, and expending their many different forms of labour-power in full self-awareness as one single social labour force. All the determinations [*Bestimmungen*] of Robinson's labour are repeated [*wiederholen*] here, but with the difference that they are social [*gesellschaftlich*] instead of individual [*individuell*]. All Robinson's products were exclusively the result of his own personal labour and they were therefore directly objects of utility for him personally. The total product of our imagined association is a social product.[170]

This passage implies that Robinson's production for need is maintained and generalised once individualised and abstract production is replaced by actually social production, realised cooperation. It could appear here that Marx thinks that a free society is simply an inversion of the capitalist production process. Yet there is more going on in this passage. Calling attention to the social recognition of Robinson's labour, Marx adds further determinations, transforming its potential. In the novel, Robinson's activity is shaped by the fulfillment of his needs and desires. In turn, this activity comes to bring him an increasing sense of happiness and satisfaction. Robinson must labour to live, but he does so in accordance with the aim of living well. He takes a kind of pride in his labour, which becomes an activity more determinate than merely for survival, the reproduction of his life. For Robinson – as for the reader of the novel – the question of the meaning of his activity becomes a matter of reflection. Marx renders visible these determinations, while bringing to the fore the immanent dimension of his critique. The freedom of productive activity, posited in Robinson, can only become actually conscious practical reasoning aimed at achieving the human good when it is constituted socially.

This self-consciousness Marx finds to be a crucial element of rational production. Labour activity is now performed in collective "full self-awareness." Not only does Marx deem the negation of capital in terms of the collective institutions of freely associated rule, but also his stress on the social character of the labour process is directly contrasted with Robinson's individual labour. Marx cannot, however, be taken to dissolve the modern individual into a return to precapitalist communalism founded "on the immaturity of man as an individual"; but he maintains that human beings are individualised and reified through modern productive processes that prevent sociality from actually being comprehended in terms of individuals.[171]

Marx's conception of free association *repeats* Robinson not to claim his industry as an example of his own ideal human being, but as an immanent critique. He seeks to present the rational aspect of Robinson's labour, its concrete expression. In the 1867 version of the chapter, Marx notes the "essential difference" in the contrast between Robinson and free association is that production "remains social." Marx does not venture an abstract future plan for the distribution of the results of production. Rather, his claim is that planning is itself a historically specific question that depends on the correlation between "the correct proportion of the various labour-functions to the various needs."[172] My interpretation runs against MacIntyre's critique in *AV*. MacIntyre argues that Marx secretes a "radical individualism" by presenting the free individual as a socialised Robinson, without making clear "on what basis he enters his free association." Accordingly, this "lacuna" becomes the association of "abstract moral principle and utility."[173]

However, Marx's conceptualisation of shared association in terms of self-consciousness is dialectically related to the rational and collective control of labour processes, practices and institutions by social agents. This position advances a normative conception of sociality in which productive activity is recognised as rational through interdependent association. The socialist Robinson makes it possible for concrete labour to be understood not in individual but in social terms as activity of practical reasoning that is free only through mutual dependence. For Marx, concrete freedom entails self-conscious awareness and recognitive association. He maintains that a form of life after capitalism would need to be "organized as a conscious association working according to a plan."[174] Marx wants to make good on Hegel's ethical claim that self-consciousness attains its satisfaction only in the self-consciousness of others.

Conclusion

Friedman and Nozick rule out ethical cooperation without the "open market," the bastion of free choice between individuals, where "each person is a miniature firm."[175] But for Marx, the domination of capital stamps social relations as value and prevents us from being at home in the world. The possibility of an ethical life requires a social form of freedom where cooperation is rational. Marx's interpretation of *Robinson Crusoe* suggests he saw the novel as an ideological buttress for the standpoint of political economy. Marx does not deny individuality or deem it simply as ideology, thereby falling victim to a one-sided collectivism. Instead, he demonstrates that "the individual" is a product of capitalist social forms. The social and individual moments of the labour process are assessed by Marx in historically specific terms as antinomies of capitalist relations that require negation. However, individuality is sublated into a realised sociality through the freedom and self-awareness of "social labour" rationally organised. The single, isolated individual and the abstract sociality of production are both moments historically determined by capital, but the struggle for recognition makes possible self-conscious and free association in an ethical form of life.

This chapter offered a characterisation of the development of Marx's critique of political economy as a challenge to early social, economic and political thought. Posited within the "science" of political economy is a presupposed ontological position which naturalises the atomist individual. Far from peripheral, this ontology furnishes a theory of human nature. The implications of Marx's critique of this position help frame what is at stake in his social ontology. In taking issue with the naturalisation of capitalist social forms, he points to the connection between the construal of human nature in political economy and bourgeois moral philosophy. On this basis, Marx's critique of political economy allows a reconstruction of a normative theory of human action and a concept of ethical life.

PART III

FIVE

Species-Being and Flourishing

The Young Marx

IN A SERIES OF ARTICLES from 1843, at once creative and explosive, the barely twenty-five-year-old Marx polemises against Hegel and the Young Hegelians. With no revolution and only the German ideology, Marx becomes increasingly frustrated by the political situation. Regularly censored by the Prussian press, Marx's thinking in these texts looks to go beyond the limits of German politics by exploring the absences and bounds of its theoretical decline. The deterioration in thought had coalesced in the democratic political movement, which floundered against the state and grew in conservatism. In May, Marx writes to Ruge:

> The philistine world is the *animal kingdom of politics* . . . Centuries of barbarism have produced it and given it shape, and now it stands before us as a complete system based on the principle of the *dehumanized world* [*entmenschte Welt*]. Our Germany, the philistine world at its most perfect, must necessarily lag far behind the French Revolution which restored man to his estate. A German Aristotle who wished to construct his *Politics* on the basis of our society would begin by writing 'Man is a social but wholly unpolitical animal [*Mensch ist ein geselliges, jedoch völlig unpolitisches Thier*].'"[1]

These reflections convey just how significantly Hegel and Aristotle factor in Marx's considerations of his contemporary conjuncture and furnish him with a philosophical point of departure. Both intellectual influences are brought together in this period as he attempts to come to grips with the dehumanisation of capitalism. Moreover, they are constitutive elements in the philosophical investigations that make possible Marx's critique of political economy. In this letter, he writes of the "sense of freedom" that "vanished" with the decline of the Greek world and with Christianity "took up residence in the blue mists of heaven." However, it is this freedom that is necessary for society to "become a community of human beings [*Gemeinschaft der Menschen*]."[2] Freedom is understood here in Hegelian terms as the self-consciousness of a historical community. The relationship between dehumanisation and a *free community of human beings* becomes a major theme in Marx's work. The thinking through of this idea is evident in the extraordinary *Economic and Philosophical Manuscripts of 1844* (*EPM*) written during a fifteen-month period of tremendous creativity in Paris from late 1843 to early 1845.

In Marx's 1844 writings—his first sustained confrontation with political economy—he develops a conception of labour that allows him to conceive of dehumanisation in terms of the alienation of human activity in capitalist social forms. In this chapter, I show the genesis of this construal of labour and argue that Aristotle decisively helps to illuminate the normative dimensions of Marx's idea of freedom.[3] In the fragmentary and unfinished *EPM*, Marx establishes an ontological conception of sociality in his theorising of alienated labour.[4] The concept of alienation in Marx's early writings is a major issue of interpretation and still divides commentators attempting to trace the lines of continuity, rupture and growth in Marx's thought.[5]

Marx's notion of *Gattungswesen*, "species-being," entails an account of human flourishing, in which to flourish is to realise both human capabilities and the immanent possibilities for freedom. For Marx, productive activity mediates human beings and nature, developing one and the other in a mutual process of interaction. This life activity strives for its own rational self-consciousness and universality. Human beings are natural and historical beings. Human life is inseparably in nature and in society. We make ourselves and our social world. In this way, productive activity is always expressed in a historical form. In our social world, in which the relation of capital and wage-labour structures private property and productive activity, this form of being is alienated.[6] A complex set of relations determines alienated labour as a historically specific form of productive activity. Being is socially constituted and mediated by the specifically human dimension of productive activity. Human beings produce rationally and in concert with others. This practice creates and transforms our being, offering both the cruelty of domination and the potential for human flourishing. For Marx, the being-and-becoming of human activity is both the self-realisation of a human essence, historically formed, and the ethical becoming of human society, rational and universal. Marx inherits from Hegel the view that freedom is the human essence.[7] Not only is this freedom historical but it requires self-consciousness. For Marx, this freedom is constituted by the rational self-control of human activity. If so, alienation is a barrier to human freedom. The relation between alienation and freedom denotes a vital aspect of the meaning of ethical life for Marx, in which in overcoming the former, the latter can be realised.

To flourish, for Marx, is to realise both the human capacities and practices of freedom. This social ontology gives initial shape to the ethical character of his critical social theory. Marx's conception of unalienated labour as human flourishing develops the Aristotelian strain of thinking about human nature in which latent human potential is formed and actualised in society by practical reasoners. It is crucial to stress that Marx's social ontology is not transhistorical or pre-political. On the contrary, since it is derived from society, his concept of labour is intrinsically historical and political. This exposition of human *beings* as rational social beings is constituted by a historical and immanent critique of alienation. Marx's idea of human flourishing as collective *becoming* gives his account of alienation normative force. The normativity of human potentiality remains present in Marx's theorisation of labour beyond the 1844 works, which sustain his conception of ethical life as the flourishing of human sociality, the actualisation of human being-and-becoming.

Significantly, the concept of alienation has had a major revival in recent critical social theory, especially in the work of Moishe Postone and Rahel Jaeggi. With its origins in Marx's *EPM*, the concept of alienation was once a central aspect of critical social theory and a compass for normative approaches to assess capitalism. But as Jaeggi points out, "not only has alienation nearly disappeared from today's philosophical literature, it also has hardly any place any longer in the vocabulary of contemporary cultural critique."[8] In Postone's highly inventive reinterpretation of Marx's thought, he sets out to recover the concept of alienation from the deficiencies of various traditional approaches, including the current of critical theory in which Jaeggi is also in dialogue.[9] As he sees it, the concept of alienation can help us better understand Marx's own critical-theoretical approach and make it relevant for today. "A central hallmark of capitalism," as Postone puts it, "is that people do not really control their own productive activity or what they produce but ultimately are dominated by the results of that activity."[10] Compellingly, Postone demonstrates the way in which the abstract domination of the social forms specific to capitalism are relations of alienation that bear upon the fundamental structures of modern society. As such, "immanent social critique with emancipatory intent must adequately grasp the determinate grounds of unfreedom in capitalism, so that the historical abolition of what they express would imply the possibility of social and historical freedom."[11]

If Postone advances an immanent critique of the social forms of economic relations under capitalism as a recovery operation for the idea of alienation, Jaeggi offers a similar corrective by focusing on the normative relations of modern life. The central concern of Jaeggi's reconstruction of alienation critique is the "*qualities*" of an individual's relation to "self and world" and the ability to discern between "successful" or "deficient" relations.[12] She examines the difficulty of making decisions about how one should live in an alienated world. As she maintains, alienation critique points to devastating absences in the meaning of practices and relationships between ourselves, our social roles and institutions. Jaeggi conceptualises this problem in terms of "impeded" or "deficient" acts of "appropriation," which affect the ability to develop "interests and capacities" to meaningfully relate to ourselves and others in social roles and institutions we have control over.[13] For Jaeggi, as for Postone, the concept of alienation articulates nothing less than a demand for social freedom in today's world.

However, both influential thinkers criticise Marx's early social ontology as transhistorical and essentialist.[14] Postone grounds his reinterpretation of alienation in the domination of abstract labour as elaborated in the *Grundrisse* and *Capital*, rather than in what he takes to be the transhistorical social ontology in *EPM*. He maintains, "traditional Marxism" is deeply mistaken by confusing what is particular about capitalism, alienated labour, with a "transhistorical 'essence' of labor."[15] Writing about the mature texts, Postone maintains that "Marx's immanent analysis is not a critique from the standpoint of a social ontology; rather, it provides a critique of such a position by indicating that what seems to be ontological is actually historically specific to capitalism."[16] Likewise, Jaeggi conceives of alienation critique in terms that explicitly eschew the notion of a human essence. She sheds the idea that alienation is a "mismatch between the nature of human beings and their social life" that looks to some kind of "return" to an unalienated essence as "the human being's purpose or nature."[17] In no uncertain terms, both Postone and Jaeggi believe that challenging the essentialist elements of the concept of alienation as derived from the *EPM* is necessary for a critical social theory that can furnish the demands of self-determination and overcome alienated relations.[18]

While Postone's explanation of the domination of capitalist social forms and Jaeggi's normative assessment of alienated relations of appropriation are enormously generative, I believe their criticisms of the early Marx are unpersuasive. Rather, his social ontology can be vindicated by bringing attention to the historical and normative aspects of the *EPM*. As I demonstrate in this chapter, contra Postone, the *EPM* does not rely on a transhistorical notion of labour.[19] Similarly, Jaeggi is right that alienation fails to be a critical concept when it relies upon a notion of transhistorical essence. But if, as I go to show, Marx's *EPM* are not transhistorical then his idea of "human essence" does not simply counterpose a true and authentic self to modern relations of alienation. Marx has no aspiration to "return" to a true essence. A closer construal of his 1844 writings helps dispel this misapprehension.

Marx's social ontology denotes an idea of *flourishing* in which alienated labour is a historical barrier to developing human potential constituted in the normative social practices of a free and rational form of life. Properly understood, Marx's early social ontology helps grasp his mature value-form theory and would, in this sense, bolster Postone's interpretation. At the same time, Marx's social ontology makes it possible to expand the Aristotelian aspirations of Jaeggi's idea of self-realisation as when "we realize ourselves in an activity to the extent that we do it for its own sake."[20] Marx absorbs and historicises Aristotle's idea of flourishing. Marx's concept of "species-being" does not denote an ahistorical human essence, but instead formulates the way in which human beings are historical and social beings. To flourish in a rational form of life, the constitutive forms of human activity must empower and enable us to reflect collectively and self-consciously about the social roles and practices that we share with others. As social beings, we must take responsibility for our shared activity together. This normative idea of cooperation requires a form of community that can fulfill its complex and expanding needs by democratic means.

Marx's vision of communism is *eudaimonia*. His 1844 writings are instructive since they establish that his ontological conception involves two closely related and inseparable aspects of human sociality. In Marx's view, human beings are in essence social beings (*gesellschaftliche Wesen*) and community beings (*Gemeinwesen*). A dialectic emerges in which the purposeful social activity of human beings produces the community as the form of life where the goods of human activity can be realised. In Marx's words,

> the essence of *man* [*menschliche Wesen*] is the *true community* of man [*Gemeinwesen der Menschen*], men, by activating their own essence, produce, create this

human community, this social being [*gesellschaftliche Wesen*] which is no abstract, universal power standing over against the solitary individual, but is the essence of every individual, his own activity, his own life, his own spirit, his own wealth.[21]

It is precisely the historical and social essence of human beings that is alienated, thereby shaping the form of life and potentiality available for political communities. To live well as social beings, we require a collective form of freedom that habituates the individual and collective flourishing of its members. The idea of species-being endows Marx's vision of communism with normative import and gives political impetus to the argument for a democratic form of life that transcends alienation and abstract social domination.[22]

To assess the merit of Marx's social ontology, it is necessary to trace the line of this conceptualisation from its first nascent expression to its fully formed shape, since as Aristotle suggests, we must investigate things in their initial form and emergence "to get the best theoretical grasp on them."[23] The intellectual lineage of Marx's concept of human sociality is the subject of this chapter and the next. First, I discuss Marx's largely overlooked "Comments on James Mill" (*CJM*). This text affords a critical vantage point for Marx's move towards the critique of political economy and contains his earliest thoughts on the fetish character of value. Next, I address the central claims of the *EPM* and trace the relation between Marx's social ontology and Aristotle. I give detail to how Marx's concept of species-being articulates his Aristotelian argument for the historical potentiality of human flourishing and the good life. My conclusion reflects upon Marx's development of the concept of value as anticipated in the *EPM*.

Critique, Economy and Normativity

Marx's emergent immanent and normative critique of economic theory is shaped by the inability of political economy to recognise the alienated form of wage-labour.[24] In *CJM*, Marx provides his first critique of political economy's naturalisation of social form as economic law.[25] This appraisal should be understood as an intervention into the growing role of credit in monetary policy as advanced by contemporary political economists and their socialist critics.[26] Through an analysis of money and credit, and in a preliminary discussion of value, Marx charges James Mill's economic theory with a presupposed notion of human nature, which posits human beings ahistorically as egotistical producers. Additionally, Marx articulates a very early conception of human flourishing beyond capital. *CJM* consolidates Marx's 1843 texts, especially *OJQ*, by developing a political critique of economic categories. This early assessment of the capitalist state as an alienated social form leads to his concept of species-being and his investigation of value.

In *OJQ*, Marx shows that a split emerges in the modern state between the public citizen and the private life of the individual in civil society (*bürgerliche Gesellschaft*). For Marx, the modern state contains a contradiction between the particularity of civil society and the universality of citizenship. The language of human rights afforded to all citizens expresses the fundamental idea that freedom is a question of recognition between those who live in political communities. Modern constitutions put into words the political emancipation and universal freedom of individuals. But this idea of emancipation presents a promise it can never deliver. Freedom is restricted by the conflictual operation of bourgeois civil society. The political universality which the bourgeoisie claimed on its ascent to power was impossible and inherently self-contradictory, since this class only exists in particularity. Warring capitalists must compete in the market. Paradigmatically, "the rights of man" claims to enshrine universal political freedom, but rather represents the rights of individuals in civil society.[27] In a significant passage, Marx writes:

> Political emancipation is the reduction of man on the one hand to the member of civil society, the *egoistic, independent* individual, and on the other to the *citizen*, the moral person [*moralische Person*]. Only when real, individual man resumes the abstract citizen into himself and as an individual man has become a *species-being* [*Gattungswesen*] in his empirical life, his individual work and his individual relationships, only when man has recognized and organized his *forces propres* [own forces] as *social forces* so that social force is no longer separated from him in the form of *political* force, only then will human emancipation [*menschliche Emancipation*] be completed.[28]

The split between political life and private life empties both spheres for the citizen and the individual, rendering both alienated and abstract. By seeking only political emancipation, political life cannot overcome this contradiction, but as Marx's argues, confirms the antinomy.[29] Moreover, the political realm is judged to exist independently of the social realm.[30] The political realm is empty if narrowly conceived as the state and divorced from the *social* dimension of freedom. Marx offers the term "species-being" as the actualisation of the individual who recognises themselves socially. Political emancipation is necessary but remains particular until mediated by an adequately universal relation of freedom. This view of politics allows for social freedom, as human emancipation, to be conceived concretely. Marx's objection to the simple equation of politics with the modern state is that "the contradiction between *public* and *private life* [and] between *universal* and *particular interests*" makes impossible a political solution to the misery of poverty.[31] Rather than serving as a necessary condition of freedom, civil society is a barrier to the freedom and equality of the modern citizen and the realisation of a form of subjectivity which is universal.[32]

In his early writings, Marx argues that the split between the political and the social must be negated and both sublated into an emancipated human community. Sociality is a form of being mediated by the particular and universal which bring together individual and collective into relations of mutual interdependence. Marx calls the social being *Gattungswesen*, "species-being," "species-essence," or "species-life." This term, which is present in his 1843 writings, becomes a central idea in 1844.[33] The phrase is borrowed from Feuerbach but imbued with an Aristotelian social ontology.[34] Its increased conceptual weight gives further strength to Marx's analysis of political *and* social alienation by assessing the ahistorical positing of the individual in economic theory. This strategy involves probing the content of the categories set out in political economy.

In *CJM*, Marx considers the economic laws theorised by Mill to be falsely abstracted from the actual functioning of economic life. Following Ricardo, Mill hangs his analysis of supply and demand and the relation of production to exchange value on the role of money as the *medium* of exchange. Money is seen as the substance of value. Marx faults this analysis since it posits money as the natural determinant of meaning between human beings and the products of their activity, which become the "*relation* between things."[35] Contra Mill, Marx inverts the money-to-production relation by suggesting that the real mediator is productive activity. That is, activity alienated and objectified by private property and money. He claims this situation is "dehumanized" and as a result, the human being becomes a slave to money.[36]

In investigating the categories of political economy, Marx pushes at the contradiction between money and "value." In response, Marx makes an ontological claim that value is a historically determined relation and so, asks *why* value appears as money. This question is absent from political economy, Mill and Ricardo included:

> Why must private property finish up as money? Because as a social animal man must finish up in exchange and exchange—given the premise of private property—

must finish up in *value*. For the mediating movement of man engaged in exchange is not a social, human movement, it is no *human relationship*: it is the *abstract relation* of private property to private property, and this abstract relation is the *value* which acquires a real existence as value only in the form of *money*. Since in the process of exchange men do not relate to each other as men, *things* lose the meaning of personal, human property. The social relationship of private property to private property is already one in which private property is estranged from itself. Hence, money, the existence-for-itself of this relationship, represents the alienation of private property, an abstraction from its *specific* personal nature.[37]

Marx notes that simple exchange is an expected form of social interaction and different in kind to the exchange principle formed by private property, where values confront each other in exchange as values. What is particular about the exchange of private property as values is the way in which human relationships become abstract. Private property begets private property, expressing social meaning as money, the form of value. Marx's identification of the abstract domination of things ties his analysis of social being with the critique of private property exchange and the form of money. His insight that value takes existent form as money is the germ of his mature value-form theory and the concept of commodity fetishism.[38]

Modern private property encompasses the relation in which productive activity and the products of that activity become social forms determined by exchange. To Marx this means that the processes and results of productive activity do not embody human relations in which artifacts of human activity are embedded with meaning as creations of our social practices of fulfilment. Instead, there is a lack of correspondence between the needs and desires of the producers and the social fabric in which those products are made. As value, productive activity forms an *abstract social relation* to private property, in effect emptying the human content. Money comes to represent this relationship. Marx writes, "the *real* value of things is their exchange value."[39] He comes to fully explain this process in *Capital*, but in *CJM* the embryo of Marx's later distinction between use and exchange value is present. This distinction has key explanatory power in both texts, although in *Capital* the unity in contradiction between use and exchange value is theorised within the value-form at a much higher level of conceptual abstraction.

Marx's discussion in *CJM* of money and value reconceives economic processes in terms of human activity and sociality as a direct challenge to political economy, whose abstractions are continually reproduced by the real abstractions of the exchange relation under private property. Implicit in Marx's critique of political economy in *CJM* is a view of productive activity in which human artifacts could embody normative meaning as expressions of our sociality and rational practices. However, the capitalist form of life subjects the primary mode of social interaction to the compulsion of exchange. Human "morality," "social worth and status" are mediated by money in the form of credit. Marx's choice of language is significant. This terminology spells out that human relationships—ethical interaction—are devalued and alienated. Money becomes "the *moral* existence, the *social* existence [*das moralische Dasein, das gesellige Dasein*], the very heart of man, and because under the appearance of mutual *trust* [*Vertrauens*] between men it is really the greatest *distrust* [*Mißtrauen*] and a total estrangement." Further, the "content of this trust according to which a man accords *recognition* [*anerkennt*] to another man" is done by "advancing money to him."[40] Marx is describing the form of *misrecognition* that arises out of the abstract but universal relation of money. Human beings now relate primarily through a "trust" which is predicated on competition and self-gain. Through the mediation of money we interact with others as persons of legal equality, each free to decide, purchase and sell as they wish. Therefore, trust between human agents is expressed as price. What appears as the basis for recognition and trust in social life is in actuality normatively impoverished: *misrecognition* and *mistrust*.

In normative terms, the significance of alienation is the limitation of human life to the conditions of unfree activity. Alienated labour means that human activity becomes a "torment" and "wealth appears as poverty," dissolving the collective character of productive activity and naturalising individual competitive experience. Real economic abstractions dominate social life.[41] Marx writes that the

> separation from other men appears to be his true existence, his life appears as the sacrifice of his life, the realisation of his essence appears as the de-realisation of his life, their production is the production of nothing, his power over objects appears as the power of objects over them.[42]

As alienated labour is determined by the necessity to reproduce, defined not as the realisation of the human good by social beings, but the profit of one over another. Alienation disfigures human life so that the very activity which could give it definition by sharing in the good of rational practices and animate its freedom becomes its unfreedom.

In Marx's account, political economy misrepresents this social form of life and the historical expression of alienation beset by wage-labour. At a fundamental level, as Marx points out, Smith's idea of "commercial society" takes the philosophical standpoint of the individual merchant. He constructs a model of history based on this standpoint, in which the individual progresses according to the natural end of commercial society.[43] The Smithian conception of social relations is that of eternally competing private property.[44] Smith's understanding of human nature is the foundation of his analysis of transhistorical economic laws. Individuals appear abstracted from society, ready to truck, barter and exchange and only entering society, as Simon Clarke notes, in an "economic function."[45] Following this model, political economy takes alienated labour simply as labour. Alienated labour is naturalised and presented as a perpetual and necessary aspect of commercial society.

Conversely, for Marx, "economic laws" reflect definite social forms. Private property represents a specific historical juncture where commodity exchange has decisively transformed the simple circuit of use-values that characterised precapitalist social forms into the circuit of capital. Marx's understanding of productive activity under capitalism as alienated labour enables him to see past the world of the merchant and the market. Individuals interact with the mutual interest of self-advantage. Marx argues the exchange of private property as an act and social relation is normatively impoverished. Citing *CJM*, Axel Honneth is right to suggest that "members of this society do not supplement each other in their 'social relationship' through their respective individual acts; rather, they perform these acts merely 'with the intention of plundering,'"[46]

The capitalist form of life equates commodity exchange and human relations. Through this historical form of domination, the mimicry of exchange becomes all too real, and alienated relations become the actual relations between human beings. However, Marx's normative discussion in *CJM* envisions a form of society beyond capital which underlines the notion of flourishing set forth with his concept of activity. "Let us suppose that we had produced as human beings," Marx ventures. This would allow

> the *expression* of my own individual *life* during my activity and also, in contemplating the object, I would experience an individual pleasure, I would experience my personality as an *objective sensuously perceptible* power *beyond all shadow of doubt*. In the individual expression of my own life I would have brought about the immediate expression of your life, and so in *my* individual activity I would have directly *confirmed* and *realized* my authentic nature, my *human, communal* nature [*wahres Wesen, mein menschliches, mein Gemeinwesen bestätigt und verwirklicht*].[47]

This flourishing society is Marx's "good life," where human activity can be recognised as enabling social meaning, connection and rationality. We produce our lives with others. This position offers a positive vision of the possibilities and capabilities of an ethical form of societal organisation, based on a negative critique of historically specific forms of domination.[48] Marx's first encounter with political economy, especially his critique of its naturalisation of alienated labour, is developed through an enrichment of the concept of human activity.

Species-Being and Aristotle

The *EPM* presents the architecture for the specific import that productive activity holds for Marx's social ontology. The mediations of labouring activity are comprehended as transformative for social being-and-becoming. In confronting the alienated form of labour under capitalism, Marx conceives of social being in modern society as constituted by productive activity. He identifies a central structural relation in the determination of wage-labour and capital. Marx's characterisation of the abstract and alienated form of labour in capitalist society and critique of the political economy of Smith, Ricardo and Mill set forth a historical and normative account of the human form of life. The concept of "human essence" is historicised in the *EPM* by the interaction and mediation of productive activity with the being and the way of becoming of human potential. The concept of species-being embodies Marx's ontological commitment to the view that human beings are socially formed self-conscious rational beings.

In what follows, I emphasise the Aristotelian character of species-being. We can better illuminate Marx's early intent to identify what a human being is with this influence in mind. For Aristotle, the good life could not be conceived without the polis. The good life necessitates the good society. *Eudaimonia*, flourishing, can only be realised through practical reasoning and judgement which pertain to the good and are lived through the institutions which embody this living good as virtues. Marx adopts this ontology in the *EPM*:

> The individual *is* the *social being* [*Das Individuum ist das gesellschaftliche Wesen*]. His vital expression—even when it does not appear in the direct form of a *communal* expression, conceived in association with other men—is therefore an expression and confirmation of *social life*. Man's individual and species-life are not two *distinct things*.[49]

The ontological importance of human sociality and its teleological realisation is in the *type* of association organised. Properly shared association, which Marx envisions as communism, has "society as its goal," but absolute ethical life can only eventuate from the actualisation of this potential.[50] The idea of the good of human life as flourishing is teleological, but what is decisive about this position is that this end is not external to human action, as in a religious notion of telos. Instead, teleology pertains to the *inner* development of an action or thing corresponding to the form and function of what that practice or object is.[51]

For Aristotle, the development of an essence or form is the actualisation of its potential. For a living being, the "actuality is the account of what is potentially."[52] In this sense, "actuality is prior to potentiality" both in its form and temporality. Aristotle offers the formula: "for that which is in the primary sense potential is potential because it is possible for it to become actual." As it applies to species, "the actual member of the species is prior to the potential member of the same species, though the individual is potential before it is actual."[53] The distinctive human function, the *action* which allows the good to be acquired, is reason.[54] Adriel M. Trott characterises the relation between actuality and potentiality as "both the principle of movement and the form or end."[55] This view corresponds to the polis, since just as living well for a human being involves logos, the form of activity adequate to political life involves the coming-to-be of human beings and political communities simultaneously, in which the activity of political deliberation is an end in itself.[56] The interrelation between human reason and political community is formed by self-activity.

Marx recasts Aristotle's logical distinction between actuality and potentiality to render intelligible the historical form of alienation. For Aristotle, this logical distinction between actuality and potentiality is crucial because it involves the movement of human activity as both logos and telos. Marx preserves this concept of coming-to-be through rational human self-activity, but reverses the relation between actuality and potentiality. Actuality is understood historically as an alienated form of life. In reality, social relations are conflictual and determined by unfree activity. But if actuality is an alienated form, Marx maintains that there is an immanent potential for alienated beings to become free. In his language, species-being is an unactualised potentiality. Productive activity is alienated in its historical articulation, its actuality, but if the capacity for creative labour is developed in accordance with the possibilities inherent in our social practices, then the flourishing Marx associates with the human essence could be realised.[57] The *capacity* for human beings to live self-consciously, to understand our activity as rational through our practices and judgement, marks human beings distinctly as a species. Marx accepts Aristotle's teleological conception of form development and the rationality of the activity which must be involved in its coming-to-be, but inverts the historical relation between actuality and potentiality. By historicising the relation, the normative dimension of a critique of actuality is made possible.[58] Marx's "renewed emphasis on potency is a critical move," as Aaron Jaffe puts it, since "[i]f the form of humanity can be understood as the power, force, or potential to become fully human, we can begin to raise the question of the *status* of potentialities."[59]

Productive activity is ontologically significant precisely because in making our lives with others, we not only produce to live, but to live well. Such an activity requires conscious and rational reflection.[60] Seen this way, productive activity is the practical reasoning about what forms of activity contribute to the good for human beings and what kind of social life could archive that end. However, Marx's concept of labour explicitly differentiates his concept of species-being from Aristotle's.[61] Aristotle makes a sharp distinction between production (poiesis) and activity (praxis) since "production has its end in something other than itself, but action does not, since its end is acting well itself."[62] Aristotle sees that craft, *technē*, also concerns the science of production but excludes things "that are and come to be by necessity; nor with things that are by nature."[63] Instead, *technē* enables the coming-to-be of a kind of reasoning that makes this creative production skillful or artful since its "principle is in the producer and not in the product."[64] In the Aristotelian view "[w]hen things are made and done, that which makes them and that which does them are not the same." For instance, the end of weaving is the production of a coat. But in playing the harp, "there is no other end, but just is the end, the activity and the doing."[65] Just as production and action "differ in kind [*eidos*]," so do their instruments, which they both require.[66] As an instrument of production, the weaving shuttle creates an object of further use in the cloth that will be taken up by the weaver. Instruments of action, which could include the coat, however, are useful in themselves. Aristotle goes as far as to say: "Life [*bios*], though, is action and not production. That is why a slave is an assistant in the things related to action."[67] Owned as property, the slave is an instrument for another's use.

Marx takes Aristotle's distinction between action and production to reflect the structure of Athenian inequality, but rather than dismissing the categories entirely, he endeavours to establish that productive activity makes action possible in a way faithful to an Aristotelian conception of the teleological end.[68] It is in part the alienated ends of wage-labour that leads Marx to find it normatively unacceptable.

However, for Marx, productive activity is not reducible to alienated labour. Rather productive activity is the mediating relation that allows rationality to be enacted, as well as the articulation of creativity, and the potential end of human sociality.[69] The contrast is not between Aristotle's condemnation and Marx's glorification of production, but between the inbuilt limitation of Aristotle's concept of action highlighted by the historical conditions in which his concept of production arose. Marx's reevaluation of Aristotle's distinction enables productive activity itself to be understood as *technē*, but transcends and transforms the relationship between what is "made" and what is "done." With his idea of unalienated labour, Marx envisions a mode of social activity in which the making of one's life with others enables production to both meet social ends and for that activity to be a form of flourishing in which the end of the activity depends upon acting well, since our lives would be made with others rationally. Marx vindicates Aristotle's idea of praxis by sustaining the view that knowledge becomes practical when rational beings direct their activity towards the good. For this reason, Aristotle's distinction between production and action is unable to grasp the movement of rationality as mediated by the social forms of our activity. For Marx, the social form of productive activity shapes the possibilities of what kind of life is lived and for what end.

As Marx helps us see, even the types of activity most conducive to Aristotle's view are only intelligible if we understand them as forms of productive activity. It helps to consider an example that involves productive processes with greater creativity than other forms of wage-labour. In neoliberal academia, I must finish this book to please my employers and secure my job as an academic. It is an act of labour for a definite end, in part detached from what exactly I argue. At the same time, this book is a real expression of my views, beliefs and identity. Its ideas have taken various forms (conference papers, dissertations, conversations, articles etc.), and bringing them together represents my extended engagement with these themes and attempt to present these ideas synthetically. The book is also a means to an end of furthering the understanding of the ideas, thinkers and themes contained in these pages for others. As the attentive reader will have no doubt ascertained by now, this book is part of a broader theorisation of the possibilities for human emancipation. Of course, none of the intended functions of this book can be picked out as the primary cause, since they dovetail together and conform with the kind of practical wisdom Aristotle's called *phronesis*. Practical wisdom forms a unity with practical reasoning: to deliberate about the right reason for action requires judgement. But moreover, the end is acting well since contemplation is "valuable in itself."[70]

While most labour under capitalism does not permit such identification, this example serves the purpose of suggesting that Marx's idea of social form weaves together the meaning of action and production, what Aristotle and Arendt see as distinct, to demonstrate their meaning for the rationality of our activity as historical and social beings. It is the relation between activities that Marx considers pertinent and needing delineation. Marx goes another step further than Aristotle to relate activity and production, maintaining that "there is no production in general."[71] Aristotle saw the technical components of production as defining, since the "ways of life" of human beings vary between forms of subsistence (nomadic, farming, raiding, fishing and hunting), which "naturally develop of themselves."[72] Need structures the "ways of life" and as crafts of "property acquisition," and human beings take subsistence from what is "given by nature itself."[73] Whereas for Marx, production always takes a historically specific social form, demarcating technological and social relations.[74] There is no activity that sits outside of the specific iteration of production. For this reason, what defines the end of production can only have historical and normative meaning in particular social forms. The farmer in Hesiod's *Works and Days* is altogether different from Marie Antoinette at her farm at Versailles, in history or in film.[75]

Further, for Marx, the flourishing form and rational end of this activity is hindered by the estrangement of the wage-labour/capital relation. Creative productive activity, that which defines human beings, is inverted into an alien power through wage-labour. Since workers are forced to sell the activity of labour (as labour-power) for a wage, Marx characterises alienation (*Entäusserung*) as a process of objectification. For Marx, alienated labour individuates by estranging (*Entfremdung*) both the relation between producer and their product, and by the act of labour itself. The worker feels the "*loss of and bondage to the object*."[76] The social form of alienated labour means that products of human activity are objectified as commodities and subsumed by the principle of commodity exchange which comes to dominate and determine production as an activity outside the control of the producer. Alienation from the product of labour and the act itself correspond with the individualisation of the human being and the separation of the individual from society at large.[77] In the *EPM*, Marx's theory of alienation requires the concept of species-being and thus can only be adequately grasped by giving conceptual definition to the interconnected notion of human essence.

While the question of human essence has frustrated Marx commentators, leading to an "anti-essentialist consensus," I seek to defend this conception.[78] Marx's conception is Aristotelian.[79] Inquiring about the nature of what a form of life is—as the unity of whole and parts—asks the normative question of what it would mean for that life to go well or poorly. An essence defines a form of life by understanding the activities and potentialities characteristic of a species of being.[80] Any such potential can only be realised historically. Crediting Hegel, Karen Ng observes that Marx's idea of species-being is an account of "the dialectics of life and self-consciousness, a relation that defines the universal form of rational, free activity."[81] Accordingly, productive activity mediates and constitutes the relation between life and self-consciousness. Ng maintains that a human life is fundamentally a *species-life* in which our "life-activity" is embodied (activity serves to produce and reproduce bodies, suffer and act with others), and relates to an external world (life-activity works on materials external to ourselves and makes the external world a concern from human beings). Life-activity is a relation between human beings which is "intersubjective" since it "depends upon necessary bonds with other human beings" shaped and sustained "through individual and collective productive activities."[82] Marx's idea of human life articulates a form of consciousness that is fundamentally normative. Similarly, species-being can be seen as a naturalist construal of what it means for a human life to be free. Marx ascribes to the Aristotelian idea that human beings are part of nature, but we are defined by a specific form of self-conscious rationality—our activity has a "rational principle"—that marks us distinctly from vegetative and nonrational animals.[83] Unlike other animals, human beings can ask what a good life would be.[84] As Mathew Abbott puts it, "Marx claims our activity is free because we distinguish ourselves self-consciously as ones of a kind," but this freedom "does not release us from being animal but transforms the way in which we are."[85] We give reasons to decide how to enact our lives as beings that can organise our practices and social forms in a plethora of different ways.

A normative account of human consciousness provides a firm basis to reassess Marx's understanding of labour. Marx often refers to transhistorical categories (such as wealth and use) as abstractions for the purpose of critique.[86] Marx's historically specific concept of value is unintelligible without the transhistorical category of wealth. But wealth itself never appears apart from a specific historical form of surplus extraction. For the same reason, labour as productive activity is constitutive of human life, but labour is always embodied in a social form. Therefore, it is a misunderstanding to take Marx's critique of value-producing abstract labour to deny a strong normative connection with fundamental features of human life enabled by our distinct form of species. Understandably, it would be hard to glean what Marx's problem is with capitalism if the domination and exploitation of capital was not conceived in terms of the barriers to a free human life. Marx's critique of capitalism depends upon a normative conception of the flourishing social life for human beings.[87]

The concept of human essence allows for a critical position that asks what it is about human life that would make it go well, given the normative dimensions of self-consciousness for us as a species. This requires giving an account of the narratives which comprise our social roles, practical identities and collective historical reflections. This view establishes an idea of social life as practices that are end-motivated goals "informed by internal criteria for their own success."[88] Marx's social ontology entails a conception of the rationality of the human form of life and the historical possibilities for productive activity to be free. Marx's notion of human essence is no ahistorical return but, based on the negative critique of alienated labour, formulates a transformative conception of free social life.

It pays to draw out the historical dimension of this claim. To say human beings have an essence is to conceive of our social formation by historical mediations. In Marx's account, human nature cannot be understood as unchanging but instead must be comprehended as historically constituted activity. For Marx, productive activity is ontologically transformative, and essence is always expressed in historical and social forms.[89] Human beings are *historical beings*. He states this emphatically in the *Theses on Feuerbach*: "The human essence is no abstraction inherent in each single individual. In its reality it is the ensemble of the social relations."[90] This remark does not deny human essence, contra Althusser, but insists that essence is a term for the historical form of relations.[91] In Ernst Bloch's apt phrase, it is a mark of "Marx's consistency."[92] To speak of the human essence is to articulate the formative activities characteristic of rational social beings. In Marx's view, productive activity moulds and is moulded by historical processes and forms that constitute such purposive sociality.

This historical aspect supports the normative point since it furnishes an immanent critique of the present form of productive activity. Indeed, Marx takes it that capitalism enhances and emancipates aspects of social life. Wage-labour permits a type of freedom unavailable in other historical forms of social life. But it is precisely the social form of "free labour" that Marx calls into question. Alienated labour cannot be actually free. As Agnes Heller argues, Marx does not see alienation as "some sort of long-standing 'distortion' of the species or of human nature; the essence of man develops within alienation itself, and this creates the possibility for the realisation of man 'rich in needs.'"[93] Marx's critique entails an account of the social dynamic of the alienation of labour, which both creates new possibilities and fundamentally restricts those possibilities from developing according to the conscious forms of rationality embedded in productive activity. This view of potentiality understands ethical life as the historical flourishing of human sociality, human being-and-becoming.

For Marx, the being-and-becoming of human activity is both the self-realisation of a human essence, historically formed, and the ethical becoming of human society, rational and universal. Not only is this freedom historical, but it requires self-consciousness. For Marx, this freedom is constituted by the rational self-control of human activity. Marx's understanding of essence is not just the particular characteristics of alienation, but entails the denial of human potential and universality. In the *EPM*, he refers to the human essence as "the alienated *capacity* of *mankind*."[94] Marx echoes Aristotle's claim that practical wisdom is the capacity for "grasping the truth, involving reasons, concerned with action about things that are good or bad for a human being."[95] If human capacities are alienated, an overcoming of the wage-labour/capital relation is a necessary condition for the self-realisation of human potentiality. A fuller sense of humans-as-we-could-be is not found in labour in its alienated form, but as the social and collective self-control of productive activity in a rational form of life. This realisation is bound up in the historically constituted transformation of social forms of life and the negation of alienated labour for human capacities and possibilities.

The capitalist division of labour embodies an alienated social form that obstructs the realisation of human potential. The division of labour, even in précis, requires a complex breakdown of labouring tasks that must be posed in terms of production in general. But there is an important distinction between the technical and social division of labour. The former relates to the labour process in general and the second to the social form in which that labour process takes place. When commodity exchange is presupposed by political economy, the social division specific to value-producing labour is projected back onto the past and eternalised. Political economy thus takes capitalist professionalisation to reflect the particular and perpetual interests of commodity exchange. In a famous passage from the 1845/6 Brussels manuscripts, posthumously compiled as *The German Ideology*, Marx and Engels ironise this assumption:

> the division of labour offers us the first example of the fact that, as long as man remains in naturally evolved society, that is, as long as a cleavage exists between

the particular and the common interest, as long, therefore, as activity is not voluntarily, but naturally, divided, man's own deed becomes an alien power opposed to him, which enslaves him instead of being controlled by him. For as soon as the division of labour comes into being, each man has a particular, exclusive sphere of activity, which is forced upon him and from which he cannot escape. He is a hunter, a fisherman, a shepherd, or a critical critic, and must remain so if he does not want to lose his means of livelihood; whereas in communist society, where nobody has one exclusive sphere of activity but each can become accomplished in any branch he wishes, society regulates the general production and thus makes it possible for me to do one thing today and another tomorrow, to hunt in the morning, fish in the afternoon, rear cattle in the evening, criticise after dinner, just as I have a mind, without ever becoming hunter, fisherman, shepherd or critic.[96]

This vexing passage has garnered a variety of interpretations.[97] My purpose is not to discuss the viability of these precapitalist and naïve examples of activities, but rather comment on the notion of cultivation which underpins the quotation. If this passage is seen to reject the social division of labour and entail activity that is not "exclusive" in the sense of a process abstracted from the social whole, then the suggestion is just that private professions restrict the furthering of human capacity and potential. Specialisation is imposed by the narrow particularity of bourgeois civil society. What Marx and Engels find problematic is the social division of mental and physical labour—the split between head and hand—into individual producers who embody that separation.[98]

Moreover, if the meaning is taken to be ironic, then the insight has much greater significance.[99] The argumentative context and tone of the 1845/6 manuscripts is highly sarcastic and sardonic, brimming with retorts to "Saint Max" and "Saint Bruno," so there is good reason to understand this passage in the same light. Read as an ironic reproach, the passage shrewdly calls into question what it means to have a particular specialisation of activity. Accordingly, the fulfillment of narrowly conceived social roles is shown to have an inbuilt limit on the development of social practice. The activities associated with each role confine practical identities to individual livelihoods rather than the good for human beings based on shared, socially decided activity and the cultivation of human potential. It becomes clear that alienated activities cannot give adequate meaning to our social roles.[100] Capitalist specialisation betrays a bifurcation between the meaning associated with professions and the manner in which alienated labour frustrates the development of actually social roles as practical identities.

A further point of clarification is necessary. Social roles in communist society are seen by Marx and Engels to be mediated by social practices. Activity cannot be defined by exclusive spheres of "professionalisation" but by shared commitment, which is not forced upon subjects but a feature of free association. A condition of political and social life in which activity could be said to be meaningful would be the sustaining of the social order by those who identify with social roles of their making.[101] In this sense, social roles have a normative structure where individual meaning and social good are interdependent. Aristotle considers virtue to be cultivated though our activities, since virtue is learnt and sustained just like a craft:

> For we learn a craft by producing the same product that we must produce when we have learnt it; we become builders, for instance, by building, and we become harpists by playing the harp. Similarly, then, we become just by doing just actions, temperate by doing temperate actions, brave by doing brave actions. What goes on in cities is also evidence for this ... Correct habituation distinguishes a good political system from a bad one.[102]

According to Aristotle, our social roles are given expression in our activities. It would be implausible to suggest Aristotle is promoting professionalisation. In this light we need to read the passage from 1845/6 manuscripts as a conception of self-actualisation in a form of life which allows the virtues to be cultivated collectively.

By replacing private professions (defined by the sale of labour-power on the market) by social cooperation and shared association (defined by rational allocation of human activity), Marx envisions the actualising of human capacity and potential as a collectively enacted process that enriches the individual through their sociality. This idea of freedom, as unfolding humanity though activity, expresses the *practice* of rational self-control. The pleasure found in these practices bears strong resemblance to Aristotle's discussion in *Nicomachean Ethics* of the "common life":

> Whatever being is for each, or whatever the goal is for the sake of which they choose living, that is the activity he wishes to pursue in his friend's company. So it is that some drink together, others play at dice, still others exercise and hunt together or philosophise together, all and each passing their days together in whatever they are fondest of in life. For since they wish to live with their friends, they pursue and share the actions in which they find their common life.[103]

For Aristotle, flourishing unifies our activities of practical reasoning and judgement in the good of ethical life. The core claim here is that living well is conditional on *living together*. Activity is shared. The end of activity is the virtue which *activity cultivates*, since action aimed at the good is itself an end.[104] The correspondence between the two conceptions of cultivation is striking. Marx and Engels write, "[o]nly within the community has each individual the means of cultivating his gifts in all directions; hence personal freedom becomes possible only within the community."[105] In this view, alienated labour makes the good for human beings external to our activity. Rather than the shared association of collective good, where the end of activity is the life well-lived, alienated labour is a means to an external end. The expression of the social dominance of means is money.

In this sense, Marx's playful quip that the "less you eat, drink, buy books, go to the theatre, go dancing, go drinking, think, love, theorize, sing, paint, fence, etc., the more you *save*" notes the contradiction and identity between *working to live* and *living to work*.[106] Such a life alienates the individual from others and constrains the fundamental ethical question of "how we should live" to ordinary expressions of individualism: the utilitarianism of individual advancement and the escapism of hedonism. Since we relate to each other through the means of money, the end of our social activity is largely shaped by the logic of exchange, and the dynamic of power reflects this domination as a "hostile opposition of interests."[107] The work we perform for others strengthens their position. The struggle over the length of the working day shapes exactly how much time is required to earn the means taken home as pay. Moreover, the logic of exchange entails that social life is defined by the imperative to valorise value and accumulate capital. As I show in the next chapter, in *Capital* Marx draws on Aristotle to demonstrate that this imperative systematically reduces the human good to the infinite accumulation of surplus value.

Marx's concept of species-being formulates a claim about *what it is* to live a free life. By analysing alienated labour in relation to *what it would mean* for a human life to be flourishing, he establishes a normative critique of the capitalist form of life—which he takes to be defective since it limits human action and the potential human good of a free rational life. However, Marx's idea of flourishing should not be understood as an overly immaculate, pristine moral category, which would offer little insight into the nature of postcapitalist ethical life.[108] Instead, for Marx, a human life necessarily requires failure and suffering. The *EPM* express a rich view of emotion, in which human beings are always "a *suffering*, conditioned and limited being."[109] Embedded in Marx's position is the Aristotelian notion that action and feeling are entwined.[110] According to Aristotle, our ability "to be capable" of feelings of "appetite, anger, fear, confidence, envy, joy, love, hate, longing, jealousy, pity and in general whatever implies pleasure or pain" is a matter of our "capacities" to not only "act well" but to "feel well."[111] With human existence comes the capability and power for self-activity, for the potential to flourish as species-beings. Yet at the same time, Marx is unequivocal: to be a human being is to suffer and risk failure. We can live well or poorly. To discover what is valuable in human life requires learning what it means to fail and feel that failure. Exercising the virtues is the ability to make judgements about our feelings, to deliberate and structure our action so we become better at reasoning about the emotional conflicts that structure the psyche. For human reasoning to flourish and achieve shared bonds of recognition between human beings, what is required is that this reasoning allows for the development of self-consciousness. This task necessitates the type of normative judgement that can only be made if there is something to be learnt about how our actions might affect ourselves and our social relationships. Reasoning is achieved by practices in which, by doing the good, we discover what flourishing really means for our lives. We need to suffer and fail for freedom to be meaningful precisely since this freedom depends on protecting and expanding the capacity for the good to be cultivated.[112]

Significantly, Marx's conception of reasoning necessitates that life activity is *self-conscious*. If "[m]an makes his life activity itself an object of his will and consciousness," then alienated labour, "reverses the relationship so that man, just because he is a conscious being, makes his life activity, his *being* [*Wesen*], a mere means for his *existence*."[113] That human beings can contemplate the meaning of our lives historically and consciously shows a kind of reflection only possible as a distinct kind of being who can deliberate about, choose and enact the practices which self-consciousness enables. In particular, we make life an object for ourselves. For Marx, the capacity to make one's life in the world involves the self-consciousness of that activity to be embedded in reason. Will and activity are fused together to reshape processes of labour from immediate and private tasks to a universalised, collective identity that stretches and incorporates into that activity self-transformation and flourishing.

In this analysis, Marx's understanding of human essence is both the specific form productive activity takes *and* the potential within that form for flourishing. This potentiality is the teleological expression of realised activity, taken from the view that human beings are rational animals who seek the good. If actualised, the creative aspects of productive activity become possible. This realisation would be a manifestation of the flourishing characteristic of human beings as essentially social and historical beings. This teleology cannot be seen as a predetermined course, but rather in a modified Aristotelian sense, as the actualisation of a potential. This latent potential is only realisable as the result of human action. For Marx, the rationality of the proletariat makes possible its self-consciousness, the moment of objectivity and subjectivity fused in praxis. The recognition of reality meets its rational alteration. This conception of praxis can only be understood with the impetus placed upon the emancipatory potential of human activity. To overcome alienated labour requires that the very activity of labour is transformed by rational agents within that social form itself and in doing so, acting for the sake of the living good. In this *praxis*, we make our lives free. Marx renders visible the way in which the question of freedom determines if productive activity is instrumental or if the end is acting well.

Conclusion: Living Labour and Capital

In the *EPM*, Marx articulates the historically and socially determinate mediations of productive activity. His social ontology pertains to the relationship between labour and capital and makes possible his theory of the value-form and his politics of class struggle. The contradiction between the capitalist and the worker (unity in opposition) expresses a relation which is mediated by labour. Marx explains this dialectic as "hostile reciprocal opposition."[114] The *EPM* puts forward his first definition of capital, which he glosses at this point as *"stored-up [aufgespeicherte] labour."*[115] This view of labour, which here Marx takes to be alienated labour, reveals a marked difference—even at this early stage of his thinking—with political economy. But only once "labour" is understood as alienated labour is the difference between Marx and political economy clear to see. According to Marx's value-form theory, the distinction between "living labour" and "dead labour" helps elucidate the unity of abstract and concrete labour within the systematic logic of capital as a social form. Marx develops a concept of value, in which wealth is not merely the movement of private property but is articulated more determinately; in H. G. Backhaus's formulation, " '[t]he *movement* of private property' is therefore the movement of the value of capital."[116] Marx's delineation of capital in this passage, as stored-up labour, provides the first articulation of a crucial aspect of this latter conception. The movement between capital and labour is shown to demonstrate a self-relation in which capital is subject.[117] Under the capitalist form, expended labour-power is a moment of capital that unfolds through the process of contradictory and alienated relations. The domination of capital is the domination of *human being*, which masks subjectivity and inverts consciousness into objectified relations.[118]

In Marx's conception of value, living labour is extracted and transformed into dead labour as capital. This ontology is shaped on one hand by the function and end of a labour process that valorises human labour-power, and, on the other, the efforts made in the class struggle to make that labour-power a capacity within rational human self-control. The dual character of living/dead labour in value points to an important political dimension of Marx's social ontology. The political upshot is that labour-power expresses the unity in opposition of human activity. This manifests in static embodiment as dead labour, activity embalmed in machinery and technology and in the living labour of class struggle. Here living labour confronts dead labour, not as a battle over automation, but as the control of human activity. Class struggle is the end-directed activity that expresses the social ontology of labouring activity—the unity of dead and living labour within the form of labour.

Further, this concept of activity is suggestive of Marx's normative idea of sociality. The "end" of labour and the realisation of self-conscious activity allows human beings to gain self-control of our specifically human capacities—rational and productive—and the coming-to-be of a form of society established by the *eudaimon* of its members. Marx and Engels oppose two different forms of society in the *Communist Manifesto*:

> In bourgeois society [*bürgerlichen Gesellschaft*], living labour [*lebendige Arbeit*] is but a means to increase accumulated labour. In Communist society [*kommunistischen Gesellschaft*], accumulated labour [*aufgehäufte Arbeit*] is but a means to widen, to enrich, to promote the life process [*Lebensprozeß*] of the labourer.[119]

In the former, living labour is a means to the end of capital accumulation, but to the latter, living labour is a means to the human end, which in turn cultivates a reciprocal relation between the human activity and the agent. Therefore, communism is a society which "[i]n place of the old bourgeois society, with its classes and class antagonisms, we shall have an association [*Assoziation*], in which the free development of each is the condition for the free development of all [*die freie Entwicklung eines jeden die Bedingung für die freie Entwicklung aller ist*]."[120] Communism is the flourishing of our individual and collective potential into a form of life that enables the living good of the political community to be realised. In his vision of the overcoming of alienation, Marx generates a normative conception of the good life and collective self-realisation of human capacities in the activity of being.

SIX

Form and Fetishism

"Capital" and Misrecognition

> I need a covering, a coat is a covering: I need a coat. What I need I ought to make, I need a coat: I make a coat. And the conclusion "I must make a coat" is an action. And the action goes back to a starting point. If there is to be a coat, there must first be this, and if this then this—and straightaway he does this. Now that the action is the conclusion is clear. But the premises of action are two kinds, of the good and the possible.
> —Aristotle[1]

MARX WAS NOT THE FIRST to present the dialectics of human action by examining the making of a coat. In this he follows Aristotle, who he considered the originator of value-form theory. As surprising as this view might at first appear, since Marx's value-form theory investigates the form of value specific to capitalism and not a transhistorical idea of value, this consideration helps motivate his entire approach in *Capital*. Marx unfolds the social and historical activities characteristic of capitalism as a dynamic inweaving of expressions and embodiments of human practices. This endeavour closely follows Aristotle's idea of substance as form and matter. Marx looks back to Aristotle—not the least since the ancient Greek could not look forward to capitalism—to elucidate the indispensable key to his analysis in *Capital*: the value-form. Marx's historicising of value develops the possibilities immanent in the Aristotelian theory of forms for his critique of political economy. As he goes on to show, the classical labour theory of value neglects the analysis of form and as a result cannot grasp the substance or expression of value as social relations between human beings. As with Aristotle, Marx brings to bear the critical insight that wealth creation is a question of ethical value.

Marx's *Capital* is the culmination of his social thought. This chapter analyses the normative content of the notion of sociality in his mature value-form theory. Economic theorists have long maintained that Marx accepts and modifies what classical political economy called "the labour theory of value" in following the efforts of Smith and Ricardo to provide an account of economic value from the embodied amount of individual units of physiological labour needed for the production of a commodity.[2] I reject this view, instead arguing Marx transforms the categories "value," "labour," "commodity," "money" and "capital," overcoming the ahistorical conception of wealth creation advanced by political economy and developing critical categories for theorising what is specific about capitalist social relations as a form of life. Marx's examination of the form-determinations specific to value, *commodity*, *money* and *capital*, substantiates his critical theory of modern society. After first outlining my interpretative approach, I trace the silhouette Aristotle and Hegel cast across the opening concepts of *Capital*. I then contrast Marx's view with Smith and Ricardo. Next, I gauge the absorption of Aristotle's ethics in Marx's value-form theory. Aristotle raises the question of justice in exchange, a normative view of relations of recognition. This theme animates Marx's critique of fetishism. Then, I assess the concept of capital and its end as accumulation. From here, I take up the Aristotelian and Hegelian elements of Marx's distinctive claim that value is an "automatic subject," which I argue must be understood as a form of misrecognition. This leads to a discussion of the abstract sociality of production in Marx's analysis of the labour process and its impact on "cooperation." Reconstructing Marx's idea of sociality gives shape to a vision of ethical life. While I focus on *Capital*, volume 1, I draw on a range of his later texts to illuminate the normative significance of the critique of political economy. Even if the "Hegelian, all-too-Hegelian" interpretations of *Capital* are well known and Aristotle's importance "has yet to register its full weight," as I see it, both thinkers must be read together for the philosophical stakes of Marx's critique to be best obtained.[3]

Marx's account of sociality imparts a way to think about ethical life in which rational relations of human activity are fully realised in shared interdependent association. Ethical life is the recognition of sociality. The analysis of the value-form that Marx advances enables a comprehension of capitalist modernity that examines how the social and asocial are bound up in the capital relation and at the same time immanently points to a "truly social" standpoint which transcends capital: absolute ethical life. Marx conceives of value as an abstract sociality. "Abstract" meaning a position removed (in thought and being) from the totality.[4] Abstract sociality is a totality of abstract thought and abstract labour, activity alienated and fetishistic under the form of value. The social forms of the modern world are defined by these abstractions, making unintelligible both the relations inherent in the collectivity of human activity and the self-consciousness of a social world of our making. Human beings cannot be at home in a world where the fetishism of value takes form. The abstract sociality of value is the misrecognition of social relations. Against the abstract, alienated person, Marx conceives a sociality beyond capital in terms of "the process of becoming" of "the social individual [*das gesellschaftlichen individuums*]," a concept of social being in which "subjects" are "individuals, but individuals in mutual relationships [*Individuen in Beziehungen auf einander*]."[5] However, he does not posit this idea in external opposition to capitalism but generates this concept from the analysis of the collective labour processes in capitalist production. In this respect, Marx's mature social theory facilitates systematic theorisation of the conditions and dynamics of modern life, both in terms of its constitutive forms and its contradictory tendencies that result in crisis. Marx conceives of modern social forms as relations of abstract domination. As *Capital* unfolds, the contraction between private and social labour is shown in increasingly concrete determinations of value as it shifts forms, striving to reproduce and accumulate. Without this understanding this movement, any theory of social interaction lacks a sufficient account of the defining features of wealth creation. It is not enough to gloss modernity as capitalist; the concept of capital must be grasped to adequately conceive social reality and subjectivity.

I interpret Marx's concept of value in relation to his social ontology. The form of value expresses the socialisation of relations of human activity shaped by the domination of capital, given in terms of its essence and appearance. Value is a *potential* which must be *actualised* through its metamorphoses of social forms. This chapter gives specific attention to the opening of *Capital* and the contribution of value-form theory to a concept of ethical life. I argue that Marx's dialectical unfolding of the categories of "commodity," "money" and "capital" tracks the social activity of human beings as ontologically expressed in relations determined by the form of value. This unfolding is historically specific to capital as the social relations of capitalism as a form of life. The analysis of objective social relations provides Marx with an immanent point of departure—a dialectical beginning—for a normative idea of social life and subjectivity that supersedes capital.

Capital as Critical Social Theory

By taking up Aristotle and Hegel, Marx's critical social theory points to absolute ethical life. *Capital* depicts the specific manifestations of "self-valorizing value" which appears as an absolute force over social life.[6] But value is nothing other than human activity. As such, the immanent potential for its sublation renders visible a form of ethical life in which the absolute is not abstract domination, but freedom. Marx probes the vicissitudes of objective processes that frustrate human flourishing and freedom; the living abstractions of time and labour, of dead labour over living labour. Human life is ruled by these abstractions, which are embodied in the capital relation. Marx's famous description of capital captures this ethical dimension: "Capital is dead labour which, vampire-like, lives only by sucking living labour, and lives the more, the more labour it sucks."[7] Capital can only exist by expanding and imposing its form, subsuming and inverting the activity of human beings into abstract and fetishistic modes of existence. Living labour is fire-like, providing the "vital energy" which makes possible the realisation of social need.[8] As dead labour, the fire of living labour is alienated and turned into its opposite.[9] If capital is "vampire-like," not only is the very content of human productive activity alienated from human agents, but the good life is made impossible.

By investigating the abstractions of social forms of life, Marx's mature writings aim to subject capital and its standpoint, as expressed in political economy, to an immanent critique.

> The exact development of the concept of capital [*Capitalbegriffs*] [is] necessary, since it [is] the fundamental concept of modern economics, just as capital itself, whose abstract, reflected image [is] its concept [*abstraktes Gegenbild sein Begriff*], [is] the foundation of bourgeois society. The sharp formulation of the basic presuppositions of the relation must bring out all the contradictions of bourgeois production, as well as the boundary where it drives beyond itself.[10]

This approach pushes the internal tensions within a dominant economic mode of thinking about social life by examining the categories of capitalist production and exchange in their own terms and assessing their conceptual content in an effort to test and move beyond their limits. Marx goes on to show what is unresolvable in the contradictions of bourgeois thought and being. The depth of influence of Aristotle and Hegel on *Capital* signifies at an immediate level why Marx saw it necessary to draw on the history of philosophy to understand the genesis and distinctiveness of capital as a social form and, in doing so, synthesise his own theoretical determinations from the Scottish Enlightenment and German Idealism back to Greek ethics.

Aristotle appears early in *Capital*, volume 1. In the first chapter, in his crucial discussion of the commodity, Marx credits Aristotle as "the first to analyse the value-form."[11] Marx draws on Aristotle's *Politics* and *Nicomachean Ethics* to conceptualise the variance between exchange relations ancient and modern—the capitalist inversions that render the needs of human beings subordinate to the needs of capital. In this historical constellation of social relations, human beings are now slaves to capital.[12] Aristotle's authoritative status in *Capital* helps illustrate Marx's critique of the quantitative rationality of Enlightenment thought culminating in political economy. The influence of Aristotle signifies the *value* of ethics in Marx's thought. By reconstructing the normative aspects of Marx's theory of value, his vision of social freedom is enriched. His mature writings preserve and expand the Aristotelian social ontology of the early texts by elaborating the way social forms of labour are shaped by value. Marx's mature work explicates a social ontology of value. The relation of labour to capital, the crux of alienation in 1844, is strengthened by the conceptualisation of the value-form and the social form of labour as abstract labour configured by the self-valorisation of value and accumulation of capital. These forms of being are specific to the modern world and to be comprehended must be understood as real abstractions, categories that pertain to social processes and relations. Marx's concept of abstract labour poses, in a more concrete and speculative manner, his early problem of alienation.

I contend that there is strong connection between Marx's early and late social thought, specifically that the ideas of human essence and alienation are maintained from the *EPM* to *Capital* and are operative in the concept of fetishism. This argument is at odds with that of many leading commentators. For example, despite Michael Heinrich's command of Marx's critique of political economy, he is unable to connect value-form theory with the normative underpinnings that make it adequately critical. Heinrich maintains (following Althusser's demarcation) that from the 1845/6 "The German Ideology" manuscripts, "the concept of a human species-being or essence no longer surfaces in Marx's work, and he only rarely and vaguely speaks of alienation."[13] On this basis, Heinrich goes on to assert that Marx's thought is constructed "without recourse to morality," yet in the same breath concludes Marx advocates for "a good and secure life, which can only be realised by transcending capitalism."[14] Heinrich demonstrates a common but contradictory position, holding that Marx can on one hand reject morality but on the other affirm a vision of the good life. This widespread view confuses the ethical importance of the concept of the good life and mobilises a narrow notion of moral thought. This line of thinking has dramatic implications for interpreting the normative meaning of Marx's critique of political economy. Following Heinrich (and drawing more explicitly on Althusser), Søren Mau makes a similar argument, but is more explicit about his nonnormative reading. Since Mau takes Marx's social ontology to advocate for a "romantic essentialism" which "construes anti-capitalist politics as the restoration of a natural order," it follows that a concept of human nature can describe "why it is possible for human beings to organise their social reproduction in so many different ways, but it can never serve as the normative basis for the rejection of a specific form of society."[15] However, Marx does not call for any return to nature, but rather articulates that human beings are social and historical beings and, as such, the forms of life that we establish, sustain and transform are normatively constituted. We cannot avoid normativity, which is embedded in our social forms and practices.[16] Marx's critique of capitalism is strengthened by making clear the extent that he believes our historical form of society is normatively unacceptable since it subsumes human activity under abstract domination and makes that activity unfree.

Marx never abandons social ontology. His early enunciation of alienation in *EPM* is developed in the analysis of value-producing, abstract labour that is so central to his mature texts. As an expression of alienated labour, understood in a more determinate way, abstract labour is both the precondition of capital and the result of capitalist production and exchange. Later in Marx's work, social ontology examines *forms* of value as expressions of alienated modes of being. The concept of alienation is deepened by his mature discussion of abstract labour.[17] The latter confirms Marx's critique of modern domination by revealing the way economic categories are held over the conditions of being—"individuals are ruled by abstractions"—and human activity is objectified by the capitalist form of private property, commodity production and exchange.[18] Modern social relations are presented as a unity of the social (production, circulation, reproduction) and the asocial (fetishistic, abstract, alienated). I term this unity of opposites "abstract sociality." In its simplest determinations, Marx notes the dialectical contradiction between use/exchange and quality/quantity in the production of commodities. These contradictions render social life abstract, detached from the creativity and purpose latent in the free control of human activity.[19] However, these abstractions can only be understood from the standpoint of the social whole.

Marx's concept of capital is carried out in terms of the dialectics of sociality. Capital is not a thing, but a relation which must be comprehended socially. By going step by step through Marx's beginning in *Capital* and stressing the significance of his mobilisation of Aristotle and Hegel, I reconstruct the normativity of this notion of sociality. Marx's procedure in *Capital* is given closest attention, but I make use of iterations of his value-form theory in other texts. *Capital* is best understood as part of a larger theoretical project in which the drafts, most notably the *Grundrisse*, play a substantial part.[20] The *Grundrisse* shines a distinctive light on Marx's critical social theory, with the prominence of the concept of alienation throughout the text and his notion of the "social individual."[21] It details how the concept of capital and the nature of social beings are intertwined. For Marx, the relation of the individual to the community can only be adequately understood by unravelling capital. In this way, a critique of modern social forms is required for any normative assessment of the spheres of rational life needed for a society of freedom. The project of *Capital* was continuously modified and ultimately left unfinished.[22] Its incompleteness makes doubtful the view that Marx's philosophy constitutes a system.[23] However, the dialectical approach I outline interprets the movement of categories in *Capital* through a systematic progression of real abstractions, in a manner closely related to Hegel.[24]

The spirit of Hegel traverses *Capital*. In Marx's words, the chapter on value is "coquetted with the mode of expression peculiar to him."[25] This chapter has been seen as his most obvious debt to Hegel. Cornelius Castoriadis fittingly describes the first chapter as "Hegelian through and through," observing that there is "something very much more than a 'coquetting' on Marx's part with Hegelian philosophical terminology; for the words in question are more than words, they correspond to philosophically laden concepts, which Marx uses in all their weight." Thereby, Marx distinguishes "value as such" in terms of "Substance/Essence" and "its Form, the Form of that Substance/Essence, the Form of Value."[26]

Marx's debt to Hegel is commonly seen strictly in methodological terms, as the mode of abstraction which supplies his particular form of "scientific" analysis.[27] However, the focus on method only goes halfway in expressing the significance of Hegel's *Logic* to *Capital*, which not only furnishes the mode of presentation but helps inform the content of Marx's critique of dualism, in his attempt to unify form/content and fact/value in a critical theory of modern society. The social forms Marx examines pertain to the social content and the empirical weight of his critique of political economy. This critique is developed immanently. Marx shares with Hegel the aim of comprehending reality in thought, a task that does not posit phenomena as pregiven but endeavours to conceptually derive reality by the ordering of categories which become increasingly concrete through their exposition. Despite his famous profession, Marx does not so much turn Hegel on his head, but rather parallels the dialectical procedure of unfolding form-determinations to go beyond pregiven realities.[28]

Marx immanently unfolds the central conceptual categories in his theory of value: commodity, money, capital. He shows how the derivations of each social form provide the necessary determinations for the conceptual movement from one category to the next. Each social form is a unity in opposition containing two sides, a positive and a negative, the latter acting as a contradictory force, "constantly striving to overcome" itself and establish a new relation that preserves its truth in a more concrete form.[29] Basic categories like use and exchange value (simple unity) are given further content, from which Marx derives a transition into a more concrete but contradictory form (opposition) and further to the fully distinguished incorporation of both previous forms as a unity of opposites. Marx's early discussion of the elementary, expanded and general forms of value leads to the money-form and demonstrates this conceptual ordering.[30] According to this view, it would be nonsensical to consider the value of a commodity without it being an object with a price. The social form of making and giving monetary value to objects of human activity is what Marx's investigations seek to render visible.

In his dialectic, Marx provides an immanent theorisation of the objective character of social being as mediated by the subjectivity of creative activity. Social relations express both the activity of human agents and the objectification of this activity into stratified and fetishistic relations that disfigure and distort social subjectivity. Marx's theorisation of value grasps social forms as activities of being. Like Hegel, his logical unfolding of categories is also an ontology. By investigating the social forms specific to capitalism, Marx conceives of capital as a process and social relation. Capital is self-expanding value, which valorises itself through the production and exchange of commodities on the market. The concept of capital demonstrates a central aspect of the role of social ontology in Marx's thought, the ontology of social forms. Seen this way, the social ontology of value is capital's self-expansion. The accumulation of value is only possible as the result of a particular social form of human activity, and it is exactly these parasitic relations that are the lifeblood of capitalism. Value expands only by human activity taking the specific social form of abstract labour and taking its necessary mode of expression in the very form that appears to everyone to have no limit whatsoever: money.

Marx's mature texts express his idea of human sociality by exposing the "asocial" character of a commodity-producing society.[31] For commodity production to be generalisable it must be predicated on the sociality of exchange relations between equals. However, these relations are necessarily particular since we appear on the market as distinct individuals. Abstract labour mediates this particularity with the universal relation of social intelligibility: the form of value. As individuals, with only our particular labour-power to sell, we confront value in its form of appearance as price. Through prices the social world is valued. Social relations founded on these abstract forms of interaction reflect an inherent asociality within a social form compelled by a universalising logic. Since this logic is premised on abstract labour, it prevents its concrete universality from being realised. Social freedom is undermined by its conditions of existence.[32] The independence of labour is conditioned by dependence on wage-labour. This contradiction requires negating the form of value and the collective recognition of human sociality in social freedom.

Entwined with the analysis of the most central concepts in *Capital*, Marx enhances his concept of labour. Construed in normative terms, it becomes possible to see the central motivations of his account of the capitalist mode of production not as a descriptive and value-free examination, but instead as an evaluative and critical account. Under capitalism, labour has a "dual character": commodity-producing labour is both concrete and abstract. While Marx makes this conceptual distinction, in the performance of wage-labour itself they are inseparable. Marx's concept pertains to the relation between human activity and the social relations that ensue in a process in which labouring activity is measured by abstract time and value is extracted and valorised. He points to the primacy of the relationship of exchange between the seller and buyer of labour-power that defines commodity production. The worker sells their labour-power for a wage, and the capitalist buys that living labour, puts it to work and sells what it creates.[33] As Isaak Illich Rubin notes, "The transformation of individual into socially-necessary labor takes place through the same process of exchange which transforms private and concrete labor into social and abstract labor."[34]

Marx has a "value theory of labour" where the form of labour contains two pairs of categories: the first, concrete and abstract labour, and second, private and social.³⁵ Marx's distinction between productive activity and wage-labour deciphers the specific character of capitalist production as predicated upon an objectified and alienated social form of labour. The implications of this analysis powerfully impact the way Marx's social thought is interpreted.³⁶ When abstract labour is considered with its full significance, the normative content of his critique of capitalism can be more fully defined. Capital is understood as the movement of value, as it self-valorises, absorbing living labour and transforming this activity into further value. Marx develops this concept to reveal the domination of abstract social forms. The fetish character of commodities, money and capital come to shape and dominate everyday life, relentlessly subsuming human activity under their logic. However central Marx's account of abstract labour is to his concept of capital, he starts his analysis instead with the commodity and its form of value:

> To develop the concept of capital it is necessary to begin not with labour but with value, and, precisely, with exchange value in an already developed movement of circulation. It is just as impossible to make the transition directly from labour to capital as it is to go from the different human races directly to the banker, or from nature to the steam engine.³⁷

To arrive at a concrete conception of capital, a categorical ordering of the prior social forms specific to the object of investigation is required for the necessary transitions to hold. Although labour "seems a quite simple category," it is shot through with modern abstractions:

> This example of labour shows strikingly how even the most abstract categories, despite their validity—precisely because of their abstractness—for all epochs, are nevertheless, in the specific character of this abstraction, themselves likewise a product of historic relations, and possess their full validity only for and within these relations.³⁸

Marx's concept of capital provides a way to comprehend modern sociality and its social forms of value as inherently asocial, abstract and fetishistic. The concept of capital makes explicit the historicity of value-producing labour and questions its conditions of existence.

Marx not only condemns capitalism in terms of its alienated and abstract forms of activity but suggests that by negating these forms new modes of social interaction based upon socially comprehended and rational forms of association could emerge. This realisation of human potentiality frames the realm of freedom. Marx conceives of the human being in terms of the "social individual," where the egotism and dualism of capitalist social relations are not simply replaced by an all-encompassing collective, but individuality is recognised in its fully determinate sociality. Capitalism is constituted by abstract social relations that are at the same time hidden behind the backs of producers and as money appear as all powerful forces beyond human control. As Marx would have it, a social form of life beyond capital could enable relations between human beings to become concretely free in institutions of social freedom, which are self-conscious and rational. This potential arises from the social aspects of labour processes, made apparent with capitalism only in an abstract alienated form. The realisation of a concretely social form of labour in recognitive institutions of universal freedom requires the negation of capital and its associated forms of labour. Marx sees human potential as fundamentally restricted by the exploitative social relations of capitalist society. This analysis underscores that capitalism reduces human life to the fetishism of exchange. At the same time, under capitalism, the contradictions inherent within abstract social forms lay the basis for their overcoming by self-conscious human action.

Marx's critical social theory identifies the domination inherent in the movement of value and the relational ontology of social forms. Hegel's *Logic* helps think about the abstractions which begin Marx's critique of political economy. The question of beginnings allows the genesis and structure of Marx's conceptual thought to be clearly outlined. After considering Hegel's place in the opening, I proceed through Marx's form-determinations, pausing to elaborate on Aristotle's role in the systematic ordering of concepts. With this systematic logic, Marx employs Aristotle's ethical thought to his immanent critique of modern sociality. Through a close reading of *Capital*, it becomes clear that in grasping the logic of social forms, Marx wants to show how capital systematically eludes an ethical life. For Marx, capital produces and reproduces the *wrong life* but in understanding it, the possibilities for its overcoming are immanent. Marx wants to identify the barriers to mutual recognition as they exist within the social forms that define the modern world.

Capital's Beginning

Hegel's *Science of Logic* starts with the question: "With What Must the Beginning of Science Be Made?". This work concerns the form and content of philosophy itself as scientific truth, self-knowledge of subject and object in consciousness.[39] Hegel's aim is to locate a speculative beginning which allows thought to proceed, not from a dogmatic and presupposed starting point, but conceptually from the most basic abstraction pertaining to its object to increasingly concrete forms derived logically through the transition of one to the next.[40] Hegel warns against modes of thinking which dogmatically assume their content from the beginning, having little regard for method, relying on assertion, faith or intuition "shot from a pistol."[41] Instead, for thought to have any claim to "genuine knowing" it "must laboriously travel down a long path."[42] In this sense, the becoming of speculative thought is known through the content and shape of thought through its emergence.[43] Method and content are united in this process, which demands that the beginning be logical.[44] The method then becomes possible only at the end, after its appearance can be grasped as a sequence of experiences. Method is then justified.

The object of inquiry, absolute truth, begins with the *abstract* immediacy of being. Only from an abstract undetermined beginning can the doctrines of being, essence and concept be traced to their full truth in absolute knowledge. For Hegel, the absolute idea becomes known at the end of this process of development, providing justification for the analysis through its exposition. Famously, thought returns within itself: "Essential to science is not so much that a pure immediacy should be the beginning, but that the whole of science is in itself a circle in which the first becomes also the last, and the last also the first."[45] For the further determinations to validate the beginning, these derivations must transition from one form to the next, sublating the previous content in the transition. Thought progresses logically through the form-determinations that pertain to the object of philosophical truth.[46] Hegel writes,

> the beginning of philosophy is the ever present and self-preserving foundation of all subsequent developments, remaining everywhere immanent in its further determinations [*Bestimmungen*]. In this advance the beginning thus loses the one-sidedness that it has when determined simply as something immediate and abstract; it becomes mediated [*Vermitteltes*], and the line of scientific forward movement consequently turns *into a circle*.—It also follows that what constitutes the beginning, because it is something still undeveloped and empty of content, is not yet truly known at that beginning, and that only science, and science [*Wissenschaft*] fully developed, is the completed cognition of it, replete with content and finally truly grounded.[47]

This mode of thinking is specific to the subject matter under investigation, which for Hegel is the activity of pure thought. The movement and mediation of thought reflects its increasing concreteness as it sublates itself in its becoming. Thereby, speculative thought proceeds from an abstract beginning through the negativity of conceptual mediation and negation to universality. Hegel describes this process in terms of the movement of the analytic (passive thought, "which takes up its object") and the synthetic (the negative, which "demonstrates itself to be the activity of the concept itself").

> The moments of the speculative method are (a) the *beginning* [*Anfang*], which is being or the immediate; for itself for the simple reason that it is the beginning. From the vantage point of the speculative idea, however, it is the speculative idea's *self-determining* [*Selbstbestimmen*] which, as the absolute negativity or movement of the concept, *judges* and posits itself as the negative of itself. *Being,* which from the vantage point of the beginning as such appears as abstract affirmation, is thus instead the *negation, positedness*, being-mediated in general and being *pre*-supposed. But as the negation of the *concept* that is simply identical with itself in its otherness and is the certainty of itself, it is the concept not yet posited as concept or, in other words, it is the concept *in itself* [*der Begriff an sich*].—For that reason, as the still undetermined concept, i.e. the concept determined only in itself for immediately, this being is just as much the *universal* [*Allgemeine*].
>
> The beginning is taken in the sense of immediate being from intuition and perception—the beginning of the *analytic* method of finite knowing; in the sense of the universality, it is the beginning of the synthetic method of such knowing. Since, however, the logical [dimension] is immediately something universal as much as something that is [*Seiendes*], just as much something presupposed by the concept as it is immediate, its beginning is as much synthetic as it is analytic.[48]

Hegel's beginning gives conceptual thinking a distinct advantage over empiricism, which as the theoretical basis of political economy, prefigures Marx's approach.[49] In Hegel's view, empiricism starts uncritically with concepts already laden with content and as a result cannot progress logically. Empiricism claims to explain reality from the immediacy of its knowledge claim; however, the conceptual starting point presupposes too much for the progression of concepts to be carried out coherently. Empiricism is predicated upon the false abstraction of a presupposed beginning without adequate justification of this beginning. By taking the sensuous and immediate of given objects as a starting point, the mediations that make it intelligible in the first place are elided. Further, conceptual mediation, the content of concepts (economy, population, etc.), is given false concreteness. He does not dismiss the necessity of empirical knowledge, but instead insists it be logically ordered.[50] Hegel's beginning is adopted in a critical manner by Marx. While the former is insistent on the presuppositionless concept of being, Marx begins with the commodity. This does not prevent a logical derivation of concepts, as I outline next, but it does stipulate the object of his investigation. However, whereas Hegel's critique is focused on the dualism of the Enlightenment expressed in the categories of pure thought, Marx focuses his critique of Enlightenment dualism in the thought of political economy expressed in the concept of capital.[51]

In *Capital*, Marx's beginning is "difficult."[52] His object of scientific inquiry, *Wissenschaft*, is not thought itself, but the categories of being specific to the social forms of capitalism. For Marx, the existence of wealth in the modern world must be understood immanently. Marx's critique of political economy takes the basic concepts as he finds them in political economy and ascertains their truth content. He does this by probing the contradictions inherent in their concepts to lend currency to their insights, while revealing what they conceal about social life, thereby historically situating the concepts at a higher, integrated and more complex level. This procedure of immanent critique can be seen in the concepts Marx borrows from other thinkers but radically develops to a point in which the content of those concepts is filled with a substantially different meaning. This approach both immanently reconfigures and appropriates the history of social thought, rejecting the fetishistic naturalisation of capital by the political economists of the Scottish Enlightenment, culminating in Smith and Ricardo.[53] Marx opens *Capital* with the claim that:

> The wealth of societies [*Gesellschaften*] in which the capitalist mode of production prevails appears as an "immense collection of commodities"; the individual commodity appears as its elementary form. Our investigation therefore begins with the analysis of the commodity.[54]

If capitalist wealth confronts us as a vast array of commodities, Marx specifies that the appearance of the commodity, as it becomes visible in its "its elementary form," is his object of investigation. From this first sentence, Marx is concerned with identifying what is specific about capitalism as a form of life. Taking the commodity as the most general social category of capitalism entitles him to ask what it is about commodity production and exchange that leads to the creation and reproduction of these appearances.[55] In Marx's value-form theory, wealth appears in the form of money. By starting with the commodity, Marx is not suggesting that the commodity comes first in capitalist society historically but that it is logically prior.[56] The most basic unit of the capitalist form of life is the commodity, products made for exchange on a commodity market. As Marx argues, the social character of the commodity is only intelligible by investigating the specific process in which a product of human labour becomes a value. Beginning with the commodity, Marx can determine how it becomes a "citizen" of the world expressing the formal freedom of bourgeois society.[57] However, he does not assume that value is a pregiven natural category. Rather, in contrast with influential interpretations, Marx argues that value is a historically specific category.[58] *Capital* opens with a reference to the first sentence of Marx's own 1859 work, *A Contribution to the Critique of Political Economy*: "The wealth of bourgeois society, at first sight, presents itself as an immense accumulation of commodities, its unit being a single commodity. Every commodity, however, has a twofold aspect—*use-value* and *exchange value*."[59] The dialectics of social form act as a compass to Marx's critique of political economy, pointing the direction from his analysis of the commodity as a value-object to the normative lights of his understanding of abstract labour.

Aristotle is indispensable for Marx's value-form theory from the very beginning of his exposition in *Capital*. To give an account of value, Marx holds that the character of the simple determinations "use" and "exchange" must be first examined.[60] To the above passage,[61] Marx notes in the Greek original a passage from book 1 of the *Politics*:

> Each piece of property has two uses, both of which are uses of it intrinsically, but not uses of it intrinsically in the same way. Instead, one properly belongs to the thing, while the other does not properly belong to it—for example, as regards a shoe, its use in wearing it and its use in exchange. For both are uses to which a shoe can be put. For someone who exchanges a shoe in return for money or food with someone who needs a shoe is using the shoe insofar as it is a shoe. But this is not the use that properly belongs to it. For it does not come to exist for the sake of exchange. And it is the same way with other pieces of property as well.[62]

The contrast Aristotle draws between the use and exchange of property informs his discussion of "wealth-acquisition," in which he distinguishes the kind of barter that allows the household (*oikos*) to be sustained through use of the article from the hoarding of coin without limit.[63] Use is the *ergon*, the proper function of the article pertaining to its nature. If a thing performs its *ergon*, Aristotle considers this end a virtue, its proper definition and "best state."[64] In this view, exchange is also useful in its ability to meet needs, but the primary function of the article is its capacity to fulfill a use. Exchange facilitates the normativity of reciprocal relations between subjects.[65]

Since Marx's task is to grasp the form of value, Aristotle's distinction helps highlight the specifically capitalist unity of use and exchange value inherent in the commodity. But Marx does not simply assume Aristotle's ancient categories apply in the same way. His concern is that the use/exchange relation takes a distinctively modern inversion under the value-form, where the *ergon* of the thing as defined by the virtue of it being a commodity, a value-object, is exchange. For this reason, the opening dialectic of *Capital* is the "doublet [*Doppeltes*]" form of use-value and value.[66] Aristotle's normative distinction becomes unviable under the capitalist form of life, leading to an inversion in the distinction and priority between use and exchange.[67] Accordingly, "[t]he historical broadening and deepening of the phenomenon of exchange develops the opposition between use-value and value which is latent in the nature of the commodity."[68] The "deepening" of exchange denotes the historical process in which commodity exchange becomes universalised and wage-labour becomes capital posting. In this way, the commodity Marx investigates is not simply an object for exchange across time, but a category that is dependent on the historically specific form of social relations in a value-producing society.[69]

The opening of *Capital* unfolds the conceptual coming-to-be of capital. Here capital appears in its "elementary forms," the commodity and money.[70] Marx's beginning grasps the most general form of capital, the commodity, and from its duality moves to a more concrete expression of value, money and then to capital fully realised. This derivation is conducted without the level of concretisation that occurs as the argument proceeds (wages, rent, etc.). These determinations are expositions of the fetish forms outlined in volume 1 (and unfolded across the manuscripts for volumes 2 and 3) culminating in the Trinity Formula of capital-profit, land-rent and labour-wages, the form which "holds in itself all the mysteries of the social production process."[71] Only from an abstraction that comprehends the most basic character of a form is it possible to logically add determinations. *Capital* identifies that his investigation will "first of all" begin with the commodity.[72] This beginning expresses the movement between two dialectical moments, two points of departure. The movement "from the abstract to the concrete" is not "abstract" as an intangible factor of thought but a *real abstraction*.[73] From grasping the most basic unit of value, the commodity, it is then possible to unfold more complex determinations through a logical derivation of categories.

The double starting point is between: first, the concrete immediacy of the individual commodity, and second, the abstract, the form of value. The commodity gives an abstract and simple starting point between the use-value of commodities and value as the universal relation of abstract social labour. Jairus Banaji notes:

> As the immediate appearance of the total process of capital (this can be called *value as a totality reflected-into-itself* for all categories of capital are categories of value), the individual commodity forms the *analytic* point of departure. From this, however, we do not pass over directly to the concept of capital. By analysing the commodity, drawing out its determinations, we arrive at the concept of *value* as the abstract-reified form of social labour. This as the ground of all further conceptual determinations (money, capital) forms the *synthetic* point of departure of *Capital*.[74]

This double starting point begins with the real abstraction of the commodity and then proceeds from this determination to the value relation as a dialectic of essence (abstract labour) and appearance (money). Marx summarises the rationale of an abstract point of departure, which also considers the concreteness of the individual commodity:

> We begin with the commodity, with this specific social form of the product—for it is the foundation and premise of capitalist production. We take the individual product in our hand and analyse the formal determinants that it contains as a commodity and which stamp it as a commodity.[75]

Here Marx should not be mistaken as making the empiricist claim that capitalism can be understood from simply physically grasping the products of capitalist production. Instead, analysis of the conceptual determination specific to capitalist social forms must proceed from abstracting the most basic form of immediacy to grasp its content. The commodity furnishes this point of departure since it expresses two moments of value, use and exchange.[76]

The "external object" of the commodity is its qualifiable *use*, the ability to satisfy human needs, whether they be of the "stomach" or "the imagination."[77] At this point, Marx puts to the side the exact nature of hypothetical needs, since his focus is the socially recognisable features of use-values.[78] Marx is not describing the use of any particular article but of the *use-value of a commodity* within its form. In this context, the seemingly less concrete category of "use" is necessary to articulate the way in which "use-value itself—as the use-value of the 'commodity'—processes a historically specific character."[79] Use-values are heterogeneous but all useful things possess specific quantities, in addition to the qualifiable utility of the object, for example, the need for two shoes or one house. Use-value relates to needs; it cannot "dangle in mid-air."[80] In this way, use-value is carried in the material character of the commodity. Use-value expresses these two poles, quality and quantity, but requires a "social *measurement* for the *quantity* of useful things" since possible uses will vary.[81] Thus a commodity must be useful to be a commodity, but not all useful things are commodities. The use-value of a product of concrete human labour is realised when it is consumed, or expended, but once quantified by exchange value, commodities make their appearance as value-objects with a price and must be socially validated by being sold:

> Exchange-value appears first of all as the quantitative relation, the proportion, in which use-values of one kind exchange for use-values of another kind. This relation changes constantly with time and place. Hence exchange-value appears to be something accidental and purely relative, and consequently an intrinsic value, i.e. an exchange-value that is inseparably connected with the commodity, inherent in it, seems a contradiction in terms.[82]

This is not an "accidental" process, as Marx explains in detail. If two commodities are to be exchanged they must be measured quantifiably. When the commodities are put next to each other, their exchangeability is measured in quantities—for example "5 beds = 1 house"—which identifies something in common of "identical magnitude" to both things, but irreducible to either. This is "reducible" to a "third thing."[83] At this point of the exposition, Marx introduces labour:

> If then we disregard the use-value of commodities, only one property remains, that of being products of labour. But even the product of labour has already been transformed in our hands. If we make abstraction from its use-value, we abstract also from the material constituents and forms which make it a use-value. It is no longer a table, a house, a piece of yarn or any other useful thing. All its sensuous characteristics are extinguished. Nor is it any longer the product of the labour of the joiner, the mason or the spinner, or of any other particular kind of productive labour. With the disappearance of the useful character of the products of labour, the useful character of the kinds of labour embodied in them also disappears; this in turn entails the disappearance of the different concrete forms of labour. They can no longer be distinguished, but are all together reduced to the same kind of labour, human labour in the abstract.[84]

The productive activity of concrete labouring is equalised as homogeneous abstract labour. This form is dualistic, a unity between concrete and abstract labour. Concrete labour makes useful things, but they do not become commodities until the labouring tasks that create those objects are compared by a social process that equalises that activity homogeneously by putting a price on it. It is not labour as such that creates value in this socially specific way, but abstract labour. Indeed, abstract labour is "the substance, and the immanent measure of value, but it has no value itself."[85] What is already evident in these passages is a strong evocation of the separation of the worker from the product of their labour—where the sensuous, human characteristics of the product are obscured—which must appear as the relation between commodities which stamps their socially recognised "value" as money.[86]

Significantly, Marx shows from the very start of *Capital* that value is a human relation, a mediation of activity and cannot be produced sui generis by a machine. Marx's conception of value specifies the social relation between human beings that products of human productive activity mediate through the buying and selling of commodities. This is at odds with reductive, simplistic understandings of value as either the immediate utility or simply the price of any given commodity. A commodity can be held, value cannot.

> We may twist and turn a single commodity as we wish; it remains impossible to grasp it as a thing possessing value. However, let us remember that commodities possess an objective character as values only in so far as they are all expressions of an identical social substance [*gesellschaftlichen Einheit*], human labour, that their objective character as values is therefore purely social [*rein gesellschaftlich*].[87]

Marx's understanding of "substance" in this passage insists that value is not physical outputs of labour, but a social form. Following Aristotle, a substance is comprised of its form (what it is) and its matter (what makes it what it is).[88] With the example of the linen and coat that run through chapter 1, Marx demonstrates the way in which the products of labour by the weaver and tailor become values.[89] Since the common social substance of value is abstract labour, as a relation it can only become actualised as the form of value in its material existence as money. Traced from its most simple relation, the form of value expresses two poles—the relative and equivalent forms of value. Through developing this example, Marx is picking apart the "mystery" of the form of value. He shows how the labour-time socially necessary to produce both linen and coats "can *only* be expressed relatively," that is, in "another commodity."[90] Thus, the linen when related to the coat, as 20 yards = 1 coat, expresses a value. At the same time, the linen expresses its use-value in the coat, it gains a value quite "distinct" from its "physical form" and becomes "abstract," that is, measurable as something quantifiable and exchangeable for the creation of coats.[91] Marx understands the value substances of coats and linen *purely* in terms of social relations.[92]

The commodity embodies the dual character of labour. The linen had to be woven by concrete labouring, but to express value this activity must become objectified as abstract labour for it to be compared with other commodities. Abstract labour is socially necessary for acts of private labour to be measured, and it is this social mediation which both commodities have in common. Private labour employed to produce commodities can therefore only be understood in terms of the social determinations that enable activity to be socially equated. Marx is investigating the process in which the relation between the labour and the product of labour are made abstract by measurement in quantities of time and money.[93] Commodities are no longer seen individually, but as value-objects take on a new life as citizens of the world. To do this, value must assume its social form as money, which makes it possible for commodities to be constituted as objects of value and exchanged. Value as a social relation expresses its necessary "form of appearance" as exchange-value.[94] Marx suggests that the "immanent" measure of value is labour-time, which "exists only as an ideal," and money is the concrete "external measure" and "material existence."[95] For value to be actualised as a *social form*, products of socially necessary abstract labour must be measured in money and validated through exchange.[96] Marx's analysis of commodity-producing labour is nothing but the analysis of the social mediations of human activity and the alienation of that activity in the social forms of abstract labour and money. As Engels warned in his correspondence with Marx in 1867, this sequence in *Capital* can seem to layer abstraction upon abstraction. However, the nub of Marx's view may become clearer when contextualised with a view of his adversaries.

The Labour Theory of Value

To appreciate the stakes of this argument fully, it pays to more clearly demarcate Marx's critique of the classical labour theory of value. To many contemporary commentators, Adam Smith's labour theory is a failure best forgotten.[97] Yet, Smith's attempt to find a measure of value opens a line of investigation that Marx transforms and transcends by conceiving value in terms of its form-determinations. According to Marx, the total value of a commodity for Smith "is determined by the amount of labour that the worker has spent in its production."[98] Smith's theory was a means to account for the price of the commodity by starting with the quantity of labour expended on its production.[99] For example, a woollen coat requires not just a detailed division of labour in its production, but a great variety of different labours to locate the materials, bring them together and a variety of labours within the means of production itself.[100] For Smith, each "add" value to the commodity as it is before them, regardless of the object's value prior to labour. The worker "creates a value in the commodity form."[101] Smith theorises the division of the technical aspects of the labour process as a virtue of the productive efficiency that has come to fruition with commercial society and the social improvement brought about by the "invisible hand" of market forces. The division of labour increases the quantities of performed labour through three factors: the dexterity of the specialised worker, the time saved in the "workhouse" and the machinery that allows "one man to do the work of many."[102] The central problem Smith is trying to address is the technical division of production, which is becoming increasingly specialised with early manufactory.

However, in Smith's conception the division of labour that accompanies commodity production is a constant feature of human interaction. This theory of human nature imagines individuals as isolated producers of commodities and posits all production as commodity production. Smith gives priority to economic factors in the operation of the market and goes well beyond causal explanations of commercial enterprise. "Economic science" is first codified by Smith.[103] However, his explanatory model of social life is premised on an idea of human beings as motivated by economic interests. In Smith's view, "commercial society" is natural since it finally allows human beings to trade at will.[104] But there is a crucial moral dimension to this argument. The market empowers people to become moral agents. Heavily indebted to Hume's empiricism, Smith's moral philosophy is founded on the individual who is connected to others by commercial activity.[105] The idea of benevolence in *The Theory of Moral Sentiments* suggests that it is not just self-interest that motivates action, but also the goods of others.[106] However, Smith's ontology is of individuals who decide to act for others, but not *with* others. According to MacIntyre:

> Adam Smith's contrast between self-interested market behavior on the one hand and altruistic, benevolent behavior on the other, obscures from view just those types of activity in which the goods to be achieved are neither mine-rather-than-others" nor others'-rather-than-mine, but instead are goods that can only be mine insofar as they are also those of others, that are genuinely common goods, as the goods of networks of giving and receiving are.[107]

With the *Wealth of Nations*, the establishment of modern economic theory went hand in hand with Smith's ontological views. Despite Smith's motivation to chart the tendencies and dynamics of the capitalist economy, he understands these dynamics to be perpetual aspects of human nature, unfettered in modern "commercial society." For Smith, the individual trader needs society to enhance their commercial interests.[108] He locates the division of labouring tasks for self-interested purposes as a feature of the earliest types of societies. Smith superimposes the logic of commodity-producing society onto all history and provides for a human nature that is by definition commercial and egotistical.[109] Accordingly, "by treaty, by barter, and by purchase" trade ensures mutually needed goods. Smith goes so far as to claim that in hunter and agrarian societies, those who made bows and arrows and thus demonstrated a greater capacity for the task used their industry to trade with others in their "own interest," becoming "a sort of armourer," that is, a specialised profession.[110] Since value comes from labour in production, Smith gives significant attention to the material and technical division of labour but insists that the division of labour in capitalist production can be read back onto all forms of society. In this sense, Smith confuses the technical and social division of labour.[111] Further, since he sees all labour as fundamentally producing exchange value, he fails to note the historically specific distinction between "labour that creates value" and "labour that creates objects of use."[112]

Alternatively, Marx points out that in early communal societies there is a social division of labour but no generalised commodity production. By contrast, in modern commodity-producing societies "labour is systematically divided in every factory, but the workers do not bring about this division by exchanging their individual products." We do not take home the products of labour and then take them to the market as we wish. Marx adds: "Only the products of mutually independent acts of labour, performed in isolation, can confront each other as commodities."[113] This distinctive social division of labour is needed for commodity production to be generalised:

> Men made clothes for thousands of years, under the compulsion of the need for clothing, without a single man ever becoming a tailor. But the existence of coats, of linen, of every element of material wealth not provided in advance by nature, had always to be mediated through a specific productive activity appropriate to its purpose, a productive activity that assimilated particular natural materials to particular human requirements.[114]

David Ricardo begins *On the Principles of Political Economy and Taxation* by criticising Smith's account for failing to consistently find a measure of value in the "quantity of labour necessary to produce" a particular object. Smith "sometimes speaks of food grain, at other times of labour as a standard measure" of value.[115] Ricardo's aim is to give a precise explanation of "value" in the labour embodied in commodities. If two capitalists employ the "same quantity of labour" per year for commodity production, the commodities will be of a different value

> on account of the different quantities of fixed capital, or accumulated labour, employed by each respectively. The cloth and cotton goods are of the same value, because they are the produce of equal quantities of labour, and equal quantities of fixed capital; but corn is not of the same value as these commodities, because it is produced, as far as regards fixed capital, under different circumstances.[116]

Ricardo's refined theory locates value in the amount of labour-time contained in the commodity.[117] This innovation, although hugely significant, is typically seen to be Marx's position.[118] This view, at first sight, is supported by Ricardo's starting point—the division between "use" and "exchange" value as abstractions measured by labour-time. Indeed, *Capital* starts with the same abstraction.

However, Marx differentiates himself explicitly from political economy in the opening of *Capital* by his claim that the commodity is the expression of value as the "*elementary form*" of capitalist wealth. When Marx introduces labour in the social form of abstract labour, he makes clear this is not measured in embodied units of labour-time, but by the social mediation of "socially necessary labour-time"; that is, value-producing abstract labour can only be understood in a society in which commodity production is generalised.[119] By representing social need through the exchange of objects, the commodity expresses a social relation.[120] Value, as Rubin notes, "does not characterise things, but human relations in which things are produced."[121] Marx argues: "The real value of a commodity, however, is not its individual, but its social value; that is to say, its value is not measured by the labour-power that the article costs the producer in each individual case, but by the labour-time socially required for its production."[122] Value-producing labour is historically specific to this social form of production. By analysing value as a social form, Marx is doing something quite different from the Ricardian construal of value as performed labour.[123] He contends,

> Political economy has indeed analysed value and its magnitude, however incompletely, and has uncovered the content concealed within these forms. But it has never once asked the question why this content has assumed that particular form,

that is to say, why labour is expressed in value, and why the measurement of labour by its duration is expressed in the magnitude of the value of the product.[124]

Despite the depth of Ricardo's efforts to make apparent the measurement of labour value, he represents the fundamental limitations of political economy. Without a comprehension of the realisation of value within its social form, the difference between labour and abstract labour is left unanalysed. Marx observes, "[i]t does not occur to the economists that a purely quantitative distinction between the kinds of labour presupposes their qualitative unity or equality, and therefore their reduction to abstract human labour."[125] Classical political economy defines value as individual units of physiological labour, but this position is abstracted from the social relations in which value-producing labour becomes a commodity and is equated on the market as a historically specific social form.[126]

As a result, Ricardo, in Marx's evaluation, is "unconcerned with 'human beings' and concentrates exclusively on the development of productive forces."[127] Political economy naturalises value by creating a dualism between the isolated and alienated worker and the social processes of capitalist production. In contrast, Marx maintains the historical and social relations of capitalist society are mediated by value. As he notes in the *Grundrisse*:

> Each individual's production is dependent on the production of all others; and the transformation of his product into the necessaries of his own life is [similarly] dependent on the consumption of all others. Prices are old; exchange also; but the increasing determination of the former by costs of production, as well as the increasing dominance of the latter over all relations of production, only develop fully, and continue to develop ever more completely, in bourgeois society, the society of free competition [*bürgerlichen Gesellschaft, der Gesellschaft der freien Concurrenz*]. What Adam Smith, in the true eighteenth-century manner, puts in the prehistoric period, the period preceding history, is rather a product of history.[128]

A further dualism arises from the naturalised standpoint, the unexplainable gulf between quality and quantity.[129] Marx attempts to overcome these dualisms to demonstrate that not only is value-producing labour distinct from other social forms, but the production and exchange of commodities are intertwined processes which together constitute value as a social relation. Since Marx construes value as self-posited through the production and reproduction of capital, it is crucial to see that value is given actuality through its metamorphosis through various shapes, starting with the value of a commodity.

Traced from its most simple relation, the form of value expresses two poles—the relative and equivalent forms of value. Marx makes clear that the "whole mystery of the form of value lies hidden in this simple form. Our real difficulty, therefore, is to analyse it."[130] The linen is the commodity which expresses itself *relatively* in the coat, when it takes value in the coat as another commodity. But at the same time, the relative form of value "presupposes" the equivalent form, where another commodity provides the material for the value to be expressed relatively.[131] Both forms "are inseparable moments of the *same value-expression*: moments which belong to one another, and determine each other reciprocally."[132] For twenty yards of linen to be worth a coat, this coat must also be worth twenty yards of linen. These equations represent dialectically opposed poles: the relative form of value where the linen finds its value in the coat; and where the coat finds its value in the commodities expressed in its equivalent form.

Marx suggests the relative form of value necessitates the equalisation of abstract labour as that which shares "*the same substance, having a like essence.*" Its "value-being" is given shape when it takes form in another commodity.[133] The problem of equating different kinds of labour (tailoring with weaving) is to account for the characteristic that is equal to both.[134] Commodity production reduces the difference of the specific character of the labour in tailoring and the weaving to the abstract quality of "being human labour in general."[135]

Marx makes two crucial points here. First, only human labour in a particular "fluid state," as labour-power, creates value. Second, "labour is not itself value."[136] The individual relation of value between different commodities observable at the most general level of abstraction allows Marx to proceed step by step through comparison of the "value-being" of the commodity. The quantity of time needed to produce linen or coats might vary, but both objects are shaped by their relation to each other as commodities. In this process, "the sensibly-concrete [*Sinnlich-Konkrete*] counts only as appearance-form of the abstract-universal."[137] Concrete qualifiable labour that creates use-values becomes abstract quantifiable labour ("no matter in which 'useful' mode it is expended") as labour-time sold on the market.[138] The contradiction and entwinement of concrete and abstract labour is only intelligible by placing this dialectic within this larger social context. Marx calls this social form—the dialectic between the relative and equivalent poles—the "value-form," the "natural form of the commodity."[139] For Marx, abstract labour only produces value through a social form of objectifying (*Gegenständlichkeit*) human activity via commodity exchange. This process is predicated on the subsumption of labour activity into specifically commodity-producing labour in which value is realised not in the commodity itself, but in its sale on the market.

Marx suggests this social relation is made all the more mysterious since the equivalent form is constituted by the process in which "private-labour becomes the form of its opposite, becomes labour in an immediately social form."[140] It is connected by a *"system of social needs [System der gesellschaftlichen Bedürfnisse]"* in which the exchange of values mediates. According to Marx, "[t]he product of private-labour therefore has a *social form [gesellschaftliche Form] only* insofar as it has *value-form* and therefore has the form of its *exchangeability* with another labour-product. It has *immediately social form* insofar as its own corporeal [*Körper*] or natural-form is *at the same time* the form of its exchangeability with another commodity [*andrer Waare*], or *counts for another commodity as its value-form*.[141]

With Marx's opening argument in *Capital* contextualised as a critique of the classical labour theory of value, it becomes easier to appreciate its advantages as a social theory of the historical constellations of human activity under capitalism. Marx's technical assessment of the value-form avails his wider concern to illuminate the aspects of social life obscured in modern thought. By naturalising wage-labour and value, political economy reduces social life to economic motivation and loses sight of the interdependence of human beings established in the very social relations they purport to give an account for. In his endeavour to consider wealth creation in terms of the social relations between human beings and our forms of activities, Marx engages an issue often obscured in economic theory. Social relations of productive activity are normatively significant for the fabric of any form of life. To speak of the operation of economics as law like science, as if secondary or independent of norms, is to replicate the fetishism and naturalisation of capitalism. The mysteries of modern economic thought, as Marx helps unravel, stem from the inability to see value as a historically specific social relation between human beings. A simple commodity, like a coat, helps unpack the value relations in the dialectics of use and exchange value, concrete and abstract labour. Marx is challenging the "bourgeois vision of the political economist" by demonstrating that value is constituted in a dialectic between the social form of human labour and money.[142]

The Value of Aristotle

In chapter 1 of *Capital*, just as Marx appears to be bogged down in the material—coats and otherwise—of political economy, in a striking move he reaches back to Aristotle. Marx suggests that the peculiarities of the equivalent form of value "will become still clearer if we go back to the great investigator who was the first to analyse the value-form, like so many other forms of thought, society and nature. I mean Aristotle."[143] Marx looks for vindication in Aristotle's account of money as a relation of normative reciprocity. This reasoning (for what might be otherwise seen as a literary divergence) indicates that the problem of value and exchange is conceptualised within the simple form of value, the basic contradiction between use-value and value and the necessary inversion of private and social labour within this form. The deficiency in political economy, which understands value as a quantitative measure, results in the one-sided equation of value with exchange value.[144] Related to this inquiry is the modern inversion of quantity and quality in the manifestation of value as the money-form. Marx contrasts the ancient idea of use and exchange with this modern dualism:

> Political economy, which first emerged as an independent science during the period of manufacture, is only able to view the social division of labour in terms of the division found in manufacture, i.e. as a means of producing more commodities with a given quantity of labour, and consequently of cheapening commodities and accelerating the accumulation of capital. In most striking contrast with this accentuation of quantity and exchange-value is the attitude of the writers of classical antiquity, who are exclusively concerned with quality and use-value.[145]

The distinction between quality/quantity and use/exchange underlies much of the analysis of the commodity, and Aristotle adumbrates the problems of this dualism for Marx. At the same time, he maintains that the social form of labour that produces commodities is privately performed by individuals and (in general) sold as quantities of labour-time. Marx establishes a parallel problem between the use and exchange of value-objects (such as coats) and the use and exchange of labour-power, insisting the exchangeability of both as commodities requires they are expressed as quantities. As quickly as he starts to unfold the social determinations of value-producing labour, which "reflects nothing apart from its own abstract quality of being human labour," Marx brings Aristotle into the picture.[146]

Aristotle calls attention to the use-values and qualities of exchange as problems of justice, since "in the category of quality there is justice."[147] For Aristotle, the craft of exchange (*metablêtikê*) is a kind of wealth acquisition that falls within the concerns of justice. He divides exchange into trading, money-lending and wage-earning.[148] Exchange differs from the other types of wealth acquisition, farming and mining.[149] The subject of *Nicomachean Ethics*, book 5 is justice (*dikaiosunê*).[150] He is interested in "[w]hat sorts of actions" are considered just as they pertain to "the state that makes us do justice and wish what is just."[151] Justice relates to our relations with others and to lawfulness (*nomos*). In Jill Frank's words, "parts of the whole of justice, distributive, corrective, and reciprocal justice share the defining characteristic of the whole, namely, lawfulness."[152] In book 5.5 Aristotle investigates the phenomenon of reciprocity, the problem of fairness in exchange.[153]

To ascertain how Aristotle's discussion of fairness and exchange is relevant at all for Marx's analysis of the value-form, the discussion in *Nicomachean Ethics* requires some attention. Marx presents the argument from book 5.5, that if 5 beds = 1 house, this effectively means that 5 beds = a certain amount of money.[154] This equation relates simple exchange to its more developed expression in some other object. First, Aristotle questions if exchange is proportionate or equal in "communities for exchange."[155] He holds that "a city is maintained by proportionate reciprocity."[156] Aristotle then gives the examples of a builder, shoemaker, house, and shoe. If the builder exchanges shoes from the shoemaker in return for a house, then "first of all proportionate equality is found, and next, reciprocity is also achieved, the proportionate return will be reached."[157] Objects of production are compared in terms of quantity and quality. However, if the products are not seen as equal, the trade would not hold, and since the qualities of each product may well be different, an equaliser must be found.[158] This principle applies for producers, too, since "no community [for exchange] is formed from two doctors. It is formed from a doctor and a farmer, and in general, from people who are different and unequal and who must be equalised."[159] The relation of trade requires equivalence and disparity of kind. What Aristotle is outlining is simply the trade of one object of use for another.

Next, as Aristotle reasons, "if things are to be exchanged, they must be somehow capable of comparison."[160] It follows that currency is needed as a middle term, "intermediate, since it measures everything." Without a socially recognised legal tender, there would be "no exchange and no community."[161] Here currency acts as a medium to circulate goods. This measure fluctuates adding a difficulty to exchange.[162] However, Aristotle claims, "in reality, this measure is need" and currency is only a reflection of need. He writes, "[c]urrency has become a sort of pledge of need, by convention; in fact it has a name (*nomisma*)¹⁶³ because it is not by nature, but by the current law (*nomos*), and it is within our power to alter it and to make it useless."¹⁶⁴ Currency is not an end in itself, and thus not "natural," but exists only as a means to make equal things of needs, qualities. As a "pledge of need" money is a normative relation that allows us to afford it particular social uses. For Aristotle, nature facilitates the good since it is through its movement in our activities of logos that we realise ourselves as human beings and our communities as political.¹⁶⁵ All natures have a telos, an end in itself. For this reason, there is a metaphysical distinction between quality and quantity in use-value and exchange-value. The problem that Aristotle is trying to pinpoint concerns the nature of the characteristic shared by human artefacts that can be held equal in exchange. What emerges is an immense tension since the end of exchange, in its own terms, is not need, but only further exchange. Aristotle takes the equalisation of beds and houses as an example of the kind of quantities that hold value in exchange.¹⁶⁶ Marx identifies this move as having an importance. Further, Aristotle

> sees that the value-relation [*Wertverhältnis*] which provides the framework for this expression of value itself requires that the house should be qualitatively equated with the bed, and that these things, being distinct to the senses, could not be compared with each other as commensurable magnitudes if they lacked this essential identity. "There can be no exchange," he says, "without equality, and no equality without commensurability" ("οὔτ' ἰσότης μὴ οὔσης συμμετρίας") Here, however, he falters, and abandons the further analysis of the form of value [*Analyse der Wertform*]. "It is, however, in reality, impossible ("τῇ μὲν οὖν ἀληθείᾳ ἀδύνατον") that such unlike things can be commensurable," i.e. qualitatively equal. This form of equation can only be something foreign to the true nature of the things, it is therefore only "a makeshift for practical purposes."¹⁶⁷

This passage points to an objective contradiction in Aristotle's thought. He realises the expression of value rests upon the house's qualitative equation with the bed, but without a measurable substance this equality would be incoherent. However, Aristotle is unable to see how the "common substance" that represents the value relation between the bed and the house is equalised. For this reason, Marx suggests that "Aristotle therefore himself tells us what prevented any further analysis: the lack of a concept of value [*Wertbegriffs*]."¹⁶⁸

Aristotle's limitation is not the line of inquiry, which yields an insight that Marx looks to pull from the agora to the Royal Exchange, but the universal restriction of his age. Aristotle did not understand freedom as the essence of being;

in Hegel's words, that "man is in and for himself free."¹⁶⁹ Consequently, Aristotle could not see the abstract equivalence of human labour premised in this freedom. The Athenian polis was dependent on slavery for surplus extraction, hence founded on inequality between human beings.¹⁷⁰ In this context, Aristotle "considered the *slave economy* as *non*-transitory."¹⁷¹ As such, the "secret expression of value; namely the equality and equivalence of all kinds of labour because and in so far as they are human labour in general, could not be deciphered." This formal equality necessitates a society based on commodity exchange, the leveller of all persons to buyer, sellers and "possessors" of commodities.¹⁷² Marx continues, "Aristotle's genius is displayed precisely by his discovery of a relation of equality in the value-expression [*Wertausdrunk*] of commodities. Only the historical limitation inherent in the society in which he lived prevented him from finding out what 'in reality' this relation of equality consisted of."¹⁷³

Accordingly, it would be impossible for Aristotle to come to a theory of value before the historical emergence of capital, for which value is an expression.¹⁷⁴ Evidently, Marx does not see capitalism as implicit in precapitalist acts of exchange. Rather, the point he is appreciating in Aristotle's paradox is that the equivalence between objects of exchange must be grasped as relations of equality. The task is to find out what these relations are composed of, and on what terms equality bears upon their social form. Marx's evocative identification of Aristotle's "discovery" of relations of equality goes on to show the novelty of commodity-producing labour. "Equality in the full sense between different kinds of labour can be arrived at only if we abstract from their real inequality," Marx observes, "if we reduce them to the characteristic they have in common, that of being the expenditure of human labour-power, of human labour in the abstract."¹⁷⁵ Reciprocity pulls in both directions, defining the relations between things and the relations between human beings as value-relations.

Aristotle's conclusion that relations between objects of production need an independent expression of equality points to an important truth about reciprocity that is obscured in the social form of the commodity under capitalism. Aristotle's search to ascertain the abstract characteristic shared by both the house and the bed is remarkable because it can only be made out if reciprocity is consistently seen in terms of equality. Just as Aristotle's belief in the natural inequality of human beings defines his view of reciprocity in exchange, the formal equality between commodity producers restricts political economy from seeing the inequality of reciprocity within capitalism. As Marx goes on to show, once naturalised, relations of inequality hinder the assessment of any historical configuration of the creation of wealth. With Aristotle's insight held up against the complexity of generalised commodity exchange, it becomes clear that commodities appear in a highly peculiar and mysterious form that obscures the relation between value-objects and human labour. Objects are equalised as values in a process that seems to be outside of human control. In contrast, Aristotle's concern with the problem of justice in exchange pertains to the very form and sociality of reciprocal relations that is so hard for us moderns to see clearly in the glistening world of commodities.

Aristotle's faltering, his claim of impossibility for qualitative equality, raises the question that Marx charges political economy with failing to answer. Aristotle establishes an analysis of the relation between quality and quantity as conditioned by exchange. That Aristotle points to a fundamental contradiction between the end of exchange and the end of human needs suggests that an account of the social world in terms of quantities alone is insufficient to comprehend the relations between human agents and the social forms of existence that mediate experience in the social world. Exchange begets no end internal to its function, but only its further expansion. In this way, as quantities, human products come to express a paradoxical relation to their qualitative requirement to fulfill human needs. With commodity exchange, value "obtains a separate existence, in isolation from the product" and "exists alongside as itself a commodity, that is—money."[176] The inversion of quality for quantity is tied to the inversion of use-value and value. Marx takes up the *Nicomachean Ethics* to insist that the problem raised by Aristotle points to the central issue of value as a social relation. In doing so, he channels Aristotle's normative account of justice in reciprocity. With Aristotle's delineation of the normative structure of exchange and the political character of currency in view, Marx's concept of value can be mapped as it flows down the same stream.

The Fetishism of the Commodity World

With indignation, Marx picks apart the constitutive forms of a social world in which the reduction of human life under value turns labour into a one-sided source of abstract activity, rather than the many-sided needs of the human producer. If Aristotle's metaphysics are situated in the world of use-values, Marx's investigation points to the domination of exchange value. What is significant in his critical absorption of Aristotle is that Marx shows the historical possibilities of comprehending social relations in the modern world.[177] In locating reciprocity in exchange as part of his ethical theory, Aristotle inaugurates a line of inquiry that Marx explicitly takes up. Not only do just relations require that the ends of particular forms of activity contribute to the human good, but in raising the relation of value to reciprocity, Aristotle puts into focus its ongoing importance for practical reasoning and judgement. In striking upon the problem of value as part of his normative theory, Aristotle establishes that reciprocative human practices are necessary to cultivate ethical life. Marx's analysis follows suit. There can be no ethical life in a world defined by the real abstractions of value.

Returning to the unfolding of form-determinations in *Capital* helps decipher the human relations that constitute such abstractions. Once the simple form of value is presented as a contradictory whole—the commodity-form expresses the dialectic of the concrete/abstract and private/social character of human labour manifest in the value relation of two commodities—the transition is now possible to the "expanded form of value."[178] This form allows many commodities, beyond the coat and the linen, with further determination of "innumerable other members of the world of commodities." Value is reflected like a "mirror" between two commodities.[179] This transition parallels Hegel's introduction of the category "quantity" from "number" in the *Science of Logic*. After being-for-self is shown to be a simple unity with being-for-one, this oneness is forced to confront other ones, repulsing and sublating the other ones in mutual attraction. This concept becomes "a state of equilibrium; and quality, driven to a head in being-for-itself, passes over into *quantity*."[180] The one meets "many ones" in its state of repulsion and in a process of becoming, forms a unity of the one and many in attraction.[181] This derivation allows Hegel to make the transition:

> Quantity is sublated being-for-itself [*aufgehobene Fürsichsein*]. The repelling one that behaved only negatively towards the excluded one, now that it has gone over in connection with it, behaves towards the other as identical to itself and has therefore lost its determination [*Bestimmung*]; being-for-itself has passed over into attraction. The absolute obduracy of the one has melted away into this unity which, however, as containing the one, is at the same time determined by the repulsion residing in it; as unity of the self-externality, it is unity with itself. Attraction is in this way the moment of continuity in quantity.[182]

While Hegel's discussion occurs at a very high level of abstraction, well before the concreteness of a commodity, this explanation is an aid to the procedure in *Capital*. Measure enables the being of two commodities to be found in each other and for this form to be considered at a more determinate level.[183] It is only by comparing the relation between two things that the inherent shape and movement can be considered as points of connection. Once commodities confront us as individual objects and quantities of a specific kind in the general form of value, a great variety of commodities can be compared against others as value-objects. But this form of value is seen to be inadequate to grasp the expression of value. Quantities need a measure that is at once alike and distinct. Such a measure requires equality between other quantities for it to represent social objectivity. This measure is money.[184]

The dialectic of the value-form reaches its adequate form in money. Money is "the universal equivalent" that has the exceptional ability to express values between commodities. The money-form gives social validity to the social process of commodity exchange.[185] Money constitutes the social connection between individuals as producers and sellers and equates values directly as price. Central to this conception is Marx's insistence that money has a historically specific form in capitalism.[186] Money is the concrete expression of value. He carefully distinguishes between pre-capitalist forms of currency, which act as a medium for the exchange of goods at a local level, and the form money takes in capitalist society as the form of value in the generalised exchange and circulation of commodities.[187] While gold and precious metals have often been linked to money, to also supply a use-value, to stabilise economies, money is no mere "symbol"; [188] it is a social relation that "presupposes general recognition [*Anerkennung*]."[189] Money acts as the "*material* representative of *universal* wealth."[190] Marx refers to the paper currency of the French Revolution as a form of money not necessarily tied to the material value of the commodity money.[191] In this account, the particular manifestation of money is fluid, but its being-and-becoming is its actuality as the form of value.

With money, the "social bond" between individuals is legitimised in the "reciprocal" equalisation of exchange value. If one side of the "isolated" production of individual exchange values is received back to the worker in the form of money (as wages), then the other side of this relation is "exercised" in the ownership of exchange value as money; here the "individual carries his social power, as well as his bond with society [*Zusammenhang mit der Gesellschaft*], in his pocket."[192] In such social relations, money provides the basis of trust between human beings. But if trust is determined by the quantifiable character of commodity exchange, then social relations are misrecognised since value is defined not by the subjects who constitute these relations, but by the omnipresence of money as the form of social objectivity of value.

The money-form makes it possible to grasp the fetishistic character of the commodity, the duality of value as use and exchange value and the substance of value as abstract human labour.[193] Money acts as both a measure of value and a "standard of price," relatable to the trade of commodities as abstract quantities.[194] Price gives a "money-name" to different commodities and objectively measures value. Through commodity exchange, money validates the entire social system. The alienated nature of commodity production gives an abstract expression to the way that human relations appear, where things mediate human relations, naturalising and fetishising human consciousness. Money serves as a "social property" precisely because the alienated relationship of individuals to isolated production creates a fetishism of things. Money embodies "the objectification [*Versachlichung*] of the social bond," reproducing the exchange fetish in such a way as to instill trust in the social operation of money (far exceeding recognition of human sociality). The exchange of money reflects the alienation of human labour and becomes a fetishistic relation, a kind of "faith."[195]

Marx calls money the "dead pledge of society," once again quoting from *Nicomachean Ethics,* book 5.5.[196] Human beings confront each other in the market, and money takes on a universal significance. The market legitimises the reproduction of this form of abstract sociality through a quantifiable indicator of one's influence. "Money is 'impersonal' property. I can carry it around with me in my pocket as the universal social power and the universal social nexus, the social substance. Money puts social power as a thing into the hands of the private person, who as such uses this power."[197] As money, social power is actualised as an impersonal force commanded by individuals. This determination of power acts to avert forms of interaction that could cultivate normative deliberation as to how human beings should interact with each other for collective goods. The idea of money as the "dead pledge of society" illuminates what is normatively absent from capitalist society: namely, sensuous, living and interdependent relationships between rational and free human agents. Money becomes the motivating force of interaction, reducing the meaning of many forms of human activity to its accruement.

With the development of the commodity-form in *Capital*, chapter 1, and Marx's unfolding of the money-form from the "germ of the commodity-form,"[198] the concept of fetishism can be seen in the crucial connection between commodities and money as "things." Marx sharpens his discussion to emphasise the fetishism that arises from this value relation:

> A commodity appears at first sight an extremely obvious, trivial thing. But its analysis brings out that it is a very strange thing, abounding in metaphysical subtleties and theological niceties. So far as it is a use-value, there is nothing mysterious about it, whether we consider it from the point of view that by its properties it satisfies human needs, or that it first takes on these properties as the product of human labour. It is absolutely clear that, by his activity, man changes the forms of the materials of nature in such a way as to make them useful to him. The form of wood, for instance, is altered if a table is made out of it. Nevertheless the table continues to be wood, an ordinary, sensuous thing. But as soon as it emerges as a commodity, it changes into a thing which transcends sensuousness. It not only stands with its feet on the ground, but, in relation to all other commodities, it stands on its head, and evolves out of its wooden brain grotesque ideas, far more wonderful than if it were to begin dancing of its own free will.[199]

When products of human labour take the particular form of commodities, their social objectivity depends not on their relation to human needs, but their exchange-value relation to other commodities. This social transformation has devastating effects on the rationality of human action since material objects take on a life of their own.[200] The form of commodity-producing labour is abstract since "the social character of activity as well as the social form of the product" face human beings as an "autonomous" thing-like power.[201] This form of labour is abstractly social, a social form based on abstract relations of activity. What is particular about commodities is that as objects created for exchange, every aspect of their use is mediated by this character.

If an object is created as a use-value to fulfill a specific human need (I need a coat: I make a coat), then since this use is visible and easily capable of fulfillment, labouring activity appears direct and apparent.[202] But if I take it that there is a social need for coats and so I produce coats as exchange values for the market, people may well buy coats on the basis of their needs, but exchange is assumed to be the adjudicator of need in a way that conceals the social relations that constitute them as commodities, things defined by their relation to exchange. While the economic "common sense" is that producing coats in this manner is fulfilling a social need, a fundamental inversion occurs in the production of commodities to which it must conform. Commodities must express their value in money terms and not by their use. In Marx's view, the inversion between use and exchange contained within the commodity form itself mystifies products of human activities and has to be traced back to the very production of those objects as commodities. We may buy commodities we need, but their social objectivity as values consists in the abstractly social and distorted relations between human beings that constitute commodity production and the exchange of the products of our activity. Commodities must be useful things, but they are measured and given value by their exchangeability. As such, the mystification of the commodity arises from the specific social process in which things are produced to be exchanged for the end of value reproduction and accumulation.

The emergence of the commodity as a social form has profound consequences for conceiving the relationship between labour and capitalism. For Marx, the "productive activities" of labour are distinct "functions of the human organicism". He writes, "whatever may be its nature or its form, [labour] is essentially the expenditure of human brain, nerves, muscles and sense organs."[203] This concrete quality of labour as activity then becomes *quantified* in a very specific manner as abstract labour, hours of labour-time sold as a commodity to produce other commodities. Labour activity is equalised and made comparable through its exchange. Marx is clear that as a human activity, labour always takes a social form.[204] Marx's ontological concept of labour cannot be understood without its determination in social form. Attempts to rip labour activity from its social actualisation would be as ahistorical as Robinson Crusoe stories.

That is why the form of value is so important for Marx's concept of social being. If the quality of labour activity becomes objectified as value and quantified as abstract labour, "the relationship between the producers, within which the social characteristics of their labours are manifested, takes on the form of a social relation between the products of labour."[205] Not only does an inversion occur between the product and the producer, but Marx also notes the commodity takes on the character of the abstract relation between producers:

> The mysterious character of the commodity-form consists therefore simply in the fact that the commodity reflects the social characteristics of men's own labour [*Menschen die gesellschaftlichen Charaktere ihrer eignen Arbeit*] as objective characteristics of the products of labour [*Arbeitsprodukte*] themselves, as the socio-natural properties of these things. Hence it also reflects the social relation of the producers to the sum total of labour as a social relation between objects, a relation which exists apart from and outside the producers. Through this substitution, the products of labour become commodities, sensuous things which are at the same time suprasensible or social ... It is nothing but the definite social relation between men [*bestimmte gesellschaftliche Verhältniß der Menschen*] themselves which assumes here,

for them, the fantastic *form* of a relation between things [*phantasmagorische Form eines Verhältnisses von Dingen annimmt*]. In order, therefore, to find an analogy we must take flight into the misty realm of religion. There the products of the human brain appear as autonomous figures endowed with a life of their own, which enter into relations both with each other and with the human race. So it is in the world of commodities with the products of men's hands. I call this the fetishism [*Fetischismus*] which attaches itself to the products of labour as soon as they are produced as commodities, and is therefore inseparable from the production of commodities."[206]

The fetishism of the commodity emerges from its very form. Objects made by human beings as commodities take on a social power abstracted from human self-understanding. Fetishism is bound to commodities and has a singular social importance: mediating the relations between human beings through exchange. As such, social relations "appear as what they are, i.e. they do not appear as direct social relations between persons in their work, but rather as material [*dinglich*] relations between persons and social relations between things."[207]

Relations between human beings are not directly apparent but dominated abstractly by the social forms of commodities and money, which conditions the way we see ourselves as human beings and the meaning of social life. Money embodies the misrecognition of social agents, since it reflects a relation of value rather than a form of interdependent interaction. This form of labour relations is inherently fetishistic: "Value, therefore, does not have its description branded on its forehead; it rather transforms every product of labour into a social hieroglyphic."[208] Transformed into a commodity defined by value, the use of such objects is determined by their exchange relation. Adorno summarises this movement as when "the social relation appears in the form of the exchange principle, as if it were the thing in itself."[209] Abstract human labour is objectified into commodities and appears as a feature of two separate processes—production and exchange. The separation of these two processes obscures their inner unity in the value-form. Therefore the fetishism of production is a result of the exchange of commodities.[210] In this way, Marx brings in the content from his discussion of money and simple circulation.

The commodity realises its value in the realm of exchange, and this mode of being shapes a specific form of domination where people confront each other as owners and sellers of commodities, which crystallise as money. Money establishes the social form in which commodities can be equated. At the same time, labour is socially divided. The performance of labour is atomised and private but requires social validation for value to be realised. As a result, individuals are alienated. The domination of value in processes of production and reproduction staves off social relations on a freely associated basis. In contrast to precapitalist communities, Marx describes a "relationship of reciprocal isolation and foreignness":

> Things are in themselves external to man, and therefore alienable. In order that this alienation [*Veräusserung*] may be reciprocal, it is only necessary for men to agree tacitly to treat each other as the private owners of those alienable things, and, precisely for that reason, as persons who are independent of each other.[211]

Separated from the products of their activity and from production itself, the form of directly social interaction is the market where value is realised. In exchange people relate to each other in a purely atomistic way, and money takes on its true and "magical" importance as mediator.[212] In this social world, human beings "relate to each other as *abstract social persons* [*abstrakt gesellschaftliche Personen*], merely representing exchange value as such before each other."[213] The objectification of production conceals the domination of the subject in commodity and exchange relations. Money provides a "material shape" for the domination of the producers, dislocating their "control and their conscious individual action."[214] It is also the direct social bond between subjects, but money is in itself fetishistic. Money not only *appears* to have a real power over human beings but compels that social life take the logic of exchange.

It is essential to Marx's account that money is not considered as per mainstream economics as the "medium of exchange," but instead as the actualised social form in which value necessarily appears. This analysis hinges on the conceptual connection between value and money. As the "universal form" of value, money makes it possible for commodities to be compared. Marx's difference with the classical labour theory of value is apparent in this respect since value is not a physical property nor an act of concrete labour independent of the system of circulation. Instead, value must take the form of money for the abstract labour which produces value to be understood as its substance. As Marx notes, "the *social* character of labour appears as the *monetary existence* of the commodity."[215] Since value is a relation, it requires a view of production and circulation as a totality. For this to happen, by necessity money must serve a number of social roles: as a measure of value, a means of circulation and as "money as money."[216] As such, money is "the sole form of value, or, in other words, as the only adequate form of existence of exchange value in the face of all the other commodities."[217]

Although often overlooked by commentators, Marx takes considerable effort to unfold the specific functions of money (as a hoard, a means of payment and, in its final form, as world money).²¹⁸ Once the concept of money is derived from its most basic character to understand international exchange, Marx can claim, "[i]t is in the world market that money first functions to its full extent as the commodity whose natural form is also the directly social form of realization of human labour in the abstract. Its mode of existence becomes adequate to its concept."²¹⁹ As Marx adds concreteness to his concept of value throughout the structure of his argument set out in the manuscripts for *Capital*, volumes 2 and 3, he builds on this understanding of money as "not a thing but a particular form of value."²²⁰ What motivates Marx's analysis is the pressing need to fully expose the pervasive dynamic of value as it comes to rule over social life and subsume ever increasing aspects of social interaction under its logic. The normative elements of this pursuit are striking, and by bringing them into view, we get a better sense of what exactly is abstract and unfree about capitalist domination.

The End of Capital

As commodities and money, objects come to dominate human subjects.²²¹ This process, however, can only be fully conceptually comprehended by moving to the concept of capital. While the discussion of the fetish character of the commodity in Marx's thought is well known, its philosophical implications for social theory is impossible without his concept of capital. After the form of the commodity and money are developed, the transition is made to the concept of capital.²²² Capital is a process between things. As a process, capital moves from money to commodity and back to money. However, as capital, this movement *self-expands*, accumulating surplus-value. The reason capital moves from money to commodity is not to satisfy the capitalist's desire for a use-value so much as to return to the capitalist the initial capital plus accumulated capital.²²³ In Marx's view, capital is itself a form of value which consists in the form of social labour specific to commodity production. Capital realises itself as value in the circulation process, in "the moments of its metamorphosis." In its change from one form to the next, capital appears as money and then as a commodity, "then again as exchange value, then again as use value." According to Marx, each part of this process is "the transition to the other. Capital is thus posited as value-in-process, which is capital in every moment."²²⁴ Actualising itself in the forms of commodities and money, capital is the self-expansion of value.²²⁵

The circulation of capital through successive stages changes commodities into money and money into commodities, antithetical processes of negation that create a circuit predicated on the sale and purchase of value expressed in its various forms. Commodity-producing abstract labour provides the social substance that can only be realised as a value relation when the commodity is actually sold.²²⁶ Contra classical political economy and traditional Marxism, value is not a property inherent in a product of labour but a social relation that requires an analysis of the process of capital production and circulation as a total concrete whole. Abstract labour produces value only as a *potential* which must be *actualised* as a social relation on the market. Marx understands value explicitly in Aristotelian terms, noting if a capitalist withdraws a commodity

> from sale, it would form only a potential (δύναμις) element of the commodity stock, and not an actual (ἐνέργεια) one. The commodity as such is still for him simply the bearer of its exchange-value, and as such it can only have its effect by and through shedding its commodity form and assuming the money form.²²⁷

Value takes shape through the metamorphosis of social forms. By using Aristotle's Greek, Marx brings to bear not just his metaphysics but the normative dynamic inherent in the movement between potentiality and actuality. Value and its manifestations are nothing but forms of human activity. The sale of C for M and M for C masks the social relation of alienated labour and makes the products of human beings secondary to the sale and purchase of things.²²⁸ Since money is also a commodity, owned as such, it privatises social power to "private people" and instills in them the priority to valorise and reproduce surplus-value. The capitalist is beholden to the "Sisyphean task" of accumulation.²²⁹

The generalised circulation of commodities allows capital to develop as it negates one form for another more unified stage in the process.²³⁰ The cycle, M-C-M' expresses the need for capital to self-expand, to valorise itself as a social relation. The simple circuit C-M-C, based on the "satisfaction of needs" as expressed by Aristotle (if we can put the language of commodities in his mouth for a moment), is inverted as "the circulation of money as capital is an end in itself," where valorisation is a "constantly renewed movement."²³¹ No longer do we sell in order to buy, but we buy in order to sell. The M-C-M' circuit points to the universal imperative for self-expansion. In this circuit, money is transformed from a simple mediator of exchange to a form of capital.

Marx's concept of capital justifies the earlier categories of analysis and distinguishes wealth from the physical embodiment of commodities and money to capital as the telos of value. Unlike wealth in the simple form of commodities or money, capital must expand to increase its value. Since capital is value-in-process, by nature its form is always in motion. The being-and-becoming of value is capital, but capital's final end is simply *more* capital. After outlining the general formula for capital, M-C-M', Marx makes a key claim that demonstrates the extent to which his unique understanding of capitalism explicitly deploys Aristotelian and Hegelian insights. Marx writes: "The movement of capital is therefore limitless."[232] Attached to this sentence, is the footnote:

> Aristotle contrasts economics with "chrematistics." He starts with economics. So far as it is the art of acquisition, it is limited to procuring the articles necessary to existence and useful either to a household or the state. "True wealth (ὁ ἀληθινός πλοῦτος) consists of such use-values; for the amount of property which is needed for a good life is not unlimited. There is, however, a second mode of acquiring things, to which we may by preference and with correctness give the name of chrematistics, and in this case there appear to be no limits to riches and property. Trade (ἡ καπηλική is literally retail trade, and Aristotle chooses this form because use-values predominate in it) does not in its nature belong to chrematistics, for here the exchange only has reference to what is necessary for (the buyer or the seller) themselves." Therefore, as he goes on to show, the original form of trade was barter, but with the extension of the latter there arose the necessity for money. With the discovery of money, barter of necessity developed into καπηλική into trading in commodities, and this again, in contradiction with its original tendency, grew into chrematistics, the art of making money. Now chrematistics can be distinguished from economics in that "for chrematistics, circulation is the source of riches (ποιητική χρημάτων . . . διὰ χρημάτων μεταβολῆς). And it appears to revolve around money, for money is the beginning and the end of this kind of exchange (τὸ γὰρ νόμισμα στοιχεῖον καὶ πέρας τῆς ἀλλαγῆς ἐστίν). Therefore also riches, such as chrematistics strives for, are unlimited. Just as every art which is not a means to an end, but an end in itself, has no limit to its aims, because it seeks constantly to approach nearer and nearer to that end, while those arts which pursue means to an end are not boundless, since the goal itself imposes a limit on them, so with chrematistics there are no bounds to its aims, these aims being absolute wealth. Economics, unlike chrematistics, has a limit . . . for the object of the former is something different from money, of the latter the augmentation of money . . . By confusing these two forms, which overlap each other, some people have been led to look upon the preservation and increase of money *ad infinitum* as the final goal of economics."[233]

Marx's lengthy footnote is remarkable for two main reasons. First, through an engagement with book 1 of the *Politics*, Marx is explicit that chrematistics (as money wealth) is a distinct form of wealth to be contrasted with "economics." The latter is the inquiry into finite uses—relevant to the polis or the *oikos*—as value in use. Aristotle's example of the "craft of commerce"[234] appears simple, as the purposeful exchange between buyers and sellers, developing from the assumptions of barter to currency. Alternatively, chrematistics is the craft of wealth-acquisition through exchange and is predicated on the notion that "wealth and property seem to have no limit."[235] This form of wealth-acquisition is not natural since its end is the "possession" and increase of money "without limit." As Aristotle sees it, what those who endeavour to acquire wealth in such a way "take seriously is living, not living well."[236] Chrematistics disavows the possibility of wealth as a normative end of the good life, instead it is directed by self-interest.

Without limit, chrematistics seeks "absolute wealth." Marx turns to Aristotle to emphasise the novelty of the modern view of wealth accumulation as a natural part of production. Rather, Aristotle finds that chrematistics (however primitive) cannot be an end in itself since its function dislocates the connection between needs and trade. Secondly, through Aristotle, Marx is making the point that wealth creation is inescapably an ethical question. By examining the way in which wealth creation is tied to the logic of the social world, Marx makes the normative claim that capital is a fundamental barrier to ethical life. The domination of capital renders abstract the forms of interaction that would enable social relationships to be mutually reciprocal and meaningfully preserved in shared forms of association. Marx endorses Aristotle's teleological conception of ethics and affirms that capital is incompatible with this view.[237] Several pages later, Marx makes this even clearer, quoting from the same sections of the *Politics* but adding that, chrematistics "is not based on Nature, but on mutual cheating."[238] For Marx, as for Aristotle, the practice of chrematistics is normatively deficient since the end for both participants is self-gain. What is shared with the other is the compulsion for advantage. This form of wealth creation is a barrier to ethical interaction since cheating and not recognition is mutual in the relationship. The ends of such interaction are normatively deficient.

Considering Marx's value-form theory as in part a colloquy with Aristotle shows that interpretations rejecting the ethical argument in *Capital* have serious failings. Not only does Marx draw constructively from Aristotle to make clear the historical character of his own concepts, but he points out repeatedly that the investigation of value enables an understanding of human activity as social relations mediated by living and dead labour. The normative import of Marx's language cannot be understated since it is precisely the life and death of human activity that is structured on a dynamic of profit-making. This process is the objectification of life to the domination of limitless accumulation. What is expressed in this process is a relation of misrecognition. Value acts to hinder human beings from recognising each other as substantively rational and interdependent social agents in a world of our own making. Human beings cannot be at home in a world defined by value, but the necessary struggle over the very existence of value suggests not just a moral rejection of money but a normative sense of the forms of activity that must be mutually recognised.

Capital as Misrecognised Subject

Marx's claim that the movement of capital is infinite looks not only to Aristotle but to Hegel. For Hegel, the movement of consciousness unfolds by the self-activity of the subject. The absolute is not just substance but equally subject, a distinct modification of Aristotle's view that put substance over subject and held that "[n]o substance, therefore, is in a subject."[239] Instead, according to Hegel,

> the living substance is the being that is in truth *subject*, or, what amounts to the same thing, it is in truth actual only insofar as it is the movement of self-positing [*Bewegung des Sichselbstsetzens*], or, that it is the mediation of itself and its becoming-other-to-itself. As subject, it is pure, *simple negativity*, and, as a result, it is the estrangement of what is simple, or, it is the doubling which posits oppositions and which is again the negation of this indifferent diversity and its opposition. That is, it is only this *self-restoring* sameness, the reflective turn into itself in its otherness.—The true is not an *original unity* as such, or, not an *immediate* unity as such. It is the coming-to-be of itself, the circle that presupposes its end as its goal and has its end for its beginning, and which is actual only through this accomplishment [*Ausführung*] and its end.[240]

The subject, as being, comes to know itself as part of reality, as a determination of the absolute as substance. Hegel conceives of the movement of the subject as self-mediated, finding itself in other forms but returning and negating into knowledge of itself. Hegel is not insisting on pure subjectivity, but putting into view the relation between the speculative absolute and the unfolding of its determinations by the force of their internal logic.

This speculative insight helps grasp value's movement and self-valorisation. First, as fetishism, where through exchange, social relations appear as relations between things, and consciousness of the dynamics of social life is expressed in the forms that pertain to value. Second is the sense that abstract labour is the substance of value with its necessary appearance as money. Capital's movement and accumulation is the being-and-becoming of the valorisation of abstract labour. The substance (abstract labour) becomes subject (value). The constant movement which characterises the shift from form to form as capital circulates transforms value into "an automatic subject [*ein automatisches Subjekt*]."[241] Capital's very process of self-valorisation is in a sense speculative since as the "dominant subject" of modern social relations, value's movement is a process determined by its own infinite self-positing:

> In truth, however, value is here the subject of a process in which, while constantly assuming the form in turn of money and commodities, it changes its own magnitude, throws off surplus-value from itself considered as original value, and thus valorises itself independently. For the movement in the course of which it adds surplus-value is its own movement, its valorisation is therefore self-valorisation [*Selbstverwertung*]. By virtue of being value, it has acquired the occult ability [*okkulte Qualität*] to add value to itself. It brings forth living offspring, or at least lays golden eggs.
>
> As the dominant subject [*übergreifendes Subjekt*] of this process, in which it alternately assumes and loses the form of money and the form of commodities, but preserves and expands itself through all these changes, value requires above all an independent form by means of which its identity with itself may be asserted.[242]

Capital seeks to perpetually increase its value, continuingly mystifying the productive activity secreted as the substance of its form. The "golden egg," abstract labour, is made to yield constant returns as surplus-value, and the worker's human activity is excluded from reciprocal human relations. Capital can only be particular, driven into internal competition and fragmented as many capitals.[243] Value appears socially only in mystified, *misrecognised* forms. In this insight, not only does Marx demonstrate that the substance of value is comprised of abstract and alienated activity, but its efforts to self-expand seem divorced from human agency. Value has no human end, only the self-preservation of its abstract form of domination.

In this account, value defines its own movement speculatively, through its validation of the social forms that give it content.[244] According to Marx's understanding that "value is subject," value acts as a *self-moving substance* determining the "mere forms" of value in the commodity and money.[245] The implications of this view are profound, since Marx replicates Hegel's speculative proposition that "subject is substance." Considered in Hegelian terms, this argument entwines the concept of capital and normative demands for social freedom. Famously, Postone argues that Marx "explicitly characterises capital as the self-moving substance which is subject."[246] While this understanding grasps something crucial about the dynamic of capital, Postone misconceives the idea of freedom in Hegel's thought.[247] Absolute spirit is the historical form of consciousness as it actualises itself as freedom in social life. The journey spirit takes is one of "despair" and affirmation as expressions of consciousness break down by the weight of their own contradictions, immanently transforming and transcending the limitations that define them. Spirit is the self-consciousness of social life becoming free through its actualisation.

While Marx grasps capital as a social form which self-expands through its own valorisation, this is a social process *without* the consciousness of its subjects. Capital is constituted by the abstract sociality of value. Marx's analysis of the subject-like qualities of capital is an adoption of Hegel's ontology, which defines subjectivity by the movement of self-consciousness as it confronts inadequate and insufficient expressions of experience.[248] Indeed, Marx affirms something crucial to Hegel: relations of recognition require intersubjective forms of consciousness. Rose's comment that Marx's critique of political economy demonstrates the way in which "substance is ((mis)-represented as) subject" captures the ethical value of his theory.[249] Capital's movement and self-expansion demonstrates systematically why sociality is premised on the abstract social forms that take on a life seemingly independent of social agents. But capital requires living labour to lay its golden eggs. There is no capital without the activity of human beings. Marx's insight is that capital is a social form that shifts shapes as it engulfs human activity in its unceasing movement for self-valorisation.[250] On this basis, the concept of capital has normative import. It provides an understanding of the social relations that shape the way human beings interact. There is no way to step outside of capitalism since its relations have long since spread across the world and increasingly subsume more aspects of social life under its logic. When social interaction is to such a great degree mediated by money, our form of life cannot escape its domination.

In Marx's account, capital is depicted as a kind of perverted spirit, in which the self-expansion of capital through its own valorisation outlines a circular movement of social forms. Capital "is not a simple relation, but a *process*, in whose various moments it is always capital."[251] It seeks to overcome every barrier, every limit, every border in its motivation to accumulate. In the modern world, capital becomes absolute. Self-moving, capital dominates social being. Its being is also its nothingness. Comprised of nothing but relation, capital objectifies life activity into alienated, abstract modes of being.²⁵² The upshot of this analysis is that it illuminates the speculative character of Marx's comprehension of capital. The self-movement of value as the substance of abstract labour and capital as value in-process shapes both the subjectivity of capital and the objectivity of alienated labour. By making explicit the valorisation process, this speculative logic binds the theory of fetishism to the objectivity of social forms propelled by the logic of capital. That this process appears mystified reflects the contradictions inherent in the social forms themselves. The fetishisation of commodities and money is inseparable from the processes of value production and reproduction. The alienation of production begets the abstraction of the market. As a form of *misrecognition*, capital upholds a unity of substance and subject in which the experience of social agents is fetishistic and the sociality of relations is abstracted.

This barrier is inherent in the form of capital itself. In a direct sense, capital has no content, it is nothing but *form*. Tony Smith suggests capital should be seen as a "pseudo-subject," since even as it subsumes "every nook and cranny of social life" to the imperatives of commodification, monetarisation, and valorisation, capital is fundamentally *empty*. Capital is "pure form" with its power derived exclusively from living labour. This unique creation means that "the capacities of living labour remain capacities of living labour, even after they have been incorporated within capital circuits as moments of capital's self-valorisation."²⁵³ This conception of capital as both absolute and pseudo-subject reflects the contradictory form of social life resulting from the value-form. Living labour is itself contradictory, expressing a concrete activity in abstract social forms. However, the centrality of this dynamic purveys a sophisticated view of capital as a relation between human beings. Since value must appear as something other than itself, it takes the shape of commodities, money and capital, relations that are only visible as form-determinations. Marx's account of fetishism maintains that appearances are deceptive. But fetishism is not mere illusion that can be simply remedied by less commercialism of consumer goods, greater redistribution of money or reappropriation of some industries. The significance of fetishism in Marx's critical social theory is that it demonstrates that value is woven into the fabric of social life. His critique of political economy develops the conceptual categories that enable capital to be grasped speculatively, step by step through the social forms specific to value. By beginning with the commodity and mapping its procession to capital, Marx establishes a speculative path to his object of investigation. Capital is unfolded from the commodity-form, and the dualism of abstract and concrete labour is grasped in its historical shape as domination.

Marx's concept of capital poses an ongoing question for social theory since any concept of subjectivity must address this relation. Without the concept of capital, the separation between economic life and political life is preserved, and the former is treated abstractly. Human subjectivity and the subjectivity of capital spring from the same relation: human activity. Marx's understanding of capital furnishes not only an analysis of "the economic," but a comprehension of the forms of social life specific to the modern world. Marx goes beyond utopian opponents of capitalism by formulating both a normative objection to its symptoms and a systematic view of the dynamics of its constitutive forms. In this analysis, Marx shows how value is composed, reproduced and necessarily misrecognised in abstract sociality. Abstract social forms subsume and shape human consciousness to the fetishism of commodities and money. Marx's critique of relations of "reciprocal isolation" puts into relief the transformative aspect of his immanent critique of capitalism.[254] With Marx it becomes possible to conceive mutually reciprocal association as the concrete universality of social life in which the purpose of human activity and the constitution of society are inseparable conditions of free deliberation.

Abstract Sociality in Capitalist Production

The categories of value—commodities, money and capital—provide the architectonic for the increasingly concrete conceptual developments in Marx's critical social theory. After treating the commodity, exchange and money in part 1 and the transformation of money into capital in part 2, part 3 of the first volume of *Capital* examines the production process. As such, capital in production is the next conceptual form examined. A key concern for Marx's idea of sociality is the way in which capital in production shapes human interaction. The production process illustrates how labour-power that is valorised in the form of abstract labour becomes capital-positing. The purpose of my discussion, however, is the way that the labour process and human cooperation operate in Marx's thinking of the social individual. His Aristotelian view informs the understanding of domination *within* the labour process and the normativity of labour as a distinctly human activity.

The labour process bridges the "potentiality" presented by the seller of labour-power to the "actuality" of the worker in the activity of value production. Marx starts with the standpoint of the worker whose purposeful activity mediates between nature and the instruments of production. This form of interaction is presented as the first-order mediation necessary for tracing second-order layers of complexity in the basic production process (such as advanced machinery etc.). Marx begins by claiming the labour process is under the control of capital, in which the capitalist buys the use-value of such activity. Before Marx outlines the specific process of commodity-producing activity, in a long passage he reflects directly on the nature of human labour. This analysis is striking because Marx deems it necessary to abstract from any specific historical manifestation of "labour-power in action" to reflect on productive activity in ontological terms. Other sections of *Capital* comprise his dissection of the social mediations of labour-power in various aspects of the capitalist mode of production, including the working day, the division of labour and machinery. In this passage, however, he offers a concept of labour as a distinctly human activity. He writes:

> Labour is, first of all, a process between man and nature [*Mensch und Natur*], a process by which man, through his own actions, mediates, regulates and controls the metabolism [*Stoffwechsel*] between himself and nature. He confronts the materials of nature as a force of nature. He sets in motion the natural forces which belong to his own body, his arms, legs, head and hands, in order to appropriate the materials of nature in a form adapted to his own needs. Through this movement he acts upon external nature and changes it, and in this way he simultaneously changes his own nature. He develops the potentialities [*Potenzen*] slumbering within nature, and subjects the play of its forces to his own sovereign power. We are not dealing here with those first instinctive forms of labour which remain on the animal level. An immense interval of time separates the state of things in which a man brings his labour-power to market for sale as a commodity from the situation when human labour had not yet cast off its first instinctive form. We presuppose labour in a form in which it is an exclusively human characteristic. A spider conducts operations which resemble those of the weaver, and a bee would put many a human architect [*menschlichen Baumeister*] to shame by the construction of its honeycomb cells. But what distinguishes the worst architect from the best of bees is that the architect builds the cell in his mind before he constructs it in wax. At the end of every labour process, a result emerges which had already been conceived by the worker at the beginning, hence already existed ideally. Man not only effects a change of form in the materials of nature; he also realises [*verwirklicht*] his own purpose [*Zweck*] in those materials.[255]

This conception is not discordant with Marx's analysis elsewhere in *Capital*, but instead points to the consistency of his social ontology.[256] As the mediation between human beings and nature, labour is the distinctly human activity that transforms nature in a double sense.[257] Human beings act on the natural world by intention and for need. At the same time, labour transforms our nature as human beings and develops the potentials within our natures for new needs. This picture does not conflict with one that sees labour in historically specific terms, but rather makes that argument possible. We are beings that labour, and it is through our productive activity we reshape ourselves as historical beings. We can only do so since human activity is conscious in a way it is not for other species. As Marx makes clear, our labour transforms us in a specific way since we self-consciously reflect on our activity, and this dual process is the being and historical becoming of human purposes.

In this view, Marx depicts the human being as a member of a species, comparable to the bee or spider. If the life activity of the bee or spider is successful, their life is sustained and good for them. However, since human beings exercise our rationality through the mediation of productive activity, such action is conscious in a way that means when human beings sustain our lives, our goods are normative in a distinct way for us.[258] The ends of our activity are always a matter of reflection and judgement since the action itself begins as an act of consciousness. The bee nest can work well or badly. But, if for example, the nest is constructed too close to a windy area and is vulnerable to rough storms this is not a normative problem for them in the same way it is for human beings.[259] They might in future attempt to find a better location for the nest to flourish, but the bee cannot question if they should be making nests at all. Despite the collective endeavour required, the activity of the bee does not involve self-conscious reflection on its purpose and goals. The bee can flourish, but it cannot ask what it means to flourish and direct its activity with this end animating its activity. However, the builder designs in a way with the aim of realising a normatively specific goal based on conscious reasons: whether to provide a habitable and comfortable home or a facility to detain as many refugees as possible. As self-conscious beings, we knowingly act on purposes and goals, which requires we give reasons and reflect on their success or failure as an end.

According to Marx, labour is creative since at the same time it shapes the world into something new, it serves a purpose and realises goal-directed activity. Labour is determined by conscious purpose, and this capacity is what constitutes it as human activity. In this sense, there is no act of human labour that is not normative, even if it appears otherwise. That labour is a mediating process of change and reflection expresses that we must give reasons for our action and hold their success or failure up to normative standards, which are constituted by the expression of activity itself and are historically transformative. In this view, human beings are rational in a way that has immense ontological and normative significance since our activity aims to fill human self-purpose and ends. Since we are "conscious" of our purposes, which are determinate and varied, if we work in ways that are unfulfilling then we are alienated from both the "nature of the work and the way in which it has to be accomplished," impacting how much "he enjoys it as the free play of his own physical and mental powers."[260]

Cashing out an Aristotelian insight, it is because our productive activity is rational in the way that Marx outlines that we are species-beings. The example Marx gives in *Capital* of the bee (without the conscious labour of the mind) invites comparison with the concept of labour he develops elsewhere. Two passages are worth alluding to. In the *EPM*, Marx writes:

> The practical creation of an *objective world*, the *fashioning* of inorganic nature, is proof that man is a conscious species-being [*bewußten Gattungswesens*], i.e. a being which treats the species as its own essential being or itself as a species-being. It is true that animals also produce. They build nests and dwellings, like the bee, the beaver, the ant, etc. But they produce only their own immediate needs or those of their young; they produce one-sidedly, while man produces universally; they produce only when immediate physical need compels them to do so, while man produces even when he is free from physical need and truly produces only in freedom from such need; they produce only themselves, while man reproduces the whole of nature; their products belong immediately to their physical bodies, while man freely confronts his own product. Animals produce only according to the standards and needs of the species to which they belong, while man is capable of producing according to the standards of every species and of applying to each object its inherent standard; hence man also produces in accordance with the laws of beauty.[261]

We have the species-specific capacity to produce universality since conscious activity enables needs to be fulfilled to the normative standard constituted by that activity. As species-beings, we act in the world to produce our needs, and in doing so it becomes possible to give our needs complexity, transforming from the bottom up what we take a flourishing life to mean. We make and remake our lives according to beauty, not only aesthetically, but inseparably from the question of what a flourishing life would be for us.

Again, in the *Grundrisse* he evokes equivalent terms to describe the social relation of two producers in the labour process. This discussion, as in chapter 7 of *Capital*, explains the use-value of labour-power for the capitalist in the formal equality of the market,

> The fact that this need on the part of one [the capitalist] can be satisfied by the product of the other [labourer], and vice versa, and that the one is capable of producing the object of the need of the other, and that each confronts the other as owner of the object of the other's need, this proves that each of them reaches beyond his own particular need etc., as a *human being*, and that they relate to one another as *human beings*; that their communal species-being [*gemeinschaftliches Gattungswesen*] is acknowledged by all. It does not happen elsewhere—that elephants produce for tigers, or animals for other animals. For example. A hive of bees comprises at bottom only one bee, and they all produce the same thing.[262]

Across *Capital*, *EPM* and the *Grundrisse*, Marx's concept of labour is motivated by a remarkably similar ontological idea, down to the examples used to illustrate the difference between the self-conscious labour of human beings and acts of non-rational animals. The social ontology contained in these pages is both normative and historical.

With this construal of Marx's social ontology, it becomes easier to understand his portrayal in *Capital* of the sociality in the productive activity of labour. He emphasises the way in which the objects of labour are mediated by human activity and serve as a "conductor" of the labour process as it transforms our relation to the world.[263] Labour activity is a living force, a Promethean "fire" which, through its "energy," allows a process of transformation; it has the power to "awaken" old materials, and beyond rust and rot, from their death into new use-values.[264] This activity Marx describes as "the functions appropriate to their concept."[265] Labour activity is ontologically constitutive, *necessarily* "simple and abstract."[266] As life activity, productive activity is "common to all forms of society in which human beings live."[267]

In *Capital*, Marx enriches his earlier conception of human essence. He asks the reader to consider general and simple features of labouring activity to make clear what is historically specific about the determinations of particular social forms. This essence can only appear in historical forms. When Marx discusses "purposeful activity [*zweckmäßige Thätigkeit*] aimed at the production of use-values" as "the universal condition for the metabolic interaction [*Stoffwechsel*] between man and nature," he provides the abstraction which permits any historical point of reflection and identification of value-producing labour as one form of human activity.[268] The analysis of labour as a specifically human activity is precisely what makes it possible to say what is historically specific about labour under capitalism. There is no production outside of historical and social forms. For this reason, Marx conceives of human essence in a detailed investigation of social forms in which his social ontology informs every layer of analysis. Thus, capitalist production is "the most tremendous waste of individual development" since it "squanders human beings, living labour, more readily than does any other mode of production, squandering not only flesh and blood, but nerves and brain as well."[269] The loss of human potential noted here highlights the continuing role of alienation in *Capital*.

This interpretation avoids claiming either that Marx never really meant these "naturalising" comments (that they present an inexplicable anomaly) or that they are marginal to his critique of political economy. Postone goes as far as to describe Marx's "biological residue."[270] Instead, in my view, *Capital* affirms the idea that "the human essence is no abstraction inherent in each single individual. In its reality it is the ensemble of the social relations."[271] Social forms are historical expressions of the human essence. In his mature social theory, abstract labour is a more determinate notion of alienation. Postone struggles to explain the presence of "species capacities" in *Capital* and glosses over Marx's argument, suspending the concept of alienation without a sense of what it is being alienated from.[272]

Marx's intent is made clear by the next step in his argument. In *Capital*, after investigating labour from its most simple ontological relation, he shifts to explain the perspective of capital in order to investigate how abstract social labour is valorised in the production process. In précis, the capitalist buys the commodity labour-power and deploys it, consuming the time purchased from the worker within the production process to create commodities. Given that the capitalist puts human beings to work with what they already own in the means of production, the "labour process is a process between things the capitalist has purchased, things which belong to him."[273] The use-value of labour-power is then objectified into commodities that bear value. The sale of this commodity and the profit of exchange motivate the whole process. With this discussion, Marx further concretises the initial dialectic of use-value and value with the unity of the labour process and value expansion (*Wertbildungsprozess*).[274] In this sequence, "productive capital becomes product, commodity, money, and is transformed back into the conditions of production. It remains capital in each of these forms, and it becomes capital only by realizing itself as such."[275]

The labour process allows value to be renewed through its valorisation. As labour-power is deployed during the labour process by producing goods from the means of production, it sets in motion the creation of new value. The capitalist attempts to use as efficiently as possible the labour-power of the worker to derive more value from the labour-power purchased than what they had to lay down in monetary terms for the price of the labour. This process ensures, in short, that the extraction of surplus-value requires that living labour is enacted upon already socially objectified dead labour, to create more value as new commodities to be sold. Marx charts out the creation of value in this process as a sequence of value relations between subjective living labour and objective dead labour as capital.[276] Labouring activity is continually directed from one object to another, a process in which "the worker's labour constantly undergoes a transformation, from the form of unrest [*Unruhe*] into that of being [*Sein*], from the form of motion [*Bewegung*] into that of objectivity [*Gegenständlichkeit*]."[277]

Living labour becomes dead and objectified "into capital, value which can perform its own valorisation process, an animated monster which begins [in Goethe's words] to 'work,' 'as though he had love in his guts! [*als hätt' es Lieb' im Leibe*].'"[278] The valorisation of new value is now possible precisely because the labour performed has a dual character as "abstract social labour" and concrete activity of a special kind.[279] The extraction of surplus value is a social relationship of exploitation and domination, in which through the labour process, labour-time is emptied of its specific qualitative function and quantified to meet the necessity of commodity production. The quicker and harder the work is done, the bigger the possible payoff for the capitalist. Thus, the extraction of surplus labour is a battle over time and conditions. But workers are not robbed of the "value of their labour"; surplus value is extracted from the labour-power that is sold to the capitalist as "living labour" to provide "fresh value" when it is used in the production process to derive value above and beyond what was paid for the labour-power.[280] Commodities come to be values only as social objects with prices, understood not by the embodiment of individual units of labour-time, but by "the labour-time socially required for its production."[281]

Marx's discussion of the social form of labour specific to capitalism becomes increasingly concrete and determinate as he elaborates on the production process generalised by industrial production: huge workplaces and many workers in large-scale, complex division of labour.[282] While *Capital* gives considerable attention to the technical division of labour, Marx demonstrates that the simple and general character of social production requires "co-operation." In chapter 1, Marx claims commodity production involves a dualism when "private labour takes the form of its opposite, namely labour in its directly social form."[283] In chapter 13, "Co-operation," Marx investigates the sociality of labour within particular instances of capital production. This expression of sociality is immanent since wage-labour involves privately undertaken social labour within the social division of labour. Despite the cooperation which underpins the activity, its end is defined by the private accumulation of capital. The historical and conceptual starting point for capitalist production is large numbers of people "working together, at the same time, in one place" under the command of a capitalist.[284] While this at first is only a matter of quantity, this method of production becomes generalised, and the "labour objectified in value" becomes a socially measurable amount of labour-power.[285] A qualitative shift has occurred. Under capital, the labour process has become collective. "When numerous workers work together side by side in accordance with a plan," as Marx explains, "whether in the same process, or in a different but connected process, this form of labour is called co-operation."[286]

In this way, isolated labour processes are brought together and unified. This dynamic involves the increasingly collective aspects of the labour process as it develops in large workplaces. The drive to revolutionise productive power by expanding industrial production on progressively mass scales brings with it more integrated labour processes between workers. This dynamic holds within it an immanent contradiction since the expansion of industrial capitalism is predicated on cooperation and social labour. Production is privatised but must be mediated by social and collective processes for it to occur at all. This social action is abstract since the fullest possible realisation of the sociality of commodity production is the exchange of commodities produced by social cooperation. "Cooperation" under capitalist production is alienated labour that must conform its norms of social interaction by the rules and regulations set upon it for the extraction of surplus value. Cooperation in the labour process serves the function of the market and not the normative practices inherent in that activity. Productive processes are configured and mediated by the exchange imperative, which in turn ensures that labouring activity is considered a private concern, from the individual wage that the worker receives after the work period has finished to the profits taken by the capitalist at the end of the financial year.

But in analysing the dynamic of cooperation within the labour process, Marx sees the possibilities for human capacities and practices to be transformed through this sociality. When exerted together, the workers' abilities are combined in their shared activity, and the individual worker is carried by the spirit and vitality of sociality. Since Marx considers capitalist production as social domination, it may seem peculiar that he finds an expression of human potential within wage-labour. However, Marx's immanent critique of the social form of labour holds that it is precisely our sociality that enables emancipation based on the potential of rational and collective decision-making. At this point of the argument, Marx again turns to Aristotle to articulate why the sociality of human beings enables reflection on the historical configuration of social life. Commenting on the social connection that arises from collective labour process, he writes:

> This originates from the fact that man, if not as Aristotle thought, a political animal (ζῷον πολιτικόν), is at all events a social animal.

Adding in the footnote:

> The real meaning of Aristotle's definition is that man is by nature a citizen of a town [*Stadtbürger*]. This is quite as characteristic of classical antiquity as Franklin's definition of man as a tool-making animal is characteristic of Yankeedom.[287]

It could seem like Marx eschews the political connotations of Aristotle's term (as used, for example, in the *Grundrisse*).[288] However, Marx stresses the political nature of human beings is interwoven with our sociality. Marx expands Aristotle's definition of the human being as having a political nature as a polis-dweller since the historical polis conditions that concept. Any move to project a concept of humanity on such a model would be another ahistorical Robinsonade. However, this remark does not set Marx at odds with Aristotle as a whole; rather, he demonstrates the essential difference between Aristotle's social ontology and his own historicising notion of being *within* the same tradition of ethical reasoning.

For Aristotle, the political animal comes after their relation to the household, a gregarious relationship of a "special" kind, in which the household founds the political being of the citizen.[289] However, Marx transforms Aristotle's model by giving sociality historical content. Not only do human beings live in political communities, but these political relationships must be understood by their historically specific social substance. Marx holds to Aristotle's idea that societal organisation is a manifestation of human nature and with it sees that our social forms of life stand in relation to our natures as rational beings that seek a flourishing life. It is not just society in general that sets the conditions for the human good to be realised but a rationally ordered society. In this way, Marx's social ontology is historically specific, incorporating a view of human capacity and ends with the historical shape of social relations. Marx's social animal denotes the shape of social relations between human beings set within specific historical forms.[290] It is precisely our sociality which makes us historical beings and empowers us to criticise a form of life in normative terms. Sociality takes self-conscious expression through the ontological form of being, as determined by definite modes of social interaction. In this way, the human essence not only expresses historical actuality, but also the immanent potentiality for a higher form of social interaction that is both rational and collective.

Marx's discussion of productive activity in chapter 7 and chapter 13 should be seen in light of this comprehension of labour as ontologically constitutive historical processes. The productive power of social labour, Marx writes, "arises from co-operation itself. When the worker co-operates in a planned way with others, he strips off the fetters of his individuality, and develops the capabilities of his species."[291] If human potentiality is conceivable only with cooperation, Marx shows how this potential is systematically restricted by the domination of capital. The capitalist defines the terrain for cooperation, purchasing the labour-power of each worker simultaneously under conditions mandated and imposed by the capitalist (however regulated). The mode of production as a whole is mediated by competing capitalists who control parts of the total capital and oversee component parts of the production process. Marx writes, "[t]he work of directing, superintending and adjusting becomes one of the functions of capital, from the moment that the labour under capital's control becomes co-operative."[292] Capitalism is fully actualised by the abstract sociality of value, conditional on alienated relationships between human beings. The individual is forced into an atomised life reproduced by their hourly sale of activity to another.[293]

Abstract sociality depends upon the relation between workers and capitalists. The asociality of the cooperative production process goes hand in hand with capitalism as a historically specific form of domination. Marx contrasts the direct domination of the labour process prior to capitalism with that of the "lords of capital" who rely on the "freedom" of the worker to sell their labour-power.[294] While capitalist domination is impersonal, capitalists often exercise cruel and arbitrary power over their workers.[295] But capitalist domination contains within it an immanent dynamic of resistance. The particularity of capitalist domination rests in the contradiction between the cooperation inherent in productive activity and abstract social forms. Class struggle is bound up in capitalism as a form of life. The mediation of social activity between worker and capitalist are in fundamental tension since cooperation enables the cultivation of collective decision-making about the ends of activity and the demand for a flourishing life. Such a life of practical reasoning and practical wisdom is in conflict with capitalist social forms. Class struggle interrupts the logic of capital accumulation and offers its fundamental challenge. There is no value without workers and no capitalists without value.

Conclusion

Marx's mature work examines the being of value. It is crucial to his concept of value as a social form that commodities be seen as products of capital and that the creation of surplus-value arising from the capitalist production process is comprehended as historically specific to capitalism.[296] In his critical theory of society, Marx illuminates the abstract forms of being that restrict human potentiality and bind social life to the domination of capital. The value-form subsumes human life under the fetishism of abstract relations, but at the same time, social processes of cooperation expose the immanent dynamic within the very lifeblood of capitalism. Viewed in this way, capitalism lays the basis for its own overcoming. If Hegel helps animate Marx's form-determinations and better capture the immanence of social processes, Aristotle throws into relief the specifically ethical dimension of *Capital*. Steeped in Aristotle's insights, Marx grasps the contradiction between actuality and potentiality in the process of capitalist production as a whole. Marx's systematic logic establishes why abstract sociality necessarily limits the logic of human interaction to exchange. Capitalism as a form of life creates a universal relation of needs mediated by the logic of exchange—a "moral imperative [for] capital [*Moral des Capitals*] to produce as much surplus value as possible."[297]

In Marx's view, since the products of labour are valued according to the logic of the market, their ability to meet a human need or enable a social good is defined by the real abstractions of exchange, rather than normative relations of social cooperation. Products of labour take power over social life as if independent of our activity. As value objects for exchange, commodities take on a life of their own. Once generalised, commodity exchange becomes the logic of society. It expresses the "natural" finished form—the truth—of capitalist social relations.[298] Drawing explicitly on Aristotle and Hegel to develop the argument, Marx's claim that the movement of capital is limitless not only distinguishes his pivotal contribution to social theory, an understanding of capital as the absolute modern social relation, but at the very same time is motivated by a normative theory of ethical life. Reality is ethical, but reality cannot be rational if it is not self-conscious and embodied in a free form of life. In this understanding, Marx demonstrates that the value-form is a structural barrier to the mutual recognition of our life activity and forms of association. Marx's concept of ethical life points to the negation of the value-form as a life-and-death struggle for self-consciousness and human flourishing.

CONCLUSION

The Song of the Weavers

CAPITAL **IS A WORK OF** tremendous texture and depth of feeling. For many readers it is not just its theoretical insight and political impetus that continue to inspire, but the rich tapestry Marx weaves together, picturing human activity as entwined in a complex and dynamic form of social relations. *Capital* pictures a world of immense materials, collecting commodities, machines and precious metals with that of abstraction, empty time and the occult quality of value. Social relations have a phantasmagoric form, where the objects of human creation appear to have a power altogether their own. The "world of commodities" adheres to us through money, the social form that obscures both the sociality of privately performed labour and the sociality of individuals "by making those relations appear as relations between material objects, instead of revealing them plainly."[1] The peculiarity of such a form of human life is that it appears natural and immutable. Marx challenges both assumptions. He brings his vision to life, finely crafting from a vast array of literary, philosophical and economic works. Its texture reflects the richness of Marx's inquiry, with vivid style, pulling as sharply from Sophocles's *Antigone* as statistics from the British government "Blue Books." The words of political economists, philosophers and historians are the warp to the weft of the voices of factory inspectors, workers and capitalists. *Capital* strings together historical figures, personifications and tropes, constructing from a lifetime of study and political activity a truly revolutionary account of modern life.

Like a thread, the character of the weaver runs across volume 1. This figure would have been familiar to Marx's initial readers. In the nineteenth century, Manchester had the moniker "Cottonopolis." Fabric production played an essential role in the origins of capitalism, just as it shapes capitalism today.[2] Nineteenth-century technological improvements, including the power loom, meant that the socially necessary labour-time required to produce cloth was dramatically reduced. When discussing surplus value, Marx examines in detail the introduction of new machinery and the transformation from small-scale manufacturing to large-scale industry. "An example of this process, on the most colossal scale," Marx writes, "is afforded by the production of 'wearing apparel.' "[3] Since the end of capitalist commodity production and exchange is accruing surplus value, Marx's theory of the value-form looks to render visible the patterns of social life constituted by human activity but concealed by the very form of their existence.

In chapter 1 of *Capital*, as traced out in detail, Marx equates two commodities—spun linen and a tailored coat—to better examine value-creating labour and the form of wealth specific to capitalism.[4] The activities of the weaver and the tailor lace through the initial pages of the book, as Marx unfolds the value-form layer by layer. In its most simple form as a commodity, the coat reflects a historically specific social form of human labour. It is a " 'bearer of value,' although this property never shows through, even when the coat is at its most threadbare ... Despite its buttoned-up appearance, the linen recognizes in it a splendid kindred soul, the soul of value."[5] The social substance that creates such life is living labour. Marx's point is to show that in the world of commodities such activity is in a crucial way abstract. The creation of wealth depends upon productive activity in the form of commodity-producing labour. By examining the simple object of the coat, Marx suggests we need to grasp it not just as a product that has been made to be sold as a value, but that the coat reflects the social relations that are spread across the contemporary world.

Marx draws us into the dialectics of value centring around the relation of the coat to other commodities. Once the simple opposition between the linen and coat are expanded to include "the whole world of commodities," Marx brings into focus the connection between one and many commodities. This discussion leads to the most vital sections of Marx's explanation of the form of value. But just as it appears that the weaver and tailor have disappeared as the story of the production of a simple, everyday commodity becomes a more determinate picture of the relation of commodities to money, Marx announces the return of the weaver. But at this point, the focus is not on his function as a producer of commodities, but as their "guardian." We "now accompany the owner of some commodity, say our old friend the linen weaver, to the scene of action, the market [*Warenmarkt*]."⁶ Marx asks us to picture the weaver entering the market to buy a Bible for his family. Through the activity of this fabricated persona, Marx traces the changing shape of value as it is alienated in its metamorphosis from one form to another in a dialectic of use and exchange.

The Bible appears in the hand of the weaver as the embodiment of the mystification of capitalism. Marx's idea of fetishism employs a religious analogy to depict the phantasmagoric life of "autonomous figures endowed with a life of their own."⁷ In the world of commodities, which glisten brightest when displayed for sale as objects of value, the weaver appears as a personification of the life of abstract domination. The weaver represents the double bind of life under capitalism, the alienation of production and the mutual antagonism of the market. The fabric of social life is abstract, and our social relations are defined by the misrecognition of commodity production and exchange. Social activity is unfree.

In this book, I have mapped the contours of Marx's theorisation of modern society, sociality and social forms. His normative objection to capitalism is that it systematically denies the good life to be lived. By posing Marx's critique of capital as a normative theory, it becomes possible to articulate a sense of the immanent potential of human activity unfettered from the domination that characterises capitalism as a form of life. Absolute ethical life is a life beyond capital. As such, it concretely unifies the universal, particular and individual forms of human life into recognitive relations of freedom. Marx's understanding of sociality relies on fundamental normative commitments, a testament of his lifelong debt to Aristotle and Hegel. However, the act of conceptual excavation I advance in this book must look forward. Marx consciously situates his social theory directly in the present, since in bourgeois society "the past dominates the present; in Communist society, the present dominates the past. In bourgeois society capital is independent and has individuality, while the living person is dependent and has no individuality."⁸ The persistence of the past is felt as a weight. Tradition appears not as a guide to the practices of the good life, but as restraint. Taking ideological forms, tradition naturalises what has come before us and declares the present as eternal. As dead labour, the past casts its shadow over social life. Capital disfigures action and limits the living good. As abstract domination, capital denies individuality while producing the isolation and estrangement of the individual. The existing relation between past and present preserves the domination of past labour. We learn from Marx, as we learnt from Sophocles, however, that our *present care is with the present*. The present offers a glimpse of what freedom and emancipation could be, the free control of human activity in a society in which the individual is socially interdependent. Marx's aversion to utopian schemes is apparent in any early remark on immanent critique:

> Nothing prevents us, therefore, from lining our criticism with a criticism of politics, from taking sides in politics, i.e. from entering into real struggles and identifying ourselves with them. This does not mean that we shall confront the world with new doctrinaire principles and proclaim: Here is the truth, on your knees before it! It means that we shall develop for the world new principles from the existing principles of the world. We shall not say: Abandon your struggles, they are mere folly; let us provide you with the true campaign-slogans. Instead we shall simply show the world why it is struggling, and consciousness of this is a thing it *must* acquire whether it wishes or not.[9]

Ethical life entails being a part of the world, living in light of the normative commitments we make with others. At the same time, the demands of social life require subjecting the modern world to relentless criticism. This cannot be an abstract critique, removed and isolated, a critique that is external and otherworldly. Instead, *absolute* ethical life is an immanent critique of society and the normative potential for a new social form. The concept of ethical life articulates a concrete totality beyond contemporary dualisms that separate morality and politics as distinct components of action. If social being is made abstract by action separate from each sphere of human experience, then ethical life unifies social action in interdependent and rational forms.

Marx confronts explicitly modern problems, and in this confrontation he develops a philosophical understanding of the relation between society and the individual. Marx's concept of labour and value-form theory expresses a rich normative critique of the alienated and abstract sociality of modern life, which looks to their negation. His early sense of the telos of the "community of human beings" is a reflection of the emergent subjectivity of the working class. For Marx, emancipation is the activity which transforms the particularity of the individual into the universality of the recognitive community.[10] Through this activity, human beings go beyond the antinomy of political and ethical life to a higher form of association. In an 1844 article for *Vorwärts!*, Marx writes of this higher form as

> The community from which *his own labour* separates him is *life* itself, physical and spiritual life, human morality, human activity, human enjoyment, *human nature*.

Human nature is the true community of men. Just as the disastrous isolation from this nature is disproportionately more far-reaching, unbearable, terrible and contradictory than the isolation from the political community, so too the transcending of this isolation and even a partial reaction, a *rebellion* against it, is so much greater, just as the *man* is greater than the *citizen* and *human life* than *political life*. Hence, however limited an industrial revolt may be, it contains within itself a *universal* soul: and however universal a political revolt may be, its *colossal* form conceals a *narrow* split.[11]

The universality of life, the essence of ethical activity and nature, is socially comprehended in the organisation of community. In this article, Marx speaks of the recent revolt by Silesian weavers as expressing the "theoretical" and "conscious" standpoint of this new society. He asks the reader to "[t]hink first of the 'Weaver's Song,' that intrepid battle-cry which does not even mention health, factory or district in which the proletariat at once proclaims its antagonism to the society of private property in the most decisive, aggressive, ruthless and forceful manner."[12]

Heinrich Heine's poem, the "Weaver's Song," repeats the refrain "We weave; we weave" [*Wir weben, wir weben!*].[13] This activity is what voices the consciousness of the work-worn figures. Published by Marx in *Vorwärts!* and translated by Engels for the English socialist paper, *New Moral World*, the "Weaver's Song" is a vivid document of the radicalisation of German thought in its deepening critique of capitalist social relations.[14] Heine's poetry was philosophical and radical. He advocated an "explicitly revolutionary" interpretation of Hegel and "forged a new kind of poetry—or, rather a poetics that informs both his prose and his verse, dialectical and critical down to its very form."[15] As Adorno suggests, "[i]n Heine commodity and exchange seized control of sound and tone, whose very nature had previously consisted in the negation of the hustle and bustle of daily life."[16] Adorno's remark again brings to mind the tailoring and weaving of linen in *Capital*, Marx's critique of *the dismal science*.[17]

In *Minima Moralia*, Adorno points to just how the logic of commodity exchange has infested *life itself*, objectifying and mechanising.[18] He formulates this analysis of domination from the first chapter of *Capital*:

Only when the process that begins with the metamorphosis of labour-power into a commodity has permeated men through and through and objectified each of their impulses as formally commensurable variations of the exchange relationship, is it possible for life to reproduce itself under the prevailing relations of production. Its consummate organisation demands the coordination of people that are dead. The will to live finds itself dependent on the denial of the will to live: self-preservation annuls all life in subjectivity.[19]

For Adorno, the good life appears lost amidst a life determined by the domination of capital. As dead labour, capital *lives* by its objectification of human experience and reduction of social life to the logic of exchange; a life which appears as dead as the capital which hangs above our heads. With the title *Minima Moralia*, Adorno reverses the Aristotelian *Magna Moralia* and ironically ventures that the philosophical pursuit of the good life must now concern the suffering of the present.

> The melancholy science from which I make this offering to my friend relates to a region that from time immemorial was regarded as the true field of philosophy, but which, since the latter conversion into method, has lapsed into intellectual neglect, sententious whimsy and finally oblivion: the teaching of the good life.[20]

He hangs together the good life with the bad one, not to sink into despair but highlight the obstacles to our freedom within this immanent relation.[21] Adorno laments the impossibility of living a good life in the atomisation of the present social order. Market relationships render human beings into objects, which means for Adorno: "Wrong life cannot be lived rightly."[22] "Life" has a Hegelian inflection, referring to *Sittlichkeit*, ethical life, with the practices and institutions of social life as the mediators of human experience. As Hegel remarks, "the *truth* concerning *right, ethics, and the state* is at any rate as *old* as its *exposition*."[23]

Adorno's comment also conveys Hegel's strong distinction between ethics and morality.[24] As J. M. Bernstein explains,

> Like Aristotle, Adorno presupposes that ethical thought is a reflective articulation of ethical experience, which itself is structured through ethical practices. This assumes that the ethical possibilities open to an individual are delimited by the state of the ethical world this individual inhabits: wrong life (the state of the ethical world) cannot be lived rightly. And this, by itself, assumes that the provenance of the meaning and force of moral terms are the practices of the community deploying them, and that outside these practices, and the history they sediment and report, such terms lose their force.[25]

After Hegel's ethical life and Aristotle's teaching of the good life, Adorno's sardonic "wrong life" points to the ongoing crisis of ethical life in our current social order. For Hegel, ethical life is a question of rational institutions. For Aristotle, the good life is already contextualised in the polis but needs to be realised through the practices of the virtues. Yet for Adorno, the good life is not possible in our contemporary world and its present institutions. Domination has all but bleached modern life, and hope of the good life is tormented by the bad life.[26] Adorno provokes us to contemplate just how unfree capitalism actually is at the most everyday level. In what might appear as exaggeration, Adorno is lending currency to Marx's analysis of abstract social forms as relations of domination. The abstraction of the labour-process is internalised and manifests itself into the instrumental rationality of commodity fetishism. As a result, "[a]tomisation is advancing not only between men, but within each individual, between the spheres of life."[27] The individual becomes a "mere reflection of property relations."[28] Adorno takes Marx's value-form theory to be a decisive prism from which to understand individual existence and action. The exchange relation "that equally deforms men and things" is a historically specific form of domination.[29] Adorno resists the false sanguinity that permeates capitalist culture and ideology and masks domination. A free society cannot be envisioned by simply wishing it to be so.[30]

For Adorno, as with Marx, the totality of life is ethical. Adorno's insights dovetail with Marx's by reinforcing the impact of social domination. This domination must be seen as transmutable, and an immanent critique must retain a theory of emancipation. The historical failure of the workers' movement and the Holocaust frame Adorno's thought as he pursues a search for meaning in the wake of these devastations. Even in our bad world, the possibilities for ethical, practical reasoning remain potentialities, and critical theory cannot lose sight of the good life. Adorno's assessment of the condition of private existence is often understood as venturing too close to the complete denial that ethical action can ever break out of the private sphere of morality.[31] But this conception loses sight of the normative importance of Adorno's thought. In an important respect, Adorno picks up where Marx left off. The infection of abstract social relations into the widest proliferation of the individual's life is brought out in great effect in Adorno's investigation. However precisely he details how devastating the "severance of morality from politics" is in modern life, Adorno does not completely lose sight of the way in which ethical life might be generated against this paradigm.[32] He even raises "democracy of councils [*Räte*]" as the contrasting picture of social needs to late capitalism.[33] Modern domination can easily seem too total, reification too deep. But it is not so. In thinking the bad life, Adorno advances an immanent critique committed to human flourishing.[34]

For Marx, the struggle for ethical life requires the action of rational agents against the domination which frames our lives. Ethical life is not a simple idealisation of a world yet to come but the unfolding of rationality through the self-consciousness of goal-directed collective action. The universality of these goods does not constrain individuality but gives it the ground to flourish. Adorno makes a similar point, "[a]n emancipated society... would not be a unitary state, but the realisation of universality in the reconciliation of differences."[35] Further, what Marx finds appealing in Heine—emancipation and rationality in a society quite unlike our own—Adorno also notes: "there is no longer any homeland other than a world in which no one would be cast out anymore, the world of a genuinely emancipated humanity. The wound that is Heine will heal only in a society that has achieved reconciliation."[36] This normative conception of emancipation grasps society in terms of the free relations of social interaction and interdependence, which not only shape economic relationships but all human experience. The *wound* of modern life requires the universality which unfolds from the struggles of rational agents. Marx's concept of ethical life looks for the reconciliation of "*life* itself" in the community of reciprocal human sociality.[37] His analysis of the modern world identifies the abstract relations that configure sociality. This diagnosis does not indicate that the denial of ethical life under the domination of capital is absolute, but instead goes on to show that secreted within such a form of life are contradiction that surface as the expression and practice of rational agency. For Marx, the negation of abstract social forms is a potential that can only be realised by virtue of its internal dynamics. The extraction of surplus value and the impersonal domination of capital are dependent upon the activity of those who suffer from it. For this reason, the praxis of rational agents presents the central prospect for challenging the abstract sociality of capitalism. Such an overcoming requires mapping the path from particularity to universality and the decree that ethical life is freedom without domination.

In my view, there are five distinct but intertwined threads in which Marx's mature thought directly reflects on ethical questions. The first is his concept of needs. Whereas capital renders human needs subservient to the need to extract and reproduce surplus value, in Marx's account human needs are "second nature," the socially determinate cultivation of the good as an expression of freedom. Second is his concept of social individuality, a form of sociality that is underpinned by a normative vision of human flourishing. Third is his insistence upon the rational control of time, where free control of time provides a basis for the radical reduction of socially necessary labour-time. Fourth is his view that the free association of producers makes it possible for human activity to be self-conscious and rational. Goal-directed practices shape our normative lives and cultivate flourishing, braiding thought and being and establishing rational association on such a basis. Fifth is Marx's conception of an emancipated society, where he expresses a concept of social freedom, in which the good life is one of mutual recognition. The good life is communism, *absolute ethical life*.

Thread 1

Marx's concept of needs is integral to his critique of political economy. The expansion of value transformed the "fixed and limited" needs of precapitalist trade to the "ceaseless" renewal of needs mediated by market exchange.[38] The logical structure of social life is determined by the needs of exchange, rather than human need. Relations of capital production and accumulation are premised on the privatisation of human social activity. Social life is structured by economic functions which serve surplus extraction. Alienated labour besets human need, tying our activity and goods to the confines of generalised commodity production and exchange. Marx remarks, "[t]he social division of labour makes the nature of his labour as one-sided as his needs are many-sided."[39] In the *Grundrisse* he contrasts this "system of labours" with a "system of needs," employing Hegel's language, while demonstrating the impossibility of civil society as such a system.[40] Marx conceives of needs at the level of necessity, but never opposes necessity to "the manner in which they are satisfied" which is always historically conditioned.[41] In this sense, even the "necessary need" to eat is historically shaped in terms of custom and tradition. "Every [natural] drive," as Adorno remarks, "is socially mediated in such a way that its natural side never appears directly, but only as something socially produced."[42] Needs are never just physical but are "historically developed social needs, which become second nature."[43] Marx takes up Hegel's idea of rational institutions, practical agency and ethical life. Second nature means that the institutional forms which constitute society enable "the discovery, creation and satisfaction of new needs arising from society itself," which expand "the cultivation of all the qualities of the social human being, production of the same in a form as rich as possible in needs."[44] Marx's tenor echoes not just Hegel, but Aristotle. Second nature is the living embodiment of good in social institutions, dependent on and constituted by the cultivation of ethical practices.

Marx's idea of an expanding system of needs corresponds to a new social form of life in which human flourishing is embedded in the production of a "total and universal social product" based on relations of interdependence. For social meaning to be "many-sided" involves a normative transformation of decision-making and the organisation of social life to meet human needs. Under capitalism as a form of life, social needs are reduced to the necessities of commodity exchange, structured upon the private sale and reproduction of labour-power. As it stands, the accumulation of surplus value is the categorical imperative of capitalism. In Agnes Heller's words, "needs as ends are turned into needs as means and vice versa."[45] Needs are robbed of their recognitive dimension since the value of the commodity is not defined by its concretely social *ergon*, but its exchange value. Marx's system of needs has considerable advantage over Hegel's idea of needs in the *Philosophy of Right* since it shows that there is no simple "use-value" easily shorn of "exchange-value" under capitalism. Insofar as human beings expand our needs, the logic of commodity exchange shapes social life. The imperative to accumulate surplus value acts as a perverse, but impersonal, force over individual and collective behaviour and ties social needs to the mute compulsion of economic logic. Value is not premised on the social development of all-sided human beings, but instead the buying and selling of commodities. We can only speak of value as price. In his concept of needs, Marx adopts Aristotle's idea of flourishing, while drawing attention to the historical social practices that shape our form of life and the normative importance of enriching human activity through cultivating and expanding human needs.

Thread 2

The individual is conceived by Marx as part of a concrete totality as *social individuals*. This idea challenges atomistic notions of moral independence. For Marx, methodological individualism is a result of the abstract sociality that detaches the individual from rational social association. While human beings are socially formed, only beyond capital does he think social individuals can realise rational and free association as an expression of the wealth of social interdependence. This process is "the absolute movement of becoming," in which "the limited bourgeois form is stripped away" to allow human beings to develop, not in isolation but in the rich determinates of a free social form of life.[46] There is no duality between developing as individuals and as social beings, since we are both at once. For Marx, the universal being-and-becoming of the social individual is a form of sociality premised on relations of freedom. Drawing attention to the normative importance of social relations, Marx's critique of political economy theorises the socially situated position of the worker who produces value seemingly independent of human need.

This activity relegates our individuality to the judicial relation of private ownership, where we recognise each other as buyers and sellers of commodities. For Marx, the labour activity performed as a social relation by individually isolated workers must be negated within this social form itself to develop the immanent potential of human life to realise "its communal, social character."[47] What outrages Marx is that our productive activity is just another thing for sale. Yet living labour, which constitutes the substance of value, can decide on the death of capital. Living labour can give life to normative social forms beyond capital that enable the good life. The contradictions within the very generation of value—the dominance of dead over living labour—provide a potentiality for a society of rational association once the living good is realised. Marx's social ontology weaves together the threads of human activity to make clear the immanent telos for collective social being. Through the free relation of our activity with others, human beings can become interdependent social agents and transcend the binaries of individualism and collectivism. Marx's hope is that in doing so, abstract social forms of life would be rendered obsolete. This eventuality would enable the flourishing of social beings as absolute ethical life.

Thread 3

For Marx, time, freedom and human potentiality are closely related. Capital reduces human labour into component parts that correspond to the temporal dimensions of production. Marx suggests that the time of the labour process is a crucial site of conflict, as workers struggle over the duration of work and the conditions of exploitation of their labour-power. By making people work harder and longer, "absolute surplus value" can be amplified. From the standpoint of capital, labour-time measures efficiency and productivity driven by the imperative to increase surplus value. Time measures domination.[48] Under the value-form, as Adorno points out, "free time is the unmediated continuation of labour as its shadow." Free time is reified and empty, the correspondence to the working day which cannot help but take on its logic. Adorno looks "to help free time turn into freedom."[49] This possibility lies in transforming and transcending capital. In a rational society, so conceived, the democratic allocation of time would serve social need. With such freedom, the social tasks of human life activity could be rationally designed and through institutions of collective decision-making enable normative social practices. Whether the practice is necessary for society to operate or the leisure of life itself, the end of both is free since the good upon which those activities depends is the recognition of our own individual freedom and flourishing in the freedom and flourishing of everybody. As Marx observes in the *Grundrisse*:

> On the basis of communal production, the determination of time remains, of course, essential. The less time the society requires to produce wheat, cattle etc., the more time it wins for other production, material or mental. Just as in the case of an individual, the multiplicity of its development, its enjoyment and its activity depends on economisation of time. Economy of time, to this all economy ultimately reduces itself. Society likewise has to distribute its time in a purposeful way, in order to achieve a production adequate to its overall needs; just as the individual has to distribute his time correctly in order to achieve knowledge in proper proportions or in order to satisfy the various demands on his activity. Thus, economy of time, along with the planned distribution of labour time among the various branches of production, remains the first economic law on the basis of communal production. It becomes law, there, to an even higher degree. However, this is essentially different from a measurement of exchange values (labour or products) by labour time. The labour of individuals in the same branch of work, and the various kinds of work, are different from one another not only quantitatively but also qualitatively. What does a solely quantitative difference between things presuppose? The identity of their qualities. Hence, the quantitative measure of labours presupposes the equivalence, the identity of their quality.[50]

The problem Marx is addressing here is the transformation of labour-time as the measure of abstract labour to free time, time that allows for the cultivation of shared aims and ends.[51] The communal determination of time parallels the possibilities for rational production conceivable with advanced technology and machinery. As Marx pointed out, modern machinery and technology herald new levels of misery, forcing the elongation of the working day, sweeping away "every moral and natural restriction" to the time a worker is expected to be on the clock.[52] Machinery generalised and deepened the centrality of industrial capital to social relations, creating a working class and labour processes with increasing automation.[53] Considering this machinery could easily give us more free time, absurdly it is inverted to become "the most unfailing means for turning the whole lifetime of the worker and his family into labour-time at capital's disposal for its own valorisation."[54] The machine becomes the very instrument to bind the working class to the dictates of empty homogeneous time. This modern actuality is a sad reversal of the potential for machinery to "help turn free time into freedom." Thus Marx writes of machinery: "Only in the imagination of economics does it leap to the aid of the individual worker."[55] Rather, the capitalist process of production transforms the instruments of labour into "a means of enslaving, exploiting and impoverishing the worker," and the "social combination of labour processes appears as an organised suppression of his individual vitality, freedom and autonomy."[56] Normative social critique should rightly magnify the modern aspirations for freedom and autonomy between "independence and dependence" of communities and individuals.[57] But as Marx goes on to show, the lesson that follows from *owning these norms as our own* means we must take seriously social practices of transformation.

This perspective stands in stark contrast to Enlightenment notions of progress and the realities of neoliberal logic that relentlessly seek to maximise profit. Such logic privileges the domination of the past over the present and dead over living labour. The tireless development of technology against (and not with) the development of the worker—"the appropriation of living labour by capital"—lays bare the rapacity of this alien force.[58] The specifically modern character of this idea appears in stark contrast to the ancients. Marx appreciates Aristotle's vision of the Greek gods who can design machines to make the weaving shuttles operate themselves, doing the work of weaving without worker or slave.[59] But Marx disavows what Arendt affirms in Aristotle: that we would want to live a life without production.[60] Marx does not depict freedom as the overcoming of production, but rather notes the dualism between freedom and necessity. The concrete "realm of freedom" requires the establishment of rational institutions and forms of association that can democratically organise production and by doing so, make possible the potential of human activity as flourishing. Like Aristotle, Marx takes human flourishing to be the vital constitutive aspect of what it means to live a good human life. Human activity is a potential that can either be actualised as a form of domination as value or in a new social form which organises free labour as a well-lived life. When Marx considers this new form as potentiality (δυνάμει), he uses Aristotle's Greek.[61]

Thread 4

Marx's concept of needs, sociality and time requires the negation of the value-form. His theory of class struggle gives agency to the working class, the subject who acts collectively against capital. Marx strives to make us alert to the possibility of the subjects who objectify their activity as the substance of value, instead becoming subjects of universal freedom. Put in this way, Marx's theory of class struggle articulates the practical consciousness and rationality of human agents engaged in a life and death struggle with capital. According to Marx, workers become increasingly self-conscious of their social world in their action against it. This challenge can be situated in the kind of Aristotelian practical reasoning that MacIntyre draws us to in all its rich possibilities.

We can value class struggle in the normative terms adequate to its practices of cultivation and wisdom. The struggle against capital resonates with Aristotle to the extent that it speaks to "truth agreeing with correct desire."[62] Marx's theory of class struggle is a form of reasoning that, like Aristotle's, wants to bring reason and desire into harmony. Reason takes the form of self-conscious and recognitive social activity and desire in the form of the satisfaction (and multiplication) of needs. Like Hegel, these needs must be mediated by membership in normatively structured institutions that further habituate ethical life in meaningful social roles. In this way, a free and rational society cannot exist with the value-form in place. Marx's opposition goes further than an abstract negation of capital, but his immanent critique hinges on the contradictions present within the capitalist form of life and his analysis of its social dynamic and constitutive logic. Marx's immanent critique does not posit a view external to the world he is analysing, but the very conception of free association and social individuality can be seen as the living good of collective forms of social activity, overcoming its present alienation and fetishism. The concept of absolute ethical life allows for the activity of reasoning in the development of human freedom.

Without this freedom, the normative ends of our social form of life cannot be rationally comprehended. Human activities are not easily comparable in terms of shared goals and collective practices. While we endeavour to make and sustain these meaningful kinds of bonds in our families and friendship, our social relations are shot through with the abstract sociality of capitalism. There is no way to avoid the selling and buying of commodities and the whole social logic that world ensures. The meaning of happiness—human flourishing—becomes much harder to discern. Presently, banal, arbitrary and demeaning tasks that contribute little to the satisfaction of the human good are measured in the same way as profound acts that foster the cultivation of the virtues. The rule of necessity that Arendt highlighted with such force stamps itself more firmly than ever. But as Marx helps us see, alienation rather than rationality adjudicates the action of individuals. As a result, individual choice and action are motivated by the same quantifiable appearance of the social forms of value. Social action that might challenge or promote the actualisation of the virtue of resistance is reduced to the empty processes of production. While resistance is socially embedded, the rationality of capital fetishises action by reducing it to the temporal logic of machines.[63] Domination flattens human life to the processes of daily routine "as a kind of substitute for happiness."[64] The abstractions of capital are held over us, increasingly atomising and distorting social life. Aristotle claims, "[f]or nothing incomplete is happy, as it does not make up the whole."[65] In a similar manner, Marx hopes for the free activity and practices that bring about the fulfillment of the good life as self-conscious, practical reasoning intertwined with the concrete sociality of human life. Class-consciousness and self-consciousness articulate the same form of freedom. Absolute ethical life requires going beyond hostile class relations to normative relations of recognition.

Thread 5

For Aristotle, the central question of ethics is "what constitutes a good life, and how it is to be attained."[66] This problematic resonates throughout Marx's writings. However, for Marx, the first question is enfolded in the second, since a recognitive social form can only be ascertained from the immanent development of subjective modes of practice. The gulf between the objective sociality of production and the limited subjectivity of workers in asserting this sociality consciously must be challenged for a human flourishing that overcomes the antinomy of subjective and objective action. If the value-form limits the activity of human beings to the logic of exchange, rather than the end in itself of flourishing, the attainment of the good life must be through the forms of sociality that establish rational association. Human-beings-as-they-could-be, under transformed conditions, demand not an abstract negation of capital, but the immanent realisation of sociality. Like Hegel, Marx's effort to understand reality as a concrete totality denotes a concept of absolute ethical life in which productive activity and time are mediated by collective agency and the institutions of shared association. The good life allows for the pursuit of commonly agreed upon ends, practices that cultivate the living good. Social agents can explore their many-sided existence as relations of social meaning in recognition with a society of their own creation. Absolute ethical life is social freedom.

Ultimately what MacIntyre finds wanting in Marx, an adequate social ontology, and what Arendt finds wanting in Marx, political action, not only can be found, but once articulated, animate the centrality of ethical and political action in his critical social theory. For Marx, a society of associated producers makes it possible for rational agents to recognise each other in terms of our shared humanity. The normative commitment that makes such a view possible suggests that ethical life is pivotal to Marx's thinking about a world beyond capital. Putting the three thinkers, Aristotle, Hegel and Marx, in dialogue amplifies what is most pertinent in their shared philosophical approach to action. Human action is a fundamental component of social life, and without its rational self-control, we cannot be free. The character of this action as thinking, consciousness and association can be brought together by tracing the lines of continuity. From this task emerges a picture of sociality in which capitalism fails systematically to allow the good life to be lived. Its very structure ensures the bad life. For all three foundational thinkers, the action of self-conscious rational beings constitutes the fabric of human sociality. This book has attempted to find within these thinkers recurring patterns and lines of continuation. My hope is that these theoretical threads can be strengthened and hold greater weight as contributions to our normative self-understanding. Such an act of weaving looks to give shape to a critical social theory of ethical life.

A concept of absolute ethical life is not external to an immanent critique of social forms but inherent in its dynamic force. Rather than separating theoretical and practical criticism by an empiricist form of science and an external conception of justice, the immanent content of Marx's critical social theory is an ethical conception of the good life understood as the telos of rational association. This end is embedded in collective agency and points to the recognition of human sociality in social freedom. Politically conceived, social freedom would enable the sociality of human activity to be as interdependent as the needs constituting its rational association. If reality itself is ethical, in the sense that subjectivity mediates the objective world, a world defined by the actuality of abstract social forms must be grasped with the potentiality to go beyond it. The real abstractions that hang over our heads can be disrupted by the sociality of human beings, becoming a collective subject that confronts and overcomes the domination of capital. This activity has the capacity to realise the free activity of the living, the present, instead of the domination of the dead labour of the past.

The contemporary political and economic conjuncture now means that Marx's analysis of capitalism appears more viable than a generation ago. However, if Marx's critical theory of society is to have a future, it must be through a renewal of his project to subject the modern world to a critique sufficient for capital's immanent challenge. Absolute ethical life sees this challenge to comprehend the world as one of the potentialities of human rationality, action and freedom present in human sociality. Living labour makes possible the living good. To comprehend the possibilities of emancipation, social theory must theorise the present, and in doing so, grasp absolute ethical life.

Notes

Introduction

1. Karl Marx to Friedrich Engels, 16 August 1867, *MECW* 42, 402–5/*MEW* 31, 323.
2. Friedrich Engels to Karl Marx, 16 June 1867, *MECW* 42, 381–82/*MEW* 31, 303–4.
3. Karl Marx to Friedrich Engels, 22 June 1867, *MECW* 42, 384–85/*MEW* 31, 306.
4. Karl Marx to Friedrich Engels, 7 November 1867, *MECW* 42, 464/*MEW* 31, 379.
5. *Cap*.1, 90/5.
6. Louis Althusser, "Preface to *Capital*" in *Lenin and Philosophy* (London: NLB, 1971), 95.
7. A representative example is Joan Robinson's belief that value is both a "metaphysical fog" and "a great fuss about nothing," *Economic Philosophy* (New York: Routledge, 2021), 30, 36. My approach is indebted to a range of value-form theorists, see note 64 below.
8. *Cap*.1, 139/52.
9. *Gr*, 646/529–30. See also, *Cap*.1, 342/241, 367/266, 416/316.
10. Karl Marx to Ferdinand Lassalle, 22 February 1858, *MECW* 40, 270/*MEW* 29, 550.
11. Karl Marx to Friedrich Engels, 2 April 1851, *MECW* 38, 325/*MEW* 27, 228.
12. *EPM*, 365/289.
13. Typically translators have rendered "Mensch" as "man." While this specific usage has some gendered connotations, it means something akin to "fraternity of human beings." Using a gendered term for "human beings" obscures the requirements of Marx's idea of social freedom, which recognises and critically challenges the oppression of gender, in conjunction with the oppressions of race and class. Instead of modifying existing translations, which is cumbersome and can read awkwardly, I have opted to use gender-neutral terms like "human being," "their," "people" etc. throughout my exposition.

14. *PR*, §135, 162/252.

15. *SL*, 15/*W* 5, 24.

16. *PhG*, ¶397, 228/294.

17. Adam Smith, *An Inquiry into the Nature and Causes of the Wealth of Nations*, vol. 1 (Indianapolis: Liberty Fund, 1981), I.ii.2.

18. Karl Marx, "Theses on Feuerbach" in *EW*, 423/*MEW* 535.

19. Karl Marx, *The Poverty of Philosophy*, *MECW* 6, 211/*MEW* 4, 181.

20. This view is still commonplace, see Axel Honneth's suggestion that Locke's concept of labour "serve[s] as a model for Marx," "Labour, A Brief History of a Modern Concept," *Philosophy* 97:2 (2022): 151.

21. To invoke Diane Elson's apt phrase from her collection, *Value: The Representation of Labour in Capitalism* (London: Verso, 2015). C.L.R. James had earlier used the phrase, *Modern Politics* (Oakland: PM Press, 2013), 83.

22. Such relations depend upon the sale and reproduction of labour-power. As Lise Vogel argues, Marx's category of "social reproduction" has dramatic implications for an analysis of gender, *Marxism and the Oppression of Women: Toward a Unitary Theory* (New Brunswick, NJ: Rutgers University Press, 1983), 136–75.

23. *Cap*.3, 953/867. My emphasis.

24. *Gr*, 327/243.

25. Frequently Marx's polemical comments against the moralists of his day are taken to be sufficient evidence that he rejected ethics altogether as part of "bourgeois philosophy." This argument, while having support in textual isolation (e.g. "Moralising Criticism and Critical Morality," *MECW* 6, 312–40/*MEW* 4, 330–59), discounts the substantive and foundational relationship between politics and ethics in Marx's thought. While Marx rejects "empty phrases about "justice"" (*MECW* 24, 268/*MEW* 19, 164), I argue that the ethical dimension of Marx's critical social theory is necessary to make sense of his analysis and rejection of capitalism.

26. In my view, not all actions are practices. For example, the action of a solider might require learning, skill and collective endeavour, but its imperialist ends require collective despair, destruction and death.

27. Alasdair MacIntyre, *Whose Justice? Which Rationality?* (Notre Dame, IN: University of Notre Dame Press, 1988), 8.

28. MacIntyre, 7.

29. Hannah Arendt, "From Hegel to Marx" in *The Promise of Politics* (New York: Schocken Books, 2005), 73.

30. For instance, seePeter E. Gordon, *A Precarious Happiness: Adorno and the Sources of Normativity* (Chicago: University of Chicago Press, 2023).

31. *EL*, §14, 43/59; §236, 299/388.

32. *EL*, §236, 299/388.

33. Gillian Rose, *Hegel Contra Sociology* (London: Verso, 2009), 97.

34. Theodor W. Adorno, *Minima Moralia: Reflections from Damaged Life* (London: New Left Books, 1974), §116, 180.

35. *AV*, 61.

36. For early versions of this thesis, see Perry Anderson, *In the Tracks of Historical Materialism* (London: Verso, 1983) and Gillian Rose, *Dialectic of Nihilism: Post-Structuralism and Law* (Oxford: Basil Blackwell, 1984).

37. This problem is evident in a recent exchange between Jacques Rancière and Axel Honneth, one a towering figure in French post-structuralism, the other in Frankfurt School critical theory. Rancière promotes a politics of equality and Honneth an ethical life of just institutions, which includes a reinvention of market socialism. The disagreement between Rancière and Honneth is at one level foundational. There is little incorporation of ethical subjectivity in Rancière, and little incorporation of political emancipation in Honneth. However, at another level the *agreement* between Rancière and Honneth is implicit. Regardless of the political and ethical conflicts of contemporary life, they share an attitude towards Marx. Marx might be part of the traditions they traverse, but for them he has a largely diminished importance in contemporary social theory. Their exchange demonstrates the interpretive barrier which my interpretation of Marx attempts to overcome. See Jacques Rancière and Axel Honneth, *Recognition or Disagreement* (New York: Columbia University Press, 2016). Also, Jacques Rancière, *Hatred of Democracy* (London: Verso, 2006), 51–70 and Axel Honneth, *The Idea of Socialism* (London: Polity, 2017), 27–50.

38. Nancy Fraser and Rahel Jaeggi, *Capitalism: A Conversation in Critical Theory* (Cambridge: Polity, 2018), 1.

39. Martijn Konings, *Capital and Time: For a New Critique of Neoliberal Reason* (Stanford, CA: Stanford University Press, 2018), 34.

40. The long-awaited translation of *Capital*, vol. 1, by Paul Reitter and edited by Paul North and Paul Reitter will hopefully furnish a new proliferation of engagement with Marx's masterwork. I am grateful to the editors for allowing me access to the proofs of this expansive new edition. Unfortunately, the proofs reached me just as I was putting finishing touches on the book.

41. Michael Sonenscher, *Capitalism: The Story Behind the Word* (Princeton, NJ: Princeton University Press, 2022), viii.

42. Sonenscher, 11.

43. Søren Mau, *Mute Compulsion: A Marxist Theory of the Economic Power of Capital* (London: Verso, 2023), 123.

44. *Cap*.1, 486/386; *Cap*.2, 185/100.

45. *Cap*.3, 965/880–81, *M* 894.

46. Fraser and Jaeggi, *Capitalism*, 2–3.

47. Konings, *Capital and Time*, 9.

48. *Cap*.3, 969–70/885.

49. See Simon Clarke, "The Neoliberal Theory of Society" in *Neoliberalism: A Critical Reader*, ed. Alfredo Saad-Filho and Deborah Johnston (London: Pluto, 2005), 50–59.

50. Lisa Adkins, Melinda Cooper and Martijn Konings, *The Asset Economy* (London: Polity, 2020), 25.

51. Critical social theory today needs to return to this task, which separates the tradi-

tional and critical theories of society. See Max Horkheimer's famous formulation in "Traditional and Critical Theory" in *Critical Theory* (New York: Herder and Herder, 1972), 225.

52. This is the great merit of Scott Meikle's *Aristotle's Economic Thought* (Oxford: Oxford University Press, 1994).

53. Patrick Murray, *The Mismeasure of Wealth: Essays on Marx and Social Form* (Chicago: Haymarket, 2017), 49.

54. Marx's portrayal of modernisation is often said to be Eurocentric. Most influentially, Edward W. Said, *Orientalism* (London: Penguin, 2003), 21, 149–57. Kevin B. Anderson's *Marx at the Margins: On Nationalism, Ethnicity, and Non-Western Societies* (Chicago: University of Chicago Press, 2016) provides a robust defence of Marx against the claims of Eurocentrism in general, and Said, in particular, 9–41. Deciphering the late "Ethnological Notebooks," Anderson details the changes and modifications in Marx's position, which becomes a strongly "multilinear" analysis of historical development. In my view, while Said is right to detect orientalism in Marx's 1853 article "The British Rule in India" (*MECW* 12, 126–27), the entire critique rests upon this text. Said overlooks the sensitivity to Indian resistance in "The Future Results of the British Rule in India," written a month later, in which Marx puts it that the colonialised Indians should throw off "the English yoke altogether," *MECW* 12, 221. It is also hard to sustain Said's thesis when Marx's idea in *Cap*.1 of "so-called original accumulation" is considered (see chapter 4, which draws on Said's *Culture and Imperialism*). See also, Aijaz Ahmad, "Marx on India: A Clarification" in *In Theory: Classes, Nations, Literatures* (London: Verso, 1992), 221–42.

55. Marx responds to the first vulgarisation of his thought in this respect in "Critique of the Gotha Program," *MECW* 24, 87–88/*MEW* 19, 21.

56. The reduction of Marxism to economic distribution is one aspect of what Moishe Postone calls "traditional Marxism," *Time, Labor, and Social Domination: A Reinterpretation of Marx's Critical Theory* (Cambridge: Cambridge University Press, 1993), 7–15.

57. This point is not to diminish the role of slavery and other subjugation, just to suggest the normative assumptions of capitalism are inherently contradictory.

58. Rahel Jaeggi, *Critique of Forms of Life* (Cambridge: Belknap Press, 2018), 203.

59. Capitalism has always relied on violence; this condition of existence is what Marx outlines as "original accumulation."

60. *Cap*.1, 280/184. Translation modified.

61. See Jaeggi's discussion of the procedure of immanent critique in *Critique of Forms of Life*, 199–206.

62. *Cap*.1, 758/640.

63. This view takes Kantianism and utilitarianism to be the dominant moral paradigms. These positions are examined in chapter 2.

64. Important contributions include the pioneering work of Isaak Illich Rubin and Roman Rosdolsky; the systematic dialectics of Tony Smith, Patrick Murray and Christopher J. Arthur; the Open Marxism of Simon Clarke and Werner Bonefeld; Diane Elson; Moishe Postone; and the Neue Marx-Lektüre associated with H. G. Backhaus and Michael Heinrich. See also, Konings, *Capital and Time*, 8–13, Stefan Eich, *The Currency of Politics:*

The Political Theory of Money from Aristotle to Keynes (Princeton, NJ: Princeton University Press, 2022), 125–33; Nick Nesbitt, *The Price of Slavery: Capitalism and Revolution in the Caribbean* (Charlottesville: Virginia, 2022) and Søren Mau, *Mute Compulsion: A Marxist Theory of the Economic Power of Capital* (London: Verso, 2023).

65. Fredric Jameson has criticised this trend, especially Pippin, as predicated on a "lowering of the volume of Hegel's dialectical claims" to a "rescue operation, which makes Hegel respectable and allows him re-entry into the fraternity of professional philosophers," *The Hegel Variations: On the Phenomenology of Spirit* (London: Verso, 2010), 10–11. Jameson obscures the insights that may be gained from such scholarship. More significantly, he too easily dismisses the philosophical significance of a revival of Hegelianism and with it, the possibilities for a positive Marxist engagement. Martin Hägglund aims at such a synthesis, bringing to bear the insights of this interpretation of Hegel and the normative value of Marx's thought, see *This Life: Secular Faith and Spiritual Freedom* (New York: Pantheon Books, 2019). Hägglund helps open the way for a renewed discussion of Hegel and Marx in light of Anglo-American Hegel scholarship and value-form theory. For a critique of Pippin, see Michael Lazarus, "The Lives of Marx: Hägglund and Marx's Philosophy after Pippin and Postone, *Historical Materialism* 29:4 (2021): 246–50. Michael Lazarus, ed., *A New Hegelian Marxism: Debating Martin Hägglund's* This Life (New York: Routledge, forthcoming), contains important debates over the Hegel-Marx relationship following Hägglund's innovative interpretation.

66. Pinkard engages with Marxism in his work, but his attention is more historical and Marx's analysis or attempted solutions to the problems of modern life is not especially bearing on his conclusions. There are important recent exceptions, including Arash Abazari, *Hegel's Ontology of Power: The Structure of Social Domination in Capitalism* (Cambridge: Cambridge, 2020), David James, *Practical Necessity, Freedom and History: From Hobbes to Marx* (Oxford: Oxford University Press, 2021) and Frederick Neuhouser, *Diagnosing Social Pathology: Rousseau, Hegel, Marx, and Durkheim* (Cambridge: Cambridge University Press, 2023).

67. In particular, Robert B. Pippin, *Hegel's Practical Philosophy: Rational Agency as Ethical Life* (Cambridge: Cambridge University Press, 2008) and Terry Pinkard, *Hegel's Naturalism: Mind, Nature, and the Final Ends of Life* (Oxford: Oxford University Press, 2012).

68. Fred Moseley and Tony Smith, eds., *Marx's Capital and Hegel's Logic* (Chicago: Haymarket, 2016).

69. Michael J. Thompson, ed., *Constructing Marxist Ethics: Critique, Normativity, Praxis* (Leiden: Brill, 2015). See my review, *Contemporary Political Theory* 15:4 (2016): 472–76. Unfortunately, Vanessa Wills's *Marx's Ethical Vision* (Oxford: Oxford University Press, 2024) will become available too late to be considered.

70. Tony Smith's *Beyond Liberal Egalitarianism: Marx and Normative Social Theory in the Twenty-First Century* (Leiden: Brill, 2017) is an illuminating account of the normative impact of Marx's concept of value. Smith's critique of contemporary liberal political philosophy has implications for Marx's relationship to ethical thought as a whole.

71. For this reason, I have decided to leave to one side the interpretive issues, however

interesting, arising from the debate on Marx and justice that was a central feature of 1980s "Analytic Marxism." See Allen W. Wood, *Karl Marx* (London: Routledge, 1981), 123–56; Richard W. Miller, *Analyzing Marx: Morality, Power and History* (Princeton, NJ: Princeton University Press, 1984); Steven Lukes, *Marxism and Morality* (Oxford: Clarendon Press, 1985); and for an assessment as well as contribution, see Norman Geras, "The Controversy about Marx and Justice" in *Literature of Revolution* (London: Verso, 1986), 3–57.

72. Robert B. Pippin, *Modernism as a Philosophical Problem* (Oxford: Blackwell, 1991), 149.

73. *Gr*, 158/91.

74. Rose, *Hegel Contra Sociology*, 232.

75. Terry Pinkard, *Hegel's Phenomenology: The Sociality of Reason* (Cambridge: Cambridge University Press, 1996), 228.

76. While I agree with crucial elements of William Clare Roberts's notion of nondomination in *Marx's Inferno: A Political Theory of Capital* (Princeton, NJ: Princeton University Press, 2017), my idea of freedom from domination runs in quite a different direction by drawing from Marx's value-form theory a normative account of (mis)recognition.

77. As I will argue throughout the book, but will just note briefly here, Marx's concept of labour involves examining productive activity in different ways, including alienated, concrete, abstract, private, social and unalienated labour.

78. Jaeggi, *Critique of Forms of Life*, 240.

79. *Cap*.1, 182/93.

80. This space has opened significantly with work that takes up Marx's analysis of capitalism to critique contemporary society, including Hägglund, *This Life* and Roberts, *Marx's Inferno*.

81. *Cap*.1, 342/241.

Chapter 1

1. Hannah Arendt and Karl Jaspers, *Correspondence 1926–1969* (New York: Harcourt, 1992), 166.

2. *HC*, 12.

3. *HC*, 40.

4. *HC*, 26.

5. For this logic under neoliberalism, see S. M. Amadae, *Prisoners of Reason: Game Theory and Neoliberal Political Economy* (Cambridge: Cambridge University Press, 2016).

6. Adriana Cavarero, *Surging Democracy: Notes on Hannah Arendt's Political Thought* (Stanford, CA: Stanford University Press, 2021), 3–5, 33; Joke J. Hermsen, *A Good and Dignified Life: The Political Advice of Hannah Arendt and Rosa Luxemburg* (New Haven, CT: Yale University Press, 2022), 78. Seyla Benhabib situates Arendt in debates about feminism and identity politics, *The Reluctant Modernism of Hannah Arendt* (London: SAGE, 1996).

7. Jacques Rancière, *Hatred of Democracy* (London: Verso, 2006); Miguel Abensour, *Democracy against the State: Marx and the Machiavellian Movement* (London: Polity, 2011); Cavarero, *Surging Democracy*.

8. Patchen Markell, "The Moment Has Passed: Power after Arendt" in *Radical Future Pasts: Untimely Essays in Political Theory*, ed. Romand Coles, Mark Reinhardt and George Shulman (Louisville: University of Kentucky Press, 2014), 130.

9. While Arendt's concept of tradition is Eurocentric, I am interested in its potential for political action that goes beyond these confines. For discussion of these issues, see Samuel Moyn, *Liberalism Against Itself: Cold War Intellectuals and the Making of Our Times* (New Haven, CT: Yale University Press, 2023), 121–39; David D. Kim, *Arendt's Solidarity: Anti-Semitism and Racism in the Atlantic World* (Stanford, CA: Stanford University Press, 2024).

10. *HC*, 327.

11. *MCT*. Arendt's *Kritische Gesamtausgabe* is also accessible at https://hannah-arendt-edition.net/.

12. See "Von Hegel zu Marx" and "The Impact of Marx" in *MCT*. The Hannah Arendt Centre at Bard College has recently made available high-quality PDFs of Arendt's personal library. Arendt read Marx and Engels in English and German, owning a Lawrence and Wishart, *Selected Works* (1951), the Dietz edition of the *Civil War in France* (1952) and the earlier Dietz edition of *Capital* (1923). The extensive underlining and marginal notes correspond with some of her most notable objections, including Engels's speech by Marx's gravesite with his famous comparison of Darwin with Marx. See https://www.bard.edu/library/arendt/pdfs/MarxEngels-SelectedWorks.pdf.

13. This omission occurs regardless of Arendt's own account of the origins of the book. Important exceptions include Hanna Fenichel Pitkin, *The Attack of the Blob: Hannah Arendt's Concept of the Social* (Chicago: University of Chicago Press, 1998); Robert Fine, *Political Investigations: Hegel, Marx and Arendt* (London: Routledge, 2001); Patchen Markell, *Bound by Recognition* (Princeton, NJ: Princeton University Press, 2003); Abensour, *Democracy Against the State*; Miguel Vatter, *The Republic of the Living: Biopolitics and the Critique of Civil Society* (New York: Fordham University Press, 2014).

14. Many Arendt scholars dismiss Marx's concept of political action as naturalist and productivist. However, without an analysis of his texts, such accounts are unable to assess the plausibility of her criticisms or to appreciate any similarity in their thinking about action. For instance, David Arndt, *Arendt on the Political* (Cambridge: Cambridge University Press, 2019), 22–24, 96.

15. Margaret Canovan, *Hannah Arendt: A Reinterpretation of Her Political Thought* (Cambridge: Cambridge University Press, 1992), 64.

16. Benhabib, *Reluctant Modernism*, 132.

17. Eric Hobsbawm, *Revolutionaries* (London: Weidenfeld and Nicolson, 1973), 205.

18. Samuel Moyn, ". . . Rights . . ." in *The Right to Have Rights*, ed. Stephanie DeGooyer et al. (London: Verso, 2018), 66.

19. Several variants of this thesis were reworked July to December 1953, see *MCT*, 89–101, 188–460.

20. Sections of this chapter, now extensively modified, were first published in Michael Lazarus, "Alienation and Action in the Young Marx, Aristotle, and Arendt," *Constellations: An International Journal of Critical and Democratic Theory* 29:4 (2022): 417–33.

21. Markell, *Bound by Recognition*, 65.

22. *HC*, 176.

23. *HC*, 178.

24. *HC*, 159.

25. *Pol* 1253a29; 1332b4–7.

26. *HC*, 22–23.

27. *HC*, 206–7. See Cavarero's illumination discussion, *Surging Democracy*, 39–41. For the difference between Arendt and Aristotle's notion of *bios* and *zoe*, see Vatter, *Republic of the Living*, 141–43.

28. *HC*, 23. As I will discuss in chapter 6, in a distinctive way Marx affirms this move (*Cap*.1, 444/342). Of course, Arendt does not miss the passage, *HC*, 159.

29. *HC*, 12.

30. Canovan calls this "a kind of myth of a philosophical Fall," *Hannah Arendt*, 258.

31. The first English edition was entitled *The Burden of Our Time*.

32. Hannah Arendt, *The Burden of Our Time* (London: Secker & Warburg, 1951), ix.

33. For the influence of Marxist theories of imperialism on sections of *Origins* written before 1947 and the subsequent "Cold War" impact on "Part 3: Totalitarianism," see Nicholas Devlin, "Hannah Arendt and Marxist Theories of Totalitarianism," *Modern Intellectual History* 20:1 (2023): 247–69.

34. Gillian Rose argues that the redemption of civil society and the state is Arendt's most important thesis in *Origins*, which is then given up in *HC* with "the rise of the social," resulting in the "ideal, transhistorical, discursive plurality" of the public realm, *The Broken Middle* (Oxford: Blackwell, 1992), 217–29.

35. Arendt wrote to Gerhard Scholem on 20 July 1963, that "I do not belong to the 'intellectuals coming from the German left' . . . If I hailed from anywhere at all, it was from German philosophy." Earlier, in a letter to Scholem from 21 April 1946, she remarks "As for me, I have never been a Marxist (nor have I ever been 'dialectical'). People here generally consider me to be an anti-Marxist, which is far closer to the truth." *The Correspondence of Hannah Arendt and Gershom Scholem* (Chicago: University of Chicago Press, 2017), 205–6, 49. Elisabeth Young-Bruehl dates Arendt's first reading of Marx to 1931, *Hannah Arendt: For Love of the World* (New Haven, CT: Yale University Press, 1977), 95

36. Arendt, *The Burden of Our Time*, 47. For a refutation of this charge, see Robert Fine, "Rereading Marx on the "Jewish Question": Marx as a Critic of Antisemitism?" in *Antisemitism and the Constitution of Sociology*, ed. Marcel Stoetzler (Lincoln: University of Nebraska Press, 2014), 137–59. For a contextual interpretation, see David Leopold, *The Young Karl Marx: German Philosophy, Modern Politics, and Human Flourishing* (Cambridge: Cambridge University Press, 2007), 163–82.

37. Arendt, *The Burden of Our Time*, 34.

38. Arendt, 325, 329.

39. Arendt, 249.

40. Canovan is wrong to claim this addition is "clearly anticipated" in the first edition

since Arendt's thesis that ties Marx's naturalism with the concept of labour is absent, *Hannah Arendt*, 57.

41. Hannah Arendt, "Ideology and Terror: A Novel Form of Government" in *MCT*, 73.

42. See the proposal to the John Simon Guggenheim Memorial Foundation quoted in Jerome Kohn, "Introduction," *Social Research* 69:2 (2002): v.

43. Two short notes in her *Denktagebuch* from April and September 1951 anticipate this interest, see Hannah Arendt, "From Hegel to Marx" in *The Promise of Politics* (Chicago: University of Chicago Press, 2005), 70.

44. Patchen Markell traces the appearance of this thesis in her notebooks from February 1952, see "Arendt's Work: On the Architecture of 'The Human Condition,'" *College Literature* 38:1 (2011): 39n8.

45. Arendt, "The Impact of Marx," 101.

46. Hannah Arendt, "Von Hegel zu Marx" in *MCT*, 94.

47. Arendt, "From Hegel to Marx," 80; "Von Hegel zu Marx", 99.

48. Arendt, "From Hegel to Marx," 74–75.

49. Hannah Arendt, *The Origins of Totalitarianism* (New York: Harcourt, 1979), 349.

50. Arendt, *Origins*, 442.

51. The "thesis-antithesis-synthesis" model is again employed in her late discussion of Hegel (and Alexandre Koyré), see Hannah Arendt, *The Life of the Mind*, vol. 2 (New York: Harcourt Brace Jovanovich, 1978), 49–51.

52. This formulation is informed by Robert Brandom's *A Spirit of Trust: A Reading of Hegel's Phenomenology* (Cambridge: Belknap, 2019).

53. Terry Pinkard, *Hegel's Naturalism: Mind, Nature, and the Final Ends of Life* (Oxford: Oxford University Press, 2012), 119.

54. In this respect, the development of capitalism and colonialisation was not the unfolding of spirit by Western modernity upon "non-historical" others. The Eurocentric aspects of Hegel's position can be challenged by interrogating the critical resources within his thought, see Erick Lima, "Hegel Contra Hegel: Eurocentrism, Colonialism, and Progress," *Hegel Bulletin*, 45:2 (2024): 237–64.

55. Young-Bruehl, *Hannah Arendt*, 116.

56. *PhG*, 78, 52/72–73.

57. Terry Pinkard, *Hegel's Phenomenology: The Sociality of Reason* (Cambridge: Cambridge University Press, 1996), 10.

58. Pinkard, 268.

59. Arendt misunderstands his idea of immanence, see "Karl Marx," 247.

60. Marx's later historical studies are nuanced and detailed investigations of specific social forms and the implications of uneven global development. See Karl Marx, *The Ethnological Notebooks of Karl Marx* (Assen: Van Gorcum, 1974); Kevin B. Anderson, *Marx at the Margins: On Nationalism, Ethnicity, and Non-Western Societies* (Chicago: University of Chicago Press, 2016); Marcello Musto, *The Last Years of Karl Marx: An Intellectual Biography* (Stanford, CA: Stanford University Press, 2020).

61. Hannah Arendt, "Concern with Politics in Recent European Political Thought" in *MCT*, 575–89.

62. Hannah Arendt, "Karl Marx and the Tradition of Political Thought" in *MCT*, 248; "Karl Marx and the Tradition of Western Political Thought" in *MCT*, 298–300.

63. Pinkard, *Hegel's Phenomenology*, 7.

64. *PhG*, ¶175, 107/144.

65. *HC*, 179.

66. *HC*, 180.

67. Brandom, *A Spirit of Trust*, 367.

68. *PhG*, ¶679, 392–93/495–96.

69. *PhG*, ¶652, 377/478.

70. Brandom, *A Spirit of Trust*, 506. See also, 509–14.

71. Brandom, 368.

72. Brandom, 370.

73. Brandom, 387.

74. Brandom, 389.

75. For the naturalism in Hegel's account, see Terry Pinkard, "The Form of Self-Consciousness" in *Hegel on Philosophy in History*, ed. R. Zuckert and J. Kreines (Cambridge: Cambridge University Press, 2017), 106–20.

76. Brandom, *A Spirit of Trust*, 395.

77. Rahel Jaeggi, *Alienation* (Columbia: Columbia University Press, 2014), 81.

78. This is a brief gloss of Brandom's view. For his own summation, *Spirit of Trust*, 645–47.

79. Brandom, 472.

80. Brandom makes several confused remarks on Marx, including the comment that fetishism is "understanding the relative and absolute value of precious metals as objective properties intrinsic to them in essentially the sense that their density is," 30.

81. Brandom, 30.

82. *Cap*.1, 92/7.

83. Jairus Banaji, "Modes of Production in a Materialist Conception of History" in *Theory as History: Essays on Modes of Production and Exploitation* (Chicago: Haymarket, 2010), 59.

84. In Hegel's *Logic*, "*Dasein*" is commonly translated into English as "determinate being" or "existence."

85. There is a prevalent view in traditional Marxism that the ingredients of "historical materialism" come together with a text called *The German Ideology*. Yet, the manuscripts that make up this posthumously fabricated text do not have any of the coherence that generations of interpreters assumed. Research made possible by the *MEGA2* critical edition has cast new light on these issues. See Sarah Johnson, "Farewell to the German Ideology," *Journal of the History of Ideas* 83:1 (2022): 143–70.

86. Karl Marx and Friedrich Engels, *The German Ideology*, MECW 5, 43/MEGA2 1.5, 20. This passage is listed as a marginal note by the editors of *MECW*.

87. Marx and Engels, 44/20.

88. Alasdair MacIntyre, "Breaking the Chains of Reason" in *AMEM*, 151, 162.

89. Arendt, "Karl Marx and the Tradition of Political Thought", 245.

90. Arendt, 247.

91. Arendt carefully read Robert C. Tucker's *Philosophy and Myth in Karl Marx* (Cambridge: Cambridge University Press, 1961). Tucker helped to establish, along with Allen W. Wood, an influential thesis that Marx's thought is "amoral." https://www.bard.edu/library/arendt/pdfs/Tucker-Marx.pdf.

92. Arendt, "Karl Marx and the Tradition of Western Political Thought," 274.

93. Arendt, 285.

94. Arendt, 294.

95. *HC*, 41.

96. Arendt's positive endorsement of Marx's recognition that "the incompatibility between classical political thought and modern political conditions lay in the accomplished fact of the French and Industrial Revolutions" seems to have *OJQ* in mind: "He knew that the equality question was only superficially posed in the idealistic assertions of the equality of man, the inborn dignity of every human being, and only superficially answered by giving laborers the right to vote." Hannah Arendt, "Tradition and the Modern Age" in *Between Past and Future* (London: Penguin, 2006), 31.

97. *HC*, 31.

98. *HC*, 39–40.

99. *HC*, 33.

100. *HC*, 79–80. As Pitkin explains, this delineation is a "blatant" misreading. Marx's German does not express the deliberate choice of "labour" (*Arbeit*) over "work" (*Werk*), but rather his use of *Arbeit*-family words allows him to characterise the product or outcome of production and describe the process, "be it labor or work," rather than the more limited *Werk*-family. Accordingly, "when Marx says *Arbeit* or *arbeiten* he is just as likely to mean work as labor, or both together." Thus, Arendt's attribution of Marx's supposed choice is a distinction she introduces herself. Pitkin, *The Attack of the Blob*, 133–34. This point pays out in Marx's use of *Arbeiter*, which is best translated as "worker" and not "labourer."

101. This phrase appears throughout *HC*, 4, 84, 85, 92, 103, 129, 316, 318. Arendt notes "Marx only radicalisation of: Labor is creator of all wealth (Smith) & Labor gives title to property (Locke)," "The Concept of Man as Laborer" in *MCT*, 443

102. *HC*, 7.

103. *HC*, 48.

104. *HC*, 89. Arendt's reference is to *Cap*.1, 284/186, see chapter 6.

105. *HC*, 316, 321.

106. Arendt, "From Hegel to Marx," 79.

107. Arendt, "Karl Marx and the Tradition of Western Political Thought," 264, 269.

108. Arendt, "From Hegel to Marx," 79. See also, "Tradition and the Modern Age," 22; *HC*, 254.

109. Arendt, "Karl Marx and the Tradition of Western Political Thought," 264.

110. Arendt, 272.

111. *HC*, 104–5.

112. *Cap*.1, 280/184.

113. Jennifer Ring puts pressure on Arendt's distinctions with the concrete example of building a stone house, a human activity in which classifying tasks as "labour" or "work" is often arbitrary, "On Needing Both Marx and Arendt: Alienation and the Flight from Inwardness," *Political Theory* 17:3 (1989): 439.

114. As Markell has pointed out, this "territorial" reading does not preclude a more nuanced "relational" reading of the concepts, especially between "labour" and "work" and "work" and "action," "Arendt's Work."

115. Arendt, "Tradition and the Modern Age," 23–24.

116. Arendt, "Karl Marx and the Tradition of Western Political Thought," 275.

117. Arendt, 275–76.

118. Arendt, 276.

119. Arendt, 277–78.

120. Arendt, 274–75.

121. Dana Villa, *Arendt* (London: Routledge, 2021), 127.

122. For my extended discussion of these points, see chapter 5.

123. Arendt, "Karl Marx and the Tradition of Western Political Thought," 280.

124. Simon Clarke, *Marx, Marginalism and Modern Sociology* (London: Macmillan, 1982), 59.

125. For instance, *Cap*.1, 173–75/85–88.

126. Marx's idea of a society of associated producers is suggestive here, *Cap*.1, 171–72/85–86.

127. *Cap*.1, 150/64.

128. Therefore, I am unpersuaded by attempts to pose Arendt's criticisms as an "innovative rereading . . . rather than a poor interpretation." Mimi Howard, "Hannah Arendt's Contribution to a Critique of Political Economy," *New German Critique* 47:2 (2020): 47–48.

129. Marx, *Cap*.1, 188/99.

130. Patrick Murray, *Reflections on Commercial Life* (New York: Routledge, 1997), 418.

131. Arendt, "Karl Marx and the Tradition of Western Political Thought," 289.

132. For the genesis of Marx's critique of political economy in the *EPM*, see H. G. Backhaus, "Some Aspects of Marx's Concept of Critique in the Context of his Economic-Philosophical Theory" in *Human Dignity: Social Autonomy and the Critique of Capitalism*, ed. Werner Bonefeld and Kosmas Psychopedis (New York: Routledge, 2005).

133. Arendt, "Karl Marx and the Tradition of Western Political Thought," 289.

134. *Pol* 1253b30–1254a18.

135. This phrase was added by Ben Fowkes in his translation. *Cap*.1, 523/428.

136. *Cap*.1, 532/428.

137. Arendt does not see that for Aristotle the household was a place of logos since the use of money entailed discussions of reciprocity and just exchange. See Stefan Eich, *The Cur-*

rency of Politics: The Political Theory of Money from Aristotle to Keynes (Princeton, NJ: Princeton University Press, 2022), 26.

138. *HC*, 121–22.

139. *Cap.*3, 959/874/*M*, 885–86. Arendt discusses this passage, *HC*, 104–5, 44.

140. Arendt's centring of this problem is significant, even if her analysis is generally implausible in terms of what Marx might have actually thought, for instance: "According to Marx, it is foolish to think that one can liberate and emancipate labors whose very activity subjects them to necessity. When all men have become laborers, the realm of freedom will indeed have disappeared." Arendt, "Karl Marx and the Tradition of Western Political Thought," 290–91. Marx cannot be said to see freedom as freedom *from* labour, but in the first instance, freedom from *alienated labour*.

141. Karl Marx, "Critique of the Gotha Program," *MECW* 24, 87/*MEGA2* I.25, 15.

142. *NW*, 235–36/362–63.

143. *NE* 1098a3–30. On the political importance of activity as human deeds in Aristotle, Jill Frank writes "[p]raxis is what lies before someone as a possibility, as something to be done," *A Democracy of Distinction* (Chicago: University of Chicago Press, 2004), 35.

144. In this way, Marx is responding to Jean-Jacques Rousseau's identification of "the fundamental problem" of finding "a form of association" which allows for the expression of collective freedom, *The Social Contract and Other Later Political Writings* (Cambridge: Cambridge University Press, 1997), 49–50.

145. Arendt, "Karl Marx and the Tradition of Western Political Thought," 276.

146. *HC*, 130.

147. *Cap.*3, 959/873.

148. For one idea of how production could be run cooperatively, see Michael Albert and Robin Hahnel, *The Political Economy of Participatory Economics* (Princeton, NJ: Princeton University Press, 1991).

149. Martin Hägglund, *This Life: Secular Faith and Spiritual Freedom* (New York: Pantheon Books, 2019), 309.

150. This idea of democracy as the space for contesting genuinely "political questions" draws on Nancy Fraser and Rahel Jaeggi, *Capitalism: A Conversation in Critical Theory* (Cambridge: Polity, 2018) 172.

151. *EPM*, 365/298.

152. Hannah Arendt, *On Revolution* (London: Faber and Faber, 1963), 181–82.

153. Karl Marx, "The Constitution of the French Republic Adopted November 4, 1848," *MECW* 10, 567–80.

154. Arendt and Jaspers, *Correspondence*, 167.

155. For the early writings see Stathis Kouvelakis, *Philosophy and Revolution: From Kant to Marx* (London: Verso, 2003) and for the later Marx, see Anderson, *Marx at the Margins*. Anderson's account disproves Arendt's claim that Marx and Engels "curiously neglected" the national question, *Origins*, 389.

156. Karl Marx, "The Civil War in France," *MECW* 22, 333.

157. Marx, 311.

158. Marx, 312.

159. Marx, 313.

160. Marx, 317.

161. Marx, 328.

162. Fundamentally Marx's analysis of abstract labour and commodity production is a conceptualisation of action.

163. *CM*, 493/471.

164. *HC*, 201.

165. By "political writings" I mean the pamphlets, newspaper articles and manifestos written to agitate and strategically intervene in the organisation of action. A more general distinction between Marx's theoretical and political writings tends to discount how integral his political activity was to the development of his theory, for example his role in the founding of the First International was also a period of clarity in the drafting of *Capital*. Of course, *Capital* was also an intervention into the worker's movement.

166. Arendt, *On Revolution*, 260.

167. The establishing documents of the First International in 1864 attest to his interest in founding; see in particular, Karl Marx, *Inaugural Address of the Working Men's International Association* (*MECW* 20, 5–13) and *Provisional Rules of the Association* (*MECW* 20, 14–16).

168. Marx, "The Civil War in France," 310.

169. Marx, 336.

170. Marx, 333. William Clare Roberts emphasises the federated nature of "communist republics," *Inferno: A Political Theory of Capital* (Princeton, NJ: Princeton University Press, 2017), 19.

171. Arendt, *On Revolution*, 225.

172. Marx's comments mirror Arendt's criticisms of those who fail to appreciate the political importance of the council movement.

173. Marx, "The Civil War in France," 333.

174. Arendt, *On Revolution*, 259.

175. Marx, "The Civil War in France," 334.

176. Arendt, *On Revolution*, 260, 322.

177. Peter Hudis, *Marx's Concept of the Alternative to Capitalism* (Chicago: Haymarket, 2013), 204.

178. Karl Marx, "Preamble to the Program of the French Workers' Party," *MECW* 24/ *MEW* 19, 238.

179. Karl Marx to Friedrich Adolph Sorge, 5 November 1880, *MECW* 46, 44/*MEW* 34, 474.

180. *HC*, 26.

181. Marx, "Preamble to the Program of the French Workers' Party," 239.

182. Marx, "The Civil War in France," 322–23.

183. Marx, 334.

184. Karl Marx and Friedrich Engels, "Preface to the 1872 German Edition of *The Communist Manifesto*," *MECW* 23, 174–75/*MEW* 18, 96.

185. *HC*, 216–17; Arendt, *On Revolution*, 266–67.

186. Hannah Arendt, "The Hungarian Revolution and Totalitarian Imperialism" in *Thinking Without a Banister* (New York: Schocken Books, 2018), 135–36.

187. On this point, see Charles Barbour, "The Republican and the Communist: Arendt Reading Marx (Reading Arendt)," in *(Mis)readings of Marx in Continental Philosophy*, ed. Jernej Habjan and Jessica Whyte (New York: Palgrave Macmillan), 58–59.

188. Abensour, *Democracy Against the State*, 66.

189. Karl Marx, *The Eighteenth Brumaire of Louis Bonaparte*, MECW 11, 104/MEGA2 I.11, 97.

190. While I agree with much of J. M. Bernstein's rendering of Arendt's idea of founding as political "promising"; his discussion injects a Hegelian flavour to her thought that Arendt made every effort to expunge, "Political Modernism: The New, Revolution and Civil Disobedience in Arendt and Adorno" in *Arendt and Adorno: Political and Philosophical Investigations*, ed. Lars Rensmann and Smair Gandesha (Stanford, CA: Stanford University Press, 2012), 56–77.

191. *HC*, 186–87. Benhabib demarcates two models of action, one agonal (or heroic) and one narrative, *Reluctant Modernism*, 125–30.

192. *HC*, 179. Markell, *Bound by Recognition*, 13.

193. Cavarero, *Surging Democracy*, 21.

194. Marx, *Eighteenth Brumaire*, 103/97.

195. On this score, there are strong similarities between Arendt and C.L.R. James. In *Modern Politics* (Oakland: PM Press, 2013), public lectures given in Trinidad in 1960, James casts the great promise of the workers' councils of Hungary in terms set out by the good life of the polis. However, James affirms this analysis primarily from Marx.

196. Pitkin, *The Attack of the Blob*, 175.

197. Benhabib, *Reluctant Modernism*, 138–39; Bernstein, "Political Modernism"; Villa, *Arendt*, 180–81.

198. Hannah Arendt, "What Is Freedom?" in *Between Past and Future*, 163–64.

199. *HC*, 198.

200. *HC*, 199.

201. See for instance, Rosa Luxemburg, "Our Program and the Political Situation" in *The Rosa Luxemburg Reader* (New York: Monthly Review, 2004), 357–73.

202. *HC*, 133.

203. *Cap*.1, 899/777.

Chapter 2

1. Reprinted as "An Interview with Giovanna Borradori" in *The MacIntyre Reader*, ed. Kelvin Knight (London: Polity Press, 1998), 265.

2. *AV*, xvi.

3. Paul Blackledge and Neil Davidson include a comprehensive, but incomplete, bibliography of over 200 publications between 1953 and 1974 in a carefully edited collection of his New Left writings, *AMEM*, lvii–lxvi.

4. Alasdair MacIntyre, "On Having Survived the Academic Moral Philosophy of the Twentieth Century," in *What Happened in and to Moral Philosophy in the Twentieth Century?: Philosophical Essays in Honor of Alasdair MacIntyre*, ed. Fran O'Rourke (Notre Dame, IN: Notre Dame Press, 2013), 20.

5. This term originates in Kelvin Knight's work, see "Introduction" in *The MacIntyre Reader* and in the same collection, Alasdair MacIntyre, "Politics, Philosophy and the Common Good," 235.

6. Joan Robinson, *An Essay on Marxian Economics* (London: Macmillan 1966), viii.

7. Alasdair MacIntyre, *Marxism: An Interpretation* (London: SCM Press, 1953), 48–58. The first partial translation in English, produced in 1947 by the Johnson Forest Tendency (which included Raya Dunayevskaya and C.L.R. James), was attached as an appendix to Dunayevskaya's *Marxism and Freedom* (New York: Bookman, 1958), 288–325. MacIntyre appreciates her Hegelianism in his review, "The Algebra of Revolution" in *AMEM*, 41–44. Dunayevskaya's interpretation of Marx is noteworthy since she retains Hegel's idea of the absolute. Frequently, Marxists attempt to affirm Hegel's revolutionary method and disavow the absolute. See Gillian Rose, *Hegel Contra Sociology* (London: Verso, 2009), 44–45.

8. MacIntyre remarks on the "very odd" Anglo-American reception of Hegel, in which "[h]e has been blamed for so much—for liberalism, the bombing of London, modern atheism, the concentration camps, communism . . . an uninformed reader who guessed that there was more than one philosopher called Hegel could be forgiven," "Introduction" in *Hegel: A Collection of Essays* (Garden City: Anchor Books, 1972), 1.

9. See Blackledge and Davidson, "Introduction," xxii–xliii.

10. Alasdair MacIntyre, "Breaking the Chains of Reason" in *AMEM*, 165.

11. MacIntyre, 153.

12. Alasdair MacIntyre, *Against the Self-Images of the Age* (London: Duckworth, 1971).

13. MacIntyre's identifies the most significant influences as Georg Lukács, C.L.R. James, Lucien Goldmann, George Thomson, Karl Mannheim and Michael Kidron. He wrote polemically on the Marxism of contemporary left-thinkers including Herbert Marcuse, Jean-Paul Sartre and Isaac Deutscher. See *AV*, 110; *Marxism*, 21; "On Having Survived the Academic Moral Philosophy of the Twentieth Century," 20, 33; *Ethics in the Conflicts of Modernity: An Essay on Desire, Practical Reasoning, and Narrative* (Cambridge: Cambridge University Press, 2016), 64.

14. Representative is Stephen Mulhall and Adam Swift, *Liberals and Communitarians* (Oxford: Blackwell, 1992).

15. Reassessments of major Enlightenment thinkers and themes have often framed their contentions in reference to MacIntyre. For example, Charles L. Griswold, *Adam Smith and the Virtues of Enlightenment* (Cambridge: Cambridge University Press, 1999), 2–21.

16. John Rawls quoted in Katrina Forrester, *In the Shadow of Justice: Postwar Liberalism and the Remaking of Political Philosophy* (Princeton, NJ: Princeton University Press, 2019), 258.

17. Forrester, 21.

18. Forrester, 256.

19. Chantal Mouffe, *The Return of the Political* (London: Verso, 2020), 19.

20. See Paul Blackledge and Kelvin Knight, ed. *Virtue and Politics: Alasdair MacIntyre's Revolutionary Aristotelianism* (Notre Dame, IN: University of Notre Dame Press, 2011); Émile Perreau-Saussine, *Alasdair MacIntyre* (Notre Dame, IN: University of Notre Dame Press, 2022); Caleb Bernacchio, Ahmad Fattah, David Kretz and Michael Lazarus, ed. *Hegel and MacIntyre: Reason in History* (New York: Routledge, forthcoming).

21. For instance, Paul Blackledge, *Marxism and Ethics: Freedom, Desire and Revolution* (Albany: State University of New York Press, 2012).

22. Terry Pinkard, "MacIntyre's Critique of Modernity" in *Alasdair MacIntyre*, ed. Mark C. Murphy (Cambridge: Cambridge University Press, 2003), 176–200.

23. *AV*, xviii.

24. *AV*, 261. The first version of this thesis appeared in Alasdair MacIntyre's 1966 work, *A Short History of Ethics* (London: Routledge, 1998), 205–7.

25. Chapter 4 tries to rescue Marx's discussion of Daniel Defoe's *Robinson Crusoe* from MacIntyre's criticism and in doing so, pursue a value-form critique of methodological individualism in terms of the naturalisation of capitalist social forms.

26. *AV*, 2, 11.

27. MacIntyre is heavily influenced by G.E.M. Anscombe's 1958 essay "Modern Moral Philosophy" (reprinted in *The Is/Ought Question*, ed. W. D. Hudson (London: Macmillan Press, 1969), 175–95. See his one paragraph anticipation of the *AV* thesis, "Hume on 'Is' and 'Ought'" in *Against the Self-Images of the Age*, 123–24.

28. *AV*, 33.

29. *AV*, 7–8.

30. Aristotle's travels ground his studies of biology and political constitutions. In contrast, Immanuel Kant famously maintained that reason can be known "even without traveling," *Anthropology from a Pragmatic Point of View* (Cambridge: Cambridge University Press, 2006), 4.

31. *AV*, 9–11.

32. *AV*, 10.

33. *AV*, 19.

34. *AV*, 33.

35. *AV*, 34. Tellingly, unless mentioning Marx directly, he shies away from the term "capitalism."

36. *AV*, 51, 55.

37. *AV*, 35. This point is similar to Hegel's claim that, "[e]very philosophy is the philosophy of its own day, a link in the whole chain of spiritual development, and thus it can only find satisfaction for the interests belonging to its own particular time." *LHP* 1, 45/*W* 18, 64.

38. *AV*, 3. MacIntyre's approach is again like Hegel's notion that the history of philosophy is itself the philosophy of history, *LHP* 1, 6/*W* 18, 18. However, save from a few passing comments, direct reference to Hegel is a noticeable absence in *AV*. Considering the character of his critique of Kant bears such a resemblance to Hegel's own, MacIntyre's account of modernity lacks a detailed engagement with subsequent "post-Kantian" critics of Kant. For

this engagement with MacIntyre, see Pinkard, "MacIntyre's Critique of Modernity," 194–98 and Robert B. Pippin, "Alasdair MacIntyre's Modernity" in *Interanimations: Receiving Modern German Philosophy* (Chicago: University of Chicago Press, 2015), 241–56.

39. This is not to suggest MacIntyre undertakes social history akin to New Left historiography, best exemplified in E. P. Thompson's *The Making of the English Working Class* (London: Penguin, 1980), but more specifically *Short History* is an account of philosophy that acknowledges the social realm as an objectively determining category. This method is more evident in *Short History*, which details the sweep of Western moral philosophy from Homer to Hare and provides the historical foundation for *AV*.

40. *AV*, 11.

41. *AV*, 23.

42. *AV*, 37. Note his framing of David Hume's thought in relation to the 1688 Glorious Revolution and a response to the Levellers and Catholicism, *AV*, 48–49.

43. Compare Heide Gerstenberger, *Impersonal Power: History and Theory of the Bourgeois State* (Chicago: Haymarket, 2005) and Neil Davidson, *How Revolutionary Were the Bourgeois Revolutions?* (Chicago: Haymarket, 2012), as well as their exchange in *Historical Materialism* 27:3 (2019).

44. *AV*, 37. See also, Lucien Goldmann's view of the contradictions within "tragic" thinking of the seventeenth-century, *The Hidden God* (London: Routledge and Kegan Paul, 1964), 33.

45. This view is expressed by the "early" and "late" Marx, see *OJQ*, 229–34/157–63; *RIPP*, 1052/27.

46. Marx notes that the advances of British political economy must be seen in relation to the consolidation of capitalism and as such, first reflect a desire to explain the social system and then a compulsion to mask and apologise for its operation. *Cap* 1, 96–97/12–13.

47. For example, Immanuel Kant's comparison of the tools of philosophy with the division of labour: "All professions, crafts and arts have gained by the distribution of labour, namely when one person does not do everything, but each limits himself to a certain task ... Where labour is not differentiated and distributed like that, where everyone is a jack-of-all-trades, professions still remain in a most barbarous state," *Groundwork of the Metaphysics of Morals* (Cambridge: Cambridge University Press, 2012), 4:388.

48. For Hegel what happens "in the form of actuality" in France is "burst forth as thought, spirit, concept" in Germany. He points to the opposition of the two nations as a dialectic in "this great epoch of the world's history." History has been brought up into the present with the conjuncture of the French Revolution and German Idealism. *LHP* 3, 409/*W* 20, 314.

49. *AV*, 37.

50. Goldmann, *The Hidden God*, 282; *Immanuel Kant* (London: NLB, 1971), 26–27, 36.

51. Goldmann, *Immanuel Kant*, 32–34, 15.

52. Goldmann, 212.

53. Alasdair MacIntyre, "Pascal and Marx: On Lucien Goldmann's *Hidden God*" in *AMEM*, 315.

54. MacIntyre, 312.

55. MacIntyre, 315.

56. Goldmann considers Kant's philosophy of religion to imply the human community of Marxist thought, *Immanuel Kant*, 205.

57. MacIntyre, "Pascal and Marx," 315.

58. Goldmann's primary influence in his critique of Kant's antinomies in relation to bourgeois thought is Lukács, a source shared by MacIntyre. See Georg Lukács, *History and Class Consciousness: Studies in Marxist Dialectics* (London: Merlin Press, 1971), 110–49. For a systematic account of this text, see Daniel Andrés Lopez, *Lukács: Praxis and the Absolute* (Leiden: Brill, 2019).

59. *AV*, 39, 43.

60. MacIntyre, *A Short History of Ethics*, 183.

61. Many Kant scholars saw fit to respond to what Henry E. Allison called "the wholescale attack on Kant's moral theory launched by Alasdair MacIntyre in *After Virtue*," *Kant's Theory of Freedom* (Cambridge: Cambridge University Press, 1990), 263n25. See for instance, Onora O'Neill, "Kant After Virtue," *Inquiry* 26:4 (1983): 387–405 and Allen W. Wood, *Kant's Ethical Thought* (Cambridge: Cambridge University Press, 1999).

62. Kant, *Groundwork*, 4:418.

63. *AV*, 43–45.

64. *AV*, 45.

65. *AV*, 46. Immanuel Kant's moral theory is not the teaching of "how to be happy, but how we should become worthy of happiness," "On the Common Saying: "This May Be True in Theory, but It Does Not Apply in Practice"" in *Political Writings* (Cambridge: Cambridge University Press, 1991), 64.

66. *AV*, 44.

67. *AV*, 46–47.

68. *AV*, 47–48.

69. *AV*, 49; "Hume on "Is" and "Ought"," 109–24.

70. *AV*, 51.

71. *AV*, 52. This phrase is perhaps an ironic reference to Kant's reflection that "if we look back on all the efforts that have ever been undertaken to detect the principle of morality to this day, it is no wonder why one and all they had to fail," *Groundwork*, 4:432. In H. J. Paton's then standard translation, the last phrase is rendered "bound to fail."

72. *AV*, 84.

73. *AV*, 79.

74. Earlier versions of this critique of positivism bear Hegel's influence. He relates physiognomy and phrenology in the *PhG* to modern empiricism, since both attempt to explain human action "in scientific clothing," Alasdair MacIntyre, "Hegel on Faces and Skulls" in *Hegel*, 225.

75. See *EL*, §37–60, 78–109/106–47.

76. *AV*, 109; also, 26–27, 86, 88–89.

77. *AV*, 86.

78. *AV*, 88–89.

79. *AV*, 71.

80. *AV*, 71.

81. *AV*, 33–34.

82. MacIntyre claims that Aristotle is not a historicist, but Hegel is "to some greater or less degree" Aristotelian, *AV*, 277. In his later work, he constantly distances himself from Hegel, suggesting his historicism "excludes all claims to absolute knowledge," *AV*, 270.

83. *AV*, 110.

84. *AV*, 215.

85. *AV*, 215.

86. Karl Marx, *The Eighteenth Brumaire of Louis Bonaparte*, MECW 11, 128/MEGA2 I.11, 122.

87. For the continued importance given to this text in his interpretation of Marx, see Alasdair MacIntyre, "The *Theses on Feuerbach*: A Road Not Taken" in *The MacIntyre Reader*, 223–34.

88. Karl Marx, "Theses on Feuerbach" in *EW*, 422/MEW 3, 5–6.

89. Ernst Bloch, "Changing the World: Marx's *Theses on Feuerbach*" in *On Karl Marx* (New York: Herder and Herder, 1971), 71.

90. Marx, "Theses on Feuerbach," 423/MEW 3, 7.

91. *AV*, 84–85.

92. MacIntyre avows his historicism against critics, see "Postscript to the Second Edition," *AV*, 266–72. Hans-Georg Gadamer is also an influence on his historicism and idea of tradition. Alasdair MacIntyre, "On Not Having the Last Word: Thoughts on Our Debts to Gadamer" in *Gadamer's Century: Essays in Honor of Hans-Georg Gadamer*, ed. Jeff Malpas, Ulrich Arnswald and Jens Kertscher (Cambridge: MIT Press, 2002), 157–72.

93. *AV*, 84.

94. *AV*, 118.

95. *AV*, 52–53.

96. *AV*, 123.

97. *AV*, 135.

98. *AV*, 148.

99. *AV*, 155.

100. L. A. Kosman, "Being Properly Affected: Virtues and Feelings in Aristotle's Ethics" in *Essays on Aristotle's Ethics*, ed. Amélie Oksenberg Rorty (Berkley: University of California Press, 1980), 115.

101. *AV*, 155.

102. *AV*, 156. Despite Aristotle's prejudice about who constitutes a citizen, I agree with MacIntyre that when conceived historically these views are not fatal to his conception of virtue. *AV*, 159–60.

103. *NE* 1155a24. For this contrast, see Susan D. Collins, *Aristotle and the Rediscovery of Citizenship* (Cambridge: Cambridge University Press, 2006).

104. *AV*, 254.
105. *AV*, 203.
106. *AV*, 159.
107. *AV*, 194–95.
108. For instance, *AV*, 29.
109. MacIntyre, *Ethics in the Conflicts of Modernity*, 177–78.
110. *AV*, 163–64. See also MacIntyre, *Ethics in the Conflicts of Modernity*, 243–315.
111. *AV*, 199.
112. *AV*, x.

113. For an assessment of MacIntyre's discussion of Marx in his most recent work, see Michael Lazarus, "Politics in the *Conflicts of Modernity*: Aristotelian and Marxist," *International Critical Thought* 9:3 (2019): 463–79.

114. *AV*, 110.
115. *AV*, 60.
116. *AV*, 215, 114.
117. *AV*, 109.
118. *AV*, 261.
119. *AV*, 261.
120. *Cap* 1, 171/84.

121. In recent work, MacIntyre does note the importance of Marx's adoption of Aristotelian social ontology in *Capital* and glosses his idea of fetishism. However, he considers that Marx's demarcation of precapitalist relations of personal dependence with capitalist impersonal power loses sight of the critical political and ethical nature of reflection on social roles made possible by mediaeval Aristotelians, including Thomas Aquinas, *Ethics in the Conflicts of Modernity*, 93–98.

122. *AV*, 107, 227–28.
123. *AV*, 262, 61.
124. *AV*, 263.

125. *AV*, 221. His later texts repeat this formulation, see Lazarus, "Politics in the Conflicts of Modernity," 474–77.

126. MacIntyre, *Ethics in the Conflicts of Modernity*, 122–23.

127. Acknowledging the problems of presenting Aristotle as "*the* protagonist against whom I have matched the voices of liberal modernity," MacIntyre attempts to circumvent this by way of placing Aristotle as part of a tradition. *AV*, 146.

128. Alasdair MacIntyre, "Marxist Mask and Romantic Face" in *AMEM*, 63.
129. *AV*, 118.
130. *AV*, 263.

131. Gillian Rose, *Mourning Becomes the Law: Philosophy and Representation* (Cambridge: Cambridge University Press, 1996), 4.

132. *AV*, 254.
133. MacIntyre, *Ethics in the Conflicts of Modernity*, 124–29.

134. This kind of position is what Michael Heinrich calls "worldview Marxism," *An Introduction to the Three Volumes of Karl Marx's* Capital (New York: Monthly Review Press, 2004), 221–22.

135. Alasdair MacIntyre, "Where We Were, Where We Are, Where We Need to Be" in *Virtue and Politics*, 320.

136. MacIntyre, *Ethics in the Conflicts of Modernity*, 106–10, 128–29.

137. *AV*, xvii.

138. *AV*, xviii.

139. Alasdair MacIntyre, "Notes from the Moral Wilderness" in *AMEM*, 57. This essay was published in *New Reasoner*, which merged with *Universities and Left Review* to become *New Left Review*.

140. MacIntyre, 51.

141. MacIntyre, 54–55.

142. MacIntyre, 56. See also Alasdair MacIntyre, "Freedom and Revolution" in *AMEM*, 124.

143. MacIntyre, 57.

144. MacIntyre, 58.

145. MacIntyre, 61. See the discussion of *Rameau's Nephew* in *PhG*, ¶545, 316/403.

146. Diderot is still the bourgeois moralist in *AV*, 47.

147. MacIntyre, "Notes," 59.

148. MacIntyre, 62.

149. MacIntyre, 63.

150. *PhG*, ¶177, 108/145.

151. MacIntyre, "Notes," 64.

152. Rahel Jaeggi, *Alienation* (Columbia: Columbia University Press, 2014), 156. She draws positively from MacIntyre's early work, 3, 181, 246. See also, the appraisal of his idea of crisis within traditions, Rahel Jaeggi, *Critique of Forms of Life* (Cambridge: Belknap Press, 2018), 250–55.

153. MacIntyre, "Notes," 65.

154. MacIntyre, 68.

155. MacIntyre, "Freedom and Revolution," 124.

156. MacIntyre, 126.

157. MacIntyre, 126–28.

158. MacIntyre, 133.

159. G.W.F. Hegel, *Philosophy of Mind* (Oxford: Oxford University Press, 2007), §482, 214/*W* 10, 301. I have replaced the Wallace translation MacIntyre uses with the revised edition by Michael Inwood.

160. Hegel, §482, 215/302.

161. Frederick Neuhouser, *Diagnosing Social Pathology: Rousseau, Hegel, Marx, and Durkheim* (Cambridge: Cambridge University Press, 2023), 257.

162. MacIntyre, "Breaking," 139.

163. MacIntyre, 139.

164. MacIntyre, 140.
165. MacIntyre, 140.
166. MacIntyre, 139. This traditional view of Hegel as an advocate of the Prussian monarchy has long been disproved. For instance, Shlomo Avineri, *Hegel's Theory of the Modern State* (Cambridge: Cambridge University Press, 1972), 176–77.
167. MacIntyre, *Ethics in the Conflicts of Modernity*, 94.

Chapter 3

1. *HC*, 192–93, also 179.
2. *AV*, 148.
3. *PhG*, ¶440, 255/326.
4. *PhG*, ¶440, 255/326.
5. Although rival traditions do take their name from these thinkers.
6. Alasdair MacIntyre, *Whose Justice? Which Rationality?* (Notre Dame, IN: University of Notre Dame Press, 1988), 8–9.
7. *EE* 1214a13.
8. Recently, the idea of *Sittlichkeit* as "the living good" has attracted considerable attention by Hegel scholars, see Frederick Neuhouser, *Diagnosing Social Pathology: Rousseau, Hegel, Marx, and Durkheim* (Cambridge: Cambridge University Press, 2023), 281–311 and Dean Moyar, *Hegel's Value: Justice as the Living Good* (Oxford: Oxford University Press, 2021).
9. I am here agreeing with John McDowell, "Virtue and Reason," *The Monist* 62:3 (1979): 331–50.
10. Recent Anglo-American scholarship has emphasised Aristotle's presence in Hegel's social thought, as well as his system as a whole. For example, Terry Pinkard, *Hegel's Naturalism: Mind, Nature, and the Final Ends of Life* (Oxford: Oxford University Press, 2012); Robert B. Pippin, *Hegel's Realm of Shadows: Logic as Metaphysics in "The Science of Logic"* (Chicago: Chicago University Press, 2019). The most systematic treatment is Alfredo Ferrarin, *Hegel and Aristotle* (Cambridge: Cambridge University Press, 2001). Seminal German interpretations of Hegel that centre Aristotle's significance include Herbert Marcuse, *Reason and Revolution: Hegel and the Rise of Social Theory* (London: Routledge, 1955) and Manfred Riedel, *Between Tradition and Revolution: The Hegelian Transformation of Political Philosophy* (Cambridge: Cambridge University Press, 1984).
11. Attempts to reconstruct Hegel's practical philosophy without his speculative logic are domesticating since they stand to lose its critical and normative force. The most representative of this approach is Allen W. Wood's *Hegel's Ethical Thought* (Cambridge: Cambridge University Press, 1990).
12. Gillian Rose, *Hegel Contra Sociology* (London: Verso, 2009), 50. See, *SL*, 729–34/*W* 6, 541–48.
13. Pippin, *Realm of Shadows*, 94–95.
14. Recent accounts of Hegel's concept of ethical life stress the normative dimensions of this concept. For Pippin, "conceptual or normative content can be understood only by un-

derstanding actual historical and social practices of claim-making and action justification," *Hegel's Practical Philosophy: Rational Agency as Ethical Life* (Cambridge: Cambridge University Press, 2008), 236–37.

15. *PR*, §108A, 137/207.

16. What would actually be "rationally organised" for Hegel is a far more open question than the final sections of the *PR* provides answers for. Marx's 1843 critique of Hegel is right in the sense that the capitalist state cannot be rational, but this does not mean that Hegel endorses the reality of this domination as a form of rationality. Rather, the point of disagreement is the conditions which allow for rationality and freedom to be realised.

17. Ferrarin, *Hegel and Aristotle*, 348.

18. I agree with Pinkard on this point, *Hegel's Naturalism*, 17.

19. *NE* 1179b2–4.

20. There is no need to agree with Alex Honneth's conception of recognition that leaves open the market as an institutional space of freedom, *The Pathologies of Individual Freedom* (Princeton, NJ: Princeton University Press, 2001), 72–80. Rose takes a different view, which sees today's world as one defined by the *misrecognition* that "arises out of the contradiction of bourgeois private property," *Hegel Contra Sociology*, 78. Following Rose, recognition can be understood as the universality of ethical life. This view demands the institutions of contemporary society be fundamentally and qualitatively altered.

21. *PhG*, ¶177, 108/145.

22. While Marx continued to learn till the very end of his life, the formation of his early philosophical positions is decisive for interpreting the development of his thought.

23. Eric Hobsbawm, *The Age of Revolution* (London: Abacus, 1977), 42–100; Marcuse, *Reason and Revolution*, 3–16. For the "possible trajectories of modernity" sensitive to decolonising universalism, see Massimiliano Tomba, *Insurgent Universality: An Alternative Legacy of Modernity* (Oxford: Oxford University Press, 2019), 1–29.

24. Consider Marx and Engels's remark, "to the German philosophers of the Eighteenth Century, the demands of the first French Revolution were nothing more than the demands of 'Practical Reason' in general, and the utterance of the will of the revolutionary French bourgeoisie signified in their eyes the laws of pure Will, of Will as it was bound to be, of true human Will generally." *CM*, 510/485–86.

25. Lucien Goldmann, *Immanuel Kant* (London: NLB, 1971), 103.

26. Contemporary Anglo-American scholarship, especially by figures like Pippin and Brandom, neglects serious refection on the passage from Hegel to Marx.

27. This point has much wider implications than just a biographical background but informs Marx's theoretical project as a whole.

28. Michael Heinrich convincingly argues that Marx does not abandon his poetry for what is usually assumed (his lack of talent), but rather for philosophical reasons related to a Hegelian critique of Romantism, *Karl Marx and the Birth of Modern Society* (New York: Monthly Review Press, 2019), 184–96.

29. Karl Marx, "Letter from Marx to His Father in Trier," 10–11 November 1837, *MECW* 1, 19/*MEGA2* III.1, 17.

30. In his later life Marx kept a portrait of Hegel, a gift from Ludwig Kugelmann. See Marx's letter of thanks to Ludwig Kugelmann 13 July 1867, *MECW* 42, 395/*MEW* 31, 552.

31. Marx, "Letter from Marx to His Father," 18/17.

32. Patrick Murray, *Marx's Theory of Scientific Knowledge* (New York: Humanity Press, 1988) 9–10.

33. Marx, "Letter from Marx to His Father," 15/11.

34. For example, the cursory treatment in Gareth Stedman Jones, *Karl Marx: Greatness and Illusion* (London: Penguin, 2017), 79.

35. I agree with the broad thrust of Heinrich's discussion, *Karl Marx*, 267–73.

36. See Stathis Kouvelakis, *Philosophy and Revolution: From Kant to Marx* (London: Verso, 2003), 236–39.

37. Karl Marx, "Difference Between the Democritean and Epicurean Philosophy of Nature," *MECW* 1, 103–5/*MEGA2* I.1, 89–91.

38. Marx, 85–86/69–70.

39. Marx, 29–30/13–14.

40. Marx, 35/22.

41. This notion parallels with Hegel's consideration that even if the philosophies of the ancients are alive in philosophy, their thought cannot be simply "revived" in the sense "there can be no Platonists, Aristotelians, Stoics, or Epicureans to-day," *LHP* 1, 46/65.

42. Marx, "Difference Between the Democritean and Epicurean Philosophy of Nature," 38/25.

43. Marx, 73/58.

44. Marx, 38, 43, 61, 64/25, 29, 46, 49.

45. Marx, 85/68.

46. See the articles collected in *MECW* 1, 109–375. As Andrew Chitty argues, Marx's early journalist work retains the influence of Hegel's concept of the state in terms of "life" and "life-processes." In emphasising political action (freedom of the press, etc.), Marx's idea of the popular will "expresses and demands the institutionalisation of the freedom, reason, and equality realised in the people's spirit." Further, the development of freedom as "life-processes" in the *EPM* and "German Ideology" manuscripts is underpinned by the Hegelian idea of freedom as provided in social and political institutions. Andrew Chitty, "The Basis of the State in the Marx of 1842" in *The New Hegelians: Politics and Philosophy in the Hegelian School*, ed. Douglas Moggach (Cambridge: Cambridge University Press, 2006), 233, 237, 240–41.

47. See *MEGA2* IV.1, 155–80. Marx cites in the dissertation and preparatory notes, *De Anima, On the Heavens, Generation of Animals, On Generation and Corruption, Physics, Metaphysics, On Dreams and Rhetoric*. For the dissertation, see Heinrich, *Karl Marx*, 279, 292–21. Hegel translated parts of *De Anima* in 1805 and was a comparatively early German reader of *NE* and *Pol*. Ferrarin, *Hegel and Aristotle*, 6; Riedel, *Between Tradition and Revolution*, 9n10.

48. William Clare Roberts, *Marx's Inferno: A Political Theory of Capital* (Princeton, NJ: Princeton University Press, 2017), 21.

49. Marx, "Difference Between the Democritean and Epicurean Philosophy of Nature," 35/22. See *De Anima*, 413a20-24; 415b26-28.

50. Marx's notes on Hegel's *Philosophy of Nature* are collected in *MECW* 1, 510–14.

51. *PR*, 22/26.

52. *LHP* 1, 29, 6/47, 19.

53. *PhG*, ¶11, 8–9/18–19.

54. To some degree Marx accepts this paradigm, although sharpening as a central dynamic the political impact of the working class as an objective historical phenomenon, expressing a new and universal form of collective subjectivity, specifically arising from the bourgeois revolutions. Marx differs with Hegel with respect to the exact implications of the French Revolution, although there are clear parallels in their theories of history. This is especially evident in the *Philosophy of History* and in the *Communist Manifesto*. Their differences cannot be reduced to tired oppositions between a bourgeois/idealist and a proletariat/materialist standpoint but instead the ramifications of modern civil society. Marx operates within the tradition set out by Hegel, although always critical of the mystifications that arise from not thinking through the fullest critique of civil society, he accepts the character of Hegel's modern standpoint, in terms of rational self-consciousness. Marx's concept of human freedom correlates to and offers greater perspective to Hegelian *Sittlichkeit*. See Karl Marx, "Critique of Hegel's Doctrine of the State" in *EW*, 70, 80, 93/*MEGA2* 1.2, 14, 24–25, 35–36.

55. G.W.F. Hegel, "Lectures on the Philosophy of History (1827–1831)" in *PW*, 215/*W* 12, 529. Of course, Hegel had a critique of the revolution itself, especially the terror. He wrote of the instrumental terror of the guillotine as "the coldest, emptiest death of all, having no more meaning than chopping off a head of cabbage or swallowing a mouthful of water," *PhG*, ¶590, 343/436. See Rebecca Comay, *Mourning Sickness: Hegel and the French Revolution* (Stanford, CA: Stanford University Press, 2011), 55–80.

56. Following contemporary interpreters, I reject the traditional reading of *Geist* as God, which would render Hegel as a straightforwardly religious thinker. See Terry Pinkard, *Hegel's Phenomenology: The Sociality of Reason* (Cambridge: Cambridge University Press, 1996), 8–9, 14, 83, 88, 220; Martin Hägglund, *This Life: Secular Faith and Spiritual Freedom* (New York: Pantheon Books, 2019), 354–55; Robert Brandom, *A Spirit of Trust: A Reading of Hegel's Phenomenology* (Cambridge: Belknap, 2019), 469–99.

57. John McDowell, "Why Does It Matter to Hegel That Geist Has a History?" in *Hegel on Philosophy in History*, ed. Rachel Zuckert and James Kreines (Cambridge: Cambridge University Press, 2017), 15.

58. G.W.F Hegel, *Introduction to the Philosophy of History* (Indianapolis: Hackett, 1988), 20–21/*W* 12, 30–31.

59. Pippin discusses this normative idea of freedom as an "achievement," *Hegel's Practical Philosophy*, 9, 61, passim. McDowell notes the Kantian assumptions in Pippin's account, "Why Does It Matter," 17–32.

60. Pippin, *Hegel's Practical Philosophy*, 43.

61. McDowell, "Why Does It Matter?," 16.

Notes to Chapter 3

62. Georg Lukács, *The Young Hegel: Studies in the Relations Between Dialectics and Economics* (Cambridge: MIT Press, 1975), 299. Hegel's *Encyclopedia*, composed after the *PhG*, develops at a systematic level the relation and passage between subjective and objective spirit.

63. Hegel himself warned against an equation of actuality with rationality: "Who would not have enough good sense to see much around him that is indeed not as it ought to be?" *EL*, §6, 34/47. Marx's youthful critique of Hegel is right to push at the most conservative aspects of the *PR* that look for the rational elements in civil society, constitutional monarchy and its supporting bureaucracy. No *rational* state can exist if the state is one of domination. However, if Hegel is held against the logic of his own thought, there is no need to confine his politics to this conservatism.

64. *PR*, §105-§114, 134-42/203-15. See Michael Quante's book length treatment of these passages, *Hegel's Concept of Action* (Cambridge: Cambridge University Press, 2004).

65. Immanuel Kant, *Groundwork of the Metaphysics of Morals* (Cambridge: Cambridge University Press, 2012), 4:440-4:445. See Robert B. Pippin, *Modernism as a Philosophical Problem* (Oxford: Blackwell, 1991), 56, 65.

66. *PhG*, ¶26, 17/30.

67. *PR*, §1-2, 25-28/29-33.

68. *PR*, §4, 35/46; 12-13/15.

69. *PR*, §182A, 220/339. For a summary of the relation between institutional spheres, see Moyar, *Hegel's Value*, 210-15.

70. *PR*, §243, 266/389-§255, 273/396.

71. *PR*, §289, 329/458.

72. *PR*, §249, 270/393.

73. C.L.R. James captures this dialectic in *The Black Jacobins* (New York: Random House, 1963). I explore the relationship between capitalism and colonialism in the next chapter.

74. Joachim Ritter, *Hegel and the French Revolution: Essays on the Philosophy of Right* (Cambridge, MA: MIT Press, 1984), 43.

75. Ritter, 47, 54.

76. Comay notes the liberalism of Ritter's position, *Mourning Sickness*, 77.

77. Pinkard, *Hegel's Phenomenology*, 187.

78. Hegel, *Introduction to the Philosophy of History*, 80, 79/102, 101.

79. Immanuel Kant, "What Is Enlightenment" in *Political Writings* (Cambridge: Cambridge University Press, 1991), 58-59.

80. *PhG*, ¶437-46, 253-57/324-29.

81. *PhG*, ¶440, 255/326.

82. *SEL*, 147-77/328-61.

83. *PR*, 9/11. For the significance of this subtitle in terms of Hegel's attempt to overcome the split "between morality and politics," see Riedel, *Between Tradition and Revolution*, 163.

84. Brandom, *A Spirit of Trust*, 726.

85. See also, Pinkard, *Hegel's Naturalism* and Pippin, *Hegel's Practical Philosophy*.

86. Brandom, *A Spirit of Trust*, 274-75.

87. Pinkard, *Hegel's Naturalism*, 186.

88. Robert B. Pippin, *The Culmination: Heidegger, German Idealism, and the Fate of Philosophy* (Chicago: University of Chicago Press, 2024), 219–20.

89. *PR*, §43, 74/104.

90. *PR*, §45, 76–77/107.

91. *PR*, §52, 82–83/115–16.

92. *PR*, §187, 244/343; §190–95, 228–31/347–51.

93. The example is used in his Jena writings in 1803/4 through to the Berlin lectures on natural law and the philosophy of right, G.W.F. Hegel, "First Philosophy of Spirit" in *System of Ethical Life* (1802/3) and *First Philosophy of Spirit* (Part III of the System of Speculative Philosophy 1803/4) (Albany: State University of New York Press, 1979), 248/*GW* 6, 323 and *Lectures on the Philosophy of Right, 1819–1820* (Toronto: University of Toronto Press, 2023), 141/*GW* 26.1, 463. For points of comparison between Hegel and Smith, see Lisa Herzog, *Inventing the Market: Smith, Hegel, and Political Theory* (Oxford: Oxford University Press, 2013). Despite her illuminating analysis of the emergence of the market, Herzog underplays the contrasting ontological positions of each thinker.

94. *PR*, §189, 227/347.

95. My purpose in the following section is to present the core features of Kant's position as Hegel sees it. For important defences of Kant, see Allison, *Kant's Theory of Freedom*; Allen W. Wood, *Kant's Ethical Thought* (Cambridge: Cambridge University Press, 1999); Christine M. Korsgaard, *The Sources of Normativity* (Cambridge: Cambridge University Press, 1996), *Self-Constitution: Agency, Identity, and Integrity* (Oxford: Oxford University Press, 2009) and *Fellow Creatures: Our Obligations to the Other Animals* (Oxford: Oxford University Press, 2018). However, I agree with Sally Sedgwick that Hegel takes his critique of Kant to concern the fundamentals problems of dualism and formalism, see *Hegel's Critique of Kant: From Dichotomy to Identity* (Oxford: Oxford University Press, 2012), 2–7.

96. Kant, *Groundwork*, 4:388.

97. Kant, 4:389.

98. Kant, 4:420.

99. Kant, 4:402, 4:440.

100. Kant, 4:396.

101. Korsgaard gives a more nuanced account of desire in *Self-Constitution*, especially 54–55. In response, Jonathan Lear argues she separates desire from reason, *Freud* (London: Routledge, 2014), 7–8.

102. Kant, 4:407. Also, 4:409; 4:418; 4:452.

103. Kant, 4:410. Also, 4:442.

104. Kant, 4:413.

105. Kant, 4:408.

106. Kant, 4:416.

107. Kant, 4:421. See the previous chapter for MacIntyre's critique of this justification.

108. Goldmann, *Immanuel Kant*, 126.

109. Kant, *Groundwork*, 4:433–4:436.

110. Kant, 4:447.
111. Kant, 4:451–4:453.
112. Kant, 4:456.
113. Kant, 4:459.
114. Kant, 4:463.
115. This argument parallels his claim in *EL*: "However, the *good* in which the ultimate purpose of the world is located is determined from the start only as *our* good, as the moral law of *our* practical reason. As a result, the unity does not extend beyond the agreement of the state of the world and of world events with our morality. Moreover, even with this limitation the ultimate purpose, the *good,* is an undetermined abstractum, as is what *duty* is supposed to be." He adds, "[t]he Kantian philosophy opposes this empiricism with the principle of thought and that of freedom in general, and sides with the first empiricism without in the least stepping outside its [that first empiricism's] general principles. The world of perception and of the understanding reflecting on it continues to exist on one side of its [the Kantian philosophy's] dualism." §60, 105–6/142–43.
116. Kant, *Groundwork*, 4:389.
117. *NL*, 109/443. See also, *PR*, §135, 162/252.
118. *NL*, 111/445.
119. *NL*, 113–15/448–51, 119/456.
120. *NL*, 105–7/438–40, 114–18/449–53. Hegel argues that the "natural" is not ethical in and of itself. See also, *PR*, §4A, 36/46–47.
121. Jonathan Lear, *Aristotle: The Desire to Understand* (Cambridge: Cambridge University Press, 1988), 156.
122. *NE* 1170a12.
123. *NE* 1177a13–32.
124. *NL*, 124/461.
125. In his dissertation, Marx follows Hegel's cue and compares the logic of Kant's argument with the ontological proof of God, *MECW* 1, 104/*MEGA2* I.1, 90.
126. Immanuel Kant, *Critique of Practical Reason* (Cambridge: Cambridge University Press, 2015), 5:28.
127. For defences of Kant against Hegel on this point, see Korsgaard, *Fellow Creatures*, 120–23; Wood, *Kant's Ethical Thought*, 89–90.
128. *NL*, 125/461–62.
129. There is a close resemblance here between Hegel's and MacIntyre's critique of Kant as discussed in the last chapter. In her defence of Kant against MacIntyre, Onora O'Neill points out his "understanding and criticism of Kant is venerable enough; in many respects it dates back to Hegel," "Kant After Virtue," *Inquiry* 26:4 (1983): 390.
130. Lukács, *The Young Hegel*, 294. See also, Rose, *Hegel Contra Sociology*, 61; Comay, *Mourning Sickness*, 47.
131. *NL*, 129/470.
132. Theodor W. Adorno captures this insight: "Freedom is not given to an individual in isolation, but with regard to the social totality in which human beings live. The concrete

specificity of the moral law can only be made a reality within a concept of social function, not on the model of a Robinson Crusoe," *Problems of Moral Philosophy* (Stanford, CA: Stanford University Press, 2000), 123.

133. *NL*, 139–40/480–81.

134. Ferrarin, *Hegel and Aristotle*, 351.

135. Lukács' *The Young Hegel* remains a seminal discussion, 319–420.

136. *NL*, 127/465; *SEL*, 104–14/282–94.

137. *NL*, 141–46/482–89. Translation modified.

138. Neuhouser, *Foundations of Hegel's Social Theory*, 128–33.

139. *NL*, 141/482.

140. *SEL*, 102–25/280–306. See also, Christopher J. Arthur, *The New Dialectic and Marx's* Capital (Leiden: Brill, 2004), 175–99.

141. Rose, *Hegel Contra Sociology*, 55–77, 169.

142. *NL*, 145–46/447–48.

143. *NL*, 147/489.

144. *Pol* 1255b33–37. See also, *Metaphysics* 981b13–982a3.

145. See Ferrarin, *Hegel and Aristotle*, 353.

146. *NL*, 147–51/489–94.

147. *LHP* 2, 209/228; *NL*, 161/506.

148. *LHP* 1, 150/174.

149. *LHP* 1, 151/175.

150. Pinkard, *Hegel's Phenomenology*, 139–43. See *PhG*, ¶450/258–59/330–32.

151. *LHP* 1, 153/177. For a discussion of his understanding of slavery in terms of action and production, see Adriel M. Trott, *Aristotle and the Nature of Community* (Cambridge: Cambridge University Press, 2014), 178–82.

152. Hegel, *Introduction to the Philosophy of History*, 21/31.

153. *PhG*, ¶463–75, 267–77/342–54. For a lucid discussion, see J. M. Bernstein, "'the celestial Antigone, the most resplendent figure ever to have appeared on earth": Hegel's Feminism" in *Feminist Readings of Antigone*, ed. Fanny Söderbäck (Albany: State University of New York Press, 2010), 111–30. For the role of tragedy in *NL*, see Miguel Vatter, *The Republic of the Living: Biopolitics and the Critique of Civil Society* (New York: Fordham University Press, 2014), 21–36.

154. *NL*, 159/504.

155. *NL*, 159–60/505. Translation modified.

156. *To koinon agathon* meaning "the common good." In their discussion of Hegel's translation, Laurence Dickey and H. B. Nisbet suggest Hegel depoliticises Aristotle by translating polis into *Volk*, by leaving out the connection between a community and its political or social ideal. However, this interpretation is put into question since no reason is given for translating *Volk*, the word Hegel's uses for polis, as "state" and not "people." *NL*, 295–96n99.

157. *Pol* 1253a25–40.

158. For the "naturalness" of the polis, Trott, *Aristotle and the Nature of Community*,

42–82. Key differences between Aristotle and Hobbes on political agency are outlined by Josiah Ober, *The Rise and Fall of Classical Greece* (Princeton, NJ: Princeton University Press, 2015), 57–60.

159. *PR*, §269A, 290/415. I am here disagreeing with Pippin, *Hegel's Practical Philosophy*, 63.

160. Robert R. Williams, *Hegel's Ethics of Recognition* (Berkeley: University of California Press, 1997), 295, 316.

161. *LHP* 2, 208/226.

162. *PR*, §121A, 149/229.

163. *NL*, 162/508.

164. *NL*, 172–73/521.

165. *PR*, 22/27.

166. G.W.F. Hegel, *Philosophy of Mind* (Oxford: Oxford University Press, 2007), §483–87, 217–19/*W* 10, 303–6.

167. *PR*, §4, 35/46. See Andreja Novakovic, *Hegel on Second Nature in Ethical Life* (Cambridge: Cambridge University Press, 2017), 173–207.

168. Shlomo Avineri, *Hegel's Theory of the Modern State* (Cambridge: Cambridge University Press, 1972), 118.

169. *PR*, §136, 163/254, §137, 164/254–55.

170. Hegel writes, "[m]orality and ethics, which are usually regarded as roughly synonymous, are taken here in essentially distinct senses. Yet even representational thought [*Vorstellung*] seems to distinguish them; Kantian usage prefers the expression morality, as indeed the practical principles of Kant's philosophy are confined throughout to this concept, even rendering the point of view of ethics impossible and in fact expressly infringing and destroying it. But even if morality and ethics were etymologically synonymous, this would not prevent them, since they are now different words, from being used for different concepts." *PR*, §33, 63/87.

171. *PR*, §2, 26/30, §4, 35/46.

172. *PR*, §33, 62/87.

173. *PR*, §123A, 151/232.

174. *NE* 1097b21–22. In a note Hegel relates Aristotle's reason with the "true principles of ethical action" *PR*, §140/170–71; *NE* 1110b27.

175. *PR*, §124, 151/233.

176. *NE* 1141b15023.

177. *NE* 1140b10. For terminological differences, see Ferrarin, *Hegel and Aristotle*, 16.

178. Riedel, *Between Tradition and Revolution*, 15, 21. Riedel notes, "[w]hat is remarkable about Hegel's method of work in this period is that his reconstruction of the ancient theory of the polis walks side by side with these contemporary studies. Just as he reached back to Aristotle's *Politics* in his struggle with natural law theory, so he now used elements of classical economics as a foil for handling the political economic problems raised by the English," 111.

179. *PR*, §142, 189/292.

180. *NE* 1139a37–38. See also, Avineri, *Hegel's Theory of the Modern State*, 65.

181. *LHP* 2, 204/223. Hegel is critical of the principle of the mean which he views as insufficient to determine the good.

182. *PhG*, ¶17, 12/23. See also, Pinkard, *Hegel's Naturalism*, 96.

183. *EE* 1231b32.

184. Williams, *Hegel's Ethics of Recognition*, 80–84.

185. Hegel, *Introduction to the Philosophy of History*, 60–61/78.

186. Hegel, *Lectures on the Philosophy of Right, 1819–1820*, 174/497.

187. *PR*, §245, 267/390; §248A, 269/392. See Frederick Neuhouser, *Foundations of Hegel's Social Theory: Actualizing Freedom* (Cambridge, MA: Harvard University Press), 171–74.

188. Comay, *Mourning Sickness*, 140.

189. Hegel, *Lectures on the Philosophy of Right*, 1819–1820, 173/*GW* 26.1, 497.

190. Neuhouser, *Foundations of Hegel's Social Theory*, 174.

191. For an account influenced by Rawls, see Moyar, *Hegel's Value*, 247–53.

192. Hägglund, *This Life*, 234. Also, Michael Lazarus, "The Lives of Marx: Hägglund and Marx's Philosophy After Pippin and Postone," *Historical Materialism* 29:4 (2021), 248–49.

193. *PR*, §192, 229/349.

194. *PR*, 22/26.

195. *LHP* 1, 295/340.

196. *EE* 1138b12–13.

197. *LHP* 3, 545/455.

198. Karl Marx, "Letters from the Franco-German Yearbooks," in *EW*, 208/*MEGA2* III.1, 55.

Chapter 4

1. *The Economist*, 20/12/2023. https://www.economist.com/christmas-specials/2023/12/20/why-economists-love-robinson-crusoe.

2. An earlier version of this chapter first appeared as Michael Lazarus, "From Shipwreck to Commodity Exchange: Robinson Crusoe, Hegel and Marx," *Philosophy and Social Criticism* 48:9 (2022): 1302–28.

3. Milton Friedman, *Capitalism and Freedom* (Chicago: University of Chicago Press, 2020), 193–200; Robert Nozick, *Anarchy, State and Utopia* (Oxford: Basil Blackwell, 1974), 183–89.

4. For an account of the relationship between market and democracy in Friedman, see Thomas Biebricher, *The Political Theory of Neoliberalism* (Stanford, CA: Stanford University Press, 2018), 81–101; for Nozick, Katrina Forrester, *In the Shadow of Justice: Postwar Liberalism and the Remaking of Political Philosophy* (Princeton, NJ: Princeton University Press, 2019), 127–32. See also, Jessica Whyte, *The Morals of the Market: Human Rights and the Rise of Neoliberalism* (London: Verso, 2019).

5. Friedman, *Capitalism and Freedom*, 167–68; Nozick, *Anarchy, State and Utopia*, 188.

6. Edward W. Said, *Culture and Imperialism* (London: Vintage, 1994), 85.

7. Recent accounts of recognition have identified its earliest expression with Rousseau, Axel Honneth, *Recognition: A Chapter in the History of European Ideas* (Cambridge: Cambridge University Press 2021), 12–41; as well as Hobbes, Frederick Neuhouser, *Rousseau's Critique of Inequality* (Cambridge: Cambridge University Press, 2014), 65. Although such genealogies point to the significance of identifying value in another's status, I develop a notion of recognition as social interdependence, which acts as a critique of individualism.

8. F. A. Hayek, *The Counter-Revolution of Science* (Indianapolis: Liberty Press, 1979), 393.

9. John Maynard Keynes, *The General Theory of Employment, Interest and Money* (London: Macmillan and Co., Limited, 1949), 20; Hal R. Varian, *Microeconomic Analysis*, 3rd ed. (New York: W. W. Norton, 1992), 350–51.

10. Lucien Goldmann, *Towards a Sociology of the Novel* (London: Travistock, 1977), 1–15. For *Robinson Crusoe* in this context, see Franco Moretti, *The Bourgeois: Between History and Literature* (London: Verso, 2013), 8–17, 25–66.

11. Alasdair MacIntyre, *A Short History of Ethics* (London: Routledge, 1998), 146.

12. For the modern person as subject, *PR*, §35, 67–68/93–94.

13. Georg Lukács, *The Theory of the Novel* (Cambridge: MIT Press, 1971), 66, 89.

14. Terry Eagleton *Marxism and Literary Criticism* (London: Methuen & Co. Ltd., 1976), 25.

15. Christopher Hill, "Robinson Crusoe," *History Workshop* 10 (1980): 7.

16. Hill, 7.

17. Eric Williams, *Slavery and Capitalism* (Chapel Hill: University of North Carolina Press, 2021), 33.

18. Robin Blackburn makes this point, while also noting that Defoe was himself "not a consistent ideologue of slavery," *The Overthrow of Colonial Slavery: 1776–1848* (London: Verso, 1988), 153–54.

19. Said, *Culture and Imperialism*, 83.

20. Said, 187.

21. Marx showed a great appreciation for Walter Scott and Honoré de Balzac, amongst other nineteenth-century novelists.

22. Daniel Defoe, *Robinson Crusoe* (London: Penguin, 2001), 5.

23. Defoe, 6.

24. Defoe, 38–39.

25. Defoe, 43–45.

26. Defoe, 108.

27. Defoe, 116.

28. Defoe, 80, 118.

29. Defoe, 101.

30. Defoe, 163.

31. Through narrative, Benedict Anderson argues the novel form produces "spectacular possibilities for the representation of simultaneous actions in homogeneous empty time." Anderson draws on Walter Benjamin to illustrate the way cultural products become a means for apprehending the world in "homogeneous, empty time." Anderson considers the novel

(and newspaper) as the technical means to reproduce the "imagined community." His concern is the genesis of nationalism, especially the spread of new world colonialism. Benedict Anderson, *Imagined Communities* (London: Verso, 2006), 194, 25. Further, Benjamin associates homogeneous, empty time with modern thought: mechanical and conformist, robbed of contradiction and riddled with a "stubborn faith in progress." He rejects time conceived in linear terms, events told and retold by "chroniclers," which flatten time to the logic of the present, wrenching history away from its past. This empty time denies the present "the fullness of the past," depicting history as a distant object that can be reshaped to any size. For Benjamin, time is filled by historical content that which bears upon the present. Walter Benjamin, "Thesis on the Philosophy of History" in *Illuminations* (New York: Schocken Books, 1968), 254–61.

32. J. M. Coetzee, *Foe* (Melbourne: Text Publishing, 2019).

33. Thomas Hobbes, *On the Citizen* (Cambridge: Cambridge University Press, 1998), 21–31. See also, Leo Strauss, *The Political Philosophy of Hobbes* (Chicago: University of Chicago Press, 1952), 30–34.

34. This raises the difficult tension between Rousseau's individualism and his idea of self-government through political community. See his discussion of particular and general wills, *The Social Contract and Other Later Political Writings* (Cambridge: Cambridge University Press, 1997), 84, 106.

35. Defoe, *Robinson Crusoe*, 94.

36. Lawrence Krader, *Dialectic of Civil Society* (Amsterdam: Van Gorcum, Assen, 1976), 31–32.

37. There is much more to be said about Hobbes's ethics. See Christine M. Korsgaard, *The Sources of Normativity* (Cambridge: Cambridge University Press, 1996), 21–28; Arash Abizabeh, *Hobbes and the Two Faces of Ethics* (Cambridge: Cambridge University Press, 2018), 183–262. Also relevant is Quentin Skinner, *Liberty Before Liberalism* (Cambridge: Cambridge University Press, 1998), 5–11. For an assessment of the origins of the social contract tradition in terms of gender and slavery, see Carole Pateman, *The Sexual Contract* (London: Polity Press, 1988), 43–76.

38. Thomas, Hobbes, *Leviathan* (Cambridge: Cambridge University Press, 1996), 88.

39. Hobbes, *Leviathan*, 87.

40. Hobbes, 89. See also Jean-Jacques Rousseau, *The Discourses and Other Early Political Writings* (Cambridge: Cambridge University Press, 1997), 135–36, 151–53.

41. Hannah Arendt identifies Hobbes as the bourgeois moralist par excellence, unequalled in his ability to "derive public good from private interest," where power "is the accumulated control that permits the individual to fix prices and regulate supply and demand in such a way that they contribute to his own advantage," *The Origins of Totalitarianism* (New York: Harcourt, 1979), 139–43.

42. Giorgio Agamben, *Stasis: Civil War as a Political Paradigm* (Stanford, CA: Stanford University Press, 2015), 53.

43. Raymond Geuss, *Changing the Subject: Philosophy from Socrates to Adorno* (Cambridge, MA: Harvard University Press, 2017), 146–50.

44. C. B. Macpherson, *The Political Theory of Possessive Individualism: Hobbes to Locke* (Oxford: Oxford University Press, 1964), 37–42, 61–65, 78–80. The interpretation of Hobbes's thought (and Locke's) as "bourgeois" has garnered a long debate. Honneth describes Macpherson's thesis as "somewhat justified," but gives no further comment, *Recognition*, 58. For a critical response, see Keith Tribe, *Land, Labour and Economic Discourse* (London: Routledge, 1978), 35–52. For a revised version of the thesis, see Michael Bray, "Macpherson Restored? Hobbes and the Question of Social Origins," *History of Political Thought* 28:1 (2007): 56–90. For an assessment of the debate in relation to Locke, closer to Marx than Macpherson, but with a convincing reply to his critics, see Onur Ulas Ince, "Enclosing in God's Name, Accumulating for Mankind: Money, Morality and Accumulation in John Locke's Theory of Property," *Review of Politics* 73:1 (2011): 29–54.

45. Strauss, *The Political Philosophy of Hobbes*, 126.

46. Hobbes, *Leviathan*, 63.

47. *Cap*.1, 274/178.

48. Adam Smith, *An Inquiry into the Nature and Causes of the Wealth of Nations*, vol. 1 (Indianapolis: Liberty Fund, 1981), I.v.3. Smith shifts the meaning of Hobbes's idea of power, which is fundamentally still a political notion, to an explicit idea of economic power.

49. Defoe, *Robinson Crusoe*, 146.

50. Locke also rejects Hobbes's absolutism, see Ellen Meiksins Wood, *Liberty and Property: A Social History of Western Political Thought from the Renaissance to Enlightenment* (London: Verso, 2012), 260–62. However, Wood mistakenly downplays Locke's influence on Defoe, 287.

51. John Locke, *Two Treatises of Government* (Cambridge: Cambridge University Press, 1998), 290. For a detailed account of Locke's view of property, including discussions of Nozick and Macpherson, see Jeremy Waldron, *The Right to Private Property* (Oxford: Oxford University Press, 1988), 137–251.

52. Locke, *Two Treatises of Government*, 350.

53. On the idea of "trust" see John Dunn, *Rethinking Modern Political Theory* (Cambridge: Cambridge University Press, 1985), 34–54.

54. Defoe, *Robinson Crusoe*, 80.

55. Locke, *Two Treatises of Government*, 296–97.

56. Ellen Meiksins Wood, *Empire of Capital* (London: Verso, 2003), 96–97.

57. Ian Watt, *The Rise of the Novel* (London: Penguin, 1957), 70.

58. Defoe, *Robinson Crusoe*, 190.

59. Karl Marx, "Economic Manuscript of 1861–3," *MECW* 34, 89/*MEGA2* II.3.6, 2120. See also, *Cap*.1, 513/409.

60. *Cap*.1, 126/40.

61. See also *NW*, 246/373.

62. Honneth's erroneous argument that Marx takes Locke's concept of labour as a "model" also wrongly assumes both conceive of value as transhistorical objects of production. Rather, Marx provides a critique of value as a social relation. Axel Honneth, "Labour, A Brief History of a Modern Concept," *Philosophy* 97:2 (2022): 151, 160.

63. *Cap*.1, 131/45. This crucial difference is not adequately noted by neo-Ricardian understandings of value, for example, G. A. Cohen, "Marx and Locke on Land and Labour" in *Self-Ownership, Freedom and Equality* (Cambridge: Cambridge University Press, 1995), 165–94.

64. Maurice Dobb, *Theories of Value and Distribution Since Adam Smith* (Cambridge: Cambridge University Press, 1973), 141, 148–49; Honneth, "Labour, A Brief History of a Modern Concept," 150–53. Key differences between Locke's notion of labour and classical political economy are noted by Patrick Murray, *The Mismeasure of Wealth: Essays on Marx and Social Form* (Chicago: Haymarket, 2017), 88–91.

65. *Cap*.1, 909/786.

66. Jean-Jacques Rousseau, *Émile* (New York: Basic Books, 1979), 185.

67. Rousseau, 188. At first, Robinson Crusoe is the only book Émile is permitted to read, 184. Hegel considered *Émile* to be a defective model for moral education since human nature was confined to the isolated individual, *PR* §153, 196/304.

68. Rousseau, *Émile*, 188.

69. See Honneth, *Recognition*, 31–37.

70. Rousseau, *Discourses*, 161.

71. Rousseau, 161–67. For an account of the models of history operative in the *Discourses*, see David James, *Practical Necessity, Freedom and History: From Hobbes to Marx* (Oxford: Oxford University Press, 2021), 46–54.

72. Rousseau, *Discourses*, 170–71.

73. Rousseau, 182.

74. Rousseau, 169. See also, Joshua Cohen, *Rousseau* (Oxford: Oxford University Press, 2010), 119–21.

75. For an in-depth account, see Neuhouser, *Rousseau's Critique of Inequality*, 63–108.

76. Rousseau, *Discourses*, 218.

77. To borrow Istvan Hont's apt phrase, *Politics in Commercial Society* (Cambridge, MA: Harvard University Press, 2015), 46. See his analysis of the division of labour between industry and agriculture, 98–99, 104.

78. Rousseau, *The Social Contract*, 43.

79. Following Rousseau, Kant noted that modern dissatisfaction and "weariness of civilised life" lead the daydreaming individual to be seduced by "tales of Robinson Crusoe," "Conjectures on the Beginning of Human History" in *Political Writings*, 233.

80. G.W.F. Hegel, "First Philosophy of Spirit" in *System of Ethical Life* (1802/3) and *First Philosophy of Spirit* (Part III of the System of Speculative Philosophy 1803/4) (Albany: State University of New York Press, 1979), 242/*GW* 6, 314–15.

81. G.W.F. Hegel, *Lectures on Natural Right and Political Science: The First Philosophy of Right (Oxford: Oxford University Press, 2012)*, §2, 52/*GW* 26, 8.

82. Free will is rendered here as "the unity of thought with itself is freedom, free will," *LHP*, 402. Brandom argues that Hegel incorporates, but goes beyond, the autonomy model of normativity in Rousseau and Kant, Robert Brandom, *A Spirit of Trust: A Reading of Hegel's Phenomenology* (Cambridge: Belknap, 2019), 262–307.

83. Rousseau, *The Social Contract*, 54.

84. For Rousseau, as Frederick Neuhouser points out, "independence is synonymous with freedom," *Foundations of Hegel's Social Theory: Actualizing Freedom* (Cambridge, MA: Harvard University Press), 64. By making clear the distinction between independence and freedom, Neuhouser's reconstruction of social dependence in Rousseau's thought is illuminating. However, he downplays the political significance of Hegel's critique of Rousseau along this line.

85. *PR*, §258, 277/400.

86. *PhG*, ¶187, 111/148–49.

87. Neuhouser, *Foundations of Hegel's Social Theory*, 177.

88. *PR*, §149, 192–93/297–98.

89. *PhG*, ¶177, 108/145.

90. Hobbes, *Leviathan*, 88.

91. *PR*, §57, 86–87/123.

92. Robert B. Pippin, *Hegel on Self-Consciousness* (Princeton, NJ: Princeton University Press, 2011), 87.

93. *PhG*, ¶178, 108/145.

94. *PhG*, ¶179, 109/146.

95. Hobbes neglects the possibility of struggles where "the desire for recognition is stronger than the desire for life itself," Terry Pinkard, *Hegel's Naturalism: Mind, Nature, and the Final Ends of Life* (Oxford: Oxford University Press, 2012), 63.

96. *PhG*, ¶187, 111/148.

97. *PhG*, ¶189, 112–13/150.

98. *PhG*, ¶191, 113–14/151–52. See also, G.W.F. Hegel, *The Berlin Phenomenology* (Dordrecht: D. Reidel Publishing Company, 1981), ¶435/87–91.

99. Pinkard, *Hegel's Naturalism*, 64.

100. G.W.F. Hegel, *The Philosophical Propaedeutic* (Oxford: Basil Blackwell, 1986), §35, 62/*W* 4, 120–21.

101. Defoe, *Robinson Crusoe*, 162–63. "I tug his woolly hair, finger the chain about his throat," writes Coetzee in his chilling take on these lines. What is spoken by the colonial subject is drowned, "caught with water and diffused. This is a place where bodies are their own signs. It is the home of Friday." *Foe*, 147.

102. *Gr*, 465/373.

103. Dispelling such depictions with a history of black revolt in the slave trade, in C.L.R. James's words, "[t]he docile Negro is a myth," "Revolution and the Negro" in *C.L.R. James and Revolutionary Marxism* (New York: Humanity Books, 1994), 77.

104. Defoe, *Robinson Crusoe*, 170–71.

105. Defoe, 168.

106. My use of male pronouns alludes to Pateman's *The Sexual Contract*, 178–79.

107. *PhG*, ¶195, 115/153.

108. *PhG*, ¶195, 115/153.

109. *PhG*, ¶196, 116/154.

110. *PR*, §57, 87/123.

111. *PR*, §153, 196/303.

112. This membership entails social roles and practical identities, see Neuhouser, *Foundations of Hegel's Social Theory*, 92–110.

113. *PR*, §260, 282/406.

114. *PhG*, ¶175, 107/143. For the importance of this claim, see Pippin, *Hegel on Self-Consciousness*, 54–87.

115. The radical implications of this idea of freedom from domination was expanded by thinkers including C.L.R. James and Franz Fanon who developed the concept in relation to their postcolonial contexts. For James and Fanon, Hegel's claim for universal freedom could only be conceived as adequate to its concept by mobilising its potential in contemporary struggles for recognition. See James, *The Black Jacobins*; "Dialectical Materialism and the Fate of Humanity" in *Spheres of Existence* (Westport: Lawrence Hill and Co., 1980), 70–105; Fanon, *The Wretched of the Earth* (London: MacGibbon and Kee, 1965), as well as his early play "The Drowning Eye" in *Alienation and Freedom* (London: Bloomsbury, 2018), 81–112.

116. From a tentative analysis of Hegel's interest in the Haitian Revolution, Susan Buck-Morss surmises that the mastery-servitude dialectic should be understood as inspired by these events. However interesting her intellectual history of the attitude towards slavery before Hegel, the argument is too literal to be convincing on the basis of the textual evidence she presents. Moreover, Buck-Morss conceives of Hegel as opening up an idea of universal history based not in Europe, but in the struggles for freedom against colonialism, *Hegel, Haiti and Universal History* (Pittsburgh: University of Pittsburgh Press, 2009). See also, Tomba, *Insurgent Universality*, 30–70.

117. C.L.R. James, "Fanon and the Caribbean" in *International Tribute to Franz Fanon* (New York: United Nations Centre Against Apartheid, 1979), 43–46.

118. Alexandre Kojève, *Introduction to the Reading of Hegel* (New York: Basic Books, 1969), 64–65; for a critique of this interpretation see Christopher J. Arthur, "Hegel's Master-Slave Dialectic and a Myth of Marxology," *New Left Review* 1/142 (1983): 67–75.

119. *Gr*, 461/369.

120. *Gr*, 461–3/369–71.

121. *Cap*.1, 271–2/175–76.

122. *Gr*, 463/371. Of course, this activity takes a different form for the worker as the commodity labour-power.

123. Karl Marx, "Letter to *Otechestvenniye Zapiski*," *MECW* 24, 199. See also Werner Bonefeld, *Critical Theory and the Critique of Political Economy* (London: Bloomsbury, 2014), 79–95.

124. *Cap*.3, 753–54/665.

125. *Cap*.1, 881/759, 915/790.

126. *Cap*.1, 915/791. Onur Ulas Ince makes a novel distinction between "capital-positing violence" and "capital-preserving violence," "Between Equal Rights: Primitive Accumulation and Capital's Violence," *Political Theory* 46:6 (2018): 885–914.

127. *Cap*.1, 925–26/800–801. Translation modified. For a rigorous value-form account of

New World slavery, and reconstruction of Marx's argument in *Capital*, see Nesbitt, *The Price of Slavery*.

128. *Cap.*1, 927/802.

129. For a historical account, see E. P. Thompson, "Time, Work-Discipline and Industrial Capitalism" in *Customs in Common* (London: Merlin Press, 1991), 352–404.

130. *Cap.*1, 932/805.

131. Franz Fanon insists recognition must go beyond liberal nationalism to socialist humanism, see *Black Skins, White Masks* (New York: Grove Press, 1967) 216–22 and *The Wretched of the Earth*, 121–63.

132. My argument in this paragraph is indebted to Murray, *The Mismeasure of Wealth*, 60–62.

133. *Cap.*1, 730/612.

134. *Gr*, 472/379.

135. *Gr*, 705–8/580–84.

136. Marx is virtually ignored in the contributions collected in *The Cambridge Companion to "Robinson Crusoe,"* ed. John Richetti (Cambridge: Cambridge University Press, 2018).

137. For example, G. A. Cohen, *Karl Marx's Theory of History* (Oxford: Oxford University Press, 1978), 408.

138. S. S. Prawer, *Karl Marx and World Literature* (Oxford: Oxford University Press, 1976), 274.

139. Theodor W. Adorno and Max Horkheimer, *Dialectic of Enlightenment* (London: Verso, 1997), 60–61.

140. Alfred Sohn-Rethel, *Intellectual and Manual Labour: A Critique of Epistemology* (New Jersey: Humanities Press, 1978), 43.

141. This is also evidenced by Engels's usage, see his letter to Marx, 19 November 1869, *MECW* 43, 379/*MEW* 32, 396. In a letter to Karl Kautsky, Engels notes Robinson's connection to the slave trade, and therefore a "proper 'bourgeois,'" 20 September 1884, *MECW* 47, 194/*MEW* 36, 210. The metaphor is also used throughout *Anti-Dühring*, although not in the short section written by Marx, *MECW* 25, 143–54/*MEW* 20, 143–54.

142. Karl Marx, "Note on *The Poverty of Philosophy*," *MECW* 24, 327.

143. Karl Marx, *The Poverty of Philosophy*, *MECW* 6, 112. See also, 142–43.

144. *Gr*, 83/21–22.

145. *Gr*, 485/390.

146. Henry Charles Carey and Frédéric Bastiat are Marx's contemporary targets. Carey is the first to evoke Robinson Crusoe as an economic parable.

147. I agree with Neuhouser that Rousseau's social contract in conceived as a critique of both Hobbes and Locke, with the aim "to set out the principles of political association that eliminate the state of war by imposing an order within which the fundamental interests of all individuals can be satisfied," *Rousseau's Critique of Inequality*, 104n37.

148. Rousseau *The Social Contract*, 49. For a book length elaboration of this argument, see Cohen, *Rousseau*.

149. Rousseau, *Discourses*, 165.

150. Rousseau warns those who "attribute to man a natural inclination to servitude," *Discourses*, 176.

151. *Gr*, 156/89.

152. For his critical remarks on Hobbes's idea of society, see Adam Smith, *The Theory of Moral Sentiments* (Indianapolis: Liberty Fund, 1983), VII.iii.1.1–VII.iii.3.9. John Dunn outlines differences in the moral theories of the Scottish Enlightenment and Hobbes and Locke (with focus on the latter), *Rethinking Modern Political Theory*, 55–67.

153. This section was added into subsequent editions of *Capital*, after it first appeared as an appendix. The discussion of Robinson Crusoe, however, appeared in the original 1867 first chapter but was concentrated in two paragraphs. *Cap*.1a, 35–36/45.

154. *Cap*.1, 165/78.

155. *Cap*.1, 168–69/81.

156. Defoe, *Robinson Crusoe*, 47.

157. Defoe, 103.

158. *Cap*.1, 188/99.

159. Adorno and Horkheimer, *Dialectic of Enlightenment*, 62

160. *Cap*.1, 169/81.

161. *Cap*.1, 169–70/82. Translation modified.

162. Max Weber, *The Protestant Ethic and the "Spirit" of Capitalism and Other Writings* (London: Penguin, 2002), 360–63. See also, Konings, *Capital and Time*, 73–74.

163. *Cap*.3, 777/689.

164. *Cap*.2, 211/128.

165. *Cap*.1, 125/39.

166. *RIPP*, 1042/111. Translation modified.

167. Michael Sonenscher fails to note this point, suggesting Robinson is simply "multitasking," *Capitalism: The Story Behind the Word* (Princeton, NJ: Princeton University Press, 2022), 169.

168. *Gr*, 361/272.

169. *Gr*, 705/581.

170. *Cap*.1, 171/84. Translation modified. Fowkes translates *"Bestimmungen"* as "characteristics" rather than "determinations," missing the dialectical meaning of the word.

171. *Cap*.1, 173/85.

172. *Cap*.1a, 36/46.

173. *AV*, 261.

174. *Cap*.3, 799/711.

175. Nozick, *Anarchy, State and Utopia*, 186.

Chapter 5

1. Karl Marx, "Letters from the Franco-German Yearbooks," in *EW*, 201/*MEGA2* III.1, 49. Many of Marx's 1843 articles are published in the single-issue *Deutsch–Französische Jahrbücher*, he edited with Ruge in 1844.

2. Marx, "Letters from the Franco-German Yearbooks," 201/49.

3. This chapter acts to reinforce the critique of Arendt offered in chapter 1 and reorient the dialogue between thinkers by showing that her commitment to the political realm of action shares something fundamental with Marx's understanding of human flourishing, once the richness of this concept is adequately articulated.

4. For the philological difficulties in treating the *EPM* as "a single work," see David Leopold, *The Young Karl Marx: German Philosophy, Modern Politics, and Human Flourishing* (Cambridge: Cambridge University Press, 2007), 94–96.

5. Most significant is the debate ignited by Louis Althusser's demarcation of an "epistemological break" occurring in Marx's 1845 *Theses on Feuerbach,* in his *For Marx* (London: Verso, 2005), 31–39. For a gloss on his position, framed autobiographically, see "The Humanist Controversy" in Louis Althusser, *The Humanist Controversy and Other Writings* (London: Verso, 2003), 222–305. Many works promoting the "humanist" Marx shortly followed; especially strong is István Mészáros's *Marx's Theory of Alienation* (London: Merlin Press, 1970) and Shlomo Avineri's *The Social and Political Thought of Karl Marx* (Cambridge: Cambridge University Press, 1968).

6. According to the formulation in the *CM*: "Property, in its present form, is based on the antagonism of capital and wage-labour," 499/476.

7. G.W.F Hegel, *Introduction to the Philosophy of History* (Indianapolis: Hackett, 1988), 20–22/*W* 12, 30–32. Alasdair MacIntyre discusses this point, "Freedom and Revolution" in *AMEM*, 124. For a convincing assessment of Marx's inheritance of Hegel's view, see Andrew Chitty, "Species-Being and Capital" in *Karl Marx and Contemporary Philosophy*, ed. Andrew Chitty and Martin McIvor (New York: Palgrave Macmillan, 2007), 123–26.

8. Rahel Jaeggi, *Alienation* (New York: Columbia University Press, 2014), xix, 10.

9. Moishe Postone, *Time, Labor, and Social Domination: A Reinterpretation of Marx's Critical Theory (Cambridge: Cambridge University Press, 1993)*, 16.

10. Postone, 30.

11. Postone, 90.

12. Jaeggi, *Alienation*, xxi–xxii.

13. Jaeggi, 37–39.

14. Postone, *Time, Labor, and Social Domination*, 61–63, 31n41; 160n96; Jaeggi, *Alienation*, 14.

15. Postone, 47.

16. Postone, 167.

17. Jaeggi, *Alienation*, 27.

18. Jaeggi, 199–200; Postone, *Time, Labor, and Social Domination*, 32, 36–42.

19. Those who identify a historically specific position in the young Marx include: Simon Clarke, *Marx, Marginalism and Modern Sociology* (London: Macmillan, 1982), 59; Patrick Murray, *The Mismeasure of Wealth: Essays on Marx and Social Form* (Chicago: Haymarket, 2017), 98n14; Christopher J. Arthur, *Dialectics of Labour* (Oxford: Basil Blackwell, 1986); Kostas Axelos, *Alienation, Praxis and Technē in the Thought of Karl Marx* (Austin: University

of Texas Press, 1976); Agnes Heller, *The Theory of Need in Marx* (London: Allison and Busby, 1976); Scott Meikle, *Essentialism in the Thought of Karl Marx* (La Salle: Open Court, 1985).

20. Jaeggi, *Alienation*, 207.

21. *CJM*, 265/451. In modern sociology there is often a sharp distinction between *Gesellschaft* (society) and *Gemeinschaft* (community). The former as "a purely mechanical construction" and the latter as "having real organic life," Ferdinand Tönnies, *Community and Civil Society* (Cambridge: Cambridge University Press, 2001), 17. This distinction does not figure in Marx's usage.

22. For this reason, Søren Mau is wrong to suggest that Marx's "romantic" position in *EPM* "tends to depoliticise" criticism of capitalism, *Mute Compulsion: A Marxist Theory of the Economic Power of Capital* (London: Verso, 2023), 80–83.

23. *Pol* 1252a24.

24. Sections of this chapter appeared in an earlier form in Michael Lazarus, "Alienation and Action in the Young Marx, Aristotle, and Arendt," *Constellations: An International Journal of Critical and Democratic Theory* 29:4 (2022): 417–33.

25. Recent scholarship places the composition of *CJM* before or at the initial stages of writing the *EPM*. See Marcello Musto, *Another Marx* (London: Bloomsbury, 2018), 34–45.

26. See Stefan Eich's analysis of *CJM* and the context, *The Currency of Politics: The Political Theory of Money from Aristotle to Keynes* (Princeton, NJ: Princeton University Press, 2022), 109–116.

27. *OJQ*, 229/157.

28. *OJQ*, 234/162–63. This passage follows an approving quotation of the "abstraction of the political man" from Jean-Jacques Rousseau, *The Social Contract and Other Later Political Writings* (Cambridge: Cambridge University Press, 1997), 69.

29. This view has similarity with Arendt's discussion of "the rights of man" as confined to positive "natural rights," rather than the rights of citizenship and freedom, Hannah Arendt, *On Revolution* (London: Faber and Faber, 1963), 104.

30. This insight is confirmed in Marx's 1844 article in the newspaper *Vorwärts!*, "Critical Notes on the Article 'The King of Prussia and Social Reform. By a Prussian'" in *EW*, 411/ *MEGA2* I.2, 455.

31. Marx, 412/456.

32. For the political use of "universal" and "particular" in Hegel and Marx, see Patrick Murray, *Marx's Theory of Scientific Knowledge* (New York: Humanity Press, 1988), 36–39.

33. In chapter 6, I show that the content of this concept is present in Marx's later works, even if the term appears only fleetingly. For one such use, *Gr*, 243/166–67.

34. Feuerbach's influence has been a major focus in the reception of the *EPM*. However, this influence is fleeting and highly pragmatic, see Arthur, *Dialectics of Labour*, 95–110. Althusser's interpretation hinges on the importance of Feuerbach's presence, see *For Marx*, 43–48 passim and "On Feuerbach" in *The Humanist Controversy and Other Writings*, 87–154.

35. *CJM*, 260/446.

36. *CJM*, 260–61/446.

37. *CJM*, 261/446–47.

38. *Cap*.1, 163–70/76–82. In Marx's later work the category "commodity" further concretises this analysis, since commodities are the general form of private property specific to capitalist production and exchange.

39. *CJM*, 262/447.

40. *CJM*, 263/448.

41. For the connection between economic theory and economic rationality, see Werner Bonefeld, *Critical Theory and the Critique of Political Economy* (London: Bloomsbury, 2014), 22–26 passim.

42. *CJM*, 266/451.

43. Adam Smith, *An Inquiry into the Nature and Causes of the Wealth of Nations*, vol. 1 (Indianapolis: Liberty Fund, 1981), I.i.

44. *CJM*, 265/450.

45. Clarke, *Marx, Marginalism and Modern Sociology*, 19.

46. Axel Honneth, *The Idea of Socialism* (London: Polity, 2017), 16. Also, Eich, *The Currency of Politics*, 112.

47. *CJM*, 277–78/462. "Authentic nature" is just to say that the human form of life is a social one.

48. For Marx's idea of negation in *EPM*, see Peter Hudis, *Marx's Concept of the Alternative to Capitalism* (Chicago: Haymarket, 2013), 72–73.

49. *EPM*, 350/267.

50. *EPM*, 365/289.

51. Jonathan Lear, *Aristotle: The Desire to Understand* (Cambridge: Cambridge University Press, 1988), 18–20.

52. *De Anima* 415b13–15.

53. *Metaphysics* 1049b4–20.

54. *NE* 1097a21–1098a8. For a defence of this argument, see Christine M. Korsgaard, *The Constitution of Agency: Essays on Practical Reason and Moral Psychology* (Cambridge: Cambridge University Press, 2008), 129–50.

55. Adriel M. Trott, *Aristotle and the Nature of Community* (Cambridge: Cambridge University Press, 2014), 36.

56. Trott, 41–45.

57. In this way, the conception of actuality/potentiality in Marx is structurally identical to MacIntyre's Aristotelian position. Telos is potentiality in MacIntyre's claim that ethics is the "science" of human understanding as we transition from *as-we-happen-to-be* to *as-we-could-be* if we realise our essence. *AV*, 52–53.

58. This argument is made forcefully by Aaron Jaffe, "From Aristotle to Marx: A Critical Philosophical Anthropology," *Science and Society* 80:1 (2016), 56–77.

59. Jaffe, 64.

60. This view has important correlations with Hegel, see *Lectures on Fine Art*, Vol. 1 (Oxford: Oxford University Press, 1975), 80/*W* 13, 113.

61. This idea of labour also separates Marx from Feuerbach who understood species-being in relation to species-consciousness and religion. For example, Ludwig Feuerbach, *The Fiery Book: Selected Writings* (Garden City: Anchor Books, 1972), 188–91. In the *EPM*, conscious and creative productive activity is fundamental to reproducing and transforming species-being.

62. *NE* 1140b6–8. Arendt upholds this distinction, *HC*, 12–13.

63. *NE* 1140b14–15.

64. *NE* 1140a6–12. In his gloss on these passages, Cornelius Castoriadis takes this "revelation of the producer as this origin of the principle of being or becoming . . . [as] more or less what Marx was to say twenty-three centuries later," "Technique" in *Crossroads in the Labyrinth* (Cambridge: MIT Press, 1984), 233.

65. *Magna Moralia* 1197a4–11.

66. *Pol* 1254a5–6.

67. *Pol* 1254a6–8.

68. *Cap*.1, 175/87, 533/429.

69. If this is correct, then Arendt's critique of Marx is undercut by the clear differentiation between his notion of production and Aristotle's.

70. *NE* 1178a15–19; 1178b29–33.

71. *Gr*, 85/23.

72. *Pol* 1256a40.

73. *Pol* 1256b26, 1256b7.

74. Thanks to Patrick Murray for discussion on this point.

75. Hannah Arendt's remark that Hesiod's depiction of labour means he is "the only Greek who unashamedly praises private life" follows directly from an early version of her critique of Marx's "production of life through labour," "The Great Tradition" in *Thinking Without A Banister* (New York: Schocken Books, 2018), 59.

76. *EPM*, 324/236.

77. *EPM*, 326–30/238–42.

78. Karen Ng, "Humanism," *Philosophical Topics* 49:1 (2021): 156. In *Hegel's Naturalism: Mind, Nature, and the Final Ends of Life* (Oxford: Oxford University Press, 2012), Terry Pinkard shows that Hegel's adopts Aristotle's essentialism as rational agency, 17–33. With a better sense of this influence, there are important implications for understanding Marx's relation to essentialism.

79. Meikle's *Essentialism* is the most convincing assessment of Marx's debt to Aristotle.

80. *NE* 1097b25–29.

81. Karen Ng, "Ideology Critique from Hegel and Marx to Critical Theory," *Constellations: An International Journal of Critical and Democratic Theory* 22:3 (2015): 393.

82. Ng, 401–2.

83. *NE* 1098a1–19.

84. Taking up Aristotle's ontological distinction, Martin Hägglund develops an account of the form of life for human being as rational and defined by a "double ought" struc-

ture, *This Life: Secular Faith and Spiritual Freedom* (New York: Pantheon Books, 178–81. See also, Korsgaard, *The Constitution of Agency*, 141–43.

85. Mathew Abbott, "Species-Being and Self-Consciousness," *Angelaki*, forthcoming.

86. Joseph Fracchia makes this observation in his criticism of Postone, "On Transhistorical Abstractions and the Intersection of Historical Theory and Social Critique," *Historical Materialism* 12:3 (2004): 125–46.

87. To be sure, Marx is concerned about the flourishing of animal and vegetative life, taking it that the dynamics of capitalism are destructive of all forms of life. See for instance, Kohei Saito, *Karl Marx's Ecosocialism: Capital, Nature, and the Unfinished Critique of Political Economy* (New York: Monthly Review Press, 2017), 208–10 and passim.

88. Frederick Neuhouser, *Diagnosing Social Pathology: Rousseau, Hegel, Marx, and Durkheim* (Cambridge: Cambridge University Press, 2023), 18.

89. For a detailed version of this thesis, see Arthur, *Dialectics of Labour*.

90. Karl Marx, "Theses on Feuerbach" in *EW*, 423/*MEW* 3, 6.

91. Althusser, *For Marx*, 227–31.

92. Ernst Bloch, "Changing the World: Marx's *Theses on Feuerbach*" in *On Karl Marx* (New York: Herder and Herder, 1971), 74. For an alternative view in accordance with Althusser, see Étienne Balibar, *The Philosophy of Marx* (London: Verso, 2017), 123–58.

93. Heller, *The Theory of Need in Marx*, 46–47.

94. *EPM*, 377/320.

95. *NE* 1140a5–7.

96. Karl Marx and Friedrich Engels, "The German Ideology," *MECW* 5, 47/*MEGA2* I.5, 22. For the problematic editing of the manuscripts, see Takahisa Oishi, *The Unknown Marx: Reconstructing a Unified Perspective* (London: Pluto, 2001), 20–31, 179–88; Sarah Johnson, "Farewell to the German Ideology," *Journal of the History of Ideas* 83:1 (2022): 150–66.

97. For an overview, Terrell Carver, *The Postmodern Marx* (University Park: Pennsylvania State University Press, 1998), 97–107. Carver makes much of this passage being in Engels's handwriting. However, even if the differences in handwriting were enough to demarcate differences in thought, the numerous versions of the manuscript do not betray significant variances between Marx and Engels on this point, save Marx wanted to "criticise after dinner," see Marx and Engels, *Marx and Engels's "German Ideology" Manuscripts: Presentation and Analysis of the "Feuerbach Chapter,"* ed. Terrell Carver and Daniel Blank (New York: Palgrave Macmillan, 2014), 89–91.

98. Marx and Engels, "The German Ideology," 45/21.

99. Here I draw on the concept of irony in Jonathan Lear, *A Case for Irony* (Cambridge, MA: Harvard University Press, 2011) especially 9–41, 154–61.

100. Jaeggi's discussion is clarifying, *Alienation*, 37–40, 122–26.

101. Hägglund gives an insightful account of the relationship between social roles and practical identities in a postcapitalist form of life, developing the dialectic between ends and means, freedom and necessity, *This Life*, 302–3.

102. *NE* 1103a32–1103b7.

103. *NE* 1172a1–9. Translation modified.

104. *NE* 1140b6.

105. Marx and Engels, "The German Ideology," 78/66.

106. *EPM*, 361/281.

107. *EPM*, 311/353.

108. Leopold considers Marx to hold to a (narrow) perfectionist notion of human capacities as inherently good, "irrespective of their hedonist consequences," because they realise human nature, *The Young Karl Marx*, 185–86. I find this characterisation overlooks the text's moral psychology.

109. Marx, *EPM*, 389–90/296; also, 351/268.

110. *NE* 1106b25.

111. *NE* 1105b23–26. For an illuminating discussion, see L. A. Kosman, "Being Properly Affected: Virtues and Feelings in Aristotle's Ethics" in *Essays on Aristotle's Ethics*, ed. Amélie Oksenberg Rorty (Berkeley: University of California Press, 1980), 104–5.

112. Significantly, the normative dimension of Marx's argument puts him close to Alasdair MacIntyre, *Dependent Rational Animals* (London: Duckworth, 1999), 81–98.

113. *EPM*, 328/240.

114. *EPM*, 341/246.

115. *EPM*, 295/339.

116. H. G. Backhaus, "Between Philosophy and Science: Marxian Social Economy as Critical Theory" in *Open Marxism* 1, 77. For the significance of Backhaus's "bridge" from the early to late Marx, see Miguel Vatter, *The Republic of the Living: Biopolitics and the Critique of Civil Society* (New York: Fordham University Press, 2014), 72.

117. Backhaus argues the *EPM* "constitute the *beginning*" of Marx's value-form theory, in which he "specifies value as the value of capital . . . its subject-character," "Between Philosophy and Science," 71, 80. Two important points must be noted about the use of "value" and "value-form" in the passage from the *EPM* to his later texts. First, Marx conceptually refines "private property" as "commodity." Second, he makes the vital conceptual distinction between value and the value-form.

118. *EPM*, 319/230.

119. *CM*, 499/476.

120. *CM*, 506/482.

Chapter 6

1. *Movement of Animals* 701a16–25. For a discussion of action in this passage, see Martha Craven Nussbaum, *Aristotle's De Motu Animalium* (Princeton, NJ: Princeton University Press, 1978), 194–95, 150–51.

2. For this view in historical treatments, see Joseph A. Schumpeter, *History of Economic Analysis* (New York: Routledge, 1987), 368–70 and Agnar Sandmo, *Economics Evolving: A History of Economic Thought* (Princeton, NJ: Princeton University Press, 2011), 127–29.

3. Nick Nesbitt, *The Price of Slavery: Capitalism and Revolution in the Caribbean* (Charlottesville: Virginia, 2022), 216n29.

4. Marx holds to Hegel's insistence that the abstract is that dislocated from the whole, rather than something thought finds intangible, *EL*, §164, 239/314.

5. *Gr*, 712/589, 708/584.

6. *Cap*.1, 255/161.

7. *Cap*.1, 342/241.

8. *Cap*.1, 289/191.

9. *Gr*, 462/370.

10. *Gr*, 331/246.

11. *Cap*.1, 151/64.

12. Marx does not equate the social forms of slavery and wage-labour, but he does understand the latter as a pervasive form of domination and often describes the domination of the worker in terms of slavery. For instance, *CM*, 491/469. Marx regularly contrasts slavery and wage-labour as historical, not natural, social forms. In reference to Aristotle's argument (*Pol* 1254a10–15; 1255b19–41), Marx notes, the worker is no more a slave by nature than "spindles and cotton are *capital* by nature just because they are consumed nowadays by the *wage-labourer* in the labour process," *RIPP*, 997/73; and *Cap*.1, 175n35/87n33. Also, "the capitalist mode of production is distinguished from the mode of production founded on slavery by the fact that the value or price of labour-power is expressed as the value or price of labour itself, i.e. as wages," *Cap*.3, 121/51. As Nesbitt argues, Marx does indeed give an account of "capitalist slave labour," which can only be grasped by understanding capitalism in terms of its social form of value, rather than the traditional focus on the presence or absence of wage-labour, see *The Price of Slavery*, 65–103.

13. Michael Heinrich, *An Introduction to the Three Volumes of Karl Marx's Capital* (New York: Monthly Review Press, 2004), 21–22.

14. Heinrich, 35–36.

15. Søren Mau, *Mute Compulsion: A Marxist Theory of the Economic Power of Capital* (London: Verso, 2023), 118.

16. Rahel Jaeggi, *Critique of Forms of Life* (Cambridge: Belknap Press, 2018), 90–96.

17. In what he calls "Rubin's Dilemma," Patrick Murray makes a distinction between the abstraction needed for an analysis of "any concrete and historically specific social type" of labour and the "practically abstract" labour that produces value under capitalism and "receives its social validation precisely insofar as it counts as abstract labour," *The Mismeasure of Wealth: Essays on Marx and Social Form* (Chicago: Haymarket, 2017), 124–25.

18. *Gr*, 164/96.

19. Karl Marx, "Theses on Feuerbach" in *EW*, 421–22/*MEW* 3, 5.

20. As Michael Heinrich has shown, based on the new *MEGA2* critical edition, the whole research project of "Capital" is essentially a series of drafts in different forms and states of completion, "Reconstruction or Deconstruction? Methodological Controversies about Value and Capital, and New Insights from the Critical Edition" in *Re-reading Marx:*

New Perspectives After the Critical Edition, ed. Riccardo Bellofiore and Roberto Fineschi (New York: Palgrave Macmillan, 2009), 71–98.

21. See Carol C. Gould, *Marx's Social Ontology* (Cambridge: MIT Press, 1978), especially 101–28.

22. The first volume of *Capital* is the most complete text from this project, the only volume prepared for publication, although it was altered significantly in subsequent editions and editorial changes. Marx made considerable alterations to chapter 1 in preparing the second edition in 1872 and further changes to the French edition in 1875. *Cap*.1, 94/10, 105/20. Kevin B. Anderson's *Marx at the Margins: On Nationalism, Ethnicity, and Non-Western Societies* (Chicago: University of Chicago Press, 2016), 171–80. While the project of *Capital* is the most systematic of Marx's intellectual endeavours, the supposed authority of the text and any detailed analysis must be sensitive to the modifications that *Capital* underwent by his own hand, as well as changes by his editors and translators. Nonetheless, *Capital* should be seen as the richest statement of Marx's theoretical project even if the work and his project remains unfinished.

23. As István Mészáros argues in *Marx's Theory of Alienation* (London: Merlin Press, 1970), 18.

24. Christopher J. Arthur, *The New Dialectic and Marx's* Capital (Leiden: Brill, 2004), 1–17. Arthur's thesis is that there is homology between the categories of the *Logic* (being, essence and concept) which correspond to the dialectic of value (commodity, money and capital), 79–110. In Smith's view, a "one-to-one" mapping is unlikely since it contravenes Hegel's rejection of the direct application of the categories of the *Logic* immediately to social philosophy. Smith instead stresses the impact of *Science of Logic*, book 2, *The Doctrine of Essence* on the dialectic of value, Tony Smith, *The Logic of Marx's* Capital*: Replies to Hegelian Criticisms* (Albany: State University of New York Press, 1990), 44–45, 51–54. Arthur suggests his difference with Smith is "at the level of ontology," *The New Dialectic*, 7. However, the discussion has progressed to some degree, with Smith mobilising a view that Marx "was correct to think that Hegelian categories illuminate the social ontology of capitalism," "Hegel, Marx and the Comprehension of Capitalism" in *Marx's Capital and Hegel's Logic*, ed. Fred Moseley and Tony Smith (Chicago: Haymarket, 2016), 29; Tony Smith, *Beyond Liberal Egalitarianism: Marx and Normative Social Theory in the Twenty-First Century* (Leiden: Brill, 2017), 73–130. Murray also defends Hegel against Marx but believes that his early misreading provides dividends when he comes to later systematically conceptualise capital, *Mismeasure of Wealth*, 376–80.

25. *Cap*.1, 103/18. Of course, elsewhere Marx tells us he is speaking in an "Hegelian fashion," *Cap*.3, 139/68; 914/829.

26. Cornelius Castoriadis, "Value, Equality, Justice, Politics: From Marx to Aristotle and from Aristotle to Ourselves," *Crossroads in the Labyrinth* (Cambridge: MIT Press, 1984), 265, 331.

27. The problem of method is a central controversy between scholars. Marx rarely wrote directly on method and commentators have been at pains to specify his approach. However, practically, Marx's attitude is closely aligned to Hegel's refusal to separate method from con-

tent. Marx's methodological approach arises from a detailed study of the content of his analysis. An assessment of the relationship between Marx's texts explicitly concerns which concepts are deemed operative in the mature texts.

28. Marx's cryptic comment in the Postface to the 1872 second edition of *Capital* states: "My dialectical method is, in its foundations, not only different from the Hegelian, but exactly opposite to it... With him it is standing on its head. It must be inverted, in order to discover the rational kernel within the mystical shell." This remark should not be read as a simple disavowal of Hegel, especially considering the sentence directly before this passage, which gives decisive intellectual contextualisation. Marx is responding to when those "ill-humoured, arrogant and mediocre epigones who now talk large in educated German circles began to take pleasure in treating Hegel in the same way as the good Moses Mendelssohn treated Spinoza in Lessing's time, namely as a 'dead dog'; I therefore openly avowed myself the pupil of that mighty thinker, and even, here and there in the chapter on the theory of value, coquetted with the mode of expression peculiar to him." *Cap*.1, 102–3/18. See also, Marx to Ludwig Kugelmann, 6 March 1868, *MECW* 42, 544/*MEW* 32, 538–39. It is worth noting that both the "dead dog" and "rational kernel" metaphors refer back to Hegel's own usage, see *EL*, 14/22 and *Introduction to the Philosophy of History*, 32–33/*W* 12, 46. Marx frequently evokes a contrast between his own rational dialectical method and Hegel's mystical method. For example, Marx to Ferdinard Lassalle, 31 May 1858, *MECW* 40, 316/*MEW* 29, 561; Marx to Joseph Dietzgen, 9 May 1868, *MECW* 43, 31/*MEW* 32, 547. Marx's ongoing view is that Hegel superimposed logical categories upon reality. However, this attitude is complicated by his approving reflections about the influence of the *Logic* on his drafting of the *Grundrisse*, Marx to Friedrich Engels 16 January 1858, *MECW* 40, 249/*MEW* 29, 260. As I see it, Marx's remarks on his relationship to Hegel are not especially reliable. Marx is not only prone to stark contrasts and polemically sharp statements (sometimes in regard to the poor readings of Hegel by Lassalle and Proudhon), but generations of commentators have taken Marx strictly at his word, which is less exact than a reconstruction of the transition of categories in *Capital*. In this sense, Althusser's discussion of Marx's comments in the Preface of *Capital* is right to present inherent problems in the possibility of a simple inversion of the dialectic and to stress its metaphorical character. Nevertheless, I disagree with Althusser's conclusion that this presents a "structural difference" between Marx's usage of Hegel's terminology, Louis Althusser, *For Marx* (London: Verso, 2005), 88–94.

29. *RIPP*, 1037/107.

30. Smith, "Hegel, Marx and the Comprehension of Capitalism," 94; Murray, *Mismeasure of Value*, 226.

31. Smith makes this point adopting from Kant the term "dissociated sociality," *Beyond Liberal Egalitarianism*, 81.

32. *Cap*.1, 272–73/176–77.

33. Smith, *Beyond Liberal Egalitarianism*, 126.

34. Isaak Illich Rubin, *Essays on Marx's Theory of Value* (Montréal: Black Rose Books, 1973), 175.

35. Diane Elson, "Value Theory of Labour" in *Value: The Representation of Labour in Capitalism* (London: Verso, 2015), 144–46.

36. This significance is first argued in depth by Rubin, *Essays on Marx's Theory of Value*, especially 131–58.

37. *Gr*, 259/183. See also, *NW*, 241–42/369.

38. *Gr*, 105/40.

39. Rocío Zambrana's gloss is helpful: "Logic is both the practice of articulating the most general assumptions involved in a historically specific conception of intelligibility and the acknowledgment that these assumptions themselves express the commitments of a concrete shape of *Geist*. Logic must externalize itself, however, it must refer to nature, to material reality, if its critical assessment of intelligibility is to be a concrete articulation of what is. This move to nature is eventually also a move back to *Geist*." *Hegel's Theory of Intelligibility* (Chicago: University of Chicago Press, 2015), 138.

40. Robert B. Pippin suggests Hegel actually presupposes "thought as such" and the investigation of "thinking as such," *Hegel's Realm of Shadows: Logic as Metaphysics in "The Science of Logic"* (Chicago: Chicago University Press, 2019), 184–85. See also, *SL*, 48/*W* 5, 69.

41. *SL*, 45/*W* 5, 65.

42. *PhG*, ¶27, 17/31.

43. *PhG*, ¶14, 10/20.

44. *SL*, 46/*W* 5, 66.

45. *SL*, 49/*W* 5, 71. Also, *PhG*, ¶20, 13/24.

46. *EL*, §1, 28/41.

47. *SL*, 49/*W* 5, 71 See also *LHP* 1, 27/46.

48. *EL*, §238, 300–301/380–81.

49. *EL*, §7, 34–36/49–51.

50. See *LHP* 3, 176/79.

51. In a letter to Engels, Marx contrasted taking "a science to the point at which it admits of a dialectical presentation" and the pseudo-Hegelian approach of applying "an abstract, ready-made system of logic to vague presentiments of just such a system," 1 February 1858, *MECW* 40, 260–61/*MEW* 29, 274–75.

52. *Cap*.1, 89/5. Hegel warns his readers of the same "difficulty," *SL*, 45/*W* 5, 65.

53. *Cap*.2, 303/222.

54. *Cap*.1, 125/39.

55. In this way, from the first sentence of *Capital*, Marx is doing something very different from "economics" or "history" conventionally defined. He approaches "economy theory" as a specific moment in social thought conceived more broadly, which attempts to understand society through determinate categories that relate to objective social forms. For Marx, the appearance of the commodity is located in an essence. This does not negate the reality of the commodity, but rather follows Hegel in claiming that appearances are relationally bound to essences, a moment of expression and both appearances and essences are vital aspects of social reality that cannot be held apart, as if "appearance" is something that comes out of thin air. *EL*, §132, 199/264.

56. The controversy about Marx's beginning goes back to Engels, who establishes the

"logical-historical" reading of *Capital*, in which starting with "simple commodity production" Marx proceeds historically. See Friedrich Engels, "Review: Karl Marx, *Contribution to the Critique of Political Economy*," *MECW* 16, 475/*MEW* 13, 475.

57. *Cap*.1, 155/68.

58. For instance, Ronald L. Meek, *Studies in the Labour Theory of Value* (New York: Monthly Review Press, 1956), 148–49, 299–305.

59. Karl Marx, *A Contribution to the Critique of Political Economy*, *MECW* 29, 269/ *MEGA2* II.2, 107. See also, *Gr*, 881/740.

60. In the *Grundrisse*, Marx rejects the false concretion of political economy which starts with "the real and the concrete," i.e. population, wages etc., 100/35–36. Accordingly, this is a false abstraction which presupposes too much. However, in the *Contribution to the Critique of Political Economy* and in *Capital* Marx advances from the starting point he offers in the *Grundrisse* of "material production" (*Gr*, 83/21), by beginning with the commodity and its form of value as the logical form specific to capital.

61. Marx uses the same quotation in his discussion of exchange at the beginning of chapter 2, in the simple opposition of use and exchange between buyer and sellers of commodities, *Cap*.1, 179/91.

62. *Pol* 1257a6–15; Marx, *A Contribution to the Critique of Political Economy*, 269/107.

63. *Pol* 1257b32–35; 1258a15–19.

64. *EE* 1219a3–13.

65. Jill Frank, *A Democracy of Distinction* (Chicago: University of Chicago Press, 2004), 85.

66. *Cap*.1a, 49/626. Replaced with *Doppelform* in the second edition.

67. Marx's attentiveness to this point bears strong comparison with MacIntyre's portrayal of the erosion of ancient moral categories in modernity, as I discussed in chapter 2.

68. *Cap*.1, 181/93.

69. Moishe Postone, *Time, Labor, and Social Domination: A Reinterpretation of Marx's Critical Theory* (Cambridge: Cambridge University Press, 1993), 139.

70. *RIPP*, 975/51–52.

71. *Cap*.3, 954/867.

72. *Cap*.1, 125/39.

73. *Gr*, 100/36.

74. This emphasis on the "abstract-reified form of social labour" makes clear that the concept of alienation is present at the very start of *Capital*, Jairus Banaji, "From the Commodity to Capital: Hegel's Dialectic in Marx's *Capital*" in *Value*, ed. Diane Elson, 39–40.

75. *RIPP*, 1059/30.

76. The distinction between "value" and "exchange value" often goes unnoticed. For instance, Frederick Neuhouser flattens value to exchange value, *Diagnosing Social Pathology: Rousseau, Hegel, Marx, and Durkheim* (Cambridge: Cambridge University Press, 2023), 60. However by doing so, it overlooks the dialectic of essence (abstract value-producing labour) and appearance (money) in Marx's account. The value-form enables value to be actualised as exchange value.

77. *Cap*.1, 125/39.
78. *Cap*.1a, 7/17.
79. *NW*, 242/370.
80. *Cap*.1, 126/40.
81. *Cap*.1a/17.
82. *Cap*.1, 126/40–41.
83. *Cap*.1, 127/41.
84. *Cap*.1, 128/42. Arthur argues that Marx brings in labour too early, risking "the appearance of model-building," *New Dialectic*, 85. Considering abstract labour is implicit in the commodity, this objection is groundless.
85. *Cap*.1, 677/562.
86. *Cap*.1, 128/42.
87. *Cap*.1, 138–39/52.
88. *Metaphysics* 1025b29–1026a4.
89. *Cap*.1, 132/46.
90. *Cap*.1, 139–40/53.
91. *Cap*.1, 147/61.
92. *Cap*.1, 149/62–63.
93. *Cap*.1, 196/107. See also Karl Marx, "Economic Manuscript of 1861–3," *MECW* 31, 12/*MEGA2* II.3.2, 443.
94. *NW*, 230/358; Karl Marx to Ludwig Kugelmann, 11 July 1868, *MECW* 43, 69/*MEW* 32 553.
95. Karl Marx, "Economic Manuscript of 1861–3," *MECW* 32, 340–45/*MEGA2* II.3.4, 1336–43; *Gr*, 140/75.
96. See Murray, *Mismeasure of Wealth*, 439; Smith, *Beyond Liberal Egalitarianism*, 81–82; Heinrich, *An Introduction*, 64.
97. Craig Smith, *Adam Smith* (Cambridge: Polity, 2020), 113.
98. *Cap*.2, 452/378.
99. Marx, *A Contribution to the Critique of Political Economy*, 299/137; "Economic Manuscript of 1861–3," 265/*MEGA2* II.3.4, 1264–65. For Smith's most discussed formulation, Adam Smith, *An Inquiry into the Nature and Causes of the Wealth of Nations*, vol. 1 (Indianapolis: Liberty Fund, 1981), I.v.1–3. More sympathetic is Samuel Fleischacker's *On Adam Smith's Wealth of Nations: A Philosophical Companion* (Princeton, NJ: Princeton University Press, 2009), 125–31.
100. Smith, *Wealth of Nations*, I.i.ii
101. *Cap*.2, 451/378.
102. Smith, *Wealth of Nations*, I.i.5–8.
103. Martijn Konings argues that Smith shapes the secular vision and fantasy of "activities centered on money-dealing" characteristic of modern economics with the idea that money is the ideal medium of exchange in a neutral market organised by the invisible hand, *Capital and Time: For a New Critique of Neoliberal Reason* (Stanford, CA: Stanford University Press, 2018), 57–58.

104. *Cap*.1, 470–75/368–73; Isaak Illich Rubin, *A History of Economic Thought* (London: Ink Links, 1979), 169. Ellen Meiksins Wood interprets Smith's "commercialization model" and idea of progress as transhistorical, technological determinism, *The Origins of Capitalism* (London: Verso, 2002).

105. See Adam Smith, *The Theory of Moral Sentiments* (Indianapolis: Liberty Fund, 1983), VI.ii.I.1–ii.3.6. Smith takes issue with Aristotle's conception of virtue, VII.ii.I.12–17. On Smith and Hume, see Dennis C. Rasmussen, *The Infidel and the Professor* (Princeton, NJ: Princeton University Press, 2017), 160–85.

106. For instance, Smith, *The Theory of Moral Sentiments*, II.i.1.1–5; VII.i–ii.4. In decisive challenges to the so-called "Adam Smith Problem" many scholars have pointed out the need to read *Wealth of Nations* in light of *The Theory of Moral Sentiments*. See Istvan Hont, *Politics in Commercial Society* (Cambridge, MA: Harvard University Press, 2015), 25–40; Axel Honneth, *Recognition: A Chapter in the History of European Ideas* (Cambridge: Cambridge University Press 2021), 69; Charles L. Griswold, *Adam Smith and the Virtues of Enlightenment* (Cambridge: Cambridge University Press, 1999), 259–66.

107. Alasdair MacIntyre, *Dependent Rational Animals* (London: Duckworth, 1999), 119.

108. Honneth is wrong to insist that Smith's "philosophical aim was to counter the spread of capitalistic convictions by formulating relations of recognition that always already join us to each other," *Recognition*, 84. For an account of Smith's "powerful *economic* justification for the untrammelled pursuit of individual self-interest," see Albert O. Hirschman, *The Passions and the Interests* (Princeton, NJ: Princeton University Press, 2013), 100. Fleischacker, on the other hand, suggests "there need be no difficulty in bringing *homo moralis* and *homo economicus* together," *On Adam Smith's Wealth of Nations*, 83, also 84–99 and 55–57.

109. *Cap*.1, 468/365; Rubin, *A History of Economic Thought*, 170.

110. Smith, *Wealth of Nations*, I.ii.3.

111. Rubin, *History of Economic Thought*, 179.

112. *Cap*.2, 453/379–80; 504/432.

113. *Cap*.1, 132/46.

114. *Cap*.1, 133/47.

115. David Ricardo, *On the Principles of Political Economy and Taxation* (London: Penguin, 1971), 55–57.

116. Ricardo, 75–76.

117. See Marx, "Economic Manuscript of 1861–3," *MECW* 31, 389–99/*MEGA2* II.3.3, 815–25.

118. Meek, *Studies in the Labour Theory of Value*, 118–20, 177.

119. *NW*, 231/358. Also, Postone, *Time, Labor, Social Domination*, 192.

120. "As "use-value on the social scale," "social need" reflects "simply the same law" that individual commodities exhibit, they must have a use-value to be an exchange value and express value. *Cap*.3, 774/686.

121. Rubin, *Essays on Marx's Theory of Value*, 69.

122. *Cap*.1, 434/332.

123. This limits political economy to the view that only labour, and not capital, is produc-

tive, which according to Marx, means "they do not conceive capital in its *specific character as form*, as a *relation of production* reflected into itself, but think only about its material substance, raw material etc. But these material elements do not make capital into capital." *Gr*, 309/228.

124. *Cap*.1, 173–74/85–86. "The value-form of the product of labour is the most abstract, but also the most universal form of the bourgeois mode of production; by that fact it stamps the bourgeois mode of production as a particular kind of social production of a historical and transitory character. If then we make the mistake of treating it as the eternal natural form of social production, we necessarily overlook the specificity of the value-form, and consequently of the commodity-form together with its further developments, the money form, the capital form, etc." *Cap*.1, 174n34/85n31.

125. *Cap*.1, 174/86.
126. Clarke, *Marx, Marginalism and Modern Sociology*, 67–68.
127. *Cap*.3, 368/288.
128. *Gr*, 156/89.
129. *Cap*.1, 148/61.
130. *Cap*.1, 139/53.
131. *Cap*.1, 140/54.
132. *Cap*.1a, 50/627.
133. *Cap*.1a, 52/629.
134. *Cap*.1, 142/56
135. *Cap*.1a, 52/630.
136. *Cap*.1, 142/56.
137. *Cap*.1a, 56–57/634.
138. *NW*, 243/370.
139. *Cap*.1, 148/61.
140. *Cap*.1a, 57/635.
141. *Cap*.1a, 56/635.
142. *Cap*.1, 149/63.
143. *Cap*.1, 151/64.
144. *NW*, 242/369.

145. *Cap*.1, 486/383. Marx echoes Aristotle when he criticises the division of labour in Plato's *Republic* and the "many-sidedness of the needs of individuals" compared to "the-one sidedness of their capabilities" which curtails Plato's understanding of Athenian society, 486–89/383–86.

146. *Cap*.1, 150/64
147. *EE* 1217b30–31.
148. *Pol* 1258b21–28.
149. *Pol* 1258b9–32.

150. I agree with Stefan Eich that between *Pol* and *NE*, Aristotle's analysis of money does not vary wildly and should be assessed together as bearing upon the normativity of wealth, *The Currency of Politics: The Political Theory of Money from Aristotle to Keynes* (Princeton, NJ: Princeton University Press, 2022), 26.

151. *NE* 1129a4–10.

152. Frank, *Democracy of Distinction*, 81.

153. There is widespread recognition that Aristotle's discussion of justice and commercial exchange in some way anticipates Marx's idea of value. See Anthony Kenny, Introduction to *EE*, xxvi, 165n. Notwithstanding generally vague suggestions, most commentators see Aristotle's discussion as confused and unworthy of serious consideration. Further, in Kenny's case, he thinks this discussion possibly "makes Aristotle an early advocate for the free market economy" (165n). The framing argument of Scott Meikle's *Aristotle's Economic Thought* (Oxford: Oxford University Press, 1994) is a critique of Anglophone scholarship that paints Aristotle in this light. Other work that challenges such assumptions include: M. I. Finley, "Aristotle and Economic Analysis" in *Studies in Ancient Society*, ed. M. I. Finley (London: Routledge and Kegan Paul, 1974), 26–52; G.E.M. de Ste. Croix, *The Class Struggle in the Ancient Greek World* (Ithaca, NY: Cornell University Press, 1981), 69–80; Frank, *A Democracy of Distinction*; Todd S. Mei, "The Preeminence of Use: Revaluating the Relation Between Use and Exchange in Aristotle's Economic Thought," *Journal of the History of Philosophy* 47:4 (2009): 523–48; Murray, *Mismeasure of Wealth*, 42–7; Eich, *The Currency of Politics*, 22–46.

154. *Cap*.1, 151/64; *NE* 1133b25. For a systematic reconstruction, see Meikle, *Aristotle's Economic Thought*, 6–42.

155. *NE* 1132b32. The *NE* shares books 5, 6 and 7 with *EE* 4, 5 and 6. Where Irwin translates "communities for exchange" and C.D.C Reeve as "communities based on exchange," Kenny renders this passage as "commercial association." This translation gives Aristotle's meaning an unwarranted and modern implication, *EE* 1132b32.

156. *NE* 1132b35.

157. *NE* 1133a9–14.

158. *NE* 1133b6–10.

159. *NE* 1133a15–19.

160. *EE* 1133a19–20.

161. *NE* 1133a25.

162. This is clear again in *EE*, "one party claims the value of money at the time of lending, and the other the value at the time of repayment" (1243a27–32), and "we must measure by a single standard, but a ratio rather than a number. We must measure by a proportion, in the way that a civic partnership is measured. How can a cobbler do business with a farmer, unless their products are equalised by proportion? In cases where exchanges are not of like for like, measurements must be by proportion" (1243b30–32).

163. Aristotle uses *nomisma*, meaning "legal currency," rather than the word for money, *chrēmata*. For the political impact of these terms, see Eich, *The Currency of Politics*, 27–29.

164. *NE* 1133a30–32.

165. Trott, *Aristotle on the Nature of the Community*, 13.

166. Meikle, *Aristotle's Economic Thought*, 14–15. For the growth of money as a "real abstraction" in Ancient Athens, see Alfred Sohn-Rethel, *Intellectual and Manual Labour: A Critique of Epistemology* (New Jersey: Humanities Press, 1978), 94–103; Richard Seaford,

"Monetisation and the Genesis of the Western Subject," *Historical Materialism* 20:1 (2012): 78–102.

167. *Cap.*1, 151/65.

168. *Cap.*1, 151/65.

169. *LHP* 1, 49/68.

170. For a seminal discussion of ancient slavery in relation to its social from of surplus extraction, see Ste. Croix, *The Class Struggle in the Ancient Greek World*, 49–55.

171. *NW*, 232/359.

172. *Cap.*1, 179/91.

173. *Cap.*1, 151–52/65.

174. *Cap.*1, 153–54/67. How can Marx praise Aristotle's foresight but then claim its historical impossibility? Castoriadis argues this conclusion is a nonsequitur and results from Marx's inability to resolve the tension between Aristotle's idea of *physis* (nature) and *nomos* (law), which becomes a metaphysical antinomy. Castoriadis rejects that the substance of value is abstract labour and mistakenly conceives Marx's critique as one of distribution rather than production. While he affirms the Aristotelian problematic Marx is steeped in, Castoriadis's core claim is weakened by the unsubstantiated assertion that Marx's idea of substance is transhistorical. See "Value, Equality, Justice, Politics: From Marx to Aristotle and from Aristotle to Ourselves," 260–339. In reply, Agnes Heller compares Castoriadis to MacIntyre and Arendt suggesting "[t]he modern person can conjure up Aristotle as either a hostile or a kindred spirit in relation to modernity. Castoriadis, similar to Arendt, chose the second path, MacIntyre the first," "With Castoriadis to Aristotle; From Aristotle to Kant; From Kant to Us," *Revue Européenne des Sciences Sociales* 27:86 (1989): 162. Heller captures something important about Arendt's and MacIntyre's use of Aristotle. As I see it, Arendt's "kindred spirit" approach preserves the Aristotelian division between labour and action in modernity, whereas MacIntyre's "hostile" Aristotle contrasts the teleological practices of the virtues with modern morality and its social structures.

175. *Cap.*1, 166/79.

176. *Gr*, 145/79.

177. Alasdair MacIntyre affirms this view: "When he moves beyond Aristotle, in order to understand the distinctive economic forms and development of the modern world, he still employs key concepts as Aristotle used them: essence, potentiality, goal directedness," *Ethics in the Conflicts of Modernity: An Essay on Desire, Practical Reasoning, and Narrative* (Cambridge: Cambridge University Press, 2016), 94.

178. Karl Marx to Friedrich Engels, 27 June 1867, *MECW* 42, 392–93/*MEW* 31, 314–46.

179. *Cap.*1, 155/68.

180. *SL*, 126/*W* 5, 174.

181. *SL*, 135–6/*W* 5, 186–87.

182. *SL*, 154/*W* 5, 211–12.

183. *Cap.*1, 155/68.

184. *Cap.*1, 162/74–75.

185. *Cap*.1, 162/74–75.

186. "In antiquity, one could buy labour, a slave, directly; but the slave could not buy money with his labour. The increase of money could make slaves more expensive, but could not make their labour more productive," *Gr*, 224/149.

187. Money is a measure and means of circulation, which must represent commodities while also acting as a commodity itself. All four functions of money establish that money is the expression of value—requiring it is distinct from other commodities as the universal equivalent and objectification of value, *Gr*, 146/80. Further, capital is the unity of the production process and circulation, *Gr*, 320/237. For Aristotle, money is only the common measure for exchange, *NE* 1163b34–37.

188. *Cap*.1, 185/96–97; 224/134; *Gr*, 170/101.

189. *Gr*, 144/79.

190. *U*, 438/26.

191. *Cap*.1, 183/95.

192. *Gr*, 157/90.

193. *Gr*, 149/83.

194. *Cap*.1, 192/103.

195. For the religious connotations of "fetishism," see Michael Heinrich, *How to Read Marx's* Capital (New York: Monthly Review Press, 2021), 143–44.

196. *Gr*, 160/93.

197. *U*, 431/20.

198. *Cap*.1, 163/76. "After money is posited as a commodity in reality, the commodity is posited as money in the mind," *Gr*, 191/121.

199. *Cap*.1, 163–64/76.

200. See *Cap*.1, 165/78.

201. *Gr*, 157/90.

202. Murray warns against "use-value Romanticism," *Mismeasure of Wealth*, 50, 313–34.

203. *Cap*.1, 164/77. The organicism is more explicit in the 1867: productive activities are "functions of a specifically *human* organism as distinguished from *other* organisms, and that every such function, whatever its content and its form, is essentially *expenditure* of *human* brain, nerve, muscle, organ of perception, etc." *Cap*.1a, 34/40.

204. *Cap*.1, 164/77.

205. *Cap*.1, 164/77.

206. *Cap*.1, 164–65/77–78.

207. *Cap*.1, 166/78.

208. *Cap*.1, 167/79–80.

209. Theodor W. Adorno and Max Horkheimer, *Towards a New Manifesto* (London: Verso, 2019), 54.

210. The distinction but inseparability between the commodity and commodity fetishism makes impossible the viability of a base/superstructure model for understanding Marx's social theory. Not only does this model rely upon a dualistic and causal determinism, but if

the commodity and its fetishism come from the same moment, base/superstructure is inadequate in grasping the beginning of Marx's understanding of capital.

211. *Cap.*1, 182/93.
212. *Cap.*1, 187/98–99.
213. *U,* 430/19. My emphasis.
214. *Cap.*1, 187/98–99.
215. *Cap.*3, 649/562. Marx notes this significance in relation to monetary crises.
216. *Cap.*1, 248/153.
217. *Cap.*1, 227/135.
218. Roman Rosdolsky, *The Making of Marx's* Capital (London: Pluto, 1977), 97–166; Suzanne de Brunhoff, *Marx on Money* (London: Verso, 2015), 19–48.
219. *Cap.*1, 241/148. Marx has great interest in the history of money, see *Cap.*3, 431–39/346–54; *Gr,* 163–185/95–115.
220. *Cap.*3, 1003/918. See also, *Cap.*2, 416/342. Cf. *SL,* 670/*W* 6, 462.
221. *Cap.*1, 187/99.
222. As Marx writes, "thus capital does not originally realise itself—precisely because the appropriation of alien labour [*fremde Arbeit*] is not itself included in its concept. Capital appears only afterwards, after already having been presupposed as capital—a vicious circle—*as command over alien labour*. Thus, according to A. Smith, labour should actually have its own product for wages, wages should be = to the product, hence labour should not be wage-labour and capital not capital. Therefore, in order to introduce profit and rent as original elements of the cost of production, i.e. in order to get a surplus value out of the capitalist production process, he *presupposes* [my emphasis] them, in the clumsiest fashion." *Gr,* 330/245.
223. Clarke, *Marx, Marginalism and Modern Sociology,* 78.
224. *Gr,* 536/435; *Cap.*2, 185/100.
225. *Cap.*2, 291/209.
226. Smith, *Beyond Liberal Egalitarianism,* 80; Murray, *Mismeasure of Value,* 19.
227. *Cap.*2, 223/140–41.
228. *Cap.*1, 200–209/111–19.
229. *Cap.*1, 230–31/138–39.
230. *Cap.*1, 247–48/153–54.
231. *Cap.*1, 253/159.
232. *Cap.*1, 253/159.
233. *Cap.*1, 253–54n6/159–60n6. See also, *Pol* 1256a1–1258b10.
234. Many translators give this term a modern rendering as "retail trade."
235. *Pol* 1256b40–42.
236. *Pol* 1257b20–41.
237. This is confirmed in the *Urtext,* "Aristotle regards the form of circulation C–M–C, in which money functions only as measure and coin—a movement which he calls economic—as natural and reasonable, and brands the form M–C–M, the chrematistic one, as unnatural and inappropriate," *U,* 488/74.

238. *Cap*.1, 267/172.
239. *Categories* 3a20.
240. *PhG*, ¶18, 12–13/23.
241. *Cap*.1, 255/161.
242. *Cap*.1, 255/161.
243. *Gr*, 590/481.
244. This part of the text (*Cap*.1, 255–56/161–62) is crucial for the value-form interpretation. See Postone, *Time, Labor, Social Domination*, 71–75; Murray, *Marx's Theory of Scientific Knowledge*, 216; Arthur, *New Dialectic*, 137–52; Smith, *Beyond Liberal Egalitarianism*, 110–12; Heinrich, *How to Read Marx's* Capital, 296–301.
245. *Cap*.1, 256/162.
246. Postone, *Time, Labor, Social Domination*, 75.
247. Smith, *Beyond Liberal Egalitarianism*, 112.
248. Neuhouser, *Diagnosing Social Pathology*, 61–62.
249. Rose, *Hegel Contra Sociology*, 232.
250. *Cap*.2, 185/101; *Cap*.3, 476/388.
251. *Gr*, 258/180.
252. Postone, *Time, Labor, and Social Domination*, 156.
253. Smith, *Beyond Liberal Egalitarianism*, 129.
254. *Cap*.1, 182/93.
255. *Cap*.1, 283–84/185–86.
256. Postone tries to side-step the problems this passage might have for his anti-ontological interpretation by omitting the full quotation and insisting the appearance of an ontological position is due to the presentation, *Time, Labor, and Social Domination*, 279.
257. For "metabolism" as the "mediation of nature through society," see Alfred Schmidt, *The Concept of Nature in Marx* (London: NLB, 1971), 76–94. An ecological strain of Marx scholarship has stressed this idea, see Kohei Saito, *Marx's Ecosocialism* (New York: Monthly Review Press, 2017), 98–137.
258. My argument in this paragraph draws on Martin Hägglund's ontological distinction between human beings as rational animals and non-rational animal life, *This Life: Secular Faith and Spiritual Freedom* (New York: Pantheon Books, 2019), 174–81 and Terry Pinkard's discussion of Hegel's recasting of Aristotle's idea of the soul, *Hegel's Naturalism: Mind, Nature, and the Final Ends of Life* (Oxford: Oxford University Press, 2012), 25–33.
259. Marx has in mind Bernard Mandeville's parable for the virtues of economic self-interest, *The Fable of the Bees or Private Vices, Publick Benefits* (Indianapolis: Liberty Fund, 1988), 62–75.
260. *Cap*.1, 284/186.
261. *EPM*, 328–29/241.
262. *Gr*, 243/166–67.
263. *Cap*.1, 286–88/188–90.
264. Of Heraclitus' "metamorphosis of fire," Hegel writes that "[t]hese are thus not

still, dead starts, but are regarded as in Becoming, as being eternally productive," *LHP* 1, 289/332.

265. *Cap*.1, 289/191.

266. Murray points out the difference between the "general abstraction" used by political economy, which naturalises wage-labour and Marx's "determinate abstraction" which uses an *abstract* category of analysis to grasp *abstract labour* under capitalism, see *Marx's Theory of Scientific Knowledge*, 121–29.

267. *Cap*.1, 290/192.

268. *Cap*.1, 290/192.

269. *Cap*.3, 182/109.

270. Postone, *Time, Labor, and Social Domination*, 144.

271. Marx, "Theses on Feuerbach," 423/6.

272. Postone, *Time, Labor, and Social Domination*, 328.

273. *Cap*.1, 291–92/193.

274. *Cap*.1, 293/195.

275. *Gr*, 724/600.

276. *Cap*.1, 316–32/216–32.

277. *Cap*.1, 296/197.

278. *Cap*.1, 302/203.

279. See *Cap*.1, 308/209.

280. Murray, *Mismeasure of Wealth*, 420; Nesbitt, *The Price of Slavery*, 183.

281. *Cap*.1, 434–35/332–33. For abstract time, see Postone, *Time, Labor, and Social Domination*, 190–200.

282. *Cap*.1, 439/337.

283. *Cap*.1, 151/64.

284. *Cap*.1, 439/337.

285. *Cap*.1, 440/337.

286. *Cap*.1, 443/340.

287. *Cap*.1, 444/342. Earlier, Marx approvingly references Benjamin Franklin's definition of human beings as "tool-making animals," *Cap*.1, 286/188. Cf. Max Weber's discussion of Franklin's utilitarianism and view of man as a money-making animal "devoid of all eudemonistic" motivations, *The Protestant Ethic and the "Spirit" of Capitalism and Other Writings* (London: Penguin, 2002), 9–13.

288. "The human being is in the most literal sense a ζῷον πολιτικόν, not merely a gregarious animal, but an animal which can individuate itself only in the midst of society," *Gr*, 84/22.

289. *EE* 1242a22–28.

290. This is what Marx means with his critique of Adolph Wagner's empty concept of "man": "he has in general, 'no' needs; if it is man who confronts nature as an individual, then he is to be understood as a non-herd animal; if it is man situated in any form of society," *NW*, 235/362.

291. *Cap*.1, 447/345.

292. *Cap*.1, 448–49/346. Marx furthers his analysis of supervision by drawing on Aristotle in *Cap*.3, 507–9/419–20; *M*, 487–88.

293. The reproduction of labour-power occurs for the "immediate production process" and "total social reproduction," Lise Vogel, *Marxism and the Oppression of Women: Toward a Unitary Theory* (New Brunswick, NJ: Rutgers University Press, 1983), 140.

294. *Cap*.1, 552–53/448–49.

295. See Ellen Meiksins Wood, *Democracy Against Capitalism* (Cambridge: Cambridge University Press, 1995), 19–48 and William Clare Roberts's important critique of "moralized accounts of exploitation," *Marx's Inferno: A Political Theory of* Capital (Princeton, NJ: Princeton University Press, 2017), 144. However, such claims should not be misunderstood as implying that capitalism has not always relied on direct cohesion.

296. *RIPP*, 949/24.

297. *RIPP*, 1051/118.

298. *Cap*.1, 148/61.

Conclusion

1. *Cap*.1, 168–69/81.

2. For a sweeping narrative, see Sven Beckert, *Empire of Cotton: A Global History* (London: Penguin, 2014). Also, Eric Williams, *Slavery and Capitalism* (Chapel Hill: University of North Carolina Press, 2021), 50–56.

3. *Cap*.1, 599/495. This phrase appears in English. In particular, Marx focuses upon the exploitation of women and children.

4. *Cap*.1, 142/56.

5. *Cap*.1, 143/56–57.

6. *Cap*.1, 199/110.

7. *Cap*.1, 165/78.

8. *CM*, 499/476.

9. Karl Marx, "Letters from the Franco-German Yearbooks," in *EW*, 208–9/*MEGA2* III.1, 56.

10. The role of community occupied Marx's thought till the very end, see Marcello Musto, *The Last Years of Karl Marx: An Intellectual Biography* (Stanford, CA: Stanford University Press, 2020), 49–76.

11. Karl Marx, "Critical Notes on the Article 'The King of Prussia and Social Reform. By a Prussian'" in *EW*, 418–19/*MEGA2* I.2, 462.

12. Marx, 415/459.

13. Heinrich Heine, "Die schlesischen Weber" in *Selected Verse* (London: Penguin, 1968), 148–49. A revolt of some thousands of weavers in June 1844 was prompted by the arrest of a weaver singing these words, Michael Löwy, *The Theory of Revolution in the Young Marx* (Chicago: Haymarket, 2005), 82n69.

14. Heine sent Marx the poem shortly before fleeing Germany; his letter to Marx from 21 September 1844 is untranslated into English (*MEGA2* III.1, 443–44). For the Marx-Heine connection, see David Leopold, *The Young Karl Marx: German Philosophy, Modern Politics,*

and Human Flourishing (Cambridge: Cambridge University Press, 2007), 26–32. Heine is a frequent reference in *The Holy Family* and the 1845/6 "German Ideology" manuscripts.

15. Stathis Kouvelakis, *Philosophy and Revolution: From Kant to Marx* (London: Verso, 2003), 46–47. For Heine's ironic style and relationship to Hegelian philosophy, see Terry Pinkard's Introduction to Heinrich Heine, *On the History of Religion and Philosophy in Germany and Other Writings* (Cambridge: Cambridge University Press, 2012), vii–xxxii.

16. Theodor W. Adorno, "Heine the Wound" in *Notes to Literature*, vol. 1 (New York: Columbia University Press, 1991), 82.

17. Not to mention the development of the working class as a "class" with "tailors here and weavers there" in E. P. Thompson's *The Making of the English Working Class* (London: Penguin, 1980), 8.

18. Theodor W. Adorno draws on Heine to make this point in reference to Freud, see *Minima Moralia: Reflections from Damaged Life* (London: New Left Books, 1974), §37, 61.

19. Adorno, §147, 229, also §146, 226–27.

20. Adorno, 15.

21. Theodor W. Adorno refers to *Minima Moralia* as a work on "the good—or rather the bad—life," *Problems of Moral Philosophy* (Stanford, CA: Stanford University Press, 2000), 1.

22. Adorno, *Minima Moralia*, §17–18, 37–39.

23. *PR*, 11/13–14.

24. J. M. Bernstein, *Adorno: Disenchantment and Ethics* (Cambridge: Cambridge University Press, 2001), 40, 58–70.

25. Bernstein, 41.

26. Fabian Freyenhagen emphasises his "negative Aristotelian," *Adorno's Practical Philosophy: Living Less Wrongly* (Cambridge: Cambridge University Press, 2013), see especially 232–54.

27. Adorno, *Minima Moralia*, §84, 130.

28. Adorno, §99, 153.

29. Adorno, §146, 228.

30. Adorno, §58, 95, §66, 102–3.

31. For a refutation of this kind of view, see Peter E. Gordon, *A Precarious Happiness: Adorno and the Sources of Normativity* (Chicago: University of Chicago Press, 2023), 7–40.

32. Adorno, *Minima Moralia*, §116, 180.

33. Theodor W. Adorno, "Theses on Need," *New Left Review* 2/128 (March/April 2021), 81.

34. Gordon makes this argument in connection to Aristotle, Hegel, Marx and MacIntyre, *A Precarious Happiness*, 69–72.

35. Adorno, *Minima Moralia*, §66, 103.

36. Adorno, *Notes to Literature*, vol. 1 (New York: Columbia University Press, 1991), 85.

37. He sees this form of life as "human society, or social humanity," Karl Marx, "Theses on Feuerbach," in *EW*, 423/*MEW* 3, 7.

38. *Cap*.1, 228/136.

39. *Cap*.1, 201/111.

40. *Gr*, 528/428.
41. *Cap*.1, 275. Also, *Gr*, 325/241.
42. Adorno, "Theses on Need," 79.
43. *Cap*.3, 999/914–15.
44. *Gr*, 409/322.
45. Agnes Heller, *The Theory of Need in Marx* (London: Allison and Busby, 1976), 97.
46. *Gr*, 488/392.
47. *Gr*, 489/393, 709/579. Marx notes that "the labour of the individual is from the very beginning posited as social labour." *Gr*, 172/103.
48. As value circulates on the market as capital, the turnover of capital imposes an increasingly abstract and empty linear time in the fragmented circuits of sale and purchase. The turnover of time (the unity of production time and circulation time of capital) determines the time from the advance of capital value and its valorisation "as it passes through different forms of existence in the course of its circuit," *Cap*.2, 233/150.
49. Theodor W. Adorno, "Free Time" in *Critical Models* (New York: Columbia University Press, 1998), 173–75.
50. *Gr*, 172–73/103–4.
51. See the discussion in Martin Hägglund, *This Life: Secular Faith and Spiritual Freedom* (New York: Pantheon Books, 2019), 260–69.
52. *Cap*.1, 532/428.
53. Tony Smith, *Beyond Liberal Egalitarianism: Marx and Normative Social Theory in the Twenty-First Century* (Leiden: Brill, 2017), 292, 139–43.
54. *Cap*.1, 532/428.
55. *Gr*, 702/578.
56. *Cap*.1, 638/531.
57. Robert B. Pippin, *Modernism as a Philosophical Problem* (Oxford: Blackwell, 1991), 149.
58. *Gr*, 703/579.
59. *Cap* 1, 532/428; *Pol* 1253b30–1254a18.
60. *HC*, 121–22.
61. *Gr*, 297/217.
62. *NE* 1139a29–30.
63. See Christopher J. Arthur, *The New Dialectic and Marx's* Capital (Leiden: Brill, 2004), 225–41.
64. Theodor W. Adorno and Max Horkheimer, *Towards a New Manifesto* (London: Verso, 2019), 54.
65. *EE* 1219b6.
66. *EE* 1214a13.

Index

Abbott, Mathew, 209
Abensour, Miguel, 40, 72
abstract labour, 12, 31, 178, 196, 220, 226–27, 232, 234, 235–37, 240, 257, 261, 263, 264; alienation and value-form theory linked by, 6, 22, 62–63, 222, 223, 269; concrete labour and, 185, 186, 235, 241–43, 253; defined, 5; Marx's critique of, 209; measures of, 183, 184, 187, 255, 286
Adorno, Theodor W., 15, 17, 32, 180, 184, 254, 279–83, 285, 321–22n132
After Virtue (*AV*, MacIntyre): 28, 29; Aristotelian roots of, 92, 96–99, 106, 107; disagreement analyzed in, 83–84; Enlightenment critiqued in, 86, 88, 90–91, 94; fact/value distinction in, 91; individual vs. community in, 82, 106–7; Kant critiqued in, 88–89; Marxist roots of, 77–78, 80–82, 92–95, 102–5, 108, 115, 189; modernity in, 77, 100–101, 105–7; response to Rawls, 79
Agamben, Giorgio, 164
alienation: Hegel's view of, 135, 136, 138; MacIntyre's view of, 108-15; Marx's view of, 3, 6–11, 14, 20, 22, 30, 31, 54, 59, 60–65, 176, 194–96, 202, 205, 208, 210-11, 222, 223, 254–55, 262–63, 277, 288-90; Rousseau's view of, 169; value-form theory linked to, 6, 22, 62–63, 222, 223, 269
Althusser, Louis, 3, 14, 210, 222, 223
American Revolution, 68, 73
Anderson, Benedict, 325–26n31
Antigone (Sophocles), 53, 97, 148, 275
Arendt, Hannah, 14, 27, 29, 208, 287–89; action theorized by, 42–43, 45, 50, 73, 74–75; Aristotle and Marx linked by, 50, 59, 119; class struggle dismissed by, 46; council movement viewed by, 42, 44, 72, 75, 120; determination and historical change linked by, 55; dialectics condemned by, 48, 50; Greek polis idealized by, 39, 42, 44, 74, 119–21; Hegel oversimplified by, 43, 48–49, 50–52; labour and praxis decoupled by, 44; MacIntyre's critique of modernity linked to, 119; Marx and Darwin linked by, 46, 48; Marx linked to, 66–67, 72;

Arendt, Hannah (*cont.*)
  Marx's Aristotelianism viewed by, 28; Marx's theory of labour refuted by, 40–47, 56–64; modern politics critiqued by, 39; as political protest theorist, 40; public vs. private realms distinguished by, 45, 57, 65, 74; social realm viewed by, 38; Stalinism analyzed by, 45–46; the *vita activa* viewed by, 38, 43–44, 45, 67, 68, 71

Aristotle: action and feeling linked by, 214–15; action and virtue linked by, 213; action vs. production distinguished by, 206; actuality vs. potentiality distinguished by, 205; "chrematistics" criticized by, 258–59; ethical virtue viewed by, 3–4, 25, 29, 121–23, 152; ethics and politics linked by, 149; *eudaimonia* theorized by, 4, 12–13, 15, 38, 45, 99, 120, 123–26, 151; freedom vs. necessity viewed by, 58; MacIntyre linked to, 77, 92–101, 105–7, 115–16, 120, 288; human being deemed political animal by, 272; Marx influenced by, 30–31, 41, 81, 83, 218; "political animal" theorized by, 45; quality of exchange and justice linked by, 244–45, 248; reciprocity explored by, 244, 245, 247, 248–49; slavery defended by, 106, 147, 206, 247; social ontology of, 3, 12–13, 30, 41, 43, 59, 77, 148, 222, 272; substance placed over subject by, 260; teleological ethics of, 122, 149–51, 154; unfreedom and, 122; wealth acquisition discussed by, 232

Backhaus, H. G., 216
Banaji, Jairus, 54–55, 233–34
Bauer, Bruno, 130
Benedict, Saint, abbot of Monte Cassino, 101, 104
Benhabib, Seyla, 42

Benjamin, Walter, 325–26n31
Bentham, Jeremy, 23–24
Bernstein, J. M., 280
Bloch, Ernst, 94, 210
Borradori, Giovanna, 76
Brandom, Robert, 24, 43, 52–54, 138
"Breaking the Chains of Reason" (MacIntyre), 114

Capital (Marx), 1, 32, 54, 56, 64, 166, 175-90, 188, 196, 201, 214, 240, 268; Aristotle's influence on, 4, 219, 222, 224, 244–48; communism discussed in, 103; as critical social theory, 221–28; exchange value in, 201, 232–33; Hegel's influence on, 4, 219, 222, 224–25; human essence in, 269; master-slave dialectic in, 175; materiality and abstraction linked in, 275; opening of, 229–37; theory of value in, 3, 4–5, 18, 26, 218, 237–48; use value in, 232–33
Castoriadis, Cornelius, 224, 336n64, 348n174
categorical imperative, 141, 143, 145, 284
Cavarero, Adriana, 40, 73
The Civil War in France (Marx), 67–71
Clarke, Simon, 203
class struggle, 216, 273; Arendt's view of, 46; Hegelian relation to, 41, 78; living labour linked to, 217; MacIntyre's view of, 93, 110–12, 115; as political struggle, 68; working-class agency linked to, 287–88
Coetzee, J. M., 163, 329n101
Comay, Rebecca, 155
"Comments on James Mill" (*CJM*, Marx), 198–204
communism, 10, 21, 50, 62, 65, 74, 103, 197-98, 205, 217, 283
Communist Manifesto (Marx and Engels), 68, 71, 217

A Contribution to the Critique of Political Economy (Marx), 232
council movement, 42, 44, 69, 72, 74–75, 120

Darwin, Charles, 46
De Anima (Aristotle), 131
Defoe, Daniel, 3, 30, 103, 159–66, 168, 169, 172–80
Democritus, 130
Diderot, Denis, 85, 90, 110
Discourse on Inequality (Rousseau), 168
division of labour, 139, 186-7, 211–12, 237-39, 270

Eagleton, Terry, 161
Economic and Philosophical Manuscripts of 1844 (*EPM*, Marx), 175, 194, 197–98, 267–68; alienation in, 208, 222, 223; capital defined in, 216; emotion viewed in, 214; "human essence" in, 204, 211, 222; Parisian working-class movement described in, 7–8
The Eighteenth Brumaire of Louis Bonaparte (Marx), 73, 92, 93
Émile (Rousseau), 163, 167–68
Encyclopedia of the Philosophical Sciences (Hegel), 2, 113
Engels, Friedrich, 56, 101, 211–14, 217, 237, 279, 337n97; theory of value viewed by, 1–2, 343-4n56
English Civil War, 86, 310n42
Enlightenment, 127, 136–37, 287; Aristotelianism contrasted with, 83; fragmented modern thought linked to, 7; Hegel's critique of, 13, 110, 231; MacIntyre's critique of, 79–80, 85–94, 96, 110; Marx linked to, 47; Marx's critique of, 222, 231; religious dogmatism vs., 136; social contract and, 11
Entäusserung. *See* alienation

Epicurus, 130
Ethics in the Conflicts of Modernity (MacIntyre), 106–8, 115
eudaimonia, 4, 38, 45, 77, 99, 120-21, 123–26, 151, 204, 217

Fanon, Franz, 330n115, 331n131
Feuerbach, Ludwig, 200, 336n61
Fichte, Johann Gottlieb, 129
Findlay, J. N., 78
First International, 68-9, 306n165
Foe (Coetzee), 163
Francis of Assisi, Saint, 101
Frank, Jill, 245
Frankfurt School, 17. *See* Adorno; Horkheimer
Forrester, Katrina, 79–80
Franklin, Benjamin, 272
Fraser, Nancy, 18, 305n150
French Revolution, 86–87, 114, 127-28, 132–33, 136-37, 193, 250
French Workers Party, 70
Freud, Sigmund, 1, 354n18
Friedman, Milton, 158–59, 190

Gattungswesen. *See* species being
Geist (spirit), 26, 41, 51-2, 133–34, 136, 154
The German Ideology (Marx and Engels), 55, 211–12, 222
Goethe, Johann Wolfgang von, 270
Goldmann, Lucien, 87–88, 128
Groundwork of the Metaphysics of Morals (Kant), 140–41
Grundrisse (Marx), 32, 175, 180–81, 196, 224, 241, 267–68, 272, 283, 286
Guesde, Jules, 70

Hägglund, Martin, 65, 155, 297n65
Hayek, Friedrich A. von, 160
Hegel, G.W.F., 2; "the absolute" posited by, 15–16, 25, 41, 123–24, 133, 146–47;

Hegel, G.W.F. (*cont.*)
"absolute" vs. "relative" ethical life distinguished by, 125, 146; action and deed theorized by, 43, 52; Adorno influenced by, 280; alienation analyzed by, 135, 136, 138; Arendt's misreading of, 43, 48–49, 50–52; as Aristotelian, 29, 121, 124–25, 132, 143, 146, 147–50; attraction and quantity linked by, 249; civil society viewed by, 11, 122, 124, 134, 135, 136, 140, 145–47, 155; dialectics of, 49; division of labour viewed by, 139; empiricism rejected by, 230; ethical life (*Sittlichkeit*) defined by, 4, 13, 15, 52–54, 123–26, 134, 137–56, 170, 280; growing interest in, 24; "inner universality" of, 174–75; Kantian morality viewed by, 140; Kant refuted by, 10, 134–35, 138, 141–44; language viewed by, 52; "living good" theorized by, 121; MacIntyre linked to, 78–79; Marx scholars' dismissal of, 14; Marx's dialectic linked to, 26; Marx's early criticisms of, 193; Marx's social thought linked to, 83, 274; mastery-servitude dialectic of, 171, 172–74, 175; as modernist, 132–37; morality vs. ethics distinguished by, 152; phenomenology of, 49–50; philosophy of right of, 135; the "rabble" discussed by, 155; rationality viewed by, 4, 81; recognition concept of, 51, 111, 112, 153, 160, 170–72, 174, 175; scientific thought viewed by, 229; social interdependence theorized by, 30, 160, 170–71, 174–75; sociality viewed by, 171; social recognition viewed by, 13, 30; spirit (*Geist*) viewed by, 133–34, 136, 154; substance and subject linked by, 260, 261; universality viewed by, 135

Hegel Contra Sociology (Rose), 25–26
Heine, Heinrich, 279
Heinrich, Michael, 222–23, 314n134, 339n20

Heller, Agnes, 210, 284, 348n174
Heraclitus, 156
Hesiod, 208
The Hidden God (Goldmann), 87, 88
Hill, Christopher, 161
Hobbes, Thomas, 11, 30, 142, 159, 163–65, 171, 174, 181–83
Holocaust, 281
Homer, 73, 97
Honneth, Axel, 203, 295n37, 316n20, 327n62, 345n108
Horkheimer, Max, 180, 184, 296-7n51
The Human Condition (Arendt): antiquity vs. modernity distinguished by, 29, 119-20; early lectures linked to, 47; erosion of public life deplored by, 38, 40, 57, 120; Marx's glorification of labour rejected by, 41, 45; Marx's Hegelianism rejected by, 28, 48; Marx's social ontology rejected by, 28, 40, 43; plurality of action, 37, 38, 44–45, 70, 120
Hume, David, 83, 85, 86, 90, 126, 238
Hungary: uprising in, 39, 72; workers' councils in, 78

Idealism, 7, 14, 87, 128, 131, 132, 222
"Ideology and Terror" (Arendt), 46–47
Immanuel Kant (Goldmann), 87, 88
Industrial Revolution, 127

Jaeggi, Rahel, 18, 22, 28, 53, 111, 195–97
Jaffe, Aaron, 206
James, C.L.R., 175, 294n21, 307n195, 319n73, 329n103, 330n115
Jameson, Fredric, 297n65
Jaspers, Karl, 37
July Revolution (1830), 86

Kant, Immanuel, 15, 83–90, 110, 123, 124, 128-29; categorical imperative of, 141, 143, 145; deposit example of, 144; duty viewed by, 140–41; enlightenment

viewed by, 137; ethical life vs. morality distinguished by, 126; Hegel's refutation of, 10, 134–35, 138, 141–45; practical vs. theoretical critique of, 131
Keynes, John Maynard, 160
Kojève, Alexandre, 49, 330n118
Konings, Martijn, 18
Korsgaard, Christine M., 320n101, 335n54
Kosman, Aryeh, 98
Krader, Lawrence, 163–64
Kritische Gesamtausgabe (Arendt), 41

labour theory of value, 3, 10, 24, 166; Marx's critique of, 12, 30, 31, 167, 185, 186–87, 218–19, 237–43, 255
Lear, Jonathan, 143, 320n101
Leviathan (Hobbes), 161, 162, 320n101
Locke, John, 11, 12, 30, 159, 163, 165–67, 178–79, 181, 186
logic of exchange, 5, 214, 255, 274, 280, 298
Louis Napoleon Bonaparte, emperor of the French, 93
Lukács, Georg, 76, 87, 161, 311n58
Luxemburg, Rosa, 45

MacIntyre, Alasdair, 14, 17, 27, 55–56, 348n177; as Aristotelian, 77, 92–101, 105–7, 115–16, 120, 288; class struggle and Hegelian reason linked by, 110–11; ethical action and reason linked by, 97, 114, 123; facticity viewed by, 91; Goldmann praised by, 88; Hegel's *Science of Logic* discussed by, 109; history of philosophy traced by, 86–91; individual vs. community viewed by, 82, 85; Kantian morality viewed by, 88–90; Marxism criticized by, 28–29, 81, 102–8, 290; Marxism defended by, 77–79, 92, 108; modernity interpreted by, 77, 78, 80–81, 83, 85, 87, 90, 100–101, 105–6, 110, 119–20, 122; moral language's inadequacy viewed by, 83–84; political emancipation and ethical freedom linked by, 111–14; *Robinson Crusoe* viewed by, 160; Smith's *The Theory of Moral Sentiments* critiqued by, 238; social roles examined by, 114; theory of human action advanced by, 109–10
Marie Antoinette, queen of France, 208
Markell, Patchen, 44
Marx, Eleanor, 101
Marx, Karl, 1; abstract labour viewed by, 5–6, 12, 22, 31, 62–63; abstract sociality and labour linked by, 220; action celebrated by, 43, 67–68, 72–73, 78–79; activity and production linked by, 208; alienation viewed by, 3, 6–11, 14, 20, 22, 30, 31, 54, 59, 61–64, 176, 194–96, 202, 208, 210, 222, 223, 254–55, 262–63; Arendt linked to, 66–67, 72; Arendt's misreading of, 27–29, 59, 60–64, 68–71; Aristotle's actuality-potentiality formula inverted by, 206; Aristotle's "chrematistics" criticized by, 258–59; Aristotelian idea of "human essence," 208-11; Aristotle's theory of wealth creation viewed by, 32; Aristotle's value relation viewed by, 246–47; base/superstructure metaphor of, 102, 109; capital analyzed by, 256–64; capital and social needs counterpoised by, 156; capital deemed social relation by, 18–19, 20; capital defined by, 216; capitalism and colonialism linked by, 178; capitalist domination and resistance linked by, 273; civil society viewed by, 199–200; class struggle viewed by, 41, 46, 68, 78, 93, 110–12, 115, 216, 217, 273, 287–88; collective agency viewed by, 126; community vs. state distinguished by, 153; council movement linked to, 74–75; "dead labour" attacked by, 175–76, 216–17, 221, 270; decline of Aristotelianism and decline of Hegelianism

Marx, Karl (*cont.*)
linked by, 130, 131; dialectical approach of, 2, 3, 50, 61; division of labour ironised by, 211–12; early writings of, 193–217; economics politicized by, 20; economic terms viewed by, 166–67; economy of time viewed by, 285–86; Enlightenment views rejected by, 11, 13, 231; essences and content linked by, 132; ethical life viewed by, 3, 9–10, 14, 22, 25, 32–33, 92, 106, 122, 155, 156–57, 190, 195, 214, 219–21, 228, 249, 259, 274, 278, 281–83; exchange value defined by, 235; failure and suffering viewed by, 214–15; fetishism viewed by, 7, 13, 16–17, 32, 33, 81, 183, 198, 201, 219, 222, 227, 248–56, 260–64, 277, 288–91; French Revolution viewed by, 87, 128, 193, 250; freedom's contradictions viewed by, 22–24, 60; freedom vs. necessity viewed by, 64–65; the good life viewed by, 7, 8, 11, 13, 14, 15, 21, 198, 204; Hegel criticized by, 193; Hegelianism adopted by, 128–29; Hegel's absolute spirit distorted by, 41; Hegel's social freedom linked to, 108–9; Hegel's speculative philosophy linked to, 26; history of philosophy traced by, 222; history theorized by, 54, 92–94; Hobbes viewed by, 165; human needs viewed by, 32, 282, 283–84; labour deemed human activity by, 265, 266; labour's social form viewed by, 253; labour theory of value critiqued by, 12, 30, 31, 167, 185, 186–87, 218–19, 237–43, 255; language viewed by, 55–56, 65; MacIntyre's misreading of, 27, 29; means vs. ends viewed by, 9; misrecognition and distrust (*Mißtrauen*) viewed by, 202; modes of production conceived by, 55; modernity critiqued by, 25, 122; money analyzed by, 200–201, 219–20, 225–28, 231–37, 243–45, 250–64, 275–76; physical ailments of, 1–2; political economy critiqued by, 25, 92, 125, 159, 185–86, 284; politics and sociality linked by, 272; postcapitalist democracy foreseen by, 66; practical consciousness viewed by, 115; price vs. value distinguished by, 5; private property exchange analyzed by, 200–201; production process analyzed by, 264–73; productive activity and rationality liked by, 207; renewed interest in, 18; *Robinson Crusoe* satirized by, 30, 159–66, 179–90; social ontology of, 24–28, 30, 41, 57–60, 81, 92, 102–3, 122, 123, 195, 197, 198, 200, 210, 216, 217, 220, 225–26, 265, 268–69, 285; "the social" theorized by, 10, 40, 75; "species being" (*Gattungswesen*) concept of, 30, 194, 197–99, 204–6, 208–99; surplus value theorized by, 5, 60, 178–79, 209, 214, 256, 270, 274; types of currency distinguished by, 250; universal vs. particular interest counterpoised by, 199–200; value-form theory of, 3, 4–5, 12, 18, 21–22, 25, 30, 31, 62, 81–83, 122, 139, 155, 159, 176, 186, 197, 201, 216–20, 231, 242, 259, 263, 275, 281, 287; value-producing labour viewed by, 5–9, 227, 240–41, 244, 268; wage-labour condemned by, 177, 206, 208, 210

Marxism (MacIntyre), 78
materialism, 12, 94-5
Mau, Søren, 18, 223
McDowell, John, 133, 315n9
Mill, James, 30, 198, 200, 204
Minima Moralia (Adorno), 279–82
Mouffe, Chantal, 80
Murray, Patrick, 20, 63

Natural Law (Hegel), 138, 141, 146, 150
Neuhouser, Frederick, 114, 155, 329n84, 343n76
Ng, Karen, 209

Nicomachean Ethics (Aristotle), 3, 152, 213, 222, 245, 248, 251
Nietzsche, Friedrich, 83
Nozick, Robert, 158–59, 190

On Revolution (Arendt), 66–67
On the Jewish Question (OJQ, Marx), 46, 57
On the Principles of Political Economy and Taxation (Ricardo), 239
The Open Society and Its Enemies (Popper), 49
The Origins of Totalitarianism (Arendt), 37, 45–47, 56
Out of Apathy (Thompson), 114

Paris Commune (1871), 67–72, 75
Phenomenology of Spirit (Hegel), 15, 43, 49, 51–52, 53, 132, 148, 171
Philoctetes (Sophocles), 97
Philosophy of History (Hegel), 129
Philosophy of Mind (Hegel), 113
Philosophy of Right (Hegel), 11, 115, 124, 134, 138-39, 150–56, 284
Pinkard, Terry, 24, 49–50, 136, 138–39
Pippin, Robert B., 24, 25, 133, 138–39
Pitkin, Hanna Fenichel, 73
political economy, 2, 123, 167, 211, 257; ethical life tradition counterpoised with, 30; Hegel's view of, 11, 139, 145–46, 152; Locke's view of, 166; Marx's critique of, 3, 7, 13, 18, 20–21, 24–25, 30, 32, 60, 63, 83, 92, 103, 125, 126, 139, 157, 159–60, 181–82, 185–86, 190, 194, 198, 200–204, 216, 218–23, 225, 228, 230–32, 240–44, 247–48, 262–63, 269, 283–84; social form of value linked to, 62
Politics (Aristotle), 63–64, 147, 149, 222, 232, 258, 259
Popper, Karl, 15, 49, 109
Postone, Moishe, 195–97, 262, 269, 296n56, 351n256
post-structuralism, 17

The Poverty of Philosophy (Marx), 180
Prawer, S. S., 179
Proudhon, Pierre-Joseph, 180
Prussia, 51, 115, 131, 193

Rameau's Nephew (Diderot), 110
Rancière, Jacques, 40, 295n37
Rawls, John, 79
Realphilosophie (Hegel), 12, 124, 169–70
recognition, 175–76; Aristotle's justice in exchange linked to, 219; Hegel's theory of, 13, 15, 30, 51–53, 126, 133–34, 137-38, 151, 153–56, 160, 170–75, 262; MacIntyre's view of, 95, 98, 110, 111; Marx's theory of, 4, 9–10, 14, 16–17, 24, 30, 175-80, 188, 190, 199, 202, 215-16, 218–74, 277, 283, 289, 290
Ricardo, David, 7, 11, 18, 167, 180–81, 204, 219, 231; labour theory of value developed by, 3, 12; Mill influenced by, 200; Smith criticized by, 239–40; value and performed labour linked by, 240–41
Riedel, Manfred, 323n178
Ritter, Joachim, 136
Robinson Crusoe (Defoe), 3, 103, 168, 169, 172–78; Marx's satire of, 30, 159–66, 179–90
Rose, Gillian, 16, 25–26, 106, 123, 146, 262
Rousseau, Jean-Jacques, 30, 159, 163, 167–69, 170, 181–82, 305n144
Rubin, Isaak Illich, 226, 240, 339n17
Ruge, Arnold, 157, 193

Said, Edward, 161, 296n54
Sandel, Michael, 79
Science of Logic (Hegel), 4, 10, 15–16, 109, 124–25, 224, 228–29, 249
Sittlichkeit (ethical life), 4, 13, 15, 52–54, 123–26, 134, 137–56, 170, 280
Smith, Adam, 3, 7, 11, 30, 85, 165, 167, 181–83, 204; capital naturalised by, 231; Hegel contrasted with, 146; Hegel

Smith, Adam (*cont.*)
  influenced by, 139; labour theory of value advanced by, 237–38; Marx's views distinguished from, 203, 219, 239; Ricardo's criticism of, 239–40; social relations viewed by, 203; social wealth viewed by, 18
Smith, Tony, 263
social contract, 11, 30, 98, 157, 159, 163, 170–71, 179, 181–82
The Social Contract (Rousseau), 169-70
social freedom: Hegel's view of, 15, 30, 114, 122, 134, 139, 151, 170, 171, 173–75; MacIntyre's view of, 99, 108–9; Marx's stress on, 4, 9, 24, 29, 40, 65, 196, 200, 222, 226, 228, 261, 289-90
Socrates, 45
Sonenscher, Michael, 18
Sohn-Rethel, Alfred, 180
Sophocles, 53, 97, 148, 275, 277
"species being" (*Gattungswesen*), 30, 194, 197–99, 200, 204–6, 208–9, 214-5, 222, 267-68
A Spirit of Trust (Brandom), 52
Stalin, Joseph, 47, 78, 109
Strauss, Leo, 164
Suez Crisis, 78
surplus value, 5, 60, 178–79, 209, 214, 256-57, 261, 270-71, 274, 276, 282, 284-85
System of Ethical Life (Hegel), 138, 146

Taylor, Charles, 79
Teresa of Avila, Saint, 101

A Theory of Justice (Rawls), 79
The Theory of Moral Sentiments (Smith), 238
Theses on Feuerbach (Marx), 12, 40, 94, 95, 210
Thompson, E. P., 114, 331n129
Time: Arendt's theory of, 75; Benjamin's view of, 325–26n31; on Crusoe's island, 162–63, 173, 185–88; labour-time, 10, 63, 64, 167, 185–87, 236-37, 240, 242, 244-45, 253, 270, 275, 276, 282; Marx's theory of, 32, 63, 178–79, 185–88, 214, 221, 226, 237, 240, 242, 269–70, 285–87; prioritization of, 60, 61, 185; Smith's view of, 238, 240, 185-88, 214, 226, 237-38, 240-42, 269, 270, 285-87, 325-6n31
Trotsky, Leon, 101
Trott, Adriel M., 205
Two Treatises on Government (Locke), 163

utilitarianism, 23, 80, 107–11, 115, 120, 214

Varian, Hal, 160
Villa, Dana, 61

Walzer, Michael, 79
Watt, Ian, 166
The Wealth of Nations (Smith), 238–39
Weber, Max, 91, 186, 352n287
Williams, Eric, 161
Works and Days (Hesiod), 208

Young Hegelians, 129–30, 193

CURRENCIES

New Thinking for Financial Times
STEFAN EICH AND MARTIJN KONINGS, EDITORS

Noam Yuran, *The Sexual Economy of Capitalism*

Joscha Wullweber, *Central Bank Capitalism: Monetary Policy in Times of Crisis*

Eli Jelly-Schapiro, *Moments of Capital: World Theory, World Literature*

Jakob Feinig, *Moral Economies of Money: Politics and the Monetary Constitution of Society*

Charly Coleman, *The Spirit of French Capitalism: Economic Theology in the Age of Enlightenment*

Amin Samman, *History in Financial Times*

Thomas Biebricher, *The Political Theory of Neoliberalism*

Lisa Adkins, *The Time of Money*

Martijn Konings, *Capital and Time: For a New Critique of Neoliberal Reason*

The authorized representative in the EU for product safety and compliance is:
Mare Nostrum Group
B.V Doelen 72
4831 GR Breda
The Netherlands

www.ingramcontent.com/pod-product-compliance
Lightning Source LLC
Chambersburg PA
CBHW031845220426
43663CB00006B/505